Macmillan Technology Series

UnixWare 7 System Administration

Gene Henriksen
Melissa Henriksen

Macmillan Technical Publishing U·S·A

FIRST EDITION

International Standard Book Number: 1-57870-080-9

Library of Congress Catalog Card Number: 98-85489

2002 01 00 99 4 3 2

Interpretation of the printing code: The rightmost double-digit number is the year of the book's printing; the rightmost single-digit, the number of the book's printing. For example, the printing code 99-1 shows that the first printing of the book occurred in 1999.

Composed in Palatino and MCPdigital by Macmillan Computer Publishing

Printed in the United States of America

Trademark Acknowledgments

All terms mentioned in this book that are known to be trademarks or service marks have been appropriately capitalized. Macmillan Technical Publishing cannot attest to the accuracy of this information. Use of a term in this book should not be regarded as affecting the validity of any trademark or service mark.

UnixWare 7 is a registered trademark of Santa Cruz Operation, Inc.

Warning and Disclaimer

This book is designed to provide information about UnixWare 7. Every effort has been made to make this book as complete and as accurate as possible, but no warranty or fitness is implied.

The information is provided on an as-is basis. The authors and Macmillan Technical Publishing shall have neither liability nor responsibility to any person or entity with respect to any loss or damages arising from the information contained in this book or from the use of the discs or programs that may accompany it.

Feedback Information

At Macmillan Technical Publishing, our goal is to create in-depth technical books of the highest quality and value. Each book is crafted with care and precision, undergoing rigorous development that involves the unique expertise of members from the professional technical community.

Readers' feedback is a natural continuation of this process. If you have any comments regarding how we could improve the quality of this book, or otherwise alter it to better suit your needs, you can contact us at `networktech@mcp.com`. Please make sure to include the book title and ISBN in your message.

We greatly appreciate your assistance.

Publisher
Don Fowley

Executive Editor
Linda Ratts Engelman

Managing Editor
Patrick Kanouse

Acquisitions Editor
Karen Wachs

Development Editor
Lisa M. Thibault

Project Editor
Theresa Mathias

Copy Editor
Bonnie Lawler

Indexer
Joy Dean Lee

Acquisitions Coordinator
Jennifer Garrett

Manufacturing Coordinator
Brook Farling

Book Designer
Anne Jones

Cover Designer
Aren Howell

Production Team Supervisor
Tricia Flodder

Layout Technician
Eric S. Miller

Proofreader
Mary Ellen Stephenson

About the Authors

Gene Henriksen is part of the SCO beta test group for UnixWare 7. He is the author of *Windows NT and UNIX Integration*, published by Macmillan Technical Publishing, and he is a private consultant and software developer who teaches courses on UNIX at SCO Training Centers and Windows NT at Microsoft Training Centers. With more than 15 years of experience with the UNIX operating system, Gene is a SCO UNIX Advanced Certified Engineer (ACE), SCO UNIX Instructor, Microsoft Certified Professional (MCP), Microsoft Certified Trainer, and is certified to teach Solaris. Gene speaks at conferences across the country, including SCO's 1996 Worldwide Systems Engineering conference on UNIX/Windows integration and at SCO's 1997 and 1998 Forums in Santa Cruz on Advanced File and Print Server. He was a trainer in October 1998 at the SCO distributors' training session. Gene contributes to *Windows NT Magazine* and *Windows Magazine*.

Melissa Henriksen has a bachelor of science in computer science from the College of William and Mary in Virginia and more than eight years of experience in the computer industry. She first used SCO UNIX as a platform on which to develop Informix programs. She now divides her time among software development, consulting, and SCO-authorized training. She and her father are partners in Henriksen's, Inc.

Melissa lives in Virginia with her two cats. She enjoys traveling, skiing, reading fiction, and listening to music.

About the Technical Reviewers

These reviewers contributed their considerable practical, hands-on expertise to the entire development process for *UnixWare 7 System Administration*. As the book was being written, these folks reviewed all the material for technical content, organization, and flow. Their feedback was critical to ensuring that *UnixWare 7 System Administration* fits our readers' need for the highest quality technical information.

John Boland is a support engineer for SCO, based in Watford, UK. He graduated from Waterford Institute of Technology (WIT) in Ireland in 1986 with a bachelor of science in applied computing. John started his career as a lecturer of Diploma and Degree students in WIT. In 1988, John moved to the UK to take up a position with WANG UK, developing and delivering training on WANG's proprietary VS operating system. Two years later, John joined SCO and became a support engineer at SCO's European Headquarters in Watford, UK. He has held various positions within the SCO support organization, including technical team leader and support manager. He currently is principal technical lead within the support group and is responsible for managing the support of UnixWare 7 and Year 2000.

Chris Jordan has been in sales and marketing positions in the microcomputer industry since the advent of the Commodore VIC 20, which heralded his entry into the field. Selling both hardware and software solutions to such customers as Fortune 1000 organizations, government bodies, and small- to medium-sized enterprises, he has more than 20 years of technology experience. His background is one of not only understanding the fast-changing technologies but successfully selling solutions that solve the problems of businesses today. Chris's understanding of technologies and their uses encompasses UNIX-based operating systems, Wide Area Networking, cable communications, mainframes, and the Internet, to name but a few.

Bruce Keitell is a UNIX Systems Specialist for Indiana University–Purdue University at Indianapolis, in the University Information Technology Services division. He graduated from ITT Technical Institute in Indianapolis in 1993 with an associate of applied science. Bruce provides consulting and system administration on UNIX platforms (SUN, DEC, HP, SGI, and Linux) and specializes in UNIX system security and PC interoperability. Bruce is a Microsoft Certified Systems Engineer.

Brendan McTague is a senior systems engineer with the Global Financial Services division of Perot Systems Corporation. He currently manages an engineering team for the investment division of a major European bank. When not working, Brendan prefers to spend his time with his wife and child in their home outside Chicago.

Tony Nelson is the founder of Open Learning Center, a SCO Advanced Education Center located on SCO's corporate campus in Santa Cruz (`www.openlearning.com`). With more than 15 years of industry experience, he teaches UNIX system administration and programming, develops curriculum, and serves on various industry boards.

A. Richard Pachter is the president of Rainier Services, Inc., in Chicago. He is also a training partner for Silicon Graphics, teaching performance and tuning. His clients have included Fujitsu, the Royal Air Force, the Ministry of Defense, the Department of Foreign Affairs and International Trade, and UNIX System Laboratories (Bell Labs). In addition, Dick joined ICL in 1982 and lectures, on behalf of the company, on technical and non-technical subjects to students across the globe.

Acknowledgments

Writing a book is not a one-person performance. I often am asked if I write a book and then look for a publisher. Without a publisher's guidance during the writing process, a book would be much less coherent. The development editor is the person who reviews the newly written material and sends it out to the technical reviewers. Lisa Thibault kept up with everything in spite of getting married in the middle of the project.

The acquisition editors determine whether the book is economically feasible. David Gibson got the paperwork rolling to get the book approved. He then moved on to another position and passed the book to Karen Wachs, who worked with me on *Windows NT and UNIX Integration*.

On the SCO side of the picture, I received an enormous amount of help. I would like to thank Scott Allen for introducing me to SCO back in 1986 in Germany. He was my pathway to meeting other SCO employees. One of those was Jim Bahn, currently the product manager for OpenServer 5 and the migration path to UnixWare 7. At the SCO Forum in August 1997, Jim and I talked about the need for a book on UnixWare 7. John Shepherd had just given me a copy of the UnixWare 7 beta, then known as the Gemini Forum beta.

Later, Dion Johnson became an evangelist for the book idea. He and Jim sold the necessary people at SCO on the need to support the book on a technical level. In March 1998, my wife Susie and I went to Santa Cruz for an all-day meeting with Jim and several people from different departments who would be our contact points. An email alias was created for Melissa and me to send questions on points we couldn't quite handle alone.

Many SCO engineers and other people, technical and non-technical, contributed to the book. In addition to their contributions, each chapter was reviewed by two SCO employees. John Boland of SCO's London office read every chapter and made many suggestions. He also offered bits of information that I had not uncovered and corrected misunderstandings. Each chapter was also read by a specialist in the subject area. Their help was crucial to the completeness and correctness of the material.

SCO employees who contributed to the book include

Karen Adams, Mike Almond, Kathryn Anderson, Jim Bahn, Simon Baldwin, John Boland, Ann Burrell, Yaping Chen, Hiram Clawson, Jon Coyle, Chris D'Arcey, Ranjit Deshpande, George F. Demarest, David Dougherty, Michael Drangula, Sue Eschweiler-Spencer, Jim Ferrigno, Mark Forry, Albert Fu, Marty Gindi, Dipak Gohil, Kurt Gollhardt, Rod Harrison, Mark Hoffmann,

Philip J. Hollenback, Mike Hopkirk, Paul Hurford, Kurt Hutchison, Dion Johnson, Brian Keegan, Wu Liu, Tony Lofthouse, Peter Knight, Bela Lubkin, Tammy McBride, Andrew Malcolm, Mary McNulty, Meg McRoberts, Rob Mills, Graham Moore, Dewi Morgan, Truls S. Myklebust, Hanna Nelson, Tamar Newberger, Clare Oakley, Kathy Petersen, Nathan Peterson, Jean-Pierre Radley, Rene Rodriguez, Richard Roscoe, Jens Scheithauer, Scott Popp, Vince Seavello, Glenn Seiler, John Shepherd, Jay Sinha, Barry Southon, Annette Sweet, Rick Thomas, Nick White, David Wight, Steve Wiley, Dave Williams, Philip Wright, Karl Young.

Help also was provided by three SCO Advanced Education Centers. David M. Clark (MUA Pty Ltd, Australia) sent a compendium of notes he had accumulated on UnixWare 7. Tony Nelson and Jim VanVerth (Open Learning Center: Santa Cruz, CA) also provided information they had uncovered.

Matt Thurmaier (The Computer Classroom: Schaumburg, IL) provided help on performance tuning. Matt has written course materials for UnixWare 7 internals and device drivers. His training staff also wrote the SCO Networking course materials. Andrew Merrill provided help on some of the networking chapters and a script on changing IP addresses and system names.

Some of the computer hardware was loaned by Hampton Roads Computer (Newport News, VA). Jim Nichols, who has been a SCO instructor as well as a Novell Gold Reseller, helped with the NetWare connectivity chapter (my knowledge of NetWare being limited to the color of the box used by Novell). DPT's Pete Bolliger provided information on SCSI standards and capabilities. For the chapter on serial communications, Mike Burris of Stallion Industries shipped us a multiport serial card with UnixWare 7 drivers.

—Gene Henriksen

I have a few thanks of my own to add to the list of folks from Macmillan and SCO who kept us afloat and on course.

First and foremost, thanks to my father, Gene, for getting me involved in this project. He has been helpful, supportive, and never stingy with the red ink when reviewing my chapters. And most importantly, he reminds me both by advice and example to, in the words of humorist Will Rogers, "Go out on a limb. That's where the fruit is."

My mother, Susie, graciously surrendered two of the bedrooms in the family home for my temporary office and living quarters during the writing. She also feigned interest when Gene and I dominated household conversation with discussion of current chapters and truly pathetic attempts at UnixWare humor.

My sister, Mina, kept me focused on the task at hand, although I suspect her interest was in part related to a desire to finally stop hearing about progress on the book at family dinners.

Jennifer Iaccarino provided the same tireless support and encouragement for this project as she does for my life in general.

And a special thanks to my feline darlings, Solstice and Kingsley, for keeping me company late at night and being generally adorable little terrors.

—Melissa Henriksen

Contents at a Glance

Table of Contents

Foreword

SCO is the leading supplier of UNIX servers with 40% market share (IDC preliminary data, December 1997). In 1995, SCO acquired the UNIX source-license business and technology from Novell along with the UnixWare product line. Following this acquisition, SCO decided to take the best of breed technologies from its two existing Operating System product lines—SCO OpenServer Release 5 and SCO UnixWare Release 2.1—and create the most advanced operating system available on the Intel platform. The operating system that was created is called *UnixWare 7*.

UnixWare 7 has been shipping since the beginning of 1998. In that time, it has attracted much press and has won *BYTE* Magazine's Best Operating System award at CeBIT 98, among other awards. UnixWare 7 also has demonstrated its performance and scalability by powering five of the 10 category-winning UNIX platforms at the recent AIM Technology "Hot Iron Awards."

UnixWare 7 is ideal as an enterprise, departmental, mail, or Internet server; it also is made available (for a small media fee) for non-commercial and educational use via the SCO Web site at

`www.sco.com/offers/`

UnixWare 7 has proven reliability and scalability, provides a robust network computing environment, and has built-in support for many types of computer clients, including PCs, network cards, character terminals, and Java-enabled "Webtop" devices.

Gene Henriksen has been an active contributor to the UnixWare 7 Beta and Early Availability programs. During the course of these programs, Gene was involved in the testing and exercising of many of the features of UnixWare 7. His background in training and his expertise with previous releases of SCO operating systems and layered products made him an invaluable contributor to these programs.

Learning how to configure a new operating system is difficult. This book is an ideal guide for helping you configure and use the many new features of the product. It takes you through the process of installation, configuration, and maintenance of your UnixWare 7 system. This book is filled with technical tips and useful hints on how to get the most from the features of UnixWare 7. It also contains many references to differences between SCO OpenServer 5, SCO UnixWare 2.1, and UnixWare 7, that existing administrators and users of these products will find useful.

UnixWare 7 contains many features that will be new to existing SCO UNIX, SCO Open Desktop, SCO Open Server, SCO UnixWare Release 1/2, and SCO OpenServer 5 users. This book approaches these features in a clear and concise way. The reader will find this book useful as both a learning aid and a reference.

—Doug Michels, CEO, Santa Cruz Operation (SCO)

Introduction

In November 1995, SCO purchased the UnixWare product from Novell. From the beginning, SCO planned to merge the UnixWare product with the OpenServer operating system to form a new operating system. The project to combine the two operating systems was code-named *Gemini*. (Gemini is a constellation containing the stars Castor and Pollux, also known as the twins.)

When the process of trying to merge the two operating systems started, it became apparent that the total merger was too large a project to be carried out in one step. The best features of each operating system were selected from UnixWare 2 and OpenServer 5 to create the new UnixWare 7.

The concept of project Gemini intrigued us: All the traditional ease of use and the graphical interface of SCO's OpenServer 5 grafted onto the newer UNIX kernel in UnixWare 2. Having worked with SCO products from the days of XENIX, having gone through the transition to SCO UNIX with the 3.2v2 and then 3.2v4 series, learning OpenDeskTop and finally OpenServer 5, Melissa and I were well grounded in SCO operating systems. We have moved with SCO up the technological ladder as Intel chips became more powerful.

Thanks to friends at SCO, I got onto the list for the beta program for Gemini. When it became apparent that SCO planned to have the majority of the UnixWare 7 documentation online rather than on paper, the idea of a UnixWare 7 book was born.

We have spent all of our computer careers working in the field without a support team behind us. We knew that the biggest problem facing technical support people in the field is having access to a good hands-on book written by people who have done the work and documented the process, the problems, and the alternatives. This book is an attempt to provide a field guide to UnixWare 7. During the writing of this book, we used UnixWare 7.0.0, the Early Access Product version of 7.0.1, and the final release of 7.0.1.

Using a network of up to 11 systems with a mix of OpenServer 5, UnixWare 2, UnixWare 7, and Windows, we tried and tested as much as we could. Many of the notes and tips are the result of personal experiences, and others came from SCO engineers. We configured Internet proxy servers, email servers, PPP, FTP, network printers, and numerous other services. We made systems unbootable and experimented with restoring them in various ways. We sent hundreds of emails to SCO engineers asking for help and for clarifications, and in some cases, improvements.

We hope this book will save you some of those terrifying moments when, as one early English pilot put it after a crash, he suddenly ran out of experience. We have tried to reduce the frustration level for you by going through it ourselves. How does DNS suddenly become enabled without your enabling it? Why does the mail system have a host name lookup failure? What does the message `The hard disk is sane` mean? It is all in this book.

Contents of the Book

We tried to organize the book in a logical manner proceeding from the theory of UnixWare 7 through installation, initial setup, disaster recovery preparation, and disaster recovery. Here is what the book covers by chapter.

Part I: UnixWare 7: The UNIX of the Future

Chapter 1, "Why UnixWare 7?" discusses the changes to UnixWare 7 and why it is now referred to as System V Release 5. The chapter also covers the migration plan for OpenServer 5 users moving to UnixWare 7. In this chapter, you will learn about Network User Licenses.

Chapter 2, "Hardware Configuration," covers the hardware configurations for UnixWare 7. The chapter also covers Host Bus Adapter diskettes.

Chapter 3, "UnixWare 7 System Configuration," explains the licensing models and system profiles. You will learn how SCO made installation easier through the grouping of services into a licensing model and what this holds for the future.

Installing the system is the subject of Chapter 4, "Installation of UnixWare 7." Installations can be run from CD-ROM or over the network. You will learn how to create new diskettes for installation as well as the network installation diskettes.

Part II: Post-Installation Tasks

The Common Desktop Environment (CDE) is the new graphical user interface replacing both the OpenServer 5 and UnixWare 2 GUIs. Chapter 5, "Console Administration, Logins, and SCOadmin," provides a guide to using the new interface as well as the Panorama and Failsafe GUIs.

Chapter 6, "LAN Network Configuration," is the largest chapter and explains not only the tried and true TCP implementations of NFS and DNS. It also has information about the new features in SCO networking: Dynamic Host Configuration Protocol, Address Allocation Server, the new Network Configuration Manager, SNMP, LDAP, and the Client Manager.

Wide area networking is a hot topic and the subject of Chapter 7, "WAN Network Configuration." The Modem Manager, Dialin Service Manager, Dialout Service Manager, PPP, and other topics are covered here.

Routing, browsers, and intranets are covered in Chapter 8, "Browsers and Intranets." See how to route with UnixWare 7. We cover the problems you may experience with Windows clients when using RIP.

Chapter 9, "NetWare," instructs you on using the NetWare Services and NetWare UNIX Client. Learn to interconnect your system with NetWare servers.

Serial configuration has changed drastically from OpenServer 5. In Chapter 10, "Configuration of Serial Ports and Terminal Devices," you learn how to deal with the new method of serial configuration using SAF, setup modems and terminals, and install a third-party intelligent serial card.

Printers are another area that has changed. The directories have moved, and the printer scripts don't look like OpenServer 5 printer scripts. In Chapter 11, "Printer Configuration," we show you how to control an HP Laser printer through a preprocessor script.

Tape drives, diskettes, and backups are the topic in Chapter 12, "Removable Media." See how easy it is to add tape drives and removable hard drives. We explain ARCserve/Open from Cheyenne and preview the beta of the next release.

Adding new software to the system involves the `pkgadd` command or the Application Installer. Both of these are covered in Chapter 13, "Software Installation."

When you get everything configured, it is time to make the Emergency Recovery Diskettes and tape. We also tell you how to license the system and index the online help in Chapter 14, "Wrapping Up the Install."

Part III: Maintaining the System

Chapter 15, "System Administration," covers an assortment of topics, including remote administration, system defaults, system reports, system logs, and other daily administration tasks.

Chapter 16, "Starting and Stopping," covers the details of starting and stopping. OpenServer 5 went to multi-user at run level 2; UnixWare 7 boots to run level 3. Learn how to boot to single-user mode.

User administration is a major part of managing an active system. Chapter 17, "User Administration," covers the user accounts and groups management from both the graphical and command line.

Process management is easier under UnixWare 7. Graphical managers allow terminating processes without using the command line. Learn about the graphical cron administration in Chapter 18, "Process Management."

New filesystem types are discussed in detail in Chapter 19, "Storage Devices, Filesystems, and Permissions." UnixWare 7 uses `prtvtoc` and `edvtoc` to accomplish what OpenServer 5's `divvy` command did.

In Chapter 20, "Mailers," learn how to use your UnixWare 7 system as a mail server.

In Chapter 21, "Performance Tuning," learn how to check your system performance and adjust it for maximum performance.

Chapter 22, "Security," covers security from the perspective of users' roles, network security with packet filters, and the file security package that verifies authenticity of the installed operating system programs.

Part IV: Disaster Recovery

Disaster recovery is an indispensable part of support. In Chapter 23, "Emergency Recovery," we dissect the emergency recovery procedures for UnixWare 7 and tell you how to boot a system when the recovery diskettes are missing.

Chapter 24, "Migrating to UnixWare 7," covers migration to UnixWare 7. Learn about what is currently available and see how to ease your migration workload.

Part V: Appendixes

Appendix A, "SCO Resources on the Web," is a list of the Web pages at SCO's Web site that are of interest to UnixWare 7 users.

Appendix B, "References," covers printed reference materials that you might want to use for additional reading.

Conventions Used in this Book

The following conventions are used in this book:

Tip

Tips provide you with helpful ways of completing a task.

Troubleshooting Tip

Troubleshooting tips provide resolutions of some problems you may encounter during deployment.

Warning

Warnings provide you with information you need to know to avoid damage to data, hardware, or software, or to avoid error messages that tell you that you are unable to complete a task.

Author's Note

In these areas I relate to you personal experiences I've encountered that give you a real-life understanding of a topic.

OpenServer 5 Tip

Information specific to OpenServer 5 users is included here to highlight changes that will affect you.

UnixWare 2 Tip

Information specific to UnixWare 2 users is included here to highlight changes that will affect you.

PART I

UnixWare 7: The UNIX of the Future

CHAPTER 1

Why UnixWare 7?

- The Santa Cruz Operation and UNIX
  Learn the genealogy of UnixWare 7.
- Network computing
  Learn how UnixWare 7 is equipped for the future of business computing.
- UNIX for the twenty-first century
  Take a look at 64-bit computing.
- What UnixWare 7 brings to UNIX: New features
  Learn about UnixWare 7's advanced capabilities, new technologies, and ease of use.

The Santa Cruz Operation and UNIX

SCO has been producing UNIX and XENIX operating systems for more than 15 years. In December 1995, SCO acquired both the UNIX system source-license business as well as the UnixWare product line from Novell. In early 1996, SCO joined with seven Enterprise hardware vendors, establishing UnixWare as the standard UNIX system on Intel servers.

From its beginnings with XENIX, carrying forward through SCO UNIX, Open Desktop, and OpenServer 5, SCO has provided user-friendly management tools. With its acquisition of UnixWare, the decision was made to combine OpenServer and UnixWare into a single product line. The management tools from OpenServer 5 and the System V Release 4 (SVR4) kernel from UnixWare 2 were combined to form the starting point for UnixWare 7.

SCO's dedication to UNIX on the Intel platform has made SCO the world's leading supplier of UNIX server operating systems with a 40% market share, shipping more licenses than Sun, HP, and IBM combined. Narrowing the focus to the Intel market, the share jumps to 85%.

Network Computing

There is little doubt that network computing is the future for business. It provides a wide array of benefits in performance and cost. These include shared access and increased availability of hardware and software, as well as the use of cost-effective devices to access both data and applications. In network computing, there are two main elements:

- Powerful, reliable, and scalable servers
- Support for a wide range of clients

UnixWare 7 meets all of the requirements and continues to expand capabilities, providing both NetWare and Windows connectivity as a basic part of the operating system.

An example of network-based computing would be running Web-enabled applications on Java-enabled clients. This provides wide-range computing access without the need for a proprietary operating system installed on the client, or even client-side installation of application-specific software.

UNIX for the Twenty-First Century

SCO has developed a comprehensive plan for UNIX and the future. The arrival of 64-bit computing is just around the corner, and UnixWare 7 already includes the capability to support memory beyond the 32-bit limits using special features of the Pentium Pro processor. Release of a full 64-bit optimized UnixWare system is scheduled to coincide with the delivery of Intel's 64-bit processor platform.

Another part of this plan is to allow OpenServer users to not only enjoy enhancements to their systems, but also to migrate smoothly to the future. A new release of OpenServer (5.0.5) was delivered in August 1998.

Users can look forward to new features, optional services, and updates to hardware and maintenance support. While SCO does not have plans to optimize OpenServer for 64-bit architecture, it will offer migration tools and purpose-built UnixWare 7 configurations for small businesses and replicated sites. These migration tools will ease the transition of OpenServer, and older versions of SCO UNIX, into the 64-bit world of UnixWare 7. See Chapter 24, "Migrating to UnixWare 7," for more information on migration.

Also of note to OpenServer 5 and UnixWare 2 users is the *UnixWare and OpenServer Development Kit* or *UDK*. The UDK is supplied as part of the UnixWare 7 media kit. It allows developers to create a common application binary that runs across OpenServer 5, UnixWare 2, and UnixWare 7 environments. This will simplify the task of supporting applications across all of SCO's operating systems. Also included in the UDK is a complete set of Java development tools, including Sun's Java Workshop, Java Studio, and the Java Development Kit (JDK).

What UnixWare 7 Brings to UNIX: New Features

UnixWare 7 offers a wide range of improvements. These include changes to the kernel; performance and scalability; management, administration, and licensing; user interface; networking, including an integrated Netscape browser and Web server; incorporated Java capabilities; and mail and messaging.

The Kernel

The kernel has been enhanced to such an extent that it has been given a new name: *System V Release 5 (SVR5)*. Numerous changes to the kernel have been implemented, some of which are listed in the following sections.

The DDI8 Device Driver

A significant change involves the DDI8 driver specification, which provides many of the new capabilities. It is the basis for UnixWare 7's dynamic kernel. This driver specification helps driver developers create dynamically loadable kernel modules. This means that drivers can actually be loaded and unloaded from a running kernel without the need for the kernel to be rebuilt, or even for the system to be rebooted.

Applications Compatibility

UnixWare 7 offers 100% applications compatibility with UnixWare 2.1 and support for all SCO OpenServer application binary formats (ELF and COFF). UnixWare 2.1 applications will install and run without modification, and a majority of OpenServer binaries will run unchanged on UnixWare 7. Chapter 24 addresses migration and compatibility.

64-bit Technology

UnixWare 7 supports 64-bit file systems and file operations, which allows file and file systems sizes up to 1TB. C, C++, and other development tools support 64-bit integer operations (the "long data type"); and applications developed on the current UDK will run on the 64-bit version of UnixWare when it is released.

Multipath I/O

Multipath I/O increases both reliability and performance. This feature supports the connection of more than one Host Bus Adapter (HBA) to a SCSI bus. Reliability is increased due to the capability of the operating system to redirect I/O through another I/O path to the device. This maintains availability to the devices when an adapter fails. Performance can be improved by the load balancing capabilities. By default, the Multipath I/O (MPIO) driver will attempt to use all paths and load balance I/O across controllers. For more information on MPIO, see Chapter 19, "Storage Devices, Filesystems, and Permissions."

Controller Hot Plug

Along with the ability to make changes to a running kernel, UnixWare 7 also provides capabilities for changing aspects of the configuration on a running system. *Controller Hot Plug* allows PCI peripherals to be added to a server with PCI slots without powering the system down. This feature has long been associated with mainframes and very high-cost UNIX systems, but is now available with a UnixWare 7 server.

Hot Pluggable Disks

In the same vein, UnixWare 7 allows for hot pluggable disks. SCSI disks, tape drives, and CD-ROM devices can be added or removed on a running system. This ability can be used to add disks into a RAID system, to provide more mirror drives, or to add hot spares. It also allows replacement of a faulty disk on a server with mirrored drives in which one of the mirrors has a failure. Because SCSI tape drives can also be added, storage can be increased on a running system and tape drives can be shared between systems. Both the controller hot plug and hot pluggable disks serve to increase uptime by eliminating the need to shut down the server to make changes or replace failed equipment. Chapter 19 covers both of these topics.

Disk Spanning and Mirroring

UnixWare 7 has built-in disk spanning and low-cost mirroring capabilities. *Disk spanning*, the ability to create a file system that spans multiple physical devices, is included without charge in UnixWare 7. *Disk mirroring* is an optional service and requires a license to enable the capability. These features were previously provided through the Online Data Manager product, which is still available as an add-on and has additional features above and beyond mirroring and spanning.

Crash and Dump Capabilities

UnixWare 7's upgraded crash and dump capabilities improve administrators' ability to diagnose a failed system through use of the `crash` command. The improvements include selective dumping, generic structure dumping, and support for large physical memories. For most system panics, the relevant information needed to diagnose the problem is contained in the kernel pages. Thus, UnixWare 7 provides the ability to dump memory selectively, only for the kernel-mapped pages and even to multiple devices, if necessary. By doing a dump of only the kernel pages, both the time and disk space required can be significantly reduced, especially on a system with a large amount of memory. See Chapter 23, "Emergency Recovery," for more information on crash recovery.

Multi-Console Support

Multi-console products from Boundless Technologies and Maxpeed are supported by UnixWare 7. These products allow a single server to provide multiple graphical logins. By using UnixWare 7's graphical capabilities and low-cost color graphics terminals, a lower-cost, lower-maintenance alternative to PCs becomes available.

Performance and Scalability

The improved scalability of UnixWare 7 has made it the choice of vendors of enterprise systems. With more than enough scalability for the enterprise, UnixWare 7 is prepared for the 64-bit computing of the future.

Over the last two years, Intel processor–based servers running UnixWare have outperformed proprietary RISC systems in performance and price/performance benchmarks. UnixWare 7 also outperforms OpenServer 5 with the same resources. Performance has been enhanced through changes in the way the system runs, as well as in new options that are available for dealing with I/O.

Large Physical Memory

A striking feature of UnixWare 7 is its support of both large physical memory and large file systems. Up to 4GB of memory can be supported as *general-purpose memory*, which can be used by applications or the system without any modifications. This first 4GB is automatically detected and used by the system.

In addition to this general-purpose memory, UnixWare 7 can support up to 64GB of *special-purpose memory*. This must be accessed through special APIs by applications requiring more memory, such as database and transaction processing. To use special-purpose memory, an application must be written to support the PAE (Physical Address Extension) mode of the Pentium Pro processor. Single-instance databases can use memory over 4GB with the *Dynamically Mapped Shared Memory* (*DSHM*) feature, which is a separately licensed add-on package.

1TB File System and File Size

In addition to the very large amount of memory that can be supported, UnixWare 7 provides impressive storage capabilities. File systems of up to 1TB (2^40 bytes) are supported. A single file can consume up to 1TB. It is recommended that files of greater than 2GB be used only in special cases, usually database applications. Only a limited number of system commands are designed to handle files of this size. At present, the maximum storage on a UnixWare 7 system stands at a whopping 78,000TB.

Automatic Kernel Tuning

Tuning the kernel to maximize performance can be a complicated task, as well as one that, when executed poorly, can have a serious negative effect on system efficiency. Behold, advanced automatic kernel tuning. Based on such factors as available memory and disk information, key kernel parameters are automatically tuned to their optimal values. This not only serves to reduce the time that must be spent on tuning a system, but also ensures optimum performance.

Reduced Per-Process Memory Usage

Another improvement to performance involves the amount of memory used per process. On large systems, the number of running processes at any given time can reach into the tens of thousands. Thus, reducing the overhead for running processes results in maintaining optimum performance on large systems, as well as offering notable benefits even on relatively small systems.

Improved TCP/IP Performance

Performance has also been boosted in the area of TCP/IP networking. Significant improvements provide increases of up to 250% for some networking services. The effects can be seen in client/server, database, and Web applications, as well as in file transfers and application access between clients and other systems.

I_2O Support

I_2O is a new technology that is supported in UnixWare 7. Developed by Intel and its partners, I_2O defines a standard architecture for intelligent I/O, one that is both operating system and device independent.

There are two key issues addressed by I_2O. First, I/O interrupts serviced by the CPU have a negative impact on overall system performance. This problem is eliminated by a special I/O processor that offloads I/O processing from the main CPU. It can be incorporated into I_2O peripherals as well as into system motherboards. The result is that the system performs better due to the removal of I/O interrupts. I/O performance is also enhanced as a result of the special processor dedicated to handling I/O requests.

The second issue is that of the time and expense required to provide drivers for each device, for each available OS. This is handled by portable drivers. All OSs that support I_2O will be able to share drivers, which allows for timely support of new peripherals and systems on the market. The UnixWare 7 I_2O HBA driver should work on any vendor's I_2O HBA.

Management, Administration, and Licensing

UnixWare 7 ushers in a new era of ease in administering and managing UNIX systems. From application brokers through UNIX host groups, managing systems and users becomes simpler.

Tarantella: Built-in Application Brokering

Tarantella is an application broker, a program that serves as middleware between application and end user. Tarantella eliminates the need for the end user to know where his applications are located or how to access them with the correct terminal emulator or other access method. It delivers any application immediately to any Java-enabled client without any additional software needed on the client end. Thus, businesses can both prolong the life of existing applications and add a new face to old applications.

Tarantella provides the UnixWare 7 Webtop interface, which allows users or administrators to configure their own set of applications and tools available to them through a browser.

Purpose-Built Configurations

UnixWare 7 introduces a new packaging strategy called *purpose-built configurations*. In the past, each system install was customer specific: It started with the base configuration, then user licenses and processor licenses could be added, followed by installation and licensing of other optional components. Purpose-built configurations were created to simplify installation and licensing through the use of a single license that activates a set of product options. This requires fewer steps and eases the task of installation.

The currently available purpose-built configurations include

- Enterprise Edition
- Departmental Edition
- Messaging Edition
- Base Edition

The eventual goal is that licenses will be available on the Web and will automatically install the configuration specified at the time the license was purchased. For more on purpose-built configurations, see Chapter 3, "UnixWare 7 System Configuration."

Media Kits and License Packs

UnixWare 7 will be distributed in a new way, using media kits and license packs. The new distribution method reduces costs and simplifies installation and licensing. In the past, users received both media and licenses when ordering a product. For instance, ordering 50 copies of a product would result in 50 CDs and 50 licenses in 50 boxes. With the new separation between media and licenses, the customer can purchase a small number of media kits, to be used to install on many servers, and simply purchase as many licenses as are needed. Reusing media reduces cost as well as storage space requirements.

Network User Licenses

The idea of *Network User Licenses*, or *NULs*, is new with UnixWare 7. NULs are floating license mechanisms that allow businesses to license any number of UnixWare 7 servers with a single NUL. NULs were created for environments with multiple UnixWare 7 servers and will reduce costs for these environments through their additive nature. For instance, if a site has three UnixWare 7 servers, each with a 50-user license, activating the NUL will upgrade access to 150 users for all three servers without any additional cost. This is the effective equivalent of having purchased 150 user licenses for each of the three servers. NULs are available through the SCO Web site; entering existing license information will return an activation key to turn on NUL capabilities.

The SCOadmin Framework

The SCOadmin framework is the foundation for system administration in UnixWare 7. Because it is also the administration framework for SCO OpenServer 5 and is the most widely used interface of any UNIX system, it provides a familiar environment to administrators. It can be accessed from the CDE graphical desktop, from the Panorama desktop, or from the command line. For more on the graphical interfaces, see Chapter 5, "Console Administration, Logins, and SCOadmin."

Host Group Management (One-to-Many Administration)

UnixWare 7 administrators can administer up to 50 systems on a network from a single console by utilizing the Host Group capabilities. A system is designated as the *master host*, and changes made to the system are distributed to the group of machines known as *managed hosts*. Host Group operations are supported in four managers:

- Account Manager
- Printer Setup Manager
- Filesystem Manager
- System Defaults Manager

User Interface

A new UNIX-standard *Common Desktop Interface (CDE)* is provided, as well as a lightweight Panorama desktop. Several new managers have been included for improved graphical administration.

CDE Desktop

The CDE is the standard graphical user interface for UNIX in corporate environments. It provides the ability to launch applications and administrative utilities, send email, and view online help, among others. CDE is offered as one of the primary graphical user interface choices in UnixWare 7.

Because CDE is available on all of the most popular UNIX implementations and is the universal UNIX standard, UnixWare 7 systems can easily be incorporated into existing UNIX environments with no disruption of the familiar interface.

Panorama Desktop

For UNIX power users and engineers who do not want or need the full range of features associated with CDE, the Panorama desktop, a lighter-weight interface, is provided. It features the *Panorama window manager (pmwm),* which allows for a working area that is larger than can be shown on the screen. The user can then use the screen to view portions of the workspace. It runs with less overhead than CDE.

Webtop Interface

UnixWare 7 also offers a *Webtop interface*. This allows users access to applications and files from any Java-enabled client, such as Netscape Navigator, Netscape Communicator, Microsoft Internet Explorer, Sun HotJava, and so forth. This Webtop is enabled by the Tarantella packages included on the Optional Services CD.

Managers

There is a large number of graphical managers available to the UnixWare 7 administrator. Most of these managers came straight from OpenServer 5. Some came straight from UnixWare 2. Some are new to both operating systems. Throughout the book, these managers are discussed in everything from user administration to DHCP.

Networking

In UnixWare 7, a number of new network features are delivered in the operating system. These features serve to improve network capabilities, improve flexibility, and reduce the administrator's workload.

Integrated Netscape Browser and Web Server

Each UnixWare 7 system functions as a full-featured Web server out of the box. Netscape FastTrack Server is included for serving Web pages and applications. For Web browsing and Web page development, Netscape Navigator Gold is provided. See Chapter 8, "Browsers and Intranets," for more on this topic.

Multi-Link PPP

Administrators can use several ISDN or modem lines to link PPP into an ISP. The use of *multi-link PPP* provides an increase in the data that can be sent and received. Data packets are sent in parallel over the available telephone lines. This allows administrators to increase or decrease their network throughput dynamically by increasing or decreasing the number of lines connected at any given time. This ability is especially useful in situations involving peak and off-peak traffic because the number of links can be manipulated to maintain smooth performance despite highs and lows in the demands placed on the network. See Chapter 7, "WAN Network Configuration," for more on multi-link.

Multicast IP Addressing and Routing

Also related to network performance is *multicast IP addressing and routing*, which is the ability to send, receive, and route TCP/IP messages to multiple recipients without having to send an individual message to each. This feature can be used to provide audio- or video-conferencing over the network.

Multihoming

Multihoming, the capability of a UnixWare 7 system to contain multiple, virtual Internet domains, provides a great deal of flexibility on a single system. Each virtual domain has a separate IP address, and IP aliases are created. This allows ISPs and network administrators to use a single server to set up several Internet domains with their respective Web sites.

IPv6 Support

Also on the subject of IP addresses is the approach of a problem with the IPv4 numbering scheme: We are running out of IP addresses. The solution is the upcoming change in IP addressing, IPv6 (version 6 Internet Protocol). With IPv4, 32-bit addresses are assigned in four octets separated by dots; IPv6 will see 128-bit addresses in colon-separated hex pairs. UnixWare 7's IPv6 API support allows developers to prepare "IPv6-ready" applications while still running on IPv4.

Lightweight Directory Access Protocol

Directory service is a standards-based information database that is used to organize objects, such as users, groups, and devices, and the properties associated with them. These services are used to automatically share information among various applications and network services. UnixWare 7 uses *Lightweight Directory Access Protocol (LDAP),* a directory service protocol that runs over TCP/IP. LDAP is the most popular directory service for TCP/IP networks and the Internet (see Chapter 6, "LAN Network Configuration").

Dynamic Host Configuration Protocol

Dynamic Host Configuration Protocol (DHCP) is used to dynamically assign IP addresses to client machines that request them. A pool of available IP addresses is configured using the DHCP Manager. By assigning addresses as they are requested, the amount of configuration that must be performed for the end user is reduced.

DHCP also reduces the chances of accidentally assigning duplicate IP addresses on the same network. Duplicate addressing causes strange network behavior and unusual failures, and is difficult to troubleshoot. Currently, UnixWare 7 can be a DHCP server, but not a client. Chapter 6 contains more information on DHCP.

Integrated Services Digital Networks (ISDN) Support

The use of *ISDN lines*—special, dedicated phone lines from local telephone and network suppliers—is an increasingly popular method of Internet connection.

UnixWare 7 supports *BRI (Basic Rate Interface),* which is made up of two 64Kbps channels used to carry voice or data traffic, as well as supporting ISDN terminal adapters (see Chapter 7).

Extensive New Modem Support

SCO offers support for more than 1,000 modem models from virtually all of the leading modem manufacturers. UnixWare 7 will auto-detect modems, using the Modem Manager (see Chapter 10, "Configuration of Serial Ports and Terminal Devices").

Java

Java is used extensively in client/server computing and is the basis for Tarantella. SCO has provided a full Java suite in UnixWare 7.

Built-In Java Runtime Environment

UnixWare 7 includes a highly optimized *Java Runtime Environment (JRE),* which allows Java applications to be run on the system without the need for any auxiliary products. In addition to the instant portability of Java applications, the optimized JRE serves to keep the performance of Java applications in line with the superior general performance of UnixWare 7.

The JRE, which is installed by default, contains a majority of the components in the Java Development Kit (JDK), which is a part of the UDK. The JRE components include a Java compiler and a Java applet viewer, as well as a host of other tools to get Java applications running. Java applications can be invoked in several ways: from a standard UNIX command line, as an applet from a Web page, or from other programs or shells.

Java Development Kit 1.1.3

The JDK release 1.1.3 is included in the UDK. It was ported and optimized in conjunction with Sun Microsystems and serves as a powerful instrument for Java development. The JDK offers a comprehensive set of tools, classes, and example programs for developing Java applications. It includes the following:

- Java compiler (`javac`)
- Java interpreter (`java`)
- Java debugger (`jdb`)
- Java applet viewer (`appletviewer`)
- Java class file dissembler (`javap`)

Java Workshop 2.0

The UDK includes the SCO Edition of Java Workshop 2.0, by Sun Microsystems, Inc. *Java Workshop* is an integrated development environment for writing Java applications and works in conjunction with the JDK. It is written totally in Java and serves to illustrate the power and flexibility of the Java development environment while providing a fully graphical platform for developing and debugging Java applications.

Java Workshop is the state of the art in Java development tools, and offers developers a rich set of development and debugging tools on a very cost-effective platform. Java Workshop can be used with a free 30-day evaluation license, or licensed directly.

Java Studio 1.0

The UDK also provides the SCO Edition of Sun Microsystems, Inc.'s Java Studio 1.0. *Java Studio* is a graphical development tool that allows non-Java programmers to create Java and Web applications without having to know Java. It enables developers to assemble Java components (called *JavaBeans*) into full applications and comes with JavaBeans ready to use. JavaBeans are also available from third-party sources, giving developers even more flexibility in selecting modules that suit their needs. As with the Java Workshop, Java Studio can either be licensed directly or used with a free 30-day evaluation license.

Mail and Messaging

Several changes have taken place in the mail and messaging area. For instance, OpenServer 5 users will find that `mmdf` is not supported on UnixWare 7 and support for UnixWare 2's `mailsur` is removed. See Chapter 20, "Mailers," for more on mail and messaging.

Sendmail as Default Mail Transport

UnixWare 7 uses *sendmail*, the standard for mail delivery on UNIX systems, to send, deliver, and route email between users.

Support for IMAP4 and POP3

The IMAP4 and POP3 protocols are used for accessing email on UnixWare 7 systems from network clients. These protocols are used as the standard method for retrieving email from UNIX servers by mail clients, such as Netscape Navigator, Netscape Communicator, and Qualcomm Eudora. Thus, any popular email package can work with UnixWare 7 without requiring any special handling or configuration on the server. UnixWare 7 provides Navigator Gold, a POP3 client, as well as two IMAP4 clients: Pine and Communicator.

Support for a Wide Variety of Email Clients

UnixWare 7 offers extensive support of mail transportation technologies, which means that virtually all of the most popular email programs can use UnixWare 7 as the email post office. These programs include standard UNIX email readers, such as mailx, pine, dtmail (from the CDE desktop), as well as newer standards, such as Qualcomm Eudora, Netscape Navigator and Netscape Communicator, Microsoft Outlook, and other network-based mail clients.

CHAPTER 2

Hardware Configuration

- Hardware compatibility
  Learn how to determine whether your hardware will work with UnixWare 7.
- Minimum hardware configuration
  Make sure your system meets the minimum requirements for installation.
- HBA diskette
  Find out what to do with an HBA diskette, and when to do it.
- Adapter configuration settings
  Learn how to avoid conflicts between peripherals.
- SCSI and RAID tutorial
  Learn how SCSI and RAID configurations offer improved system performance.

Hardware Compatibility

A crucial task when selecting hardware components for a UnixWare 7 system is verifying that the particular items are supported. Hardware compatibility can be checked in either the Runtime Release Notes or the online Compatible Hardware Web Pages.

Troubleshooting Tip

UnixWare 7 contains Host Bus Adapter (HBA) drivers for all supported hardware. If you use vendor-supplied drivers for peripherals that are not listed in SCO's Compatible Hardware Web Pages, your system may not function properly.

Compatible Hardware Web Pages (CHWP)

The *Compatible Hardware Web Pages (CHWPs)* are the most up-to-date source for finding hardware compatibility information. They are located at `www.sco.com/chwp`.

Searches can be performed based on the hardware manufacturer, product category, and SCO product family (see Figure 2.1).

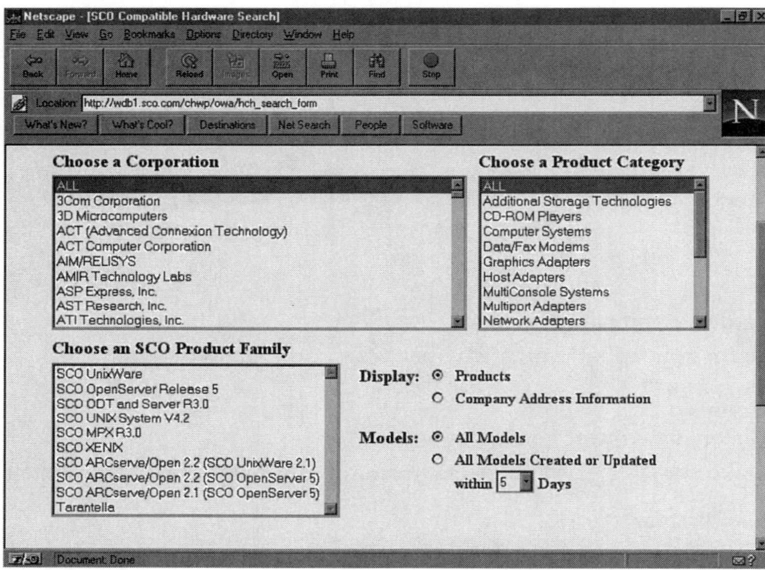

FIGURE 2.1 *Compatible Hardware Web Pages search screen.*

Upon execution of the search, a table will be returned listing products that match the criteria entered, as well as some data about the products themselves. The information displayed is dependent on the category searched. For instance, a search of `Host Adapters` shows the device interface, such as SCSI-1 or SCSI-2, and whether the device supports caching. In comparison, a `Network Adapter` listing includes the adapter type (Ethernet, Token Ring, ISDN, and so forth), media type (thick or thin coax, twisted pair, and so forth), and data path (8-, 16-, or 32-bit).

Figure 2.2 illustrates the data returned from a search. The columns under each operating system indicate the level of support, including T (Tested and Certified by SCO), V (Supported by Vendor), R (Reported by Vendor to Work), and NS (Not Supported in This Release). All abbreviations are footnoted at the end of the onscreen listing.

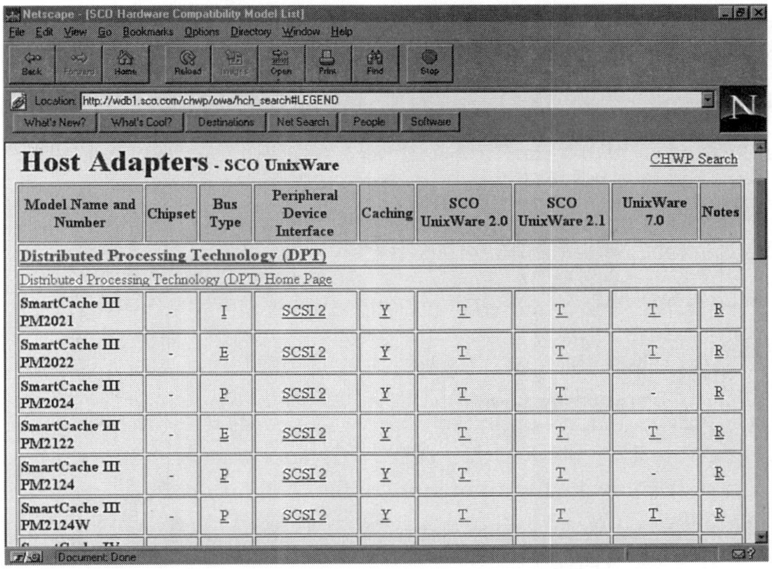

Host Adapters - SCO UnixWare

CHWP Search

Model Name and Number	Chipset	Bus Type	Peripheral Device Interface	Caching	SCO UnixWare 2.0	SCO UnixWare 2.1	UnixWare 7.0	Notes
Distributed Processing Technology (DPT)								
Distributed Processing Technology (DPT) Home Page								
SmartCache III PM2021	-	I	SCSI 2	Y	T	T	T	R
SmartCache III PM2022	-	E	SCSI 2	Y	T	T	T	R
SmartCache III PM2024	-	P	SCSI 2	Y	T	T	-	R
SmartCache III PM2122	-	E	SCSI 2	Y	T	T	T	R
SmartCache III PM2124	-	P	SCSI 2	Y	T	T	-	R
SmartCache III PM2124W	-	P	SCSI 2	Y	T	T	T	R

FIGURE 2.2 *CHWP search results.*

Some devices supported in OpenServer or previous versions of SCO UNIX may not be supported in UnixWare 7. Floppy-tape is one example. Devices that conform to SCSI or IDE/ATAPI should work in UnixWare 7, with the exception of IDE Tape.

Runtime Release Notes

A wealth of information on hardware peculiarities can be found in the Runtime Release Notes. This is the place to look for specific solutions to problems, such as corrupted cursors, display corruption, and general hardware maladies. The Release Notes can also be found online at `doc.sco.com`, as well as in the /info hierarchy on the CD-ROM.

Minimum Hardware Configuration

SCO recommends that hardware for a UnixWare 7 system meet the requirements listed in the following sections.

Processor

At least one Pentium, Pentium II, or Pentium Pro microprocessor, or one that is 100% compatible, is recommended.

The Intel486DX is the minimum processor supported, and the Intel486SX with math coprocessor is not supported.

Architecture

The following architectures are supported:

- Industry Standard Architecture (ISA)
- Extended Industry Standard Architecture (EISA)
- Micro Channel Architecture (MCA)
- Peripheral Component Interface (PCI)
- cache coherent Non Uniform Memory Architecture (ccNUMA)
- Intelligent I/O (I_2O)

There currently is no limit on the number of PCI cards that can be supported under UnixWare 7. Systems with up to 32 PCI slots have been reported to work. The restrictions really apply more to the total number of a particular type of card. Presently, up to four network interface cards (NICs) are supported, and this number is expected to increase to 32.

ccNUMA support is built into the kernel, but has not been certified on any specific hardware as of the time of this writing.

UnixWare 7 does not currently have PCMCIA support, but a support supplement is planned. For this reason, UnixWare 7 must be installed on laptop computers from CD-ROM or a docking station, because the PCMCIA NICs are not yet supported. PCMCIA drivers from SCO UnixWare 2.1 can be used with UnixWare 7, but cannot be used for a network install because they must be loaded after installation. The CHWPs contain the latest information on PCMCIA drivers for UnixWare 7.

Memory

Small Footprint systems can run with 16MB of RAM, and all other installations require a minimum of 32MB. For optimum CDE performance, 64MB is recommended. Increasing RAM further will enhance system performance.

UnixWare 7 supports up to 4GB of general-purpose memory and up to 64GB of special-purpose memory.

Disk Size

Small Footprint systems can run with as little as 300MB in the UNIX partition. All other systems have a minimum requirement of 500MB, and a disk size of 1GB or more is recommended.

Mouse

To effectively use the graphical desktop, a serial, bus, or PS2-compatible mouse should be used.

Video

To run the graphical desktop, a Super VGA monitor and video adapter offering at least 800×600 resolution are required.

> **Tip**
>
> *When installing on a Toshiba Tecra, the VGA Segment Address in the Display section of the ROM BIOS is set to* `E400H` *by default and will work this way with OpenServer 5. However, for UnixWare 7, it needs to be set to* `C000H-CBFFH`*. In the video configuration, set the adapter type to Chips 65550/65554 Super VGA 1024×768 256-color and the monitor to 14" Other. This seems to work for UnixWare 7, OpenServer 5, Windows 95, and Windows NT.*

Media

A 3.5-inch diskette drive is needed to boot the system and install additional software. Aside from the floppy drive, a system must also have at least one of the following:

- CD-ROM drive
- Supported network adapter and another UnixWare 7 machine on the network, configured as an install server

Systems with these network adapters cannot be used to perform a network installation:

- 3Com 3C507 EtherLink 16 Series
- 3Com 3C523 EtherLink MC Series

In addition, FDDI, Token-Ring, and DDI8 network adapters will not work for a network installation.

HBA Diskettes

If an HBA diskette was supplied to you by your hardware or software vendor, it must be loaded during system installation. Starting with UnixWare 7.0.1, an HBA driver diskette is included in the media kit. See Chapter 4, "Installation of UnixWare 7," for information on creating this diskette from the CD-ROM. If the HBA diskette is not loaded, UnixWare 7 may not be able to see the hardware for which the diskette was supplied. Diskettes must have been created specifically for UnixWare 7 systems in order to load successfully.

Adapter Configuration Settings

There are several configurations of which you need to be aware in order to avoid conflicts in your hardware setup. The allowable settings can be found in the manufacturer's documentation for a given piece of hardware. Chapter 4 discusses the use of the Device Configuration Utility (DCU) for checking the information discussed in the following sections.

I/O Base Addresses

Each controller that performs I/O on a system needs to have a unique space in memory to exchange messages with the operating system. The starting location of this memory is called the *I/O base address*. It is represented as a three-digit hexadecimal number. No two components on a system should use the same base address, and the address assigned to a driver must match the address settings on the associated adapter. For example, standard settings for a parallel and serial port are 378 and 3f8, respectively.

Shared RAM Addresses

The shared RAM address represents an area of system RAM used for data transfer between an adapter and the operating system. Each adapter needs a unique address. An example of a shared RAM address is c8000.

Shared ROM Addresses

Some adapters require a ROM base address. As with shared RAM, the ROM address sets aside an area of system memory to be used exclusively for that adapter. This is used in some cases for the boot ROM on a SCSI controller.

Interrupt Vectors

Interrupt Vectors (IRQs) serve to alert the CPU to a request by a device. Each device on a system must have its own IRQ, and conflicts can result in anything from unreliable activity to a total lack of response from a device.

Direct Memory Access Channels

There are different ways the CPU can exchange data with a controller. *Direct Memory Access (DMA)* allows the device to place data into memory without CPU intervention. This saves CPU cycles by eliminating the need for the CPU to retrieve data from the controller. Devices capable of DMA transfers must be configured with a DMA channel. There are eight channels available, numbered from 0 to 7.

A SCSI and RAID Tutorial

The best way to speed up a server computer is by optimizing disk access. Both SCSI and RAID contribute to an enhanced server solution.

Small Computer Systems Interface

The *Small Computer Systems Interface (SCSI)* offers better performance than other interfaces due to its use of multitasking. SCSI has the ability to process multiple overlapped commands, which allows reads and writes to be performed simultaneously on multiple SCSI drives, rather than serially. The data can then be buffered and transferred over the SCSI bus at high speeds.

Another feature of SCSI is that, unlike previous interfaces, it is not device specific. The same SCSI adapter can be used with hard drives, tapes, CD-ROMs, scanners, and so on.

Physical SCSI Configuration

SCSI controllers essentially function like a network. Signals travel along the length of the cable. Each end of the SCSI bus must be terminated, much like a thinnet network. Termination should occur at the physical end of the cable. If a cable is terminated somewhere in the middle, the remaining part of the cable essentially becomes an antenna and will have serious repercussions on signal integrity. When using a SCSI controller with either internal or external devices, but not both, the controller itself is located at one end of the bus and should be terminated. When using both internal and external SCSI devices, the controller ends up in the middle of the bus and should not be terminated.

Improper termination is the most common cause of SCSI problems. An improperly terminated SCSI bus will exhibit intermittent failures. Using terminators at each end of a SCSI bus, rather than relying on a device to act as a terminator, ensures proper termination when devices are moved on the SCSI bus. For instance, with hot-swappable devices, if the device needing to be swapped was acting as the terminator, true hot swap capability is lost because the system will likely fail when the terminating device is removed.

SCSI cabling guidelines allow a maximum cable length of 10 feet at 10MHz, and there should be a minimum of 12 inches between connectors.

SCSI devices are uniquely identified by four values:

- Controller number
- Bus number
- Target ID
- Logical unit number (LUN)

The host adapter is usually assigned ID 7. This is because the highest target ID carries the highest priority. The LUN is generally 0 for SCSI devices. A bridge controller, which can support up to eight devices, may use LUNs from 0 to 7 to identify the devices attached. A CD-ROM tower, for instance, may use this sort of numbering.

SCSI-1

SCSI-1 was the first SCSI standard, approved in 1986. SCSI-1 supported up to seven devices per adapter. It had some limitations, including not being as fast as it needed to be. SCSI-1 allowed transfer rates of 1.5MB/sec for asynchronous data transfer, and a maximum of 5MB/sec for synchronous data transfer.

SCSI-2

The SCSI-2 standard was developed to offer several improvements over SCSI-1. The clock rate of the SCSI bus was doubled from 5MHz to 10MHz, which increased the synchronous data transfer rate to 10MB/sec. This was called *Fast SCSI*.

SCSI-2 also offers Wide SCSI. With *Wide SCSI*, the bus bandwidth is doubled, using a 16-bit rather than an 8-bit bus width. The result is twofold. First, the number of devices that can be handled by a single adapter jumps from 7 to 15. Second, the data transfer rate is doubled. By combining Fast SCSI and Wide SCSI, the maximum rate is bumped to 20MB/sec.

Two SCSI-2 features have enhanced performance:

- Command queuing
- Scatter/gather

Command queuing rearranges I/O commands in order to optimize overlapping and maximize throughput. Scatter/gather applies to virtual memory addressing, in which memory may appear contiguous to the user, but is in fact quite fragmented. Consequently, when a large chunk of data is read from a device, it is broken up into different locations in memory. Scatter/gather is a method of including multiple host addresses for data transfer in one command packet. It significantly boosts performance in UNIX environments.

Other SCSI-2 advances include improved connectors, parity checking, and better reliability through synchronous negotiation.

There are some things to keep in mind when moving from SCSI-1 to SCSI-2. Narrow SCSI devices can be used in conjunction with a Wide SCSI bus, but will need adapters for the connectors. A key thing to remember involves termination. Because a narrow SCSI device is accessing only half of the Wide SCSI bus, it cannot function as the terminating device. Attempting to do so would result in terminating only the lower half of the bus width, with signals bouncing out of control on the second half. Clearly, this would be a bad thing. Termination must be associated with a Wide SCSI device. If you are working with a scenario in which a Wide SCSI controller resides in the middle of the bus, and one side has only narrow devices, the controller must be set to terminate "high only" on the bus with narrow devices.

SCSI-3

The SCSI-3 specification, which is still being ratified, takes advantage of technological advances made since the development of SCSI-2. A notable change from prior SCSI specifications is the addition of serial interconnect capabilities to the standard SCSI parallel interconnect.

Fast-20 Wide SCSI, or *Ultra SCSI,* is an improvement on the parallel side. It is backward-compatible with SCSI-1 and SCSI-2 systems and peripherals. With Ultra SCSI, the Fast SCSI bus clock rate of 10MHz is doubled. With a 20MHz clock and 16-bit Wide SCSI bus, Ultra SCSI offers data transfer rates of up to 40MB/sec.

On the serial side, there are three technologies offered by SCSI-3:

- Serial Storage Architecture (SSA)
- Fibre Channel
- IEEE P1394

Serial SCSI is not backward-compatible with SCSI-1 and SCSI-2 devices. It does, however, offer several advantages over parallel SCSI. More devices can be attached to a single bus, cables can be longer, connectors are simplified, and data transfer rates are improved. The improved transfer rates make Serial SCSI ideal for use with disk arrays. For this reason, the serial interconnects were designed to support true hot swapping without needing any special connectors.

SCSI Versus EIDE

While EIDE (Enhanced IDE) offers improvements over IDE, it still faces significant limitations. Data transfer rates remain limited to between 9 and 16MB/sec. A single EIDE controller can support only two devices; and the configuration is limited to hard drives, CD-ROMs, and tape drives. By comparison, Wide SCSI can handle 15 devices without restrictions as to type and Wide Fast SCSI transfer rates reach 20MB/sec, with Ultra SCSI capabilities reaching 40MB/sec.

In addition, EIDE is not capable of handling overlapped commands, command queuing, or scatter/gather data transfers, all of which are present in SCSI. This is because EIDE is still tied to the old WD1003 (ST506) interface. Another shortcoming of EIDE is the inability to support external devices. While SCSI is capable of handling devices connected to the computer externally, EIDE requires that all devices physically reside in the computer box.

Caching

Because disk drives perform at significantly slower speeds than system memory, they tend to create the primary bottleneck in server computers. One approach to easing this problem is the use of *caching*. This solution can be implemented in both software and hardware.

Software Caching

An OS's software cache increases performance in two ways:

- Software read caching is designed to eliminate disk reads. If the cache already contains the data requested, the disk need not be accessed.
- Software write caching works by holding data that needs to be written to the disk in the cache, then actually writing it to the disk when the system is idle. The idea here is to postpone the write until it can occur without competing for system resources.

Read caching is the more beneficial of the two types of caching because, when successful, it eliminates the need to access the disk, while write caching can only delay the access.

Software caching works best on systems with a small number of users and a small load on the system. This is true because of the way write caching works. Because write caching needs the system to have periods of idle time to flush the dirty data in the cache to the disk, the cache on a busy system tends to fill up with data waiting to be written. The cache must eventually be emptied, resulting in competition for resources on a heavily loaded system. In such a case, the benefits of write caching disappear completely. In addition, having the cache full of data waiting to be written reduces space available for read caching, which is more effective.

Software caching is built into the operating system. See Chapter 21, "Performance Tuning," for information on tuning the software buffer cache.

Hardware Caching

While software caching can serve to reduce the need for disk access and delay disk access until times when the system is idle, *hardware caching* is meant to reduce disk access time. When hardware cache is added to a system, the software cache still needs to empty its buffers, but can do so much more quickly. The time required to write data to the caching adapter is much less than that required to write to a disk. Once the software cache has been flushed, the hardware cache is written to the disk concurrent with other system activity.

In addition to allowing disk writes to be performed without interfering with system activity, hardware caching also reduces the time required for the writes themselves. This is accomplished through the use of *elevator sorting*. The purpose of the sort is to write the data to the disk in order of increasing cylinder, head, and sector number, which reduces time spent on seeks and missed rotations.

An elevator in a tall building is a good illustration of how this sort works. Suppose a group of people board in the lobby, each pressing the button for his or her desired floor. The elevator then moves up, stopping on each requested floor as the elevator reaches it. Had the requests not been handled this way, but rather in the order the buttons had been pressed, passengers would have ended up riding up and down as those who entered before them were taken to the proper floors.

Another way hardware cache serves to reduce disk access time is through *read ahead caching*. Data tends to reside in clumps on the drives, and read ahead caching is designed to take advantage of the good chance that the bytes on disk just after the last byte read will be the next requested. Those bytes are therefore read into the hardware cache. If there is a cache hit, the disk access time is greatly reduced.

Hardware caching is implemented as a physical memory add-on to a disk controller.

RAID

A *redundant array of inexpensive disks (RAID)* is a data storage solution intended to exceed the capabilities of a *single large expensive disk (SLED)* by combining a group of smaller drives. The array appears to the system as a single drive. Because of the increased number of drives, individual components of the array are likely to fail far more often than a single drive would.

The computed mean time for the array as a whole is the mean time between failures (MTBF) for each drive divided by the number of drives. For this reason, fault tolerance is a critical issue for RAID systems.

Basic to RAID is the idea of *disk striping*. Individual drives are partitioned into *stripes*, which can range in size from 512 bytes to several megabytes. When data is written, it is placed into stripes aligned across the array. Whether to use small stripes or large stripes is determined by whether the application is I/O or data-intensive.

Multiuser environments are I/O intensive, with many users simultaneously placing I/O demands on the system. For the best overall disk access performance, I/O should be balanced across the array of drives. In this case large stripes should be used in the hope that a single record can fit within a stripe. This would result in each individual drive being able to perform a complete I/O operation simultaneously.

Single-user and data-intensive environments benefit from small stripes. The result of using small stripes is that the data is spread across all of the drives in the array, which can perform I/O simultaneously. This increases performance when accessing large records. It does not, however, allow for the overlapping I/O that can be accomplished with large stripes. In addition, when small stripes are used, synchronized spindle drives are recommended to eliminate wasted spin time.

RAID Configurations

There are five defined RAID configurations, RAID-1 through RAID-5, which offer different combinations of features. Although RAID, by definition, is meant to be a redundant array, the term *RAID-0* has emerged to refer to a non-redundant array.

RAID-1 is also known as *disk mirroring*. In this configuration the drives are arranged in pairs, with both drives in a pair containing identical data. If a drive goes down, its mirrored partner is there to stand in its place until the faulty drive can be replaced and re-mirrored. Disk writes take no more time than without mirroring because the two writes are performed simultaneously. Read times stand to be improved because they, too, can be performed simultaneously on both drives in the pair. Because reads are performed independently on each of the mirrored drives, two pieces of data from different physical locations on the identical drives can be retrieved at the same time. The amount of storage available to the system with RAID-1 is one-half of the total space on the drives in the array because each piece of data will reside in two physical locations. RAID-1 also requires an even number of drives. This RAID configuration offers the best performance, especially in multiuser systems. Although not one of the initially defined RAID configurations, multiple RAID-1 arrays can be striped together to form a larger array known as a *dual-level* array, or *RAID-10*.

RAID-2 stripes data across the array and uses some drives for ECC (Error Correcting Code) information. Because ECC information is commonly embedded in drives today, RAID-2 offers no advantages over RAID-3 and is not commonly used.

RAID-3 also sector-stripes data across the drives in the array, but lets the ECC embedded in the hardware handle error correction. A single drive in the array is used as the parity drive. If a drive in the array fails, its data can be reconstructed by calculating the exclusive OR of the remaining data.

RAID-4 uses the same parity drive setup as RAID-3, but uses large stripes. Read operations on the drives can be performed simultaneously, and the large stripes are likely to contain complete records, so read requests can be overlapped. However, because write operations must always access the parity drive, overlapped writes are not possible.

RAID-5, like RAID-4, uses large stripes, which allow for overlapping I/O (see Figure 2.3). The difference is in the way parity information is stored. The drive used to store parity information is not fixed, but instead rotates through the array. Because each record stores its parity information on a different drive, both read and write operations can be overlapped. With RAID-3 through RAID-5, one drive, whether dedicated or rotating, is dedicated to storing information for data recovery. Thus, the maximum storage available to the system on one of these arrays is the total space on all drives in the array, less the space on a single drive.

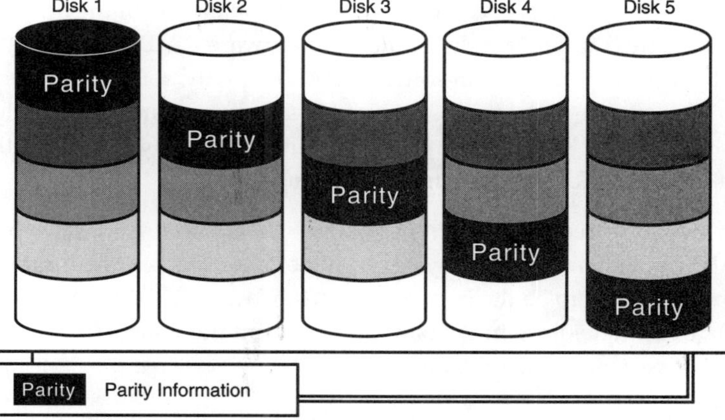

FIGURE 2.3 *RAID-5 striping with parity.*

Comparing RAID-1 and RAID-5

The trade-offs to consider when choosing between a RAID-1 and RAID-5 configuration involve storage capacity and performance. RAID-5 clearly offers more storage capability than RAID-1. For instance, in an array of six drives of 4GB each, a RAID-1 configuration would offer 12GB of storage, while a RAID-5 would have 20GB available. RAID-5 is a good solution in environments where storage efficiency is desired.

RAID-1 offers superior performance to RAID-5, for an obvious reason. When data is written to the drive in RAID-1, each of the disks in the mirrored pair records the data simultaneously; and the time required to complete the storage is simply that required to perform a single write. In RAID-5, the parity must be recomputed when data is changed. This process actually involves two reads, two performances of an exclusive OR operation, and two writes. For this reason, RAID-5 is not recommended for environments where write-performance is critical and should not be implemented in software.

RAID Implementations: Hardware and Software

RAID can be implemented in either hardware or software. The big difference between the two is in the impact of the RAID configuration on system performance. In hardware implementations, the adapter itself handles the array, eliminating the need to use CPU time. Software RAID uses system resources to perform the calculations and operations necessary to maintain the array. Its performance will vary with the load on the system at a given time and competes with other applications for system resources.

Hardware RAID, in contrast, can be performing operations on the array while the system carries out other tasks. Although hardware RAID implementation is likely to be more expensive than software RAID initially, software implementation may well require subsequent increases in system resources to handle the new load. Hardware RAID is also more fault-tolerant than software RAID, regardless of which RAID configuration is being used.

Consider two mirrored drives with IDs 0 and 1, in which drive 0 fails. In a software RAID implementation, the system will not boot because the hardware BIOS expects drive 0 to be the boot device. A hardware RAID would recognize the failure of a single drive in the pair and run from the other drive, while alerting the operator to the problem.

In a RAID-5 array, software implementations essentially require a separate boot drive not included in the array. This is necessary because the boot loader would not have the drivers to deal with the failure of one drive in the array.

The drivers needed to handle the array are loaded after the operating system loads. Because hardware RAID does not require operating system drivers, and the hardware handles reconstruction of lost data as a result of failure, hardware RAID is transparent to the operating system and is suitable for storage of the operating system itself.

UnixWare 7 offers several options for disk management. Disk Spanning is included in the base product for all editions. Disk Mirroring is offered as an add-on (UnixWare 7 Disk Mirroring Release 3.2), or as a subset of the ODM add-on (UnixWare 7 Online Data Manager Release 3.2). The ODM also offers additional services beyond those found in the Disk Mirroring add-on. Hardware RAID can be implemented with products from DPT, Adaptec, 1776, Mylex, and others.

CHAPTER 3

UnixWare 7 System Configuration

- Licensing
  Learn the new approach to licensing with UnixWare 7.
- System profiles
  Four system profiles offer different degrees of package selection customization at installation.
- Information required at install
  Know what information you will need to install.
- Printed documentation for install
  Find out what can be found in the Installation Guide, Release Notes, and System Handbook.
- CD documentation
  Additional documentation and man pages can be found on the installation CD.
- Filesystems, slices, and sizes
  Learn how UnixWare 7 partitions are managed.
- Coexistence with other operating systems
  Other operating systems can coexist on a UnixWare 7 system.

Licensing

With UnixWare 7, licensing is handled in a new way. Rather than purchasing a license for each feature or service, purpose-built licenses are used. With this method, systems have a single license for a group of services. These services are grouped according to what will be needed for a particular environment. These groups of features are referred to as *editions*.

Each of these editions can be used as a basis for installing Optional Services. Add-on user licenses are available in 10, 25, 100, and 500 network user license packs. The processor upgrade increases the number of supported CPUs to a maximum of 32. Maximum supported RAM varies by edition, and upgrades can be used to bring RAM support to the 4GB or 64GB levels if needed.

A future enhancement is planned to the licensing mechanism in which licenses will be generated based on the services required for each particular environment rather than having preconfigured editions.

Licensing Configurations

The following UnixWare 7 editions are currently available:

- Base Edition
- Departmental Edition
- Enterprise Edition
- Messaging Edition

For an updated listing of available editions, see `www.sco.com/unixware/model_numbers/`.

Base Edition

The Base Edition includes a one-user license. Support for two processors is built in. It supports RAM up to 512MB. Networking features are included, along with SCO ARCserve/Open Lite for data backup and restoration.

The Base Edition is a good basic system that, with add-ons, is suitable for dedicated and replicated environments. It is also suitable for general workstation use.

Departmental Edition

The Departmental Edition offers a 25-user license and support for two CPUs as well as built-in capabilities for up to 4GB of RAM. It includes SCO VisionFS, which allows Windows File and Print Sharing, as well as a full version of SCO ARCserve/Open, which can be used for unattended backups.

This edition is meant for medium to large business computing. It functions as an effective application and database server, and, with VisionFS, is well suited to environments in which users have Windows-based PCs.

Enterprise Edition

The Enterprise Edition includes a 50-user license and support for four processors. It supports up to 64GB of RAM and includes SCO VisionFS for Windows File and Print Services. A full version of SCO ARCserve/Open provides utilities for backup and restoration of data as well as unattended backups. Also included is a full version of the Online Data Manager (ODM), which includes software RAID support. For more on RAID, see Chapter 2, "Hardware Configuration."

The Enterprise Edition is suitable for use as a high-end application and database server. The built-in data mirroring and striping give this configuration the flexibility and reliability needed for a business-critical system.

Messaging Edition

The Messaging Edition provides a one-user license, built-in support for two processors, and 4GB RAM support. It has a full version of SCO ARCserve/Open and adds the Netscape Mail Server and 50 Netscape mailbox licenses.

This configuration is well suited for use as a high-performance, ready-to-deploy messaging server.

Optional Services

The Optional Services are a group of products that work with UnixWare 7 to add on to the built-in capabilities.

Universal Development Kit

The Universal Development Kit (UDK) provides development tools for Java, C, and C++ programming. It runs on UnixWare 7, SCO OpenServer 5, and SCO UnixWare 2.1, which enables you to write a single application for deployment over three operating systems. For more information on the Java tools, see the Java Development Kit (JDK) in Chapter 1, "Why UnixWare 7?"

Netscape Proxy Server 2.5

The Netscape Proxy Server helps reduce the load on a busy intranet or Internet server. It allows administrators to replicate WWW servers and distribute them throughout the network, reducing both network traffic and user wait times. It provides increased network security by controlling access to data, and it filters content to increase user productivity.

Netscape LiveWire 1.0

Netscape LiveWire is a set of tools that allows developers to create programs that reside on the server, and allows browsers to run database applications. It can be used to provide search and update access to relational databases through a browser.

Netscape Messaging Server 3.5

The Netscape Messaging Server provides the ability to communicate with virtually all mail systems and gateways. It offers superior performance in speed-of-message processing, queue handling, and power of directory lookups. It also can handle mail with embedded sound, graphics, video files, HTML forms, Java applets, and desktop applications.

Netscape Directory Server 3.0

The Netscape Directory Server is a Lightweight Directory Access Protocol (LDAP) client that gives administrators of Netscape servers a single management point for users, groups, and other shared data. The Netscape Messaging Server can be automatically updated with data from the Directory Server. This product is available with the Messaging Edition.

NetWare Services 4.10

This component can be used to provide both UnixWare 7 and SCO UnixWare 2.1 with Novell NetWare 4.10a File, Print, and Directory Services, which allow NetWare clients to transparently access a UnixWare 7 server. This means that a UnixWare 7 server can be introduced into an existing Novell environment without necessitating any reconfiguration. A 0 user version of NWS is provided with all UnixWare 7 editions.

Tarantella

Tarantella software provides the capability for applications to be delivered to any client, without any additional software needed on the client side. Tarantella offers simple access to network computing capabilities, particularly in heterogeneous networks. A single-user version of Tarantella is provided with all UnixWare 7 editions.

Tarantella allows clients to run applications through a Web browser. It acts as an intermediary between the servers running the applications and the clients accessing them. Tarantella uses a specially developed protocol, Adaptive Internet Protocol (AIP), to constantly reevaluate communication conditions in order to deliver data in the most efficient manner. AIP makes possible the display of graphics on very slow networks. For more on Tarantella, visit `tarantella.sco.com`.

SCO Advanced File and Print Server 4.0

SCO Advanced File and Print Server (AFPS) enables file and printer sharing with PCs running Windows (3.x, 95, or NT), OS/2, and MS-DOS. It has peer-to-peer compatibility with Microsoft NT 4.0, which allows a UNIX system to appear as an NT server to desktop clients. AFPS performs as either a Primary or Backup Domain Controller in an NT 4.0 environment. AFPS is perfect for environments requiring UNIX-to-Windows NT domain integration.

SCO ARCserve/Open from Cheyenne 2.2

This product provides data backup, restoration, and data management capabilities for networked environments. It offers unattended, automated backup management, multiclient and server network backup and restore, high-capacity data storage, and support for online backup of mission critical databases. These features make it ideal for large servers and heterogeneous networks.

UnixWare 7 ReliantHA 1.1

The newest ReliantHA software for UnixWare 7 is a nonproprietary solution, which supports off-the-shelf solutions for networking and RAID. It provides high-availability data processing through loosely coupled clustering. ReliantHA does not use redundant systems and peripherals; therefore, all the nodes in a cluster are usable.

UnixWare 7 Online Data Manager 3.2

The Online Data Manager offers software RAID support for levels 0, 1, 5, and 10 (see Chapter 2 for RAID information). It also includes disk-spanning capabilities, which allow single files and filesystems to span multiple physical devices. Filesystem resizing, migration, and RAID level changes can be performed while the system is online.

UnixWare 7 Disk Mirroring 3.2

Disk mirroring increases data availability by building in fault tolerance against disk failures. When disk mirroring is enabled on a system with two disks, a single disk failure will not result in any data loss or even a period of unavailability because a complete duplicate of the lost disk is in place and ready to use. Disk mirroring also provides faster access because it can perform overlapping reads. For more on disk mirroring (RAID-1), see Chapter 2.

RealNetworks

Several RealNetworks products are available for UnixWare 7. They allow delivery of live and on-demand RealAudio and RealVideo broadcasts on the Internet. For individuals and small workgroups, the RealNetworks Basic Server Plus 5.0 offers a low-cost, easy-to-use streaming media server solution. It is available licensed as part of the operating system and can be installed from the Optional Services CD-ROM. RealNetworks RealSystem 5.0 Internet and intranet products are also available for those requiring a more complete and powerful server.

The RealNetworks RealAudio 3.1 Encoder is licensed as part of the operating system and is available at no extra charge. It can be installed from the Optional Services CD-ROM. This product allows encoding of audio signals for broadcast through the RealNetworks Basic Server Plus or RealSystem 5.0 servers.

Evaluation Licensing

If you install UnixWare 7 and choose to defer licensing, or install products that are not included in the license you purchased, a 60-day evaluation license is generated for most unlicensed packages. The evaluation license selects the packages and services included in the Departmental Edition as a default configuration. When a license is purchased, the evaluation license needs to be removed, and the software needs to be relicensed. New licenses can be applied through the SCOadmin License Manager.

Free UnixWare 7

A free, one-user license for non-commercial or educational use is available through SCO's Web site. The UnixWare 7 Media Kit can be purchased for a small cost. Free UnixWare 7 licenses are available at `www.sco.com/offers/`.

Licensing Terms

There are some new terms to go along with the new licensing methodology.

An *End User Licensing Agreement (EULA)* is the agreement between SCO and the customer about the use of the software. The *Certificate of License Authority (COLA)* refers to the "extent of use" that applies to the purchase of a single license.

A *site* refers to a single physical location. This could be a single office, an office building, or an adjacent grouping of several buildings.

An edition of a user license for UnixWare 7 can be converted into a *Network User License (NUL)* by registering it on the NUL Web site. To access the NUL site, go to `www.sco.com/licensing` and select the option to upgrade user licenses to NULs. NULs allow a set number of users to concurrently access all UnixWare 7 servers at a single networked site. For instance, if two networked servers each had 50 user licenses, converting to NULs would allow 100 users to access both servers.

Author's Note

When keeping a standby system, it is not necessary to duplicate the NULs for the standby system; but separate licenses are required depending on whether the standby system is powered on concurrently with the main system. If the two systems will be running concurrently, a separate license is needed. If the standby system is stored with the power off, it is acceptable to use the standby system as an "archive copy" and not purchase an additional license.

System Profiles

At install time, there are four system profiles from which to choose:

- License-Based Defaults
- Small Footprint
- Full
- Customize

License-Based Defaults

By selecting to install based on the license information entered, you can be certain that no unlicensed software will be installed on your system.

Small Footprint Server

The Small Footprint option is offered as a solution for systems with limited memory and disk space. It can be installed on systems with as little as 16MB of RAM and 300MB available on the UNIX partition. The services are optimized for systems with limited resources. Networking utilities are included along with the base operating system. Small Footprint installation does not, however, contain graphics support, nor does it include SCO ARCserve/Open. Verifying that the settings for system resources are at acceptable levels is recommended before going on with the install.

Full (All Packages)

When a Full install is chosen, all services and packages on the installation media, except for supplemental languages and multiprocessor support, are selected. This does not, however, mean that all of the installed packages are licensed. See the "Evaluation Licensing" section earlier in the chapter on free evaluation licensing.

Customize Installation of Packages

The Customize option allows you to select and deselect the packages to be installed. The defaults offered are based on the configuration of the license entered. Additional packages selected for which no license has yet been purchased can be tried for 60 days with evaluation licensing, as explained in the "Evaluation Licensing" section.

When the Customize profile is used, it selects by default the packages included in the last profile selection made. It will initially include the license-based defaults profile if no profiles have yet been selected.

Information Required at Install

Before beginning an installation there are several pieces of information that should be obtained. Unless an evaluation license is being installed, the license information (License Number, License Code, and License Data, if shown on your license sheet) will be needed during the installation. You should also know the node name for the system being installed, its IP address, and the domain name, as well as the model of network card being used if you are installing for network usage. It is possible to defer network configuration until after installation.

In the case of a network install, some information is needed about the install server. For a TCP/IP install, you will need to know the netmask, default router, and server IP address. For an IPX install, you will be asked for the frame type and IPX server. If the server is not known, a search will be made for a server.

For a complete account of the questions that must be answered at install time, see Chapter 4, "Installation of UnixWare 7."

Printed Documentation for Install

Several pieces of documentation are included in the media kit. They are the Installation Guide, Runtime Release Notes, and System Handbook. You can check SCO's Web site for the most up-to-date information. All SCOhelp documentation is available on the Web at `doc.sco.com`.

Installation Guide

The Installation Guide contains information to help you before, during, and immediately after the install, and provides some configuration instructions. Appendix B of the Installation Guide provides a list of the HBAs built into UnixWare 7 and the devices they support.

Runtime Release Notes

The Runtime Release Notes have the latest information about installation, as well as up-to-date data on hardware, including a full table of supported devices. The Release Notes also offer some help with known limitations and workarounds.

System Handbook

The System Handbook picks up after the install with common administration tasks. It discusses the responsibilities of the system administrator and briefly covers such basic tasks as user management, system startup and shutdown, dealing with file systems, and configuring peripherals.

CD Documentation

In addition to the printed documentation, a full set of UnixWare 7 documentation is included on the install CD. Also included are the man pages, which provide comprehensive information on commands, and the Web-based SCOhelp documentation, which encompasses all of the UnixWare 7 manuals. See Chapter 5, "Console Administration, Logins, and SCOadmin," for more on online documentation.

Filesystems, Slices, and Sizes

A UnixWare 7 disk can be divided into contiguous data areas called *partitions*. For better management, partitions are divided into contiguous sections called *slices*. Slices can contain filesystems or swap space, or can be left for organization by an application. When installing a new non-root drive, each partition can have a maximum of 184 slices. A primary partition can contain more than the default 16 slices, but you will have to use `prtvtoc` and `edvtoc` to do this after it is installed. A maximum of two disks can be configured at the time of system installation. The maximum filesystem size or file size under vxfs is 1TB. See Chapter 17, "User Administration," for further discussion of filesystems.

Coexistence with Other Operating Systems

A UnixWare 7 system can have from one to four partitions. This allows other operating systems (OSs) to reside in their own partitions. For more on handling additional OSs and multibooting, see Chapter 16, "Starting and Stopping."

CHAPTER 4

Installation of UnixWare 7

- Installation methods
  We discuss how to install UnixWare 7 over the network as well as a local install.
- Installation media
  Learn how to replace lost or damaged disks and how to create network install disks.
- Step through the installation
  Follow along as we step through an install.
- Troubleshooting installations
  Learn how to resolve installation problems.

Installation Methods

UnixWare 7 can be installed from a CD-ROM drive or over the network. Systems without a CD-ROM drive can be installed over the network only. Systems with a CD-ROM can be installed over the network or from the local CD-ROM drive. Installations can be performed over the network, using either TCP/IP or IPX/SPX, if a suitable install server is available.

A single UnixWare 7 install server with a CD-ROM drive can be the basis for installs to numerous systems that do not have CD-ROM drives.

SCO has separated license packs from media packs, and an organization could purchase one media pack and multiple licenses. Depending on the location, time requirements, and the network interface cards (NICs), network installs may be the preferred method of installation. Network installs may be ideally suited for installation of UnixWare 7 on several systems with only one set of installation media available.

Installation Media

The installation media pack comes with the UnixWare 7 operating system CD (all versions on one CD), an Updates CD, a Vision Products CD, a CD of Optional Services, the Skunkware CD, two Installation Disks, Development Kits, and third-party CDs.

The UnixWare 7 CD can be read from either UNIX or Windows systems. Readme and release notes files are included on the CD in the /info directory. In addition, disk images for the installation disks, network install disks, a host bus adapter disk, and a troubleshooting disk named "magic" are included in the /info/images directory.

Creating Installation Disks

A set of installation disks can be created to replace lost or damaged disks. The disks can be created from UNIX or Windows.

The files required for creating the disks are in the /info/images directory on the CD. The files are boot.image.C.1 and boot.image.C.2. Starting with version 7.0.1, an HBA disk is also included as hba.image. The same instructions for creating the installation disks apply to the HBA disk.

Creating Installation Disks from UNIX

To create the disks from UNIX, mount the CD. For SCO OpenServer 5 or its predecessors, use

```
mount -r /dev/cd0 /mnt
```

For UnixWare 7, use

```
mount -r -f cdfs /dev/cdrom/cdrom1 /mnt
```

If the UnixWare 7 computer has multiple CDs, the device will be /dev/cdrom*x*/cdrom*x* where *x* is the number of the CD.

Use the `dd` command to create the disks. For OpenServer 5, use

```
dd if=/mnt/info/images/<filename> of=/dev/rfd0
```

For UnixWare 7, use

```
dd if=/mnt/info/images/<filename> of=/dev/rdsk/f03ht
```

Creating Installation Disks from a Windows System

To create boot disks from Windows, you will need a copy of DD.EXE or RAWRITE.EXE. A search of the Web for either name will turn up multiple sources. SCO plans to include a copy of a DOS program for creating the disks in the future. Check the /info/images directory for a DOS executable.

Author's Note

I have used DD.EXE from Sun's Solaris Web site and RAWRITE.EXE from the SCO Web site. Both are available free of charge. To download SCO's RAWRITE.EXE, see Technical Article 107214 and download TLS096. Follow the instructions to uncompress the download to create the RAWRITE.EXE program. To download a copy of the DOS executable DD.EXE, use FTP to download from `ftp.uu.net:/vendor/sun/solaris/x86/dd.exe`.

Insert the CD into the Windows CD-ROM drive; use the RAWRITE or DD command to copy the disk. It is not sufficient to drag and drop the disk image file onto the A: drive in Windows. The drag-and-drop operation will not replace the boot code on the disk. Also, the drag-and-drop operation will fail due to lack of space.

To copy the files with DD, use the following format:

```
DD E:\info\images\<filename> a:
```

To copy the files with RAWRITE, use the following format:

```
E:\INFO\IMAGES>rawrite

Enter disk image source file name: boot_ima.1

Enter target disk drive: a:

Please insert a formatted disk into drive A: and press -ENTER- :
```

CD Install

To install the operating system on a computer with a CD-ROM requires a CD-ROM drive that can be recognized by UnixWare 7 at boot time. Unless the manufacturer of a Host Bus Adapter (HBA) has provided an HBA disk for use with UnixWare 7, the HBA and CD-ROM drive should appear on the Hardware Compatibility List. For an up-to-date list of SCO-compatible hardware, check the Compatible Hardware Web pages (`www.sco.com/chwp`).

Network Install

A network install requires booting the target computer from the install disks and then using the network install disks to initialize the network configuration. A network install must have a network install server configured and enabled. To set up an install server see Chapter 13, "Software Installation."

Creating Network Install Disks

For a network install you will need to create a pair of network install disks. These disks are not target computer specific. The pair of disks can be used repeatedly on installs. These disks include the NIC drivers that can be used to configure the network interface on the target computer.

To create the disks, use the procedures listed in the previous section, "Creating Installation Disks." The files that need to be copied to the disks are in the /info/images directory with the boot disk images. The files required are netinstall.image.1 and netinstall.image.2.

NIC Configuration

Select a NIC from the approved hardware list. UnixWare 7 will auto-detect many cards. Those that are not autodetectable are provided in a list for the installer to select.

Install Packages

The packages that will be installed automatically are based on the license information. Chapter 2, "Hardware Configuration," discusses the system profiles and the packages included in each. When a CD-ROM install is performed, all the licensed packages will be included unless you select a custom install.

With a network install, if the images are left on the CD-ROM on the install server, only the Core Systems Services package is installed. The system must then be rebooted. Once the system is up, the Application Installer may be used to complete the installation of the packages. If all of the install packages are copied to the install server's disk, then all the packages install properly.

Replicated Installs

UnixWare 7 allows the responses to the installation questions to be written to a response disk. The response disk was designed to be used on a re-install of the same system. It can be used for answering questions on a similar install. The node name, license data, IP configuration, and other items may change. The advantage of using the response disk is that the answers are already there when questions are displayed.

Once both installation disks have been read, the option to use the response disk is displayed. The response disk does not allow the installer to press F3 to use the disk and then walk away. The same questions will have to be answered even if the answers are already filled in from the disk.

At the completion of the Installation Query Manager phase of an install, the option is displayed to create a response disk. A formatted disk is required.

Warning

Replication of a system cannot be done using the Emergency Recovery Media because, according to the man page on `emergency_rec`*:*

> *"Attempting to use the* `emergency_rec` *command to copy UnixWare from one system to another system is prohibited. The emergency recovery tape is customized for the system on which it is created and may have unpredictable ramifications if used on another system."*

There are two reasons for the preceding restriction:

- *You should not replicate an install unless you have additional licenses to avoid violating the licensing agreement.*
- *Any differences between systems will result in the need to reconfigure one or more components. In a worst case scenario, different SCSI adapter drivers would prevent the replicated computer from booting.*

Installation Step-by-Step

The installation process consists of a series of prompts for installation information. When answering the prompts, function keys and other keys are used to communicate with the install program. Table 4.1 explains the keys used and their meaning. Function keys F1, F9, and F10 are generally available. The other keys are active when needed. A help line is displayed at the bottom of the screen to guide choices.

TABLE 4.1 FUNCTION KEYS USED DURING INSTALLATION

Key	Purpose
F1	Help
F2	Display or toggle choice
F3	Read or write to media
F6	Configure advanced parameters
F8	Defer configuration
F9	Move back one window
F10	Move forward one window
Down arrow	Move down
Up arrow	Move up
Tab	Move through selections
Space	Select items in a list
Enter	Accept an item

Loading the operating system is referred to as the *Initial System Load (ISL).* During the ISL, a series of prompts is presented to the installer. The process of presenting the prompts and getting the answers is referred to as the *Installation Query Manager*. The ISL consists of several main sections:

- Initial System Load
- Hardware Configuration
- Selecting the Install Method
- Network Install
- Disk Configuration
- System Profile Selection
- Network Configuration
- System Control Entries
- Software Load

Author's Note

These sections are presented in detail. It should be noted that the wording or options may change with future releases. The dialogue presented here was taken from versions 7.0.0 and 7.0.1.

Initial System Load

Step 1. Insert the disk labeled Installation Disk Volume: 1 of 2. Turn on the power to the computer. After the BIOS checks have been performed, the UnixWare 7 logo is displayed.

Starting with version 7.0.1, a language selection menu is presented. Select the language to be used during the ISL.

Prompt: Remove the disk from the drive and insert the disk labeled UnixWare 7 Installation Disk 2 of 2. Press Enter to continue.

Step 2. Insert the requested disk and press Enter. The F10 key is not active at this point. Files are extracted from the disk.

Prompt: Information on the general installation procedure is displayed. If an installation response disk was saved on a previous install, it may be used at this point.

Step 3. If an installation response disk is available, insert it and press F3; otherwise, press F10 to continue.

Prompt: Choose a zone for this system and press F10.

Step 4. Select the appropriate zone (the default is the Americas). Zones influence the keyboard types and locales offered for configuration on the following two screens.

Prompt: Choose a locale for this system and press F10.

Step 5. Select the locale from the list shown. If you made a mistake in selecting the zone, press F9 and return to the zone. Choices for the Americas include Spanish for Argentina, Chile, Mexico, and Venezuela; Portuguese for Brazil; French and English for Canada; C (English), which is the default; USA English; and POSIX English.

Troubleshooting Tip

Do not select the default; instead, pick a geographical locale. The C locale has unexpected effects on sort order in indexes and other sorted lists.

Prompt: Keyboard

Step 6. Select the keyboard from the list provided.

Prompt: System License

Step 7. Enter the License Number, License Code, and License Data (if shown on your license sheet). Licensing may be deferred by pressing F8.

You may want to defer licensing to run an evaluation of UnixWare 7 or because you will obtain a license later. A bug in early editions will not generate a SCO System ID if the licensing is deferred. The lack of the SCO System ID will prevent licensing, and the system must be re-installed when the license is obtained. When licensing is deferred, the system runs for 60 days as a Departmental Edition.

Hardware Configuration

Prompt: If you do not have an HBA, press F10 to continue.

Step 8. Starting with version 7.0.1, SCO supplies an HBA disk. If you have HBA disks from a vendor or SCO, insert them and select Install HBA Disk. Repeat until all HBA disks are installed. If none is required or when all have been installed, press F10.

Tip

Appendix B of the UnixWare 7 Installation Guide lists the supported HBAs and their drivers.

Prompt: After Host Bus Adapter drivers are loaded, you are asked if you need to enter the Device Configuration Utility (DCU). Normally, you should not have to manually configure the HBA. Defer configuration of other devices until after the install.

Step 9. Enter the DCU if necessary. The DCU is discussed later in this chapter. Press F10 to continue.

Prompt: The loading and configuring of the system hardware drivers take place. Watch for the drivers you know should be loaded for your configuration.

> *Tip*
>
> *By pressing Ctrl+Alt+Esc, you can switch to the console screen and see the HBAs and the attached devices that were recognized. If your primary hard disk is not present, you will not be able to install. Switch back to the installation with Ctrl+Alt+F1.*

Prompt: An entry for the Node Name (*system name*) is displayed. Unlike OpenServer 5 and its forerunners, the node name is not limited to eight characters. The node name is an alphanumeric string from 3 to 63 characters in length. The only special character allowed is the dash (–). Do not enter the fully qualified domain name.

Step 10. Enter the node name and press F10.

Selecting the Install Method

Prompt: Installation Method:

Install from cartridge tape

Install from CD-ROM

Install from TCP network server

Install from IPX network server

Cancel installation and shut down

> *Tip*
>
> *Although tape is listed here, SCO does not provide the operating system on tape. It is possible for a vendor to supply tape media.*

Step 11. Depending on the resources located on the computer, you may have options for cartridge tape and CD-ROM. If a CD-ROM is on the system but the option does not appear in the list, shut down and check the setup. (If the

CD-ROM is not listed, check the HBA and device recognition as shown in step 9.) Select the method of installation and press F10.

Prompt: If the CD was selected, a message is displayed that the CD media is verified.

Network Install

For Network installs, the following menu appears:

Configure Networking Hardware

Configure Networking Protocol

Continue with Installation

Configure Networking Hardware is highlighted. Select Configure Networking Hardware by pressing F10.

If the network card is detected, it is displayed and you are asked to confirm it. If it is not detected, a list of undetectable (ISA) adapters is displayed.

Prompt: Insert the networking disk 1.

Insert the disk and press F10.

Prompt: The program steps back to the Network Install menu seen in step 11.

Configure Networking Protocol is highlighted. Press F10 to continue. For TCP/IP, you are prompted for

IP address

Netmask

Default Router

Server IP Address

The server IP address is the UnixWare 7 install server address.

Tip

If a bootp server is advertising an address, it will be automatically filled.

For IPX, you are prompted for

Frame Type

IPX server

If the server is not entered, a search will be made for a server.

The installation verifies that the install server has the required data stream for an install available. It does not check for all data streams, as mentioned earlier on the subject of the install server.

Prompt: The program steps back to the Network Install menu shown in step 11.

Continue with Installation is highlighted. Press F10 to continue.

Disk Configuration

The disk(s) is displayed for configuration. For a single disk system, the display is

Disk Number	Character Mode	Action
1	/dev/rdsk/c0b0t0d0s0	Use Whole Disk for UNIX

The Action section is highlighted; press F2 for choices. The choices are

Use whole disk for UNIX

Customize partitions

Re-load partition information from disk

If a second hard drive is detected, select the Do Not Modify option to defer configuration of the disk if you do not want the second drive configured. It may already contain data from a previous UnixWare installation that will be usable.

Selecting Customize Partitions allows the creation of up to four disk partitions for multiple operating systems.

Step 12. Partition the disk for your requirements. Press F10 to continue.

Prompt: Choose to configure slices and filesystems on the active partition, or to accept default sizes and filesystem types for /, /tmp, and other standard filesystems.

Warning

Do not eliminate the /tmp and /var/tmp memory filesystem (memfs) entries. For the emergency recovery disks to work, memfs work areas must be enabled.

The filesystem and raw disk slice setup screen format is shown below for an 8011MB disk drive with 64MB of RAM:

```
/              root filesystem       vxfs     7712
/stand         boot filesystem       bfs      20
/dev/swap      swap slice            slice    118
```

```
/dev/dump          dump slice              off
/home              user file system        off
/home2             2nd user file system    off
/var               addons file system      off
/tmp               temporary filesystem    memfs    10
/var/tmp           temporary filesystem    memfs    40
/dev/volprivate    private volume          slice    1
ALTS TABLE         ALT/sector slice        slice    160
```

Note that all disk space not assigned to other partitions is placed in root. For a full discussion of UnixWare 7 filesystems, see Chapter 19, "Storage Devices, Filesystems, and Permissions."

The Departmental server profile requires 358MB of disk, and the Enterprise version requires 364MB of space on the root filesystem. The minimum install root filesystem should be at least 500MB.

Use the arrow keys and the Enter key to move through the type and size of partitions. If desired, create a filesystem in /home and use the excess space in root for the /home filesystem.

OpenServer 5 Tip

There is no default /u filesystem, and you cannot change the name of these filesystems at this point. If you want a /u filesystem, create the /home filesystem and edit the /etc/vfstab to change /home to /u. Create a /u directory. Check the change by umounting /home and executing the `mountall` *command. Check to see that /u is mounted.*

Calculating Swap Space

Swap space for 64MB of RAM is 118MB. The formula used to compute swap space depends on the amount of memory dedicated to the memfs. If the system has at least 32MB of RAM, then /tmp is 10MB memfs and /var/tmp is 40MB of memfs.

The formula to compute swap is:

1. SWAP = memfs total – ((3 × memory) /20)
2. If SWAP < 0, then SWAP = 0
3. SWAP = SWAP + 17
4. If memory < 32, then SWAP = SWAP + memory
5. If memory > 32 and memory < 64, then SWAP = SWAP+(((9×memory)+32)/10)
6. If memory > 64 and memory < 128, then SWAP = SWAP+(((7×memory)+160)/10)

7. If memory >128 and memory < 256, then SWAP = SWAP+(((5×memory)+416)/10)
8. If memory >256, then SWAP = SWAP+(((3×memory)+928)/10)

Swap Space for a 64MB Memory System

For a system with 64MB of memory:

The memfs = 50MB (10 for /tmp and 40 for /var/tmp)

SWAP = 50 – ((3 × 64) / 20) = 40.4

SWAP = SWAP + 17 = 40.4 + 17 = 57.4

SWAP = SWAP + (((9 × memory) + 32) /10)

= 57.4 + (((9 × 64) + 32) /10)

= 57.4 + 60.8 = 118.2

> *Warning*
>
> *If configuring swap space larger than 256MB, you may have a problem with depletion of kernel virtual space. The kernel parameter* SEGKMEM_BYTES *should be increased by 0.4% of the swap space being added. For more information, see "Adding swap space" in SCOhelp.*

Step 13. Unless you prefer all free space in the root filesystem, select Customize Filesystems and Slices and press F10.

> *Tip*
>
> *All vxfs filesystems are created with an inode limit of 64Kb. The limit is for backward-compatibility with software written for version 1 vxfs. After the system is installed, user vxfs filesystems can be re-created with no inode limit if desired.*

Customize the filesystems for your requirements and press F10.

Prompt: Choose to customize surface analysis, boot block, and disk geometry options.

Step 14. Read the warnings. If you have non-UNIX partitions, changing the disk geometry will destroy all existing data. The options for customizing the disk default are

- Install new boot sector
- No scan for bad blocks
- No disk geometry changes

Press F10 to continue.

System Profile Selection

Prompt: Choose the profile to select packages based on the type of license you entered earlier. The options are License Based Defaults (364MB for Enterprise), Small Footprint Server (95MB), Full (all packages, 364MB), or Customize.

Customize will allow you to delete or add packages to the installation. Adding unlicensed packages will result in warnings of unlicensed software residing on the system.

To install a package, such as the Kernel Debugger, follow these steps:

1. Select the package from which the package is to come, in this case the Core Services, and press F10. The Select/De-select Services menu appears.
2. Place the cursor in the row with the service desired. In this case, the cursor is on the row with Extended OS Utilities, which are marked as `PART` for partly installed. Press F2 for Details.
3. Three selections are offered: Individual, All, or None. Select Individual and press Enter. User the down arrow key to move to Kernel Debugger, press the space bar to select the package (an asterisk appears beside the Kernel Debugger), and press the Enter key.
4. You are now back at the Select/De-select menu. Press F10 if you are finished.

Step 15. Select the profile you require and press F10.

Network Configuration

Step 16. The network configuration steps will be performed only if the network software was installed with the profile or manually selected.

If no network card is detected, the prompt is

```
No network adapter was detected.
```

If the network adapter is not detected, you are given the opportunity to select from a list. While the prompt suggests you may select from the full list, a short list is provided. If the network card in the system is not detected and is not displayed in the list on the screen, press F8 to defer configuration. If the correct network card is detected, you may choose to configure during install or defer configuration. If you choose to defer TCP/IP configuration, all network configuration is deferred.

If you choose to configure the network adapter, you will be prompted for the following TCP/IP parameters:

- IP address
- System netmask
- Broadcast address
- Default router
- Domain name
- Primary DNS server
- Other DNS address
- Other DNS address
- Frame Format (Default is Ethernet_II. You may change it.)

After pressing F10 you will be asked for the IPX net number and Frame Format. If you do not use IPX, press F8 to defer.

The next screen prompts for NIS information: NIS Type, NIS Domain, and three optional NIS server addresses. If you do not use NIS, press F8 to defer.

Warning

If you do not use NIS, do not accept the default setting of NIS client. Creating an NIS client when no NIS service exists will result in failure of network utilities started by the inetd daemon and very slow performance for some functions. This is caused by the client searching for an NIS server.

System Control Entries

Prompt: Date and Time

Step 17. Enter the correct date, time, and time zone, and press F10 to continue.

Prompt: Choose the desired security level.

Step 18. Select Low, Traditional, Improved, or High, depending on your security needs and press F10 to continue.

Prompt: System Owner Name

Step 19. UnixWare has a concept new to OpenServer 5 users called the *System Owner*. The System Owner is a local administrator with less than root privileges. Enter the system owner's name and login name. The UID for the system owner defaults to 101. You may override the UID. Enter the system owner's password and repeat the entry to ensure correctness. Press F10.

Prompt: Root Password

Step 20. Enter the root password twice to ensure correct spelling. Press F10.

Warning

Do not forget the root password. You will have to reinstall or contact SCO support to fix it.

Prompt: Optional Services

Step 21. The optional services screen is for information only. You may choose to read about other services or press F10 to continue with the installation.

Prompt: License Agreement

Step 22. To continue installation, you must agree to the licensing terms. Selecting Do Not Agree will terminate the installation. Press F10 to continue.

Prompt: The installation is now ready to write data to your hard disk.

Step 23. This is the last chance to exit the installation without writing to the hard disk. Press F10 to begin the installation onto the hard disk. If you want to save the installation answers for other installs on a response disk, insert a formatted disk into the floppy disk drive and press F3.

The Software Load Stage

After the F10 key has been pressed to begin the install, the user interaction ceases.

If you have selected to format the hard disk, a bar graph will appear showing the percent completion. The screen display refers to checking the hard disk, not formatting the disk.

The packages selected for install are displayed as they are installed with a bar graph depicting the progression. You should not have to do anything until the installation has completed this phase. Each package will display its own progress bar. There is no overall progress indicator.

At the completion of the system load, you will be prompted to remove disks and CDs. Reboot the system.

After the Initial Reboot

The system now runs through configuring the keyboard, network card, and other devices. The system will ask you to identify the type of mouse on the computer. Enter the correct mouse parameters and press F10.

A mouse test will begin. Move the mouse to ensure that it works. Click the mouse button to terminate the test.

Switch screens to the Console screen (Ctrl+Alt+Esc). Log in as root. You will be able to see the end of the boot messages. You should see that VisionFS is configured and running, if it was a part of your profile or you manually selected it. If IPX was deferred during install, a message stating that IPX is disabled is also visible.

Shut down and reboot your system.

Troubleshooting the Install

Problems may arise during installation. Several steps can be taken to try to resolve these problems. Most importantly, make sure that the hardware is supported by UnixWare 7. Check the SCO Compatible Hardware Web site for the latest information. Starting with version 7.0.1, the Updates CD will have a /info/hardware area with updated information.

Initial Install Problems

If you are using a SCSI controller, check the display from the SCSI BIOS to ensure the recognition of the peripheral devices attached to it. You may also check during the install phase to ensure that the installation software recognized them.

Check for vendor-supplied HBA disks. The hardware drivers may not be available from SCO.

Check for hardware conflicts. IRQs, DMAs, and memory addresses that conflict will cause problems. Strip out unnecessary devices to see if they are the source of the problem.

If the system will not boot from the boot disk, check the disk on another machine. Check the system by booting from another disk. Create a new disk if necessary.

If the system hangs or resets during boot, run diagnostics and hardware setup programs supplied by your hardware vendor to verify that the system is set up correctly. Turn off caching of video and other cache settings in the BIOS. Many of the cache settings were originally intended for the DOS memory model and have nothing to do with 32-bit computing.

If the hard disk is not found, check for SCSI settings, if applicable. The SCSI drive should be at ID0, but does not have to be. The first SCSI disk detected on the primary controller will be used as the boot disk.

Check for the compatibility of the disk controller. Look for a vendor-supplied HBA disk.

If the SCSI CD-ROM is not recognized at installation, check the ID of the CD-ROM. Check termination on the SCSI bus. If the CD-ROM is not on the primary SCSI bus, check the DCU and see if the adapter with the CD-ROM is recognized. Move the CD-ROM to the primary bus if necessary.

If you are using an IDE system, the ISL may not recognize a CD-ROM drive on the secondary IDE controller. You will need to enter the DCU and configure the secondary. SCO has Technical Article 105929 on setting up the secondary IDE CD-ROM on a Compaq ProSignia. The boot disk should be the master device on the primary IDE controller.

If you are mixing IDE and SCSI disk drives, the IDE must be the boot device.

The Device Configuration Utility

During the install, you are offered the opportunity to enter the *Device Configuration Utility (DCU)*. The DCU enables you to manipulate the hardware configuration.

OpenServer 5 Tip

UnixWare 7 does not support the display of the hardware configuration at boot time in the same manner as OpenServer 5. There is no `hwconfig` *command to list the hardware. The DCU is currently the best way to determine the hardware configuration. To list the contents of the DCU, run the* `resmgr` *command with no options.*

After install, you may enter the DCU from a terminal window by executing /sbin/dcu. Alternatively, you may enter the DCU from the graphical user interface by selecting SCOadmin, Hardware, Device Configuration Utility. The DCU is illustrated in Figure 4.1.

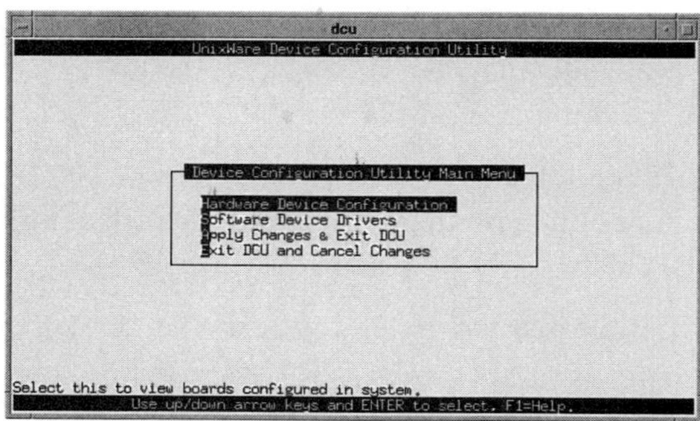

FIGURE 4.1 *The Device Configuration Utility.*

> *Warning*
>
> *The DCU should be used with care. Serious damage may be done to the ability of the system to operate by removing vital devices.*

Hardware Device Configuration

The hardware configuration is shown in Figure 4.2. The fields that may be changed by the user are shown with a black background. Devices that are not configurable have a light background, and you may not enter those fields.

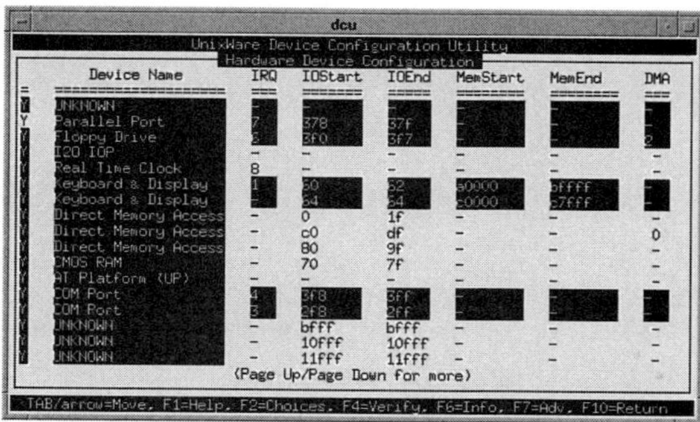

FIGURE 4.2 *The DCU Hardware Device Configuration.*

To navigate through the data, use the arrow keys to move up and down the rows in a column. The left and right arrows will move within a field, but will not move to an adjacent field. The Tab keys (shifted or not) move forward one field. The Enter key moves forward one field.

The data fields in the DCU are described below.

Configuration Status	The first column, which has all Ys in this case, is the Configuration status. If a device is configured into the kernel, a `Y` is present; otherwise an `N` is present. If the background is light, such as the entry for the Parallel Port, that line is the current or selected line.
Device Name	The name of the device. It may contain the device name (such as Parallel Port, Floppy Drive, and Real Time Clock) and the driver name (such as `adsl` for an Adaptec 294x SCSI host adapter). Starting in version 7.0.1, these are listed in the Updates CD in the /info/hardware/hba.txt file. `UNKNOWN`: The DCU cannot assign a name. An example is when hardware is installed, but no software drivers have been loaded. `UNUSED`: An ISA driver is disabled, but the device settings have been retained.
IRQ	The interrupt vector used by the device.
IOStart, IOEnd	The range of I/O port addresses through which the device can communicate.
MemStart, MemEnd	The range of valid memory addresses through which the device can communicate. Valid addresses are in hexadecimal format and range from `10000` through `FFFFFFFF`.
DMA	The channel number for devices that use DMA channels. The valid range is 0 through 7. For devices that do not use DMA, a `-1` value is used.

Function keys provide help (F1); choices of values (F2); verification of settings (where supported) (F4); more information, including software drivers (F6); and advanced settings (F7).

Figure 4.3 illustrates the F6 Info display for a SCSI adapter. Some items that may be changed will be available through the F7 option.

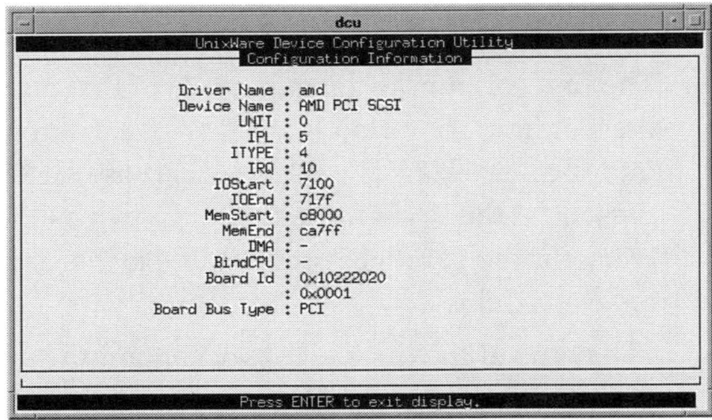

FIGURE 4.3 *The DCU configuration information displayed by F6.*

Additional pieces of information from the Info option include the following:

UNIT	The unit number for controllers that support multiple devices.
IPL	The Interrupt Priority Level for devices that have a priority handling capability. Valid values run from `1` to `7`, with `7` being highest.
ITYPE	IRQ sharing type. If not used this must be set to `0`.
BindCPU	For multiprocessor systems, specifies the CPU on which the driver will execute.

The information in these fields is not normally changed by the end-user. It is specified by the device driver writer.

Software Device Drivers

The software portion of the DCU is used only when you need to activate a driver, and the hardware device is manually configured without software setup utilities.

Figure 4.4 shows the menu for software drivers.

Figure 4.5 shows the listing for all software drivers. The drivers that have an asterisk to the left of the driver name are enabled. Pressing F6 will provide information that reflects the same data seen in the hardware configuration.

Exiting the DCU

Exit the DCU by selecting either of the last two options on the main menu, depending on whether you want to update the information or exit without changes. The changes should be reflected in the next boot.

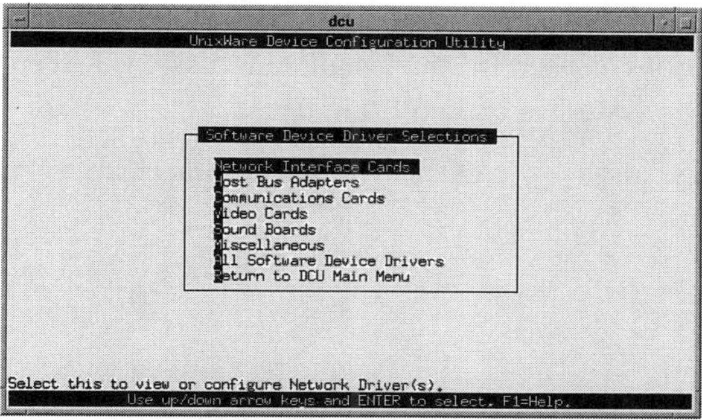

FIGURE 4.4 *The software device driver selections.*

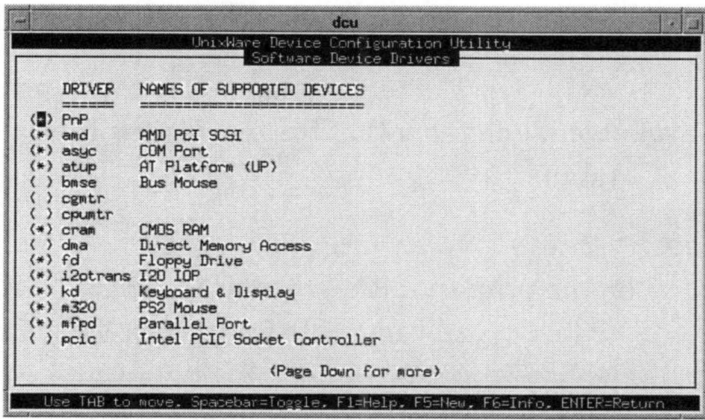

FIGURE 4.5 *The software device drivers.*

The DCU updates the resmgr database. The *resmgr program* is normally used for changing in-core resources or in-script files. Administrators should use the DCU, not resmgr, to make changes.

Another way to see the information found in the DCU is to execute resmgr with no options. The data format is not pretty and looks nothing like OpenServer 5's /etc/hwconfig listing, but it does provide a snapshot of the data.

Creating a Magic Disk

Unfortunately, in the early releases of the CD there is a reference to the *magic disk* that points to the release notes text file; but there is no information on the magic disk to be found. The magic disk is designed for use by SCO support personnel troubleshooting install problems. It can be used to provide additional tools for a system administrator who is attempting to troubleshoot an ISL or has booted from emergency disks.

The magic disk can be created with `dd` from the /info/images directory of the CD with the same instructions as used for the installation disks. When created, it can be mounted when the system is booted from disks.

The magic disk contains usr and etc directories. In the usr/bin directory are the following programs:

- find
- pg
- ps
- resmgr
- strings
- sum
- tail
- truss
- vi
- what

To mount the magic disk, type **`magic`**. The Kernel Debugger is loaded and these listed commands become available. Remember that the magic disk is an undocumented tool designed for SCO support.

Loading Multiple Operating Systems

UnixWare 7 must be installed on the primary disk, whether it is SCSI or IDE. If an IDE disk is installed, it will be the logical candidate for default boot. Check the BIOS of your computer. Some have only the options to boot from A or C, while some support boot from SCSI, A, or C in several different sequences.

Install the non-UnixWare 7 operating system first. Make sure that UnixWare 7's root filesystem lies within the 1024-cylinder boundary. To boot the other operating system, see Chapter 16, "Starting and Stopping," on starting the system. You will need to use the boot command processor (BCP) to boot the other operating system. Alternatively, purchase a software program, such as System Commander, that controls the boot process.

Author's Note

I have UnixWare 7 and Windows NT loaded on my Toshiba laptop. UnixWare 7 is the default boot. I have to boot into DOS to get NT.

Post-Install Problems

Post-install problems generally revolve around two issues: mouse and video. Both of these can be reconfigured.

Mouse Reconfiguration

UnixWare 7 supports the following mouse types:

- Any PS2–compatible/keyboard mouse
- Logitech serial, bus, or Mouseman
- Microsoft serial and bus mouse
- Mouse Systems Corporation–compatible mouse

The above types all fall into one of three categories: serial, PS2, or bus mouse devices.

Mouse failures may result from IRQ and I/O address conflicts. Use the DCU to check the resources used and to look for conflicts.

Bus mouse devices use an I/O address range of `23c` through `23f`. If this address range is not free, they will fail.

PS2 compatible/keyboard mouse devices use IRQ 12. If the IRQ is in use, the mouse will fail. Check the hardware manual for PS2 mouse resources; the DCU will not display that they are reserved for the mouse.

Serial mouse problems center around the serial port resources. Ensure that the serial port is recognized in the DCU and available (not in use by a modem or printer).

Mouse administration is performed from a console screen, not the graphical screen. Log in as **root** on the console and run mouseadmin. The mouseadmin menu follows:

```
The following terminals have mice assigned:

Display terminal          Mouse device
----------------          ------------
console    PS2 mouse

Select one of the following:
     B) Bus mouse add
     P) PS2 mouse add
     S) Serial mouse add
     T) Test your mouse configuration
     R) Remove a mouse
     U) Update mouse configuration and quit
     E) Exit (no update)
Enter Selection:
```

To remove a mouse and add a new mouse requires that you select R to remove a mouse and U to update and quit. Re-execute mouseadmin and add the mouse type. Select U to update and quit.

To test the mouse, you will need to run mouseadmin a third time.

The mouse drivers are Demand Loadable Modules (DLMs) and do not require relinking the kernel to test the mouse. This means that you do not have to reboot after changing the mouse configuration.

Video Reconfiguration

Setting the video mode can be tricky. If you make a mistake, you may not be able to see anything.

Author's Note

While configuring the video on my Toshiba Tecra with UnixWare 7, I tried to set the video mode to 1024 × 768. The software recognized the video adapter but I had to guess at the monitor type. As a result of an incorrect configuration, I lost all video. Keep the following instructions in mind when working with video.

If you accidentally set your video to an incompatible mode, both the graphical and character screens may be unusable. To resolve this problem without reinstalling, boot to single user mode (see Chapter 16).

Once in single user mode, run

```
/usr/bin/X/setvideomode -stdvga
```

or

```
/usr/bin/X/setvideomode -default
```

then reboot.

Video settings can be changed from the graphical desktop through the SCOadmin, Hardware, Video Configuration Manager. UnixWare 7 will attempt to identify the video adapter. Figure 4.6 illustrates the Video Configuration Manager. Clicking the Modify button will open a window and UnixWare 7 will attempt to autodetect the video adapter.

If the graphical screen is unusable, but the character based screens are available, run

```
scoadmin video configuration manager
```

For help in identifying the video adapter, run

```
/usr/bin/X11/VideoHelp
```

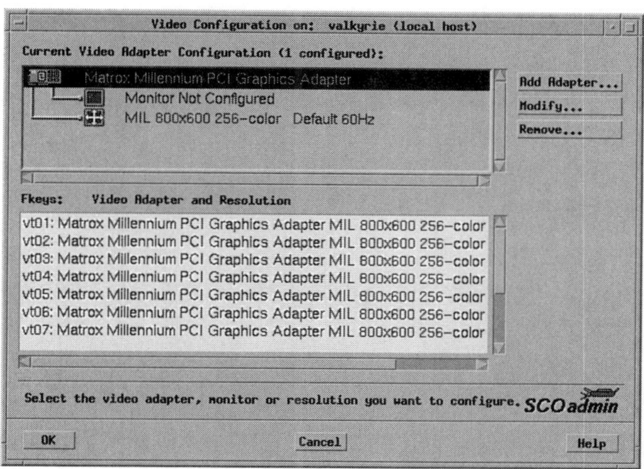

FIGURE 4.6 *The Video Configuration Manager.*

Note that /usr/bin/X11 is a link to /usr/X/bin, so /usr/X/bin/VideoHelp will also work.

The output of VideoHelp is shown below:

```
IBM COMPATIBLE MATROX/MILLENNIUM VGA/VBE BIOS (V1.6 )
Copyright  1995, Matrox Graphics Inc.
DATE: 02/08/95
Revision: 0.19
VGA/VBE BIOS, Version V1.6
```

To change the adapter or monitor type from Video Configuration Manager:

1. Select Modify. The manager will attempt to identify your adapter.
2. Select the video adapter or a compatible type. Click OK.
3. Select Change Monitor. Select the monitor type.
4. Click OK for the monitor.
5. Click OK for the modification.

To change the resolution:

1. Select the Resolution icon. Select Change Resolution. Select the desired resolution and click OK.
2. Select Test to test the resolution. Click OK after reading the warning message. A 30-second test is performed.

Warning

By selecting an incorrect resolution, you can lose the ability to return the video to a sane state. If this should occur, press Ctrl+Alt+Backspace simultaneously to exit the X server. If the display is not usable, you may have to turn the power off and on to reboot.

3. Click Cancel if the video test was not successful. Click OK if the test was successful.
4. Click OK to complete the resolution configuration changes. Changes will not take effect until your next login.
5. Exit the Video Configuration Manager.

The next 10 chapters cover the post-install procedures for configuring networking, printers, tape drives, serial ports, installing software, and wrapping up the install. Even if you are not responsible for all of those features, do not overlook Chapter 14, "Wrapping Up the Install." In particular, the sections on emergency recovery diskettes and emergency recovery tapes should be read.

PART II

Post-Installation Tasks

CHAPTER 5

Console Administration, Logins, and SCOadmin

- Console logins
  How many ways and how many times can you log in at the console? Learn about the three graphical screens available at login.
- SCOhelp
  The new SCOhelp is HTTP-driven. See how easy it is to use.
- SCOadmin
  The SCO administration managers have expanded considerably. This chapter provides a list and the chapters where they are covered.

Console Logins

The UnixWare 7 console provides both graphical- and character-based logins. In keeping with past SCO practices, multiple login screens may be used at the console.

The initial screen to greet the user is shown in Figure 5.1. The Options button provides the opportunity to choose the language the user prefers for login and the type of graphical environment the user will get when the login is completed:

- UnixWare 7 CDE
- Panorama Session
- Failsafe Session

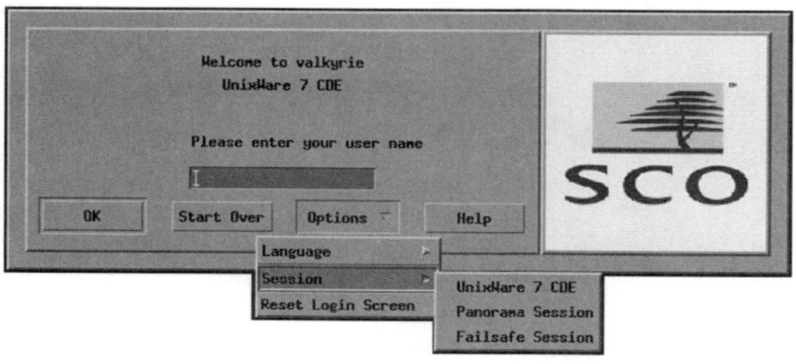

FIGURE 5.1 *The initial login screen for UnixWare 7.*

Character-based screens are also available. The character-based console login is available by simultaneously pressing the Ctrl+Alt+Esc key combination.

OpenServer 5 Tip

By comparison with the OpenServer5, OpenDesktop, and earlier SCO operating systems, the key combinations for each screen have shifted one position to the left. The first character screen is ESC instead of F1; the graphical screen is F1 instead of F2 and so on. When the GUI is disabled, it is not replaced by a character-based login, as OpenServer is.

Using the default setup, the graphical screen is on F1. The screen for Ctrl+Alt+Esc is /dev/console. The screens Ctrl+Alt+F2 (vt02) through Ctrl+Alt+F8 (vt08) are available.

UnixWare 2 Tip

UnixWare 2 users will find that the `newvt` *command is still available along with the virtual terminal manager (vtlmgr). The terminology for tty has been replaced by vt, so Ctrl+Alt+F1 switches you to vt01, which is the GUI. Ctrl+Alt+H will reach the first multiscreen as will Ctrl+Alt+Esc.*

The first free multiscreen is vt09 because screens up through vt08 are brought up to login prompts automatically for screen switching. To regain the traditional SCO UnixWare 2 multiscreen capability, enter:

```
sacadm -d -p contty
```

To re-enable the login prompts on the console screens, enter:

```
sacadm -e -p contty
```

For users from either background, it is possible to get logins on all 12 screens (F1-F12) plus the Console login with function key and Esc key switching. The script in the release notes (for version 7.0.0), under Console Multiscreens, will attempt to create the other four logins; however, there are errors in the script. The following script was tested on my system and works; it is now in the release notes for version 7.0.1.

```
for i in 09 10 11 12
do
pmadm -a -p contty -s $i -S login -fu -v `ttyadm -V` \
-m "`ttyadm -d /dev/vt$i -l console -s /usr/bin/shserv -p \"Login (vt$i): \"`"
done
```

Executing this script allows a total of 13 logins at the console: Ctrl+Alt+Esc (character login), Ctrl+Alt+F1 (graphical login), and Ctrl+Alt+F2 through Ctrl+Alt+F12 (character logins).

The CDE Graphical Login

The default login provides the UNIX standard CDE user interface. Figure 5.2 illustrates a CDE graphical environment. The bar across the bottom, the CDE front panel, contains the menus.

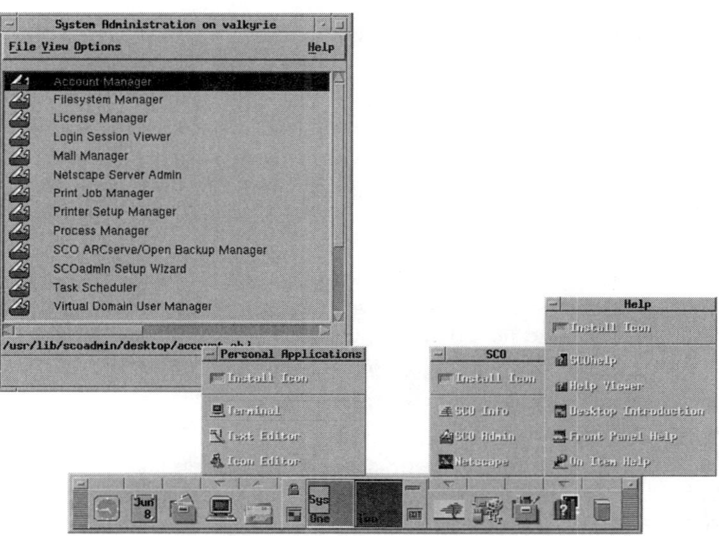

FIGURE 5.2 *The CDE graphical environment.*

The CDE Front Panel

The buttons, or controls, on the CDE front panel enable you to perform many tasks, as described in Table 5.1. When selecting items, you need to click only once to execute. Table 5.1 uses the following terms:

Click	What happens when you single-click the control.
Right-click	What happens when you right-click the control.
Drop	What happens when you drop a file or folder icon on the control.
Indicator	What the control displays or represents.

TABLE 5.1 THE CDE FRONT PANEL

Control Icon	Name/Indicator/Actions
	Clock Indicator: Displays the current time.
	Calendar Click: Starts the Calendar application. Indicator: Opens a schedule program allowing scheduling of appointments. Indicator: Displays the current date.
	File Manager - Home Directory Click: Opens the user's home directory (or folder) with a File Manager view. Drop: Opens the dropped folder in File Manager view.
	Text Editor Click: Starts the desktop text editor. Drop: Opens the dropped file with the desktop editor.
	Mailer Click: Starts the Mailer. Drop: Opens the Mailer in New Message mode with the contents of a dropped file in the body of the message. Indicator: Reveals presence of new mail.
	Lock Click: Locks the workstation—requires the user's password to unlock. (This is not the same as the OpenServer 5 lock program that asks for a password and uses that password for locking the terminal.)
	Graphical Workstation Manager (GWM) Click: Starts the GWM.
	Workspace Manager Click: Double-click another workspace to switch to that workspace. Right-click: Displays a menu of options to add, rename, and delete workspaces, and lock the screen. Indicator: Shows a miniature version of workspaces with open windows.
	Busy Light Indicator: Blinks when a requested action is running.
	Exit Click: Logs out of the current session. Presents a confirmation window prior to logging out.
	SCO Info Click: Displays copyright information.
	Style Manager Click: Starts the Style Manager which allows changes to colors, background, fonts, and the like.
	Application Manager Click: Opens the Application Manager window.

Control Icon	Name/Indicator/Actions
	Help Manager Click: Opens the SCOhelp window in Netscape.
	Trash Can Click: Opens the Trash Can window. Drop: Moves a file or folder into the Trash Can.

The CDE Subpanels

Submenus, called *subpanels*, can appear above any of the icons other than the lock, GWM, Busy Light, Exit, or Workspace Manager. In Figure 5.2, note the arrow indicators above the Text Editor, Mailer, SCO Info, and Help Manager icons. When the arrow points up, the menu is not shown. When the menu is shown, as is the case with the Personal Applications, SCO, and Help subpanels, the arrow points down.

To open or close a subpanel, click the arrow. The default action of a subpanel is to close after you execute an application from the subpanel. To keep the subpanel open, move it to another location. To move the subpanel, click the title bar of the subpanel and drag it. A Move option appears in the drop-down menu in the title bar; click the button to the left of the title.

The default subpanel contents are

Personal Applications:	Terminal, Text Editor, Icon Editor
Mailer:	Mail, Vacation
SCO:	SCO Info, SCOadmin, Netscape
Help:	SCOhelp, Help Viewer, Desktop Introduction, Front Panel Help, On Item Help

The Front Panel Help provides documentation on the front panel and the subpanels in detail. The Desktop Introduction guides you through how to use the CDE interface effectively. CDE help is not part of SCOhelp.

Each subpanel also has an Install Icon option. To add a new command or folder to a subpanel, drag the icon from an open window, such as the Calculator in the Application Manager's desktop applications, and drop it onto the Install Icon option in the Personal Applications subpanel. The Calculator will then be available from the Personal Applications subpanel.

The SCO subpanel contains the SCOadmin icon, which is one you will use more often than the SCO Info icon that appears on the main panel by default. To place the SCOadmin icon on the main panel, right-click the SCOadmin icon in the subpanel. From the menu that appears, choose Copy to Main Panel. The SCOadmin icon now appears on the main panel.

The CDE desktop provides good user functionality. Modifications to the front panel and subpanels make the user environment even more flexible and usable. The Style Manager provides the ability to modify color and background to your requirements. To easily tell one workspace from another, for example, you can choose different backgrounds.

Tip

What if you don't want background wallpaper? From the Style Manager, click the Backdrop icon. The window shown in Figure 5.3 will appear. Use the scrollbar to locate NoBackdrop. Click Apply. To turn the background gray, open a terminal window (dtterm) and execute `xsetroot`. *You can set the background to a color with* `xsetroot -solid blue`. *Instead of NoBackground, choose Foreground or Background for two solid-color options.*

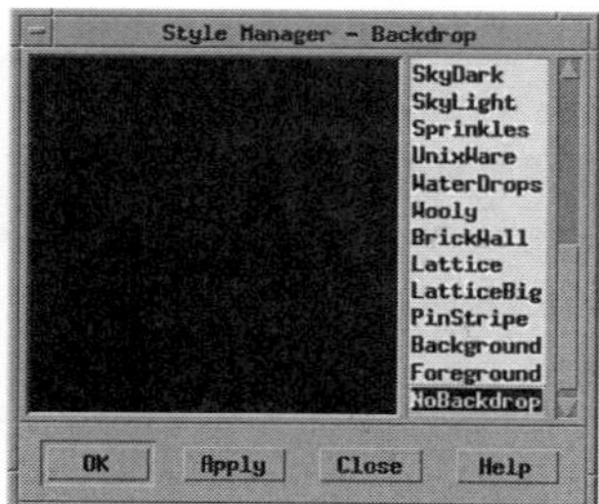

FIGURE 5.3 *Setting the background from the Style Manager.*

You can manipulate windows with keystroke combinations instead of mouse clicks. Table 5.2 lists the keystrokes and their purposes.

TABLE 5.2 FUNCTIONS AND CORRESPONDING KEY COMBINATIONS

Function	Key Combination
Window pull-down menu	Shift+Esc
Move window to back	Alt+F3
Close window	Alt+F4
Move window	Alt+F7
Resize window	Alt+F8
Switch windows	Alt+Esc or Alt+Tab
Minimize a window	Alt+F9
Workspace menu	Alt+F10

The Panorama Desktop

The Panorama desktop should be familiar to the OpenServer 5 users. It does not start with the familiar icons on the OpenServer desktop, but does have the panner in the bottom-left corner.

The Panorama desktop uses fewer system resources than the CDE desktop. On a system with 64MB of RAM, while logged in on the Panorama desktop, 5644 pages of memory and 37,575KB of swap were free. After logging in to the CDE desktop, 5,087 pages of memory and 36,303KB of swap were free. This was a drop in RAM of 557 pages and a drop in swap of 1,272KB.

Figure 5.4 illustrates the Panorama desktop with the menu (SCO logo) displayed. To display the menu, left-click in the background.

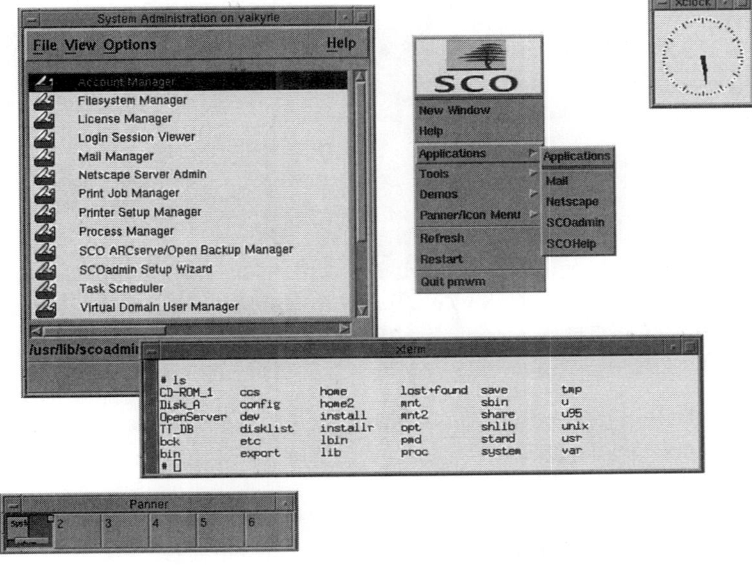

FIGURE 5.4 *The Panorama desktop with open applications.*

The panner at the bottom-left corner allows creation of jobs in multiple windows and panning to them as required.

To change the background wallpaper of a Panorama session, from an Xterm window use the `xsetroot` command to change the background as desired. To change the background to solid blue, use the following command:

```
xsetroot -solid blue
```

The Failsafe Login

The Failsafe login provides a terminal window on a gray background. The purpose of the Failsafe login is to provide an unadorned login to allow correcting a problem that is preventing the CDE or Panorama login from succeeding. Figure 5.5 illustrates the Failsafe login. To log out, you should exit the Xterm and right-click the background to get a menu. Select Quit from the menu.

FIGURE 5.5 *The Failsafe login.*

The Character-Based Screens

UnixWare 7 supports eight character-based screens by default, and four more can be added: the Console (/dev/vt00) and the screens that can be switched to by the function key. These screens use the AT386-ie emulation. The AT386-ie emulation is the UnixWare version of the ANSI terminal emulation.

If your application depends on the scoterm (SCO ansi) terminal emulation, download and install TLS701. For a scoterm window, execute:

```
/usr/lib/X11/app-defaults/ScoTerm
```

Troubleshooting the Graphical Windows

Problems with graphical screens are usually related to hardware configuration. Improper configuration of the video or mouse can create problems with the graphical login screen and cause it not to start.

Improperly Configured Video Card

Selecting an incorrect video setup can result in no graphical screen and, in extreme cases, in no video on any screen.

To recover from a misconfigured video that allows access to the character-based screens, run SCOadmin from the command prompt. Change the video to the correct settings. If in doubt, use standard VGA settings with 640×480 resolution.

If the video does not display to graphical- or character-based screens, see Chapter 4, "Installation of UnixWare 7," on video reconfiguration with the `setvideomode` command.

Improperly Configured Mouse

If the graphical screen does not start on vt01 and no graphical login appears, the mouse may be improperly configured. Check the /var/dt/Xerrors file. If the mouse is the problem, you will see a message like:

```
Cannot open /dev/mouse
: no such device or address
Mon June 8 08:10:12 1998
Error (pid 338): server for display valkyrie:0 terminated unexpectedly 3
A pointer device (such as a mouse) is not configured for this display
```

Check the mouse. Use mouseadmin, a non-graphical program, to configure the mouse. Chapter 15, "System Administration," discusses mouse administration.

Starting and Stopping the Graphical Logins

To stop and start the graphical screens, use the OpenServer 5 commands or the UnixWare 2 commands. At the present time, these work for backward compatibility.

The `scologin` command is from OpenServer 5. The command and its options are shown below:

`stop`	Stops the graphical login.
`start`	Starts a graphical login.
`query`	Returns the current status.
`enable`	Enables the graphical login to start at boot.
`disable`	Prevents the graphical login from starting at boot.

Unlike OpenServer 5, disabling the scologin GUI does not replace it with a character-based login.

With UnixWare 2, the following commands were used:

`enable_glogin`	Enables the graphical login to start at boot and starts it if not already running under UnixWare 2. This command does not work in UnixWare 7. It gives an error message that it takes no arguments but does nothing.
`disable_glogin`	Disables the graphical login at boot and stops it if currently running on UnixWare 2. It does not work on UnixWare 7, giving the same error message as `enable glogin`.

If you are making the move to UnixWare 7 or are new to SCO products, you should use the native UnixWare 7 commands. The `dtconfig` command (/usr/dt/bin/dtconfig) has options to accomplish the following:

`-d`	Disable at boot.
`-e`	Enable at boot.
`-kill`	Stop the current session.

There is no `dtconfig` option to restart the desktop.

An alternative to `dtconfig` is the startup script /etc/rc2.d/S99dtlogin, which can be used to stop the graphical screen.

Configuring a *dtterm*

From the graphical screen, you can execute terminal windows. These can be customized to include a window name, colors, font, and other options.

To create the file, use a text editor to create a file with a name such as "myapp."

The text

```
dtterm -name "my Application" -fg snow -bg cornflowerblue -font ibm10x20
```

will start a `dtterm` with the name `"my Application"` and the foreground in snow white, the background in blue and using a 10x20 IBM font.

Adding

```
 -e /usr/bin/telnet remotemachine
```

will start a telnet session on the machine named `remotemachine`.

SCOhelp

SCOhelp runs from a Netscape HTTP application. To access SCOhelp, click the Help icon on the menu bar in the CDE screen. Netscape starts and then SCOhelp appears.

SCOhelp can also be accessed from a terminal window by typing:

```
scohelp&
```

Clicking Help in any SCO application window also brings up SCOhelp.

The first SCOhelp display is shown in Figure 5.6. The frame on the left side of the window is the topics area. Select what you want to see in the topics area.

For example, clicking the first topic, Backup and Restore, will bring up a new left frame, Backup and Restore. Clicking the Backup and Restore title in the new left frame brings up a new right frame. The window now looks like Figure 5.7.

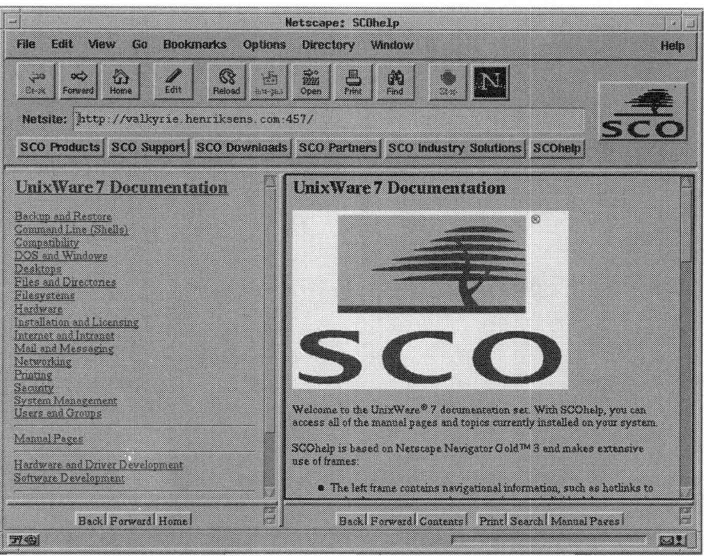

FIGURE 5.6 *The initial SCOhelp window.*

Clicking the linked text on the right page, such as SCO ARCserve/Open from Cheyenne, will bring up the frame associated with that topic. Clicking the commands that have a man pages' reference behind them, such as `emergency_disk`(1M), will bring up the associated man page.

Navigation buttons ease movement through the documents. A search capability with the Verity search engine is available by clicking the Search button in the bottom of the right frame.

Print capability has been enhanced. Clicking the Print button provides the opportunity to print only the frame being viewed or to assemble the topic and print it.

The man pages are available in two forms:

- First, selecting the manual pages from the initial screen allows browsing the manual pages by section.
- Second, clicking the manual pages button at the bottom of the right frame allows a man page command with options for the section and the `apropos` command. The `apropos` command is the same as executing `man -k`.

Within the second man page option, if you enter a word, such as **boot**, it will list the sections in which the word occurs in the right frame, allowing a choice of which one to view. For instance, boot will list `boot(1M)` and `boot(4)`. If you select the apropos search, it will list all commands found in the right frame.

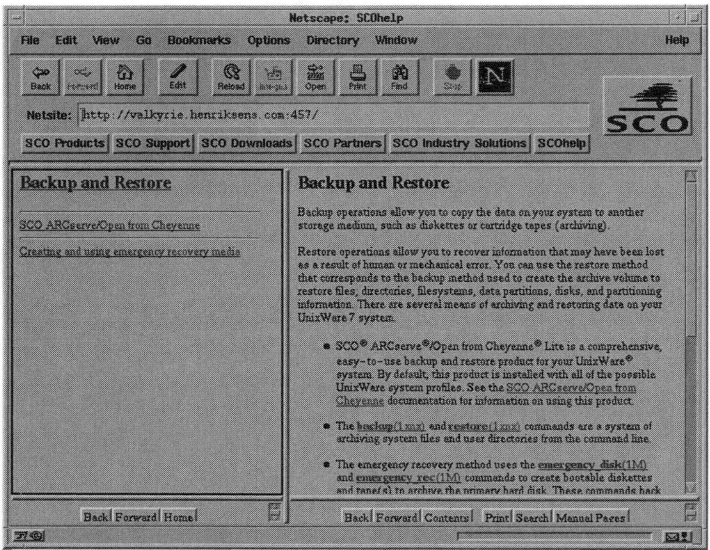

FIGURE 5.7 *Searching for backup and restore information.*

OpenServer 5 Tip

The manual page sections have changed the naming scheme. No longer is C the command section of the man pages. Now `cat(C)` *is referenced as* `cat(1)`. *The new scheme is:*

1	*Unrestricted commands that can be run by any user*
1M	*Administrative commands, which may be fully or partially restricted in use*
2	*System calls*
3	*Library routines*
4	*System files*
5	*Miscellaneous*
7	*Device drivers and driver interfaces*

In addition, there are prefixes: `X` *for X window commands,* `D` *for driver development commands. There are suffixes to subdivide the sections; for example,* `1nfs` *is for unrestricted* `nfs` *commands.*

To use the search facilities of SCOhelp, you must run `/usr/man/bin/config_search -f`, as pointed out in Chapter 14, "Wrapping Up the Install." Help can also be run from another computer with a browser. Start the browser and enter the URL `http://<machine name or IP address>:457`, with the machine name or IP address being that of a UnixWare 7 system, and SCOhelp will appear.

SCOadmin

SCOadmin is the primary method of managing a UnixWare 7 system. The different managers within SCOadmin will be covered in the appropriate chapters. The following discussion should provide you with the knowledge to navigate through the managers without problem.

From the CDE desktop, SCOadmin can be executed by clicking the arrow above the SCO logo on the main panel and clicking SCOadmin.

From a terminal window in a graphical interface (CDE Panorama or Failsafe), enter:

```
scoadmin&
```

From the Panorama desktop, left-click the background, select Applications, and then select SCOadmin from the submenu.

Individual managers can be executed from the command line with the `scoadmin` command followed by the manager name. To get a list of the managers, run `scoadmin -t`. (The list of managers at the end of this chapter is from a `scoadmin -t` listing.)

To start a manager, such as the video manager, type:

```
scoadmin video&
```

You do not have to spell out the entire manager name. There are four managers that start with the letter A: Accounts, Address Allocation, Application Installer, and Audio configuration. If you specify only the first letter, the first name that appears in the `scoadmin -t` list will be executed. So

```
scoadmin A&
```

will execute the Accounts manager.

To execute the Audio manager, specify enough letters to make the name of the manager unique:

```
scoadmin au&
```

Graphical SCOadmin

The first level graphical managers are shown when SCOadmin opens as depicted in Figure 5.8. The folders in the bottom of the list reveal other managers: 12 in the Networking folder, 10 in the System folder, 5 in Hardware, 2 each in NetWare and Software Management. UnixWare 7 is oriented toward graphical administration in a way that surpasses both UnixWare 2 and OpenServer 5.

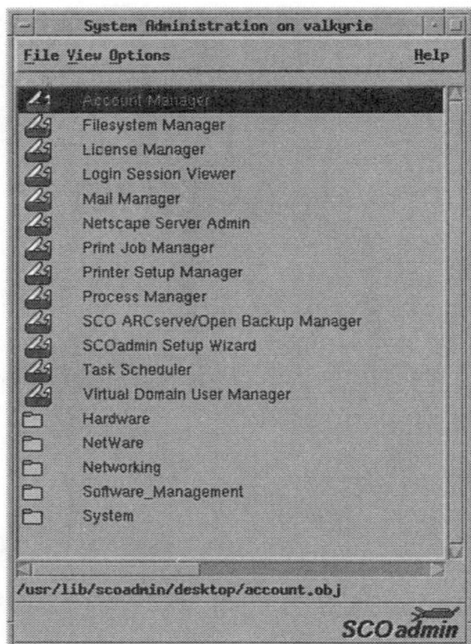

FIGURE 5.8 *The SCOadmin program with the first level of managers.*

To start a manager, double-click the Manager icon. For purposes of illustration, we will use the Accounts Manager to show the functionality of the manager. Figure 5.9 is the Accounts Manager.

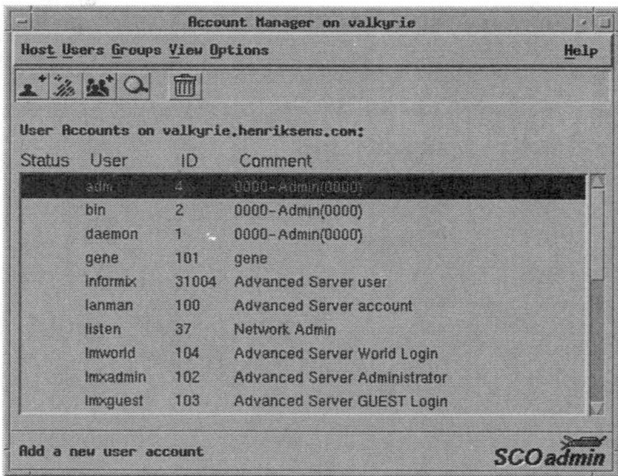

FIGURE 5.9 *The Accounts Manager.*

The Accounts Manager window is divided into several areas. At the top are the menus. Each of the menus has a drop-down menu with menu options. For instance, under Hosts are the options to select a new host, select a host group (a new concept in UnixWare 7), and exit. In all menus, the option to exit the function is in the drop-down menu list for the left-most menu item. Usually the left-most menu item is labeled Host, but not always.

Under the menus are the control buttons (icons) in a toolbar. The buttons are shortcuts to items in the menus. The toolbar can be deleted through the Options menu. On some applications, the toolbar can be customized with additional buttons through the Customize option within the Options menu.

The area from the statement `User Accounts on valkyrie.henriksens.com` to the bottom of the scroll area is the display area. This is where the main information is displayed. In the case of the Accounts Manager, an account may be modified by selecting Users, Modify or by double-clicking the account.

The bottom of the window, where `Add a new user account` is displayed, is the status line. The display of the status can be turned off in the Options menu (Point Help). Point Help provides the message in the status line. The Options menu also enables you to see the status of the account, with icons for locks and people appearing in the status column.

When using the graphical managers, use these guidelines:

- Use the mouse to navigate the screen areas.
- Select a menu by clicking it. A drop-down menu will appear; select items by clicking them.
- Use the arrow keys to move left and right within options such as menu items.
- Activate buttons by clicking them.
- Select an item in the display area by clicking it.

To delete the account for gene, for example, click on gene; then click Users, Delete.

Character-Based SCOadmin

SCOadmin runs in the character-based screens as well as the graphical. The interface is called the *CHARM (Character Motif) interface*. For systems that are running close to the limit on resources, from a character-based telnet session, or if the graphical screen is not working, the CHARM interface works well.

If you desire to run the CHARM mode even when the graphical system is running, use the following technique:

```
#CHARM=true
#export CHARM
# scoadmin
```

For comparison, the screens shown in Figures 5.10 and 5.11 are the same as the ones in the graphical section. The first things you notice are the lack of color and graphics. Figure 5.9 is the SCOadmin main menu. Not all managers run in CHARM mode. The icons from the GUI mode will display as characters in CHARM mode. There is no toolbar in CHARM mode because icons are not displayed.

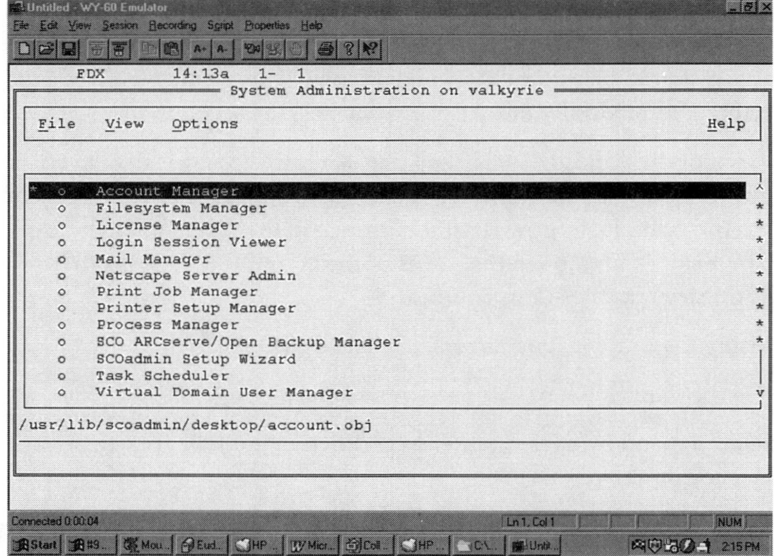

FIGURE 5.10 *The CHARM SCOadmin main menu.*

Author's Note

You are seeing these in black-and-white or shades of gray. The actual screens were displayed in the color set Delphinium. The "Swiss Army Knives" in the graphical shots are red; the folders are yellow. The CHARM screens were made using TermVision Wyse 60 emulator over TCP/IP with a black-on-white display.

There are no control buttons on the CHARM display and the "Swiss Army Knives" are displayed as small circles, the folders as dashes.

Navigation in the CHARM interface does not include a mouse. The Tab keys are used to move from one area to another. Usually, this is between the menu and the display area. In Figure 5.10, none of the menu items is highlighted.

Press Tab to highlight the File command. Use the right and left arrows to navigate in the menu. Use the up and down arrows to access drop-down menus. The Alt+F combination used to access the File menu in Microsoft Windows does not work here. It will be of use only if you are running a telnet session and want to activate the File menu in the Windows program that is running the telnet session.

If one of the menu items is highlighted, press the Tab key to move to the display area. Use the up and down arrows to move through the display area. Press the spacebar to select an item. Press the Enter key to execute an item.

Troubleshooting Tip

*In some screens, you may need to press the spacebar to select an item, such as a user account, before tabbing to the menu to perform an action on the selected item. Not pressing the spacebar can result in unexpected and undesirable results. If you want to de-install software, for instance, be sure to remove the * symbol next to the packages you do not want to remove. Because the Operating System is usually the default, an * is beside it. If you leave the * and also place one beside the software you want to remove, you will remove the Operating System.*

There are not as many options available in the Options submenu because the character-based environment has fewer capabilities. For instance, with no toolbar there is no reason for an option to turn it off or on.

If you accidentally open a pull-down menu, press Esc to get out of it. On the SCOadmin main menu, use the Enter key to open the folders into additional menu items.

The column of * characters on the right edge of the display area is a character representation of the scrollbar, providing two pieces of information:

- First, there is more information below the information displayed.
- Second, the height of the * column provides a rough scaling of how much information is hidden. Compare the length of the * to the line beneath it going down to the V.

For comparison, Figure 5.11 shows the character view of the Account Manager. Compare this with Figure 5.10. The GUI version is easier for most people to use.

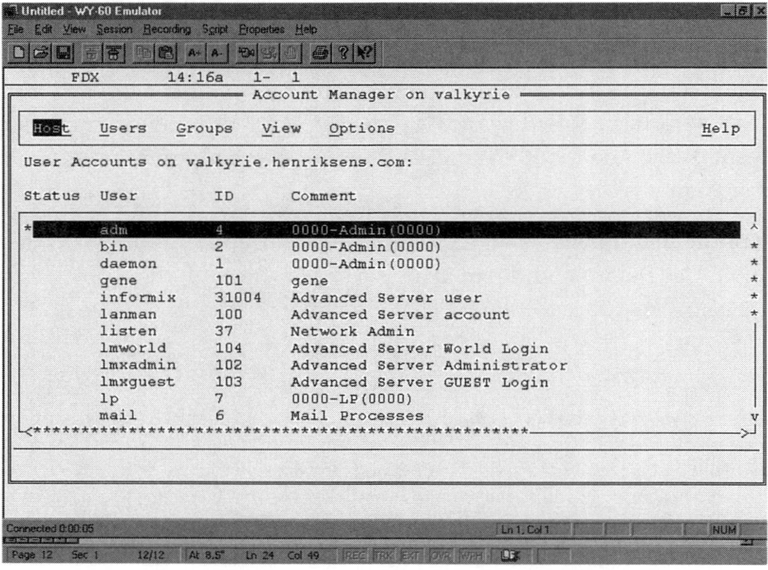

FIGURE 5.11 *The character-based Account Manager.*

The SCOadmin Managers

SCOadmin has, at this time, 44 administrative managers. The following list shows the managers and the chapters in this book that cover them in detail. This listing was made with the `-t` option to the `scoadmin` command.

Account Manager	Chapter 17
Address Allocation Manager	Chapter 6
Application Installer	Chapter 13
Audio Configuration Manager	Chapter 12
Client Manager	Chapter 6
Device Configuration Utility (DCU)	Chapter 4
DHCP Server Manager	Chapter 6
Dial-in Services Manager	Chapter 7
Dialup Systems Manager	Chapter 7
DNS Manager	Chapter 6
Filesystem Manager	Chapter 19
FTP Server Manager	Chapter 6
Install Server	Chapter 13
International Settings Manager	Chapter 15

Intranet Manager	Chapter 8
LDAP Manager	Chapter 6
License Manager	Chapter 14
Login Session Viewer	Chapter 18
Mail Manager	Chapter 20
Modem Manager	Chapter 7
Netscape Server Admin	Chapter 8
NetWare Settings	Chapter 9
NetWare Setup	Chapter 9
Network Configuration Manager	Chapter 6
Packet Filter Manager	Chapter 7
Print Job Manager	Chapter 11
Printer Setup Manager	Chapter 11
Process Manager	Chapter 15
Reports Manager	Chapters 15 and 17
SCO ARCserve/Open Backup Manager	Chapter 12
SCOadmin Setup Wizard	Chapter 15
Security Profile Manager	Chapter 23
Serial Manager	Chapter 10
SNMP Agent Manager	Chapter 6
System Defaults Manager	Chapter 15
System Information	Chapter 15
System Logs Manager	Chapter 15
System Monitor	Chapter 21
System Shutdown Manager	Chapter 16
System Time Manager	Chapter 15
System Tuner	Chapter 21
Task Scheduler	Chapter 18
Video Configuration Manager	Chapter 15
Virtual Domain User Manager	Chapter 8

CHAPTER 6

LAN Network Configuration

- TCP/IP concepts
  Learn how to configure TCP/IP addresses and netmasks.
- Network hardware
  Understand the considerations involved in selecting network interface cards. Understand the physical layer of networking.
- TCP/IP configuration
  Learn how to configure TCP in UnixWare 7. Learn how to test the TCP connectivity. See how the `ifconfig` command is used. Understand the problems in changing network addresses.
- Dynamic Host Configuration Protocol
  DHCP is now a part of UnixWare. Learn how to configure DHCP and how it can ease your administrative burden.
- Domain Name System
  See how UnixWare 7 implements DNS in a graphical environment.

TCP/IP Concepts

The *TCP/IP protocol* is the primary method of communicating between computers in LANs using UNIX. System administrators should have an understanding of the TCP/IP protocol to enable them to install, maintain, and troubleshoot their networks.

TCP/IP is an acronym for *Transmission Control Protocol/Internet Protocol*. TCP/IP encompasses a suite of programs and tools for networking.

Computer Network Addresses

For a system to communicate with another system using TCP/IP, the originating computer must know the address of the target system. When a message is sent from one system to another, both the sender's and recipient's addresses are included in the message. This allows systems to examine the message to determine if it is destined for them. It also allows the recipient to determine the return address of the sender.

Hardware Addresses

Networked systems communicate by means of hardware addresses, also known as *Media Access Control (MAC) addresses*. The hardware addresses for Ethernet networks are 48-bit (6 byte) hexadecimal values configured into the network interface card (NIC) at the time of manufacture. Each hardware address is unique. An example of a hardware address is 00:60:97:5F:0E:94. For Token-Ring networks, the card addresses are 8-bit (1 byte) numbers that may not be duplicated within a ring. An example of a Token-Ring address is 37.

Hardware addresses are sufficient for a small network where all computers can communicate over the same medium. Hardware addresses do not provide a method of locating a computer that is not on the local network.

Software Addresses

Software addresses in TCP/IP are referred to as *IP addresses*. The format of IP addresses is dotted decimal notation. The address consists of four decimal numbers separated by periods. An example of an IP address is 209.67.28.227. This IP address is for a SCO World Wide Web server.

Each IP address is composed of four 8-bit numbers ranging from 0 to 255. Each number is referred to as an *octet*, not a byte. The reason for the use of the octet terminology is that some operating systems use 7-bit bytes.

The IP address must be unique within the network. If the computer is to be connected to the Internet, the number must be unique within the entire Internet.

The Network and Host Numbers

IP addresses are composed of two parts:

- Network number
- Host number

The network portion of the address separates one network from another. The host numbers will be repeated within networks. The combination of network number and host number must be unique. This is similar to post office box numbers being unique within a postal code.

The network addresses are classified based on the value of the first octet. Each class uses a different number of octets to represent the network number and the host number.

Class	1st Octet Values	Network Octets	Host Octets	Leading Bits in 1st Octet
A	0-127	1	3	0
B	128-191	2	2	10
C	192-223	3	1	110
D	224-239	NA	NA	1110
E	240-247	NA	NA	11110

Classes A, B, and C will be the addresses that you will assign to your hosts. Class D is used for multicasting, and Class E is reserved for future use.

An example of a Class A address is 12.1.1.1. The network number (one octet) is 12 and the host number (three octets) is 1.1.1. A Class B address could be 132.101.14.27. The network number (two octets) would be 132.101 and the host number (two octets) would be 14.27. A Class C address could be 209.67.28.227. The network number (three octets) would be 209.67.28 and the host number (one octet) would be 227.

In a Class C network address, such as 209.67.28, the host numbers could range from 1 to 254, for a total of 254 hosts or nodes on the network. If an organization receives a Class C network from the Internet authority, it can assign up to 254 hosts. If it has more than 254 hosts, it would need more Class C addresses, assuming it wants the hosts to be connected to the Internet.

Author's Note

Another way of looking at addresses is from a binary number perspective. Class A addresses start with a 0 in the first bit of the first octet. If the first bit is a zero, the maximum number of networks is determined by the seven remaining bits. The maximum number of networks for Class A is ($2^7 - 2$), or 126. The first address would be 0000000 (0) and the last would be 1111111 (127). Because all zeros and all ones are not allowed in the network number, we are left with a range from 1 to 126.

A Class B network has the first two bits as the class designator (10). The remaining six bits of the first octet and all eight bits of the second octet are used to determine the network number. The total number of bits available for network numbering is 14. Class B can contain ($2^{14} - 2$) or 16,382 networks ranging from 128.1 through 191.254.

Class C networks have a leading 110 in the first three bits of the first octet. The network number is the first three octets providing (8 – 3) + 8 + 8 or 21 bits in the network portion. With 21 bits, there can be ($2^{21} - 2$) or 2,097,150 networks with Class C addresses.

The same method of binary mathematics can be used to compute the number of hosts. A Class C address has eight bits for host addresses or ($2^8 - 2$) or 254 hosts. A Class B can have ($2^{16} - 2$) or 65,534 hosts, and a Class A can have ($2^{24} - 2$) or 16,777,214 hosts.

Netmasks

If an organization had a Class A network of 12, it would have more than 16 million possible host numbers ranging from 12.0.0.1 to 12.255.255.254. Limitations on cable lengths and number of nodes per segment for ethernet cable would prohibit 16 million computers from existing on a single LAN. To use the numbers efficiently, the organization should subnet the Class A network into multiple Class C networks.

The subnetting of a network is accomplished by using a *netmask* to indicate the number of bits or octets used in the network number. Class A networks use one octet for the netmask by default. The default netmask for a Class A network is 255.0.0.0. The value 255 is the maximum number that can be created in the octet by setting all eight bits to 1s.

To understand network addresses and netmasks requires knowledge of binary arithmetic. Each octet contains eight bits. If all the bits are off (00000000), the value is 0. If all the bits are on (11111111), the value is 255. To compute the network number, TCP/IP compares the netmask to the IP address. Given an address of 10.1.20.4 and a netmask of 255.255.255.0, the comparison would be represented in binary as

```
11111111.11111111.11111111.00000000  netmask 255.255.255.0
00001010.00000001.00010100.00000100  address 10.1.20.4
```

By performing a logical AND operation on the netmask and the address, the result would be

```
00001010.00000001.00010100.00000000 network 10.1.20.0
```

By using a Class C subnet mask on a Class A address, the network designer has the ability to create (2^{16} – 2) subnets to organize the hosts into manageable units. By using the second and third octets as a part of the network number, an additional 16 bits are available for creating network numbers.

When a message is sent to another host, the netmask is compared to the IP address of the sending and receiving host. If the comparison yields the same network number, the receiving host is on the local network. If the network number is different, the message will have to be routed through other networks to get to the receiving host.

All hosts on the same LAN should use the same netmask. If the netmask is not set correctly, the system with the different netmask may not be able to communicate with other hosts on the LAN. Your network administrator is responsible for setting up the netmasks.

When a host receives a message, it uses a logical AND of its own IP address with the target computer's IP address to see if the message is for itself. A message sent out to all the hosts on a subnet is called a *broadcast message*. A broadcast has all host number bits turned on (set to 1s) so the logical AND operation matches every host number.

For the Class A network number of 12 that has been subnetted into Class C networks, all of the hosts would use the same netmask, 255.255.255.0. Within each subnet all the hosts would use the same broadcast address. For subnet 12.1.1, the broadcast address would be 12.1.1.255 and the hosts would range from 12.1.1.1 to 12.1.1.254. The network would be referred to as the *12.1.1.0 network*.

It is not necessary for the subnet portion of the address to be aligned with the octet boundaries. If you only have a Class C network and need to allow for multiple subnets, the fourth octet could be broken down into network bits and host bits. Many texts are available on subnetting. The SCO Network Administration class is a good source of training on subnetting as well.

Host Names and IP Addresses

To make the TCP/IP addressing user-friendly, host names can be used to represent IP addresses. When a user needs to access another host, the host name may be used in place of the IP address. TCP/IP must translate the host name into an IP address.

There are two main methods of enabling the host name to IP address resolution. The first method is the */etc/hosts file*. The /etc/hosts file is a simple text file with the IP address and the host name plus any aliases for the host name.

The following code is an /etc/hosts file. The special network 127 is reserved for testing. The IP address is listed with the host name and the fully qualified domain name (FQDN). The FQDN includes the registered domain name, in this case, henriksens.com.

Author's Note

You may register your domain name directly with the InterNIC at `www.internic.net`. *It maintains a search capability to allow you to determine if your desired domain name is already registered. Alternatively, your Internet service provider may register and host your domain for you.*

```
#
# Internet host table
#
127.0.0.1       localhost
10.1.1.3        valkyrie.henriksens.com valkyrie
10.1.1.2        beowulf.henriksens.com beowulf
10.1.1.1        thor.henriksens.com thor
10.1.1.4        gandalf.henriksens.com gandalf
10.1.1.9        lorelei lorelei.henriksens.com
10.1.1.10       tuscany.henriksens.com tuscany
10.1.1.101      kingsley.henriksens.com kingsley
```

As a network grows, or when it becomes a part of the Internet, the /etc/hosts file is too cumbersome. An alternate method of resolving names to IP addresses is the *Domain Name System (DNS)*. DNS uses a hierarchical system, with each organization responsible for maintaining a name resolution server. DNS is covered later in this chapter.

Resolving IP Addresses to Hardware Addresses

Hosts communicate with hardware addresses to make the transfers more efficient. Each message is checked for the destination hardware address by logically ANDing the destination address with the local host hardware address. If the addresses match, the NIC passes the message into the local host's TCP/IP software for further processing.

To determine a remote host's hardware address, a host sends out an *address resolution protocol (ARP) message*. The ARP message has a destination hardware address of

```
ff:ff:ff:ff:ff:ff
```

which is the "all bits on" hardware address. Each NIC accepts the message and passes it to the IP. The IP routines recognize the message as a request for the hardware address for a host with the targeted IP address. If the IP address matches the local IP address, a return message is sent to the originating host providing the hardware address.

Both hosts record the IP address and hardware address of the remote host in their arp cache. This enables the two hosts to communicate with each other without having to rediscover the hardware address of the remote host. The arp command can be used to list the contents of the arp cache. The information includes the host name (if it can be found by the local host), the IP address, and the hardware address.

```
arp -a
beowulf.henriksens.com (10.1.1.2) at 0:60:97:5f:e:94 (802.3)
gandalf.henriksens.com (10.1.1.4) at 0:80:5f:bc:da:e0 (802.3)
guiness.henriksens.com (10.1.1.103) at 0:20:af:dc:98:76 (802.3)
kingsley.henriksens.com (10.1.1.104) at 0:60:8:9b:8c:d (802.3)
```

The arp command can also be used to add a hardware address and IP address pair for hosts that cannot be directly configured and that require Telnet or a Web interface for configuration.

```
arp -s <ip_address> <hardware_address>
```

A static arp entry is particularly useful for print servers that require configuration by Telnet.

The behavior of arp is controlled by entries in the /etc/inet/inet.dfl file. By default the entries in the arp cache are dropped after 1,200 seconds (this parameter can be changed from 1 to 2,400 seconds). Normally, it should not be necessary for the administrator to change the default arp entries.

The TCP/IP Protocol Stack

TCP/IP is a modular protocol composed of separate components that comprise the *TCP/IP protocol stack*. Each layer of the stack performs specific functions and passes messages to the layers above or below.

Applications using TCP/IP use a client-server model. The *client* is the system requesting the service and the *server* is the system that provides the service. Applications that are network enabled send their messages to the TCP/IP protocol stack for transmission to the other system. Applications may also use the IPX/SPX protocol, which is described in Chapter 9, "Netware."

Figure 6.1 illustrates the TCP/IP protocol stack. Messages are passed through the stack on their way in and out of the system. The layers of the protocol stack each perform specific functions. The *Application Layer* provides the user interface. For example, Telnet is the client-side application layer and Telnetd is the server-side application layer of a Telnet session.

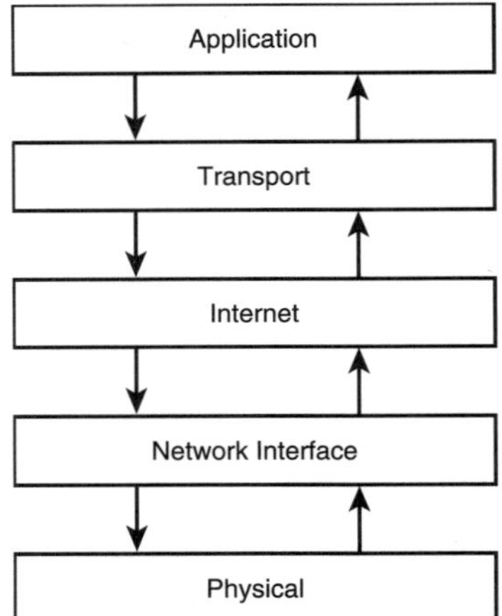

FIGURE 6.1 *The TCP/IP protocol stack.*

The *Transport Layer* creates a unique port number that identifies the recipient of return messages. The application selects either *Transport Control Protocol (TCP)* or *User Datagram Protocol (UDP)*, depending on the needs of the application program. UDP is used for one-packet messages or where loss of a packet is not of consequence. UDP is used by the `ping` command. TCP is used to guarantee delivery of packets in order. TCP is used by rlogin, Telnet, and other programs that require multiple packets of data requiring guaranteed delivery. For outgoing messages, the Transport Layer adds a header to the message received from the Application Layer and passes the information, now known as a *packet*, to the Internet Layer. On the receiving side the Transport Layer strips off the header and passes the message to the appropriate application.

The *Internet Layer* checks for an arp cache entry for the recipient. If the arp entry does not appear, the Internet Layer, also known as the *IP Layer*, directs an arp broadcast to determine the hardware address of the recipient. For outgoing messages, the Internet Layer adds an IP header to the packet received from the Transport Layer and sends the information, now called a *datagram*, to the Network Interface Layer. For incoming messages, the Internet Layer receives a message from the Network Interface layer, strips off the IP header, and sends the packet to UDP or TCP in the Transport Layer.

The *Network Interface Layer* is the NIC driver. This layer creates the physical frame by adding a header to the datagram that will travel across the network medium and will put the frame on the medium. On the receiving side, the Network Interface Layer checks the hardware or MAC address of each packet that arrives at the network interface to determine if the recipient address matches the local NIC address. If it is a packet for the local system, the frame is stripped of the frame header and passed to the Internet Layer as a datagram.

The *Physical Layer* is the medium over which the network traffic travels. Data from each layer is encapsulated by the layer below it and passed to the remote system by the Physical Layer. Upon receipt, each layer strips away the header added by its corresponding layer on the sending system. With the stripping of headers to reveal the encapsulated data on the remote system, each layer is essentially dealing with its equivalent layer on the remote system. The header information instructs each layer as to what it should do with the data. In the case of the Internet Layer, information in the header indicates whether the packet is destined for UDP or TCP in the Transport Layer.

Figure 6.2 illustrates how data from the client passes through layers from Application to Physical, across the Physical Layer to the server, and then up through the layers to the application.

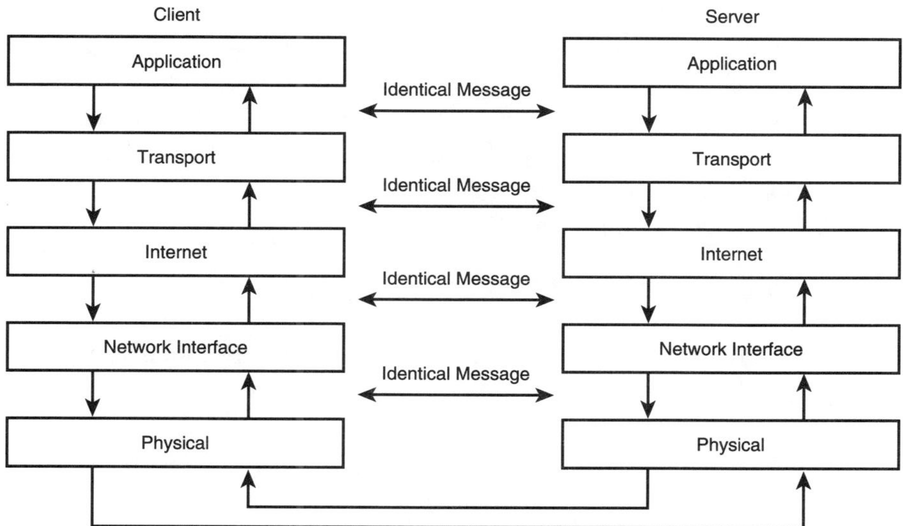

FIGURE 6.2 *The path of data from the client's application to the server's application.*

Network Hardware

To implement networking in a LAN, special hardware must be installed in the computer, along with a medium for connecting the computers. Check the SCO hardware compatibility lists to ensure that the hardware you select is usable with UnixWare 7. The Web address for the Compatible Hardware Web page is `www.sco.com/chwp`.

Network Interface Cards

In LANs, the connection to the network medium is through the *network interface card (NIC)*. NICs are specific to the Physical Layer, such as Ethernet, Token Ring, FDDI, ISDN, and the like. NICs may have one or more connectors for connecting different cabling types, such as twisted pair, thinnet, or thicknet. The speed of the network also governs choice of the NIC. Ethernet commonly runs at 10 MB/sec or 100 MB/sec. Some NICs support both and auto-sense the speed of the network.

UnixWare 7 is designed as a server and may be subjected to heavy network loads. To reduce network congestion, buy fast NICs. PCI bus NICs are currently the state of the art. Older ISA NICs are limited by slower bus speeds. NICs come in 8-, 16-, and 32-bit versions. The 32-bit NICs are faster than the 8- and 16-bit NICs. NICs also vary in buffer size. Larger buffers improve performance. Some old NICs had only 1K buffers, which created problems for NFS. With gigabit networking and the 64-bit Intel processors on the horizon, newer and faster cards will appear.

UnixWare 7 can auto-detect some NICs. Of those it cannot auto-detect, all of which are ISA, some have verify routines that can check the NIC settings. Table 6.1 is current as of version 7.0.1. Use this as a guide to selecting NICs for your systems. Always double-check the SCO compatibility lists before buying new NICs.

TABLE 6.1 UNIXWARE 7 AUTO-DETECTION OF NICS

NIC Types	NIC Name/Model
Non-ISA cards supported Should be auto-detectable (EISA Bus)	Compaq Netflex-2 series Compaq Netflex-3 series Digital DE425 EISA Ethernet Adapter Digital DEFEA FDDI Adapter 3Com 3C509EISA EtherLinkIII 3Com 3C579 EtherLinkIII 3Com EtherLink3 3C59X Novell NE3200 Bus Master and Compatible
Non-ISA cards supported Should be auto-detectable (MCA Bus) Adapter/A	3Com 3C523 EtherLink/MC 3Com 3C529 EtherLinkIII IBM Token-Ring Network Adapter/A and 16/4
	IBM PS/2 Adapter/A (WD8003E/A– and SMC8013E/A–compatible) for Ethernet Western Digital/SMC 8003/8013 Microchannel Series

NIC Types	NIC Name/Model
	IBM EtherStreamer Family Adapter Driver IBM LAN Streamer MC Family Adapter Driver
Non-ISA cards supported Should be auto-detectable (PCI Bus)	Compaq Netflex-3 series Digital EtherWORKS DE434/5 PCI Adapter Digital EtherWORKS DE450 PCI Adapter Digital EtherWORKS DE500 Adapter Digital DEFPA FDDI Adapter 3Com EtherLink3 3C59X 3Com EtherLink XL Intel PRO/100B / PRO/100+ AMD PCnet family MDI driver SMC EtherPower 8432/8434 10 MB/sec PCI Ethernet Adapter SMC EtherPower 9332DST/BDT/BVT 10/100 MB/sec PCI Adapter SMC EtherPower II 10/100 IBM PCI Ethernet Adapter IBM PCI Token-Ring Family Adapter Intel 2104x–based 10 MB/sec Ethernet Controller Intel 2114x–based 10/100 MB/sec Ethernet Controller SysKonnect FDDI PCI Adapter IBM Auto LANStreamer PCI Adapter Driver Eicon Diva Pro 2.0 PCI USA 5ESS CUSTOM Eicon Diva Pro 2.0 PCI Australia Eicon Diva Pro 2.0 PCI Euro-ISDN Eicon Diva Pro 2.0 PCI Japan Eicon Diva Pro 2.0 PCI USA National ISDN 1
ISA cards (not auto-detectable)	Digital EtherWORKS 3 Adapter 3Com 3C503 EtherLink II 3Com 3C507 EtherLink 16 Series 3Com 3C509 EtherLink III NE2000 Series SMC 8416 EtherEZ SMC 8216 Ultra IBM Auto 16/4 Token-Ring Network ISA-16 (Shared RAM) IBM Turbo ISA Token-Ring Adapter (Shared RAM) IBM Token-Ring Network ISA Series (Shared RAM) SMC/Western Digital 8003 Series SMC/Western Digital 8013 Series Eicon Diva Pro 2.0 ISA USA 5ESS CUSTOM

continues

TABLE 6.1 CONTINUED

NIC Types	NIC Name/Model
	Eicon Diva Pro 2.0 ISA Australia Eicon Diva Pro 2.0 ISA Euro-ISDN Eicon Diva Pro 2.0 ISA Japan Eicon Diva Pro 2.0 ISA USA National ISDN 1
ISA cards that have verify routines *	3Com 3C503 EtherLink II 3Com 3C507 EtherLink 16 Series 3Com 3C509 EtherLinkIII SMC/Western Digital 8003 Series SMC/Western Digital 8013 Series

** Although the card itself isn't auto-detectable, some of its parameter settings can be found when netcfg asks to look for current settings for these cards.*

Author's Note

The Eicon NICs are ISDN WAN adapters.

Many NICs come with DOS-based configuration and test routines. You may need to boot your system into DOS to configure the NIC. Some administrators install a small DOS partition on the hard disk to allow installation of test software. This will allow the administrator to boot into DOS without being limited to floppy disks.

Physical Layer

The Physical Layer is the medium over which the network traffic flows. Usually this is copper wire. It may be fiber-optic cable or a wireless method, such as laser beams or radio waves.

The Ethernet specifications cover several physical media. Commonly seen is the twisted-pair cable for running both 10 MB/sec (10BaseT) and 100 MB/sec (100BaseT) networks. For 100 MB/sec, be sure to specify Category 5 (CAT 5) cabling. Twisted-pair cables are connected to hubs. Signals transmitted by one node are seen by all nodes, essentially connecting all the devices on a hub into a single cable. One advantage of twisted pair is that a break in one cable affects only the node on that cable.

Thinnet coax cable (10Base2) has been used for years in running office networks. Thinnet is run from one system to the next. A Tee connector attached to the NIC provides a connection to the node, and cables extend from the two ends of the Tee. Each end of the network is terminated to prevent signal bounce back. A disadvantage of thinnet is that a break in the cable can bring the entire network to a halt.

Fiber-optic is an excellent Physical Layer, although expensive. Fiber has two major advantages:

- Because it is fiber, not copper, it does not conduct electricity, therefore reducing lightning strike damage.
- Fiber has very high speed and low resistance, allowing much longer cables than either thinnet or twisted pair. Typically, twisted pair is limited to 100 meters per cable; thinnet is limited to 185 meters per cable, while fiber can run up to 2 km.

For a UnixWare 7 system to participate in a LAN, it must have a NIC configured. The NIC must be connected to the LAN, and the UnixWare 7 system must be uniquely identified to the LAN. The NIC should be installed in the system while the system is shut down, unless you are using hardware that supports hot plug PCI card capability. Connect the LAN cable to the NIC and turn the power on. This boots the operating system to multi-user mode.

Author's Note

To obtain the information for the configuration on an ISA installation, you should have booted the system into DOS and run the vendor-supplied diagnostics and configuration programs. The diagnostics should warn you if you have a possible resource conflict. Look at the DCU to find available resources to help you configure an ISA card.

TCP/IP Configuration

TCP/IP is started in the /etc/rc2.d/S69inet script. Configuration files for networking are contained in the /etc/inet directory. The inetd.conf file is used by the inetd daemon to start daemons for network requests. A file that will be new to OpenServer 5 users is the /etc/inet/config file. The config file is used to start up services such as named. An extract of the file is shown here:

```
5:/usr/sbin/in.named::y:/etc/inet/named.boot::
3:/usr/sbin/in.pppd::y:/etc/inet/ppphosts::
# The next line can be read:
# If field 3 is a Y, and /etc/inet/gated.conf exists, then run
# /usr/sbin/in.gated with no optional arguments.
4a:/usr/sbin/in.gated::Y:/etc/inet/gated.conf::
```

Configuring a NIC

To configure a NIC, choose Network Configuration Manager, SCOadmin, Networking, Network Configuration Manager, or at the login prompt run `netcfg`.

OpenServer 5 Tip

The command is `netcfg`*, not* `netconfig`.

From the Network Configuration Manager's Hardware menu, select Add New LAN Adapter. Figure 6.3 illustrates the windows that are open when adding a new LAN adapter. Select Ethernet or Token-Ring. In the installation pictured here, we are installing an additional adapter. An AMD PCnet adapter is already installed.

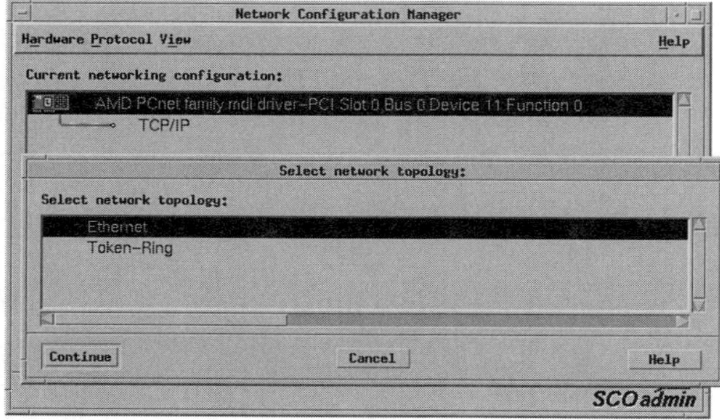

FIGURE 6.3 *The initial windows when adding a new LAN adapter.*

The NIC being added is an ISA 3C509. It is not auto-recognized by UnixWare 7. As a result, we are presented with a selection screen of NICs. Had the NIC been auto-recognizable, the window for Ethernet/Token-Ring would not have appeared. A window would have appeared stating

```
The following adapters have been found:
```

and listing the NIC.

Figure 6.4 shows the selection window of NICs. Select the NIC you are using and click the Continue button.

When the 3C509 is selected, a window appears asking if you wish to search for a 3C509. Figure 6.5 illustrates the window.

Author's Note

I found that when I allowed it to search, it did not discover the 3C509.

After the search request, you must supply the ISA configuration parameters. This window does not appear for PCI NICs. Figure 6.6 illustrates the configuration of the driver. This must match the NIC settings.

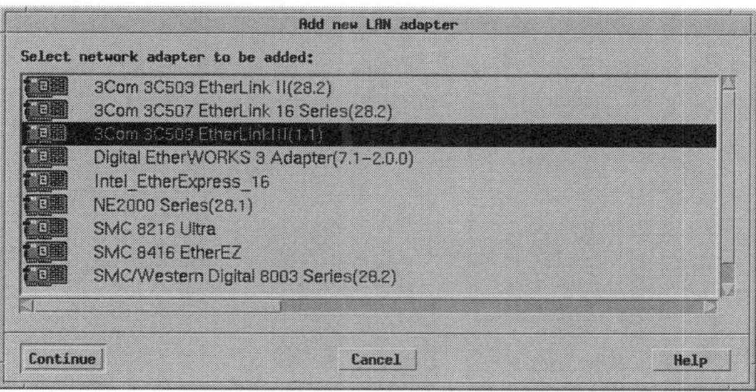

FIGURE 6.4 *The selection for non-recognized NICs.*

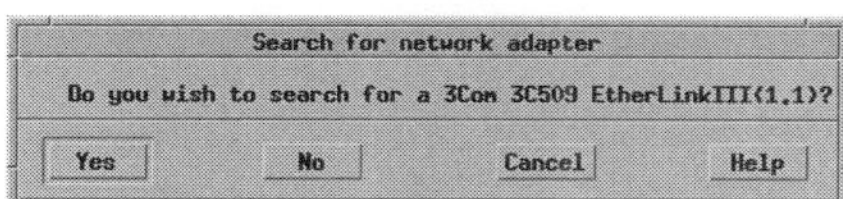

FIGURE 6.5 *The search request window.*

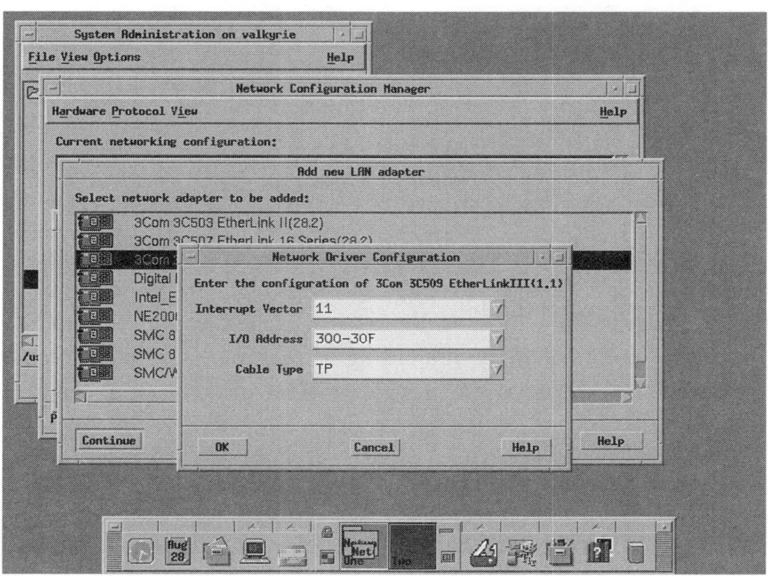

FIGURE 6.6 *The Network Driver configuration.*

After the card configuration stage has been completed, you enter the TCP/IP configuration. The Add protocol window appears offering a selection of IPX/SPX and TCP/IP for configuration. For IPX/SPX configuration, see Chapter 9, "NetWare." Figure 6.7 illustrates the Add protocol window.

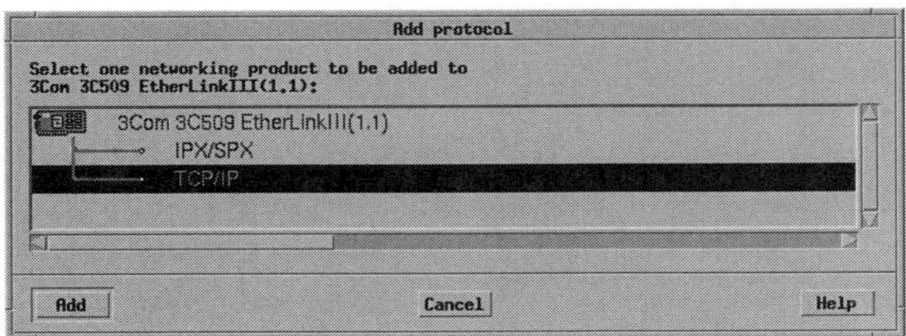

FIGURE 6.7 *The Add protocol window.*

When TCP/IP is selected as the protocol, the Internet Protocol Configuration window appears. The host name should already be configured. Enter the domain name, if you use one. Enter the IP address, the netmask, and the broadcast address. Enter a default router if you have one. The router address is not required on a single LAN not connected to other LANs or WANs.

OpenServer 5 Tip

In OpenServer 5, the default router did not appear as part of the configuration. It had to be manually configured in the /etc/tcp file.

Click the Advanced options button to see the Advanced Configuration window. Figure 6.8 illustrates both the Internet Protocol Configuration and Advanced Configuration windows. By default, 32 pseudo-ttys should be preconfigured; you may need more depending on the number of users connecting to the UnixWare 7 system via Telnet or rlogin. The default frame format is Ethernet-II.

Tip

You may enter an administrator's name and system location for documentation purposes.

When you click the OK button on the Internet Protocol Configuration window, a window recapping the successful NIC configuration should appear. Figure 6.9 shows the confirmation.

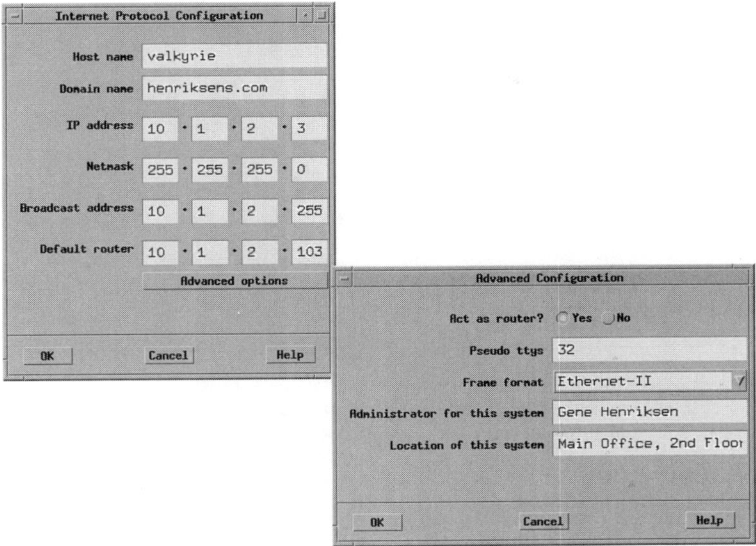

FIGURE 6.8 *The Internet Protocol Configuration and Advanced Configuration windows.*

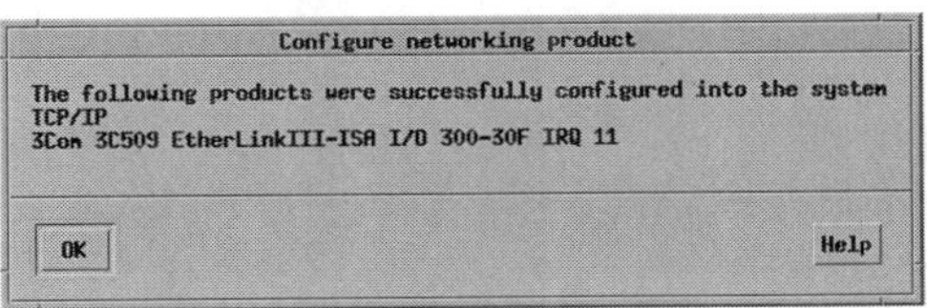

FIGURE 6.9 *The confirmation of NIC configuration.*

The Network Configuration Manager window shows the new NIC with the protocol. From the Protocol window you can add, remove, modify, or view the configuration information. Figure 6.10 shows the updated Network Configuration Manager window.

Author's Note

When adding a NIC, it is not necessary to relink the kernel and/or reboot the system to make it effective. After the sequence of adding the 3C509 card, I was able to use it immediately.

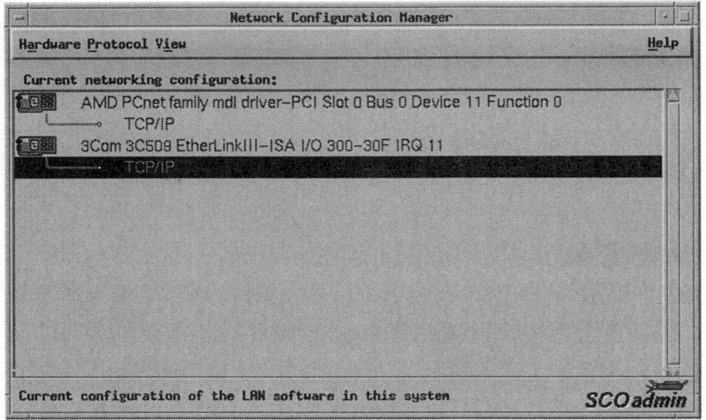

FIGURE 6.10 *The updated Network Configuration Manager.*

Testing the Connection

After the NIC has been configured, you can test for connectivity. In the Network Configuration Manager's Hardware menu is an option to Test Network Connectivity. Do not mistake this for a test of the TCP/IP protocol stack. Even if the network stack is down, running this option will test the hardware's ability to put packets on the network. The system sends out a test poll packet. The packet is a hardware broadcast (destination Ethernet address `ff:ff:ff:ff:ff:ff`) with an 802.3 frame type. Network devices, such as routers, OpenServer 5, and UnixWare 7 systems, will respond.

Author's Note

In my test of this function, I turned on my network monitor, disabled the network interfaces, and ran the test. Both UnixWare 7 and OpenServer 5 responded. No Windows operating systems responded.

This test checks the NIC, its driver, and the connection to the network. It does not use the TCP/IP layers involved in IP addressing. This provides a method of verifying the lower layers of the network stack.

The *ping* Command

The `ping` command is a network connectivity tester. From the system with the new NIC, use `ping` to echo a signal from another system.

```
ping 10.1.1.1
```

If the network interface is working and the remote host is working, you should receive a message back reporting the status of the remote host.

```
10.1.1.1 is alive
```

OpenServer 5 Tip

OpenServer 5 would default to continuous pings. This is not the behavior of `ping` on UnixWare 7.

The `ping` command has several options worth noting. To run `ping` a preset number of times, the `-s` option must be used with a number for the number of pings. However, to get it to work, you must also supply the size of the packet, which defaults to 64 bytes.

```
ping -s 10.1.1.1 64 5
```

The preceding `ping` line will ping the 10.1.1.1 IP address five times with 64 bytes per packet.

OpenServer 5 Tip

OpenServer 5 used the `-c` option to limit the number of pings (`-c 5`) to a "count" number of pings. The `-s` option was used to set the packet size. UnixWare 7 combines these in the `-s` option. If you forget to use the packet size in `-s` while trying to limit the count, the packet size defaults to the desired count and the `ping` runs continuously. For instance,

```
ping -s 10.1.1.1 5
```

will ping with 5 bytes, not for five iterations.

To test your network, use the `-f` option to flood the network with ping packets. The `-f` will print a dot for every packet transmitted and backspace once for every packet received. The number of dots showing on the screen represents the dropped packets. This option is restricted to privileged users.

To test the local TCP/IP stack Application, Transport, and Internet layers, use

```
ping localhost
```

You may substitute `127.0.0.1` or the system's IP address in the `ping`. The message from `ping` will travel down the stack to the Internet Layer. The Internet Layer performs the address lookup, determines that the address desired is local, and passes the message back up the stack.

Tip

To determine if networking connection problems are software or hardware related, use `ping` to test the top three layers of the stack. Use the Network Configuration Manager's Test routine discussed earlier to test the hardware and driver access to the network.

The *ifconfig* Command

To check the configuration of your network interfaces, use `ifconfig -a`:

```
# ifconfig -a
lo0: flags=4049<UP,LOOPBACK,RUNNING,MULTICAST> mtu 16384
        inet 127.0.0.1 netmask ff000000
        perf. params: recv size: 4096; send size: 8192; full-size
➥frames: 1
net0: flags=4043<UP,BROADCAST,RUNNING,MULTICAST> mtu 1500
        inet 10.1.1.9 netmask ffffff00 broadcast 10.1.1.255
        perf. params: recv size: 24576; send size: 24576; full-size
➥frames: 1
        ether 00:80:5f:52:13:4c
net1: flags=4043<UP,BROADCAST,RUNNING,MULTICAST> mtu 1500
        inet 10.1.2.9 netmask ffffff00 broadcast 10.1.2.255
        perf. params: recv size: 24576; send size: 24576; full-size
➥frames: 1
        ether 00:10:4b:96:4c:7f
```

The output of the `ifconfig -a` command includes information that is helpful in troubleshooting. Looking at the `net1` entry, we can determine that the interface is up and running. The IP address is `10.1.2.9` and the netmask, reported here in hexadecimal `ffffff00`, is `255.255.255.0` in dotted decimal notation. The broadcast address is `10.1.2.255`. The receive and send size window is 24,576 bytes, and the full-size frames set to `1` indicate it will use the full 24,576 bytes. The window is the NIC buffer size. The final piece of information is the MAC or Ethernet hardware address.

Problems with TCP on UnixWare 7

There are known configuration problems in early versions of UnixWare 7. These have been discovered while writing this book and by training centers. The problems listed in the following sections have been reported to SCO and should be fixed in the future.

Initial Configuration

One training center has reported that occasionally during the ISL the NIC is detected and configured properly, but afterward the GUI is not enabled and only a character-based login is available. The NIC is not detected by `ifconfig -a` and `netcfg` will not add it. This problem can be fixed by using the DCU to disable (toggle Y to N) the duplicate entries for IRQs 11-14-15 (the ones with resources shown in the dark-blue screen areas). This problem has been seen on several different brands of computer systems.

NIC Deletion

Deleting a NIC can cause all networking to cease. If the NIC is the second NIC in the system, the first NIC will quit working. `ping` will return errors even on `localhost`. The `ifconfig -a` command returns no output at all.

```
ping localhost
UX:ping: Error: sendto: Cannot assign requested address.
```

This problem can be fixed by a reboot. If you do not want to reboot, use the undocumented command:

```
initialize -U
```

This will bring the remaining network interfaces back to a running state. The command will display some error messages, but the networking will resume.

> *Troubleshooting Tip*
>
> *SCO engineers have said that the* `initialize` *command is a back-end tool for* `netcfg`. *It should not be relied on as an administrator's tool because it may change. Only use it to correct this problem. SCO is aware of the problem, and it should be fixed in a future release. Do not rely on* `initialize -U` *for other uses! This problem exists in both version 7.0.0 and version 7.0.1.*

Changing the IP Address

To change the IP address, use the graphical Network Configuration Manager or `netcfg` from the command line. Unfortunately, changing the IP address this way does not change all occurrences of the IP address. The other places it occurs are

```
/etc/inet/nb.conf
/etc/hosts
/usr/ns-home/admserv/ns-admin.conf
/var/adm/isl/ifile
```

`/etc/inet/nb.conf` is used in the configuration of NetBIOS networking. `/usr/ns-home/admserv/ns-admin.conf` is the Netscape configuration file. If this is not set correctly, Netscape Server Admin will give errors on startup and not allow you to manage Netscape. `/var/adm/isl/ifile` is a record of the install and is probably of consequence after installation is complete.

After the IP address has been changed, you must reboot to make the change effective. In lieu of rebooting, go to single-user mode and back to multi-user mode.

Warning

When changing the IP address, watch the netmask. If you are using any netmask other than the default for the class of address you are using, the netmask will revert to the default when the address is entered. As soon as you exit the IP address field after changing any part of the IP address, the system resets the netmask.

If you need to change the address for a short time only to fill the place of another system that is offline, use the ability to create an additional IP address on the system. You can create an alias without going through the hassle of changing the address. For a system with the IP address `10.1.1.9` on the NIC identified as `net0`, the `ifconfig` command that follows will make it also respond as though it were `10.1.1.222`. To find a graphical tool for creating aliases, check the Skunkware CD for the IP Address Alias Manager.

```
# ifconfig net0 alias 10.1.1.222 netmask 255.255.255.0
```

After the `alias` command has been run, `ifconfig` reports the alias.

```
# ifconfig -a
lo0: flags=4049<UP,LOOPBACK,RUNNING,MULTICAST> mtu 16384
        inet 127.0.0.1 netmask ff000000
        perf. params: recv size: 4096; send size: 8192; full-size
➥frames: 1
net0: flags=4043<UP,BROADCAST,RUNNING,MULTICAST> mtu 1500
        inet 10.1.1.9 netmask ffffff00 broadcast 10.1.1.255
        perf. params: recv size: 24576; send size: 24576; full-size
➥frames: 1
        ether 00:80:5f:52:13:4c
        (alias) inet 10.1.1.222 netmask ffffff00 broadcast 10.1.1.255
```

Note the last line of the output lists the alias. Pinging the system from another system yields the same result on both IP addresses.

```
# ping 10.1.1.9
10.1.1.9 is alive
# ping 10.1.1.222
10.1.1.222 is alive
```

Tip

One use of IP aliasing would be for a backup server. In lightning-prone areas, businesses need a backup server in the event a strike takes out the primary. To avoid having the network users telnet to a different server, alias the backup to the primary's IP address when the backup moves to primary. When the primary returns, un-alias the IP address.

Another use is for multihoming, which is the ability to have multiple IP addresses on a single NIC. If you intend to use multihoming for routing, be sure to read about the limitations in Chapter 8.

Host Name Resolution

As was mentioned previously, host names must be resolved into IP addresses before communication can take place between hosts. TCP/IP has no method of broadcasting or responding to broadcasts for host names. Host names can be resolved into IP addresses using the local /etc/hosts file, DNS, or with host files from a Network Information Service (NIS) server.

The Client Manager

The UnixWare 7 system can be configured as a client for any of three methods listed in the previous section. To configure these options, select the Client Manager from the Networking folder in SCOadmin. Figure 6.11 illustrates the default settings for the configuration. The network client service configured by default is the /etc/hosts file.

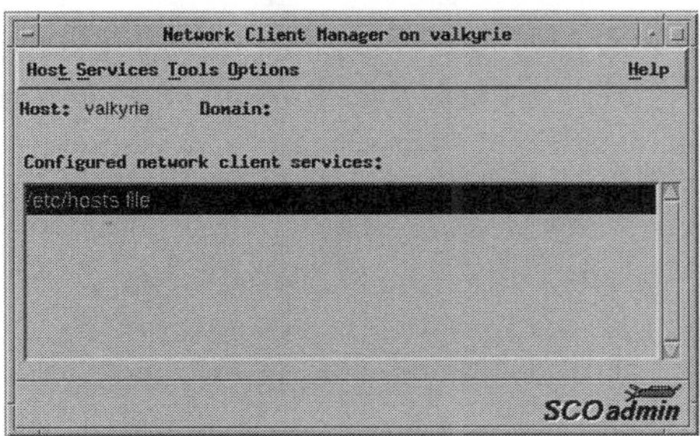

FIGURE 6.11 *The Client Manager.*

The Name Resolution Order

Under the Services menu, the first item is the Name Resolution Order. Figure 6.12 illustrates the Name Resolution Order configuration window. To add DNS or NIS, highlight the desired item under Available services and click Add to add them to the Configured services. When items are in the Configured network clients services column, the Promote and Demote buttons may be used to place them in the desired order for host name resolution. You may prefer to have one form of resolution take place over another. For example, the NIS system to be contacted may be across a WAN connection, while a DNS server is local.

To add a service, such as a DNS client, select Services, Add and select the service. Four options appear in the menu. By default, the Hosts Database option is grayed out because it is established at initial system load. The other three options are DNS client, NIS client, and NTP client.

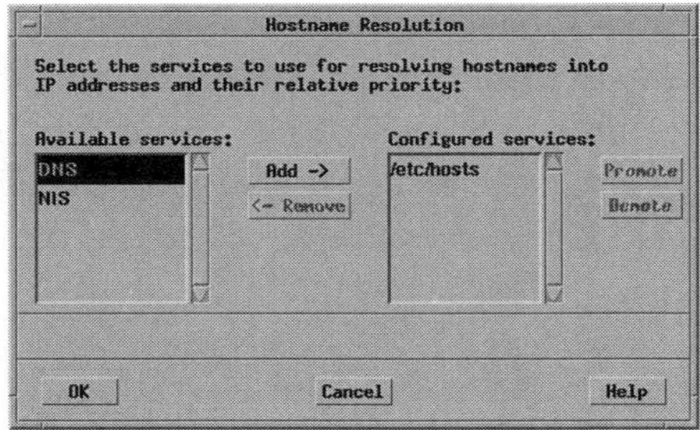

FIGURE 6.12 *The Hostname Resolution Order configuration.*

The DNS Client Service Configuration

Figure 6.13 illustrates the DNS Client Service Configuration window. To become a DNS client, enter the local domain name; enter domain names in the domain search order; and add the DNS nameserver IP addresses. Note that after nameservers have been added, you may use the Promote and Demote buttons to arrange the search order.

The *domain search order* is a list of domain names that will be used as suffixes for a DNS resolution request for a host name. For example, if the domain search order contained `santacruz.sco.com`, `murrayhill.sco.com`, and `leeds.sco.com`, a request for name resolution for a host named uw7 would result in attempts to resolve `uw7.santacruz.sco.com`, `uw7.murrayhill.sco.com`, and `uw7.leeds.sco.com`.

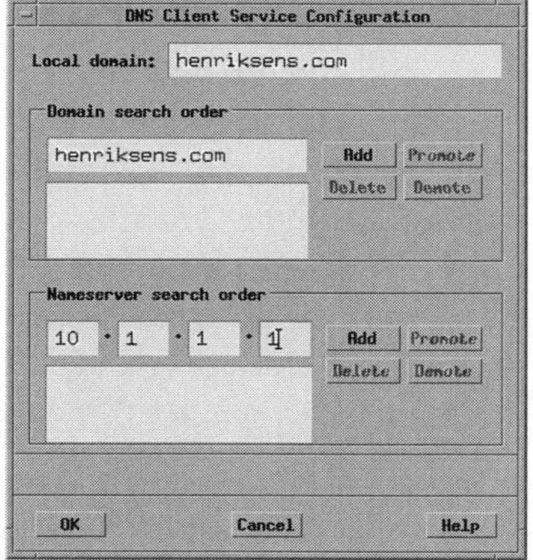

FIGURE 6.13 *The DNS Client Service Configuration window.*

The NIS Client Service Configuration

Figure 6.14 illustrates the NIS Client Configuration window. To become part of an NIS domain, enter the domain name. If you would like the client to broadcast for NIS servers, select the Yes button.

Warning

An NIS domain and a DNS domain are not the same. Entering a non-existent NIS domain will create name resolution problems that will slow the system dramatically. Each name resolution request will have to timeout on NIS before moving to the next method.

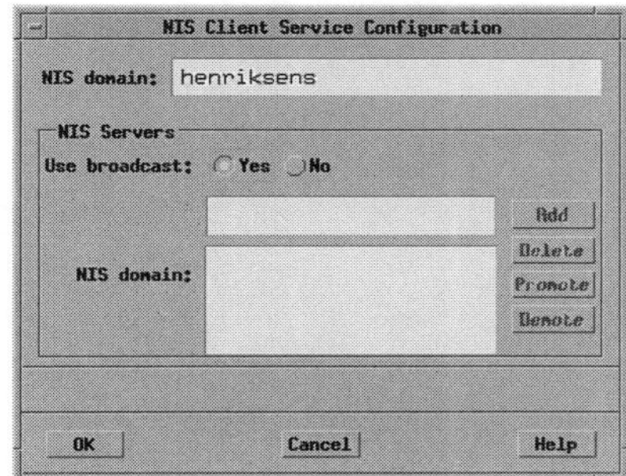

FIGURE 6.14 *The NIS Client Service Configuration window.*

Network Time Protocol Client

To have your system adjust the system time based on a time server, make it a Network Time Protocol (NTP) client. In the configuration, you may set it up to listen for time broadcasts, in which case that is all you need to set; or you can have it poll specific servers. When it polls specific servers, you can select to have it set the time at boot. Figure 6.15 illustrates setting up an NTP client.

Warning

Simply entering the Client Manager will cause it to create the /etc/inet/named.boot and /etc/inet/named.d/db.local files. As a result of these files being created, DNS will start on the next boot. This can create a problem with Netscape because it will attempt to use the DNS that is not configured to point at any DNS servers. DNS configuration without a server can also make booting very slow. In our test system, we observed 5- to 10-minute boot times as DNS attempted to communicate with a nonexistent DNS server. If this happens, remove the /etc/inet/named.boot. You may then kill the named process.

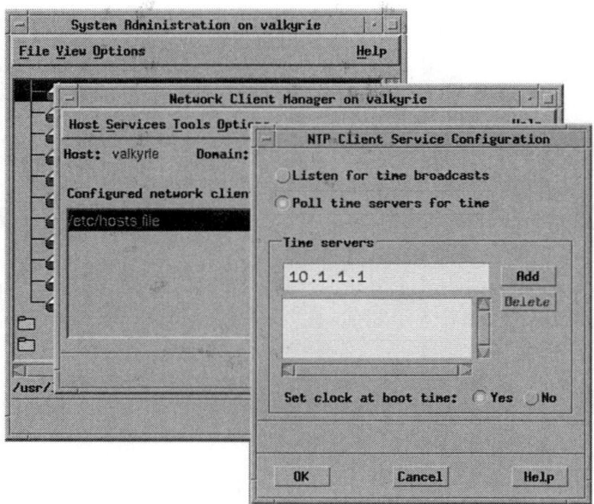

FIGURE 6.15 *The NTP Client Service configuration.*

Dynamic Host Configuration Protocol

Dynamic Host Configuration Protocol (DHCP) is a method of assigning IP addresses to client systems. The advantage of DHCP for the administrator is the ease of administering the DHCP clients. There is no requirement to keep a list of all the desktop PCs' IP addresses. The problem of duplicated IP addresses is reduced. Additional information can be sent to the DHCP clients along with the IP address, such as the default router, the netmask, DNS server addresses, and more.

A DHCP server, such as UnixWare 7, is assigned a pool of IP addresses that it uses to fill requests from DHCP clients. DHCP is an extension of the bootp protocol. As a client boots, it sends a discover packet for a DHCP server. The DHCP server sends back a DHCP offer. The client accepts the offer by returning an acceptance of the offered address. The server then sends an acknowledgment of the acceptance.

When new TCP/IP clients are installed on the network, they can be configured to be DHCP clients. No other IP configuration is necessary. In addition to the IP address, other information can be sent by the DHCP server, such as the broadcast address, DNS servers, and so on. For a Windows 95 client, in the Network applet select TCP/IP for the NIC and select Properties. In the IP Address tab, select Obtain an IP Address Automatically. When the system boots, it will broadcast for a DHCP server.

DHCP is particularly useful in a volatile office environment. When many laptop computers are brought in and out of the office on a regular basis, there may be more laptops than available addresses. DHCP will assign and unassign addresses as computers are added and removed from the LAN.

Tip

At the present time, UnixWare 7 can be configured as a DHCP server, but not as a DHCP client. A future release will allow UnixWare 7 to become a DHCP client.

Address Allocation Manager

To allocate addresses, an *Address Allocation Server (AAS)* is needed. The AAS may or may not be the same system as the DHCP server. To create an AAS, use the Address Allocation Manager in the Networking menu. Figure 6.16 illustrates creating an address range to an address pool. Individual addresses may also be specified.

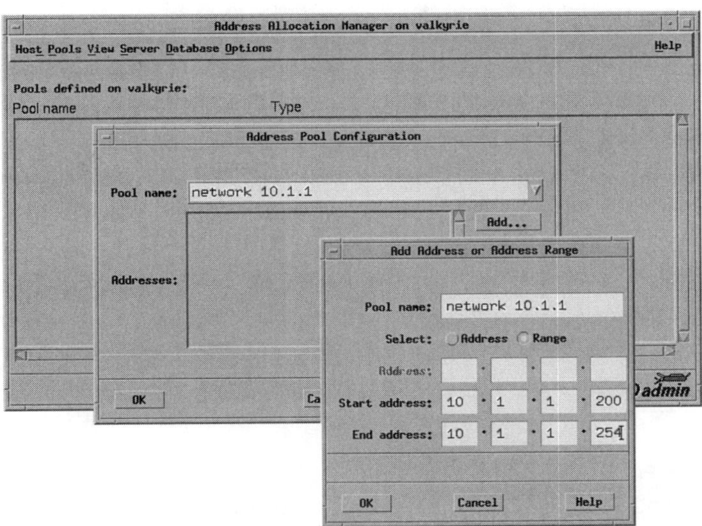

FIGURE 6.16 *Creating an address pool.*

Warning

The name of the address pool in Figure 6.16 contains a space. This will create an error in AAS, causing it to exit with an `error` *255 message, and the address pool will not be created. Do not include spaces in the pool name.*

DHCP Server Manager

The *DHCP Server Manager* uses the information configured in the AAS plus parameters configured through the DHCP Manager to supply information to the clients. Several subnets can be serviced by a single DHCP server.

Configuration Parameters

IP parameters may be configured that will be sent to the DHCP client along with the IP address. The parameters are assigned in a hierarchy. There are five classes in the hierarchy. Three are more commonly used: Global, Subnet, and Client. All parameters may be overridden by parameters at a lower (more specific) level. The classes are

- *Global*—Applies to all clients.
- *Subnet*—Applies to all clients in the subnet.
- *Client*—Applies to a specific client, specified by MAC address. This may be used to specify an IP address for a particular client.
- *Vendor*—Requires the client to specify a vendor in its broadcast for an address.
- *User*—Requires the client to specify a user in its broadcast for an address.

Tip

Why would you want to assign a specific IP address for a DHCP client? If the client is a server, it needs a static address for clients of its services to be able to locate it reliably. To avoid additional reconfiguration if parameters change, such as the DNS server's IP address, the statically assigned server will be sent the current parameters at reboot.

Global Parameters

When configuring the DHCP server, the Global class parameters can be configured by selecting View, Global Options; and then from the Entry menu, select Add. When options have been added, the Modify and Delete menu options become active.

Many of your client systems will be Microsoft Windows. These systems do not use all the DHCP options available. The parameters that can be used by Windows clients are

- *3*—Router IP address
- *6*—DNS servers
- *15*—DNS domain name

- *28*—Broadcast address
- *44*—WINS or NetBIOS nameserver, provides NetBIOS name to IP address resolution
- *46*—WINS or NetBIOS node type, instructs the Windows client on how to resolve NetBIOS names
- *47*—NetBIOS scope ID, a seldom-used option to subdivide a workgroup

Figure 6.17 illustrates the Global Options Configuration.

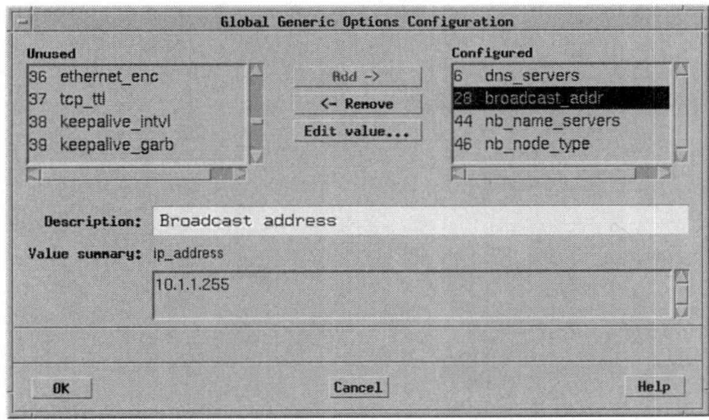

FIGURE 6.17 *Setting Global options.*

Subnet Configuration

Subnet configuration is where the addresses from the AAS are used. Figure 6.18 illustrates the Add Subnet Entry window. The subnet should have zeros in the host portion of the address. If a Class C netmask is used on a network of 10.1.1, for example, the subnet is 10.1.1.0. The address pool is assigned to the subnet (note the Pool `net1` entry in the figure). An optional description may be added to the subnet entry.

Three buttons allow setting options. Clicking the Lease button will start the window shown in Figure 6.19. Lease lifetimes can be controlled through these settings. You may select unlimited lease times. If the office is very stable and systems seldom move, unlimited lease times may be a good option. For an office with transient workers using portable computers, lease times should be set to short time periods, perhaps in hours. The maximum lease time may be set to unlimited or may be limited to a number of days, hours, and minutes. For both the default and maximum, the value must be greater than 0 and less than or equal to 49,674 days (about 136 years).

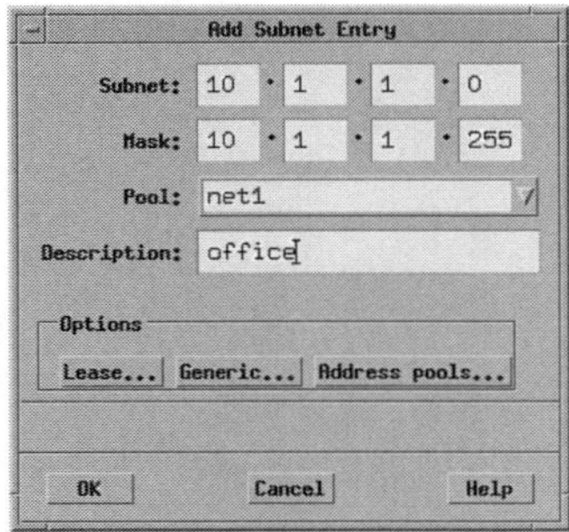

FIGURE 6.18 *Adding a new subnet to the DHCP server.*

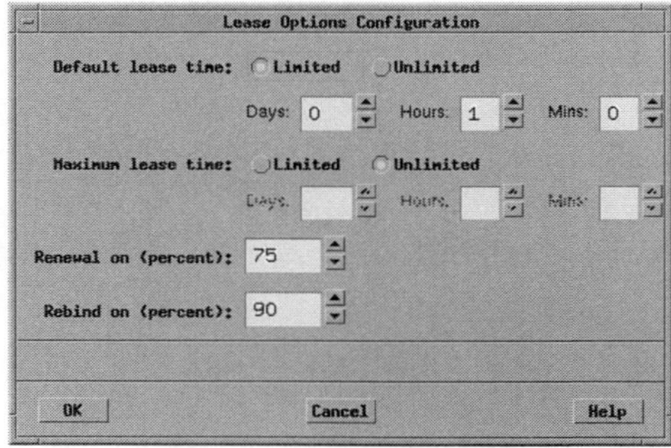

FIGURE 6.19 *The Lease Options Configuration window.*

The effect of lease times is to force the client system to ask for renewal of the lease after a specified period. While this is additional network traffic, it normally consists of two packets per renewal. The Renewal on (percent) option specifies at what percentage of lease life the client will attempt to renew the lease. If the renewal attempt fails, the DHCP server is offline or the address has been removed from the pool; the client will broadcast for a new IP address at the Rebind on (percent) time.

The Generic button brings up the same window as the Global options. This time the options will override the Global options and apply only to the subnet for which they are set.

The Address Pools button starts the AAS Manager. This provides quick access to the AAS information for modification or review.

Client Options

Figure 6.20 illustrates adding an individual client. The Hardware type is either Ethernet or 802 (Token-Ring). The Hardware address specifies the particular client. Clicking the Client button opens the Add Client Option Configuration window. Enter the desired IP address for the client. The Generic options are the same as for Global and Subnet; this time they apply only to the individual client.

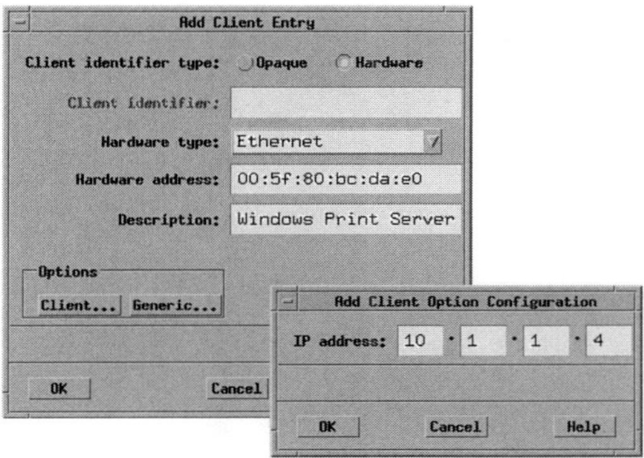

FIGURE 6.20 *Adding an individual client system IP reservation.*

Server Parameters

Under the Server menu option are the Server Parameters. Four items are in the window, as shown in Figure 6.21.

- *Initial Lease Reservation Time*—After an IP address has been offered, this is how long it is held out of the pool pending acceptance. The purpose is to avoid assigning the same address to multiple clients before the first one accepts the offer. The default is 10 minutes.
- *Pad Lease By (Percent)*—What percent of the Initial lease reservation time should be added to the time. The default is 1%.
- *Probe Addresses*—If set to Yes, the server will ping the address prior to assigning it to ensure that it has not been used. (Even with DHCP, someone can manually assign an address in the middle of your address pool without your knowledge.)
- *DHCP Option Overload*—Allows overflow of excessive option information into additional fields.

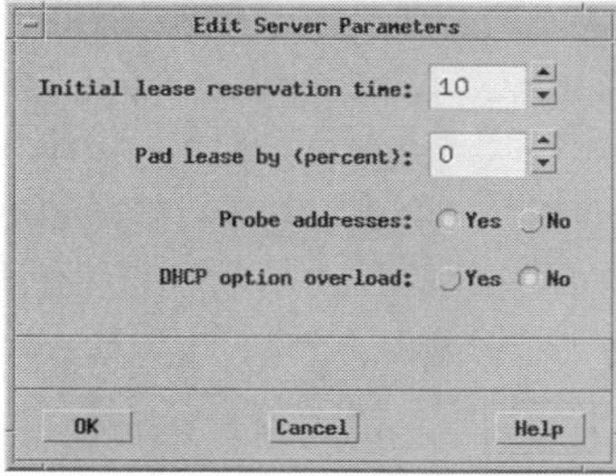

FIGURE 6.21 *The Server Parameters.*

/etc/inet/dhcpd.conf

The data from the previous configuration is stored in the `/etc/inet/dhcpd.conf` file. Shown here is the file configured during a session.

```
subnet 10.1.1.0 {
         comment Office
         mask 10.1.1.255
         pool net1
         lease_dflt 3600
         lease_max infinite
         t1 750
         t2 900
}
global {
         dns_servers 10.1.1.1
         broadcast_addr 10.1.1.255
         nb_name_servers 10.1.1.4
         nb_node_type m
}
```

Checking Assigned Addresses

After the server has been configured, clients can request IP addresses. The record of used addresses is kept in the AAS Manager, not the DHCP Manager. To view the usage of IP addresses, start the AAS Manager. Select View, Address Allocation. Select View, Expand All. The information shown in Figure 6.22 will be displayed.

To enable, disable, or release particular addresses within a pool, double-click the address or select Pools, Control. Figure 6.23 illustrates disabling a single address within a pool. If the address is currently assigned, the Disable action does not take place until the lease expires.

> **Tip**
>
> *You may want to disable an address if you have a large pool with an address within it that has been manually assigned to another device.*

Address Allocation Manager on valkyrie

Host Pools View Server Database Options Help

Address allocation by pool on valkyrie:

Address	Status	Service	Lease	Allocated	Released
net1		INET	21	1	
10.1.1.20	ALLOCATED	DHCP	000:01:00	18:12 09/04/98	
10.1.1.21	RELEASED	DHCP	000:01:00	17:35 09/04/98	18:12 09/04/98
10.1.1.22	UNUSED				
10.1.1.23	UNUSED				
10.1.1.24	UNUSED				
10.1.1.25	UNUSED				
10.1.1.26	UNUSED				
10.1.1.27	UNUSED				
10.1.1.28	UNUSED				

SCOadmin

FIGURE 6.22 *The Address Allocation Manager showing leases.*

You may also select an address and click Release. Release will release the address immediately. Address 21 in Figure 6.22 shows the status as RELEASED.

Warning

Releasing an address does not cause the client to disable its TCP stack. The Release option should be used when a system has been removed but the address is still listed as allocated by AAS. When released, it is available for a client.

If you release a currently active address, you could have the address assigned to a client while still being used by the original client.

The time under the Allocated heading is not the time of original allocation by the client, but is the time it was originally allocated or renewed.

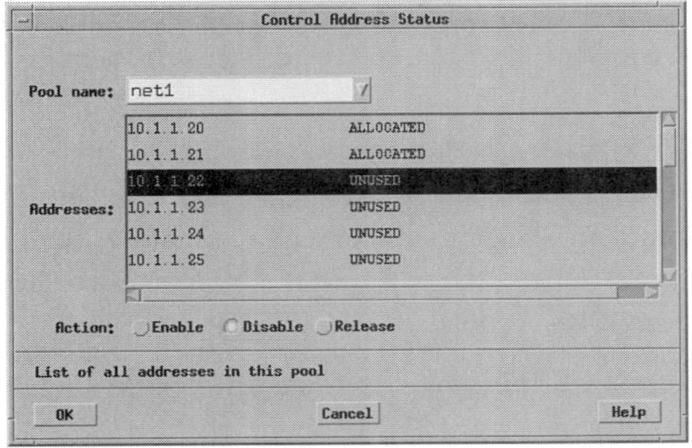

FIGURE 6.23 *The Control window for enabling, disabling, and releasing addresses.*

When an address is disabled through the Control window, a red X appears to the left of the word UNUSED. Refer to address 22 in Figure 6.22.

DHCP Over Subnets

DHCP clients use broadcasts to find a server. Broadcasts are not normally propagated by routers to reduce network traffic. For a DHCP client to find a DHCP server, you may implement a boot protocol (bootp) gateway. UnixWare 7 includes a bootp gateway. To implement the bootp gateway, include the following line in the /etc/inet/inetd.conf file:

```
bootps dgram/i upd wait root /usr/sbin/in.bootpgw in.bootpgw server_name
```

Replace *server_name* with the name or IP address of the DHCP server. You will need to restart inetd to reread the inetd.conf file:

```
#sacadm -k -p inetd
#sacadm -s -p inetd
```

The `bootpgw` will be started by inetd whenever a DHCP discover packet arrives. The `bootpgw` will remain active for 15 minutes. If no further requests arrive, it will exit.

DHCP and bootp

If you need to run both DHCP and bootp on UnixWare 7, a conflict will occur because they both use the same port for Internet communication. This can be resolved by a change to the /etc/inet/inetd.conf file. The following lines appear in inetd.conf; uncomment the two lines that begin with `#bootps` by removing the # at the beginning of the lines.

```
# in.bootpd and in.dhcpd both use the same port; to use both services
# the following entries can be used. They configure in.dhcpd to forward
# bootp packets to in.bootpd which listens on a different port.
#
#bootps dgram/i udp wait root /usr/sbin/in.tcpd in.dhcpd -b boot ps-alt
#bootps dgram/i udp wait root /usr/sbin/in.dhcpd in.dhcpd -b boot ps-alt
```

Simple Network Management Protocol

UnixWare 7 provides an SNMP agent for networking management. The SNMP agent will report information to an SNMP management application, such as HP OpenView. The SNMP agent is used to configure the information that the agent will report and to whom it will report.

To start the SNMP agent from SCOadmin, select Networking, SNMP Agent. Figure 6.24 illustrates the initial window for SNMP agent.

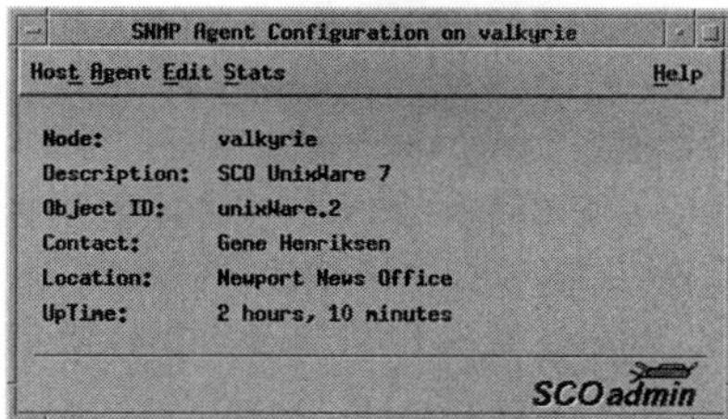

FIGURE 6.24 *The SNMP agent.*

Under the Agent menu, the options are to halt or start the agent. Under the Edit menu, several options to configure the agent are available:

- System
- Community
- Traps
- Peers

Under the Stats menu are several data-reporting windows that are all based on the `snmpstat` command. The data shown in these windows may be of interest for reasons other than SNMP. Included in the information are remote systems and their MAC addresses, currently active TCP and UDP sessions, routing information, and SNMP statistics.

The first option under the Edit menu is the System Information. This includes information on the local system, as shown in Figure 6.25. The SMUX Reserved Sub-Trees is for SMTP information that will be maintained by other agents.

The second option is the SNMP community. A *community* is used to determine which SNMP management systems have access rights to the local system. Figure 6.26 illustrates creating a community named localoffice with the management computer at `10.1.1.1` over IP protocol with Write privileges on the local system. In the background, the Community Names Editor lists the public community, which allows other community members read access. Public access could be restricted by modifying the privilege to None.

Traps are unusual events that the SNMP agent reports to management systems. The Trap Names Editor, shown in Figure 6.27, allows maintaining the list of systems to which traps will be sent.

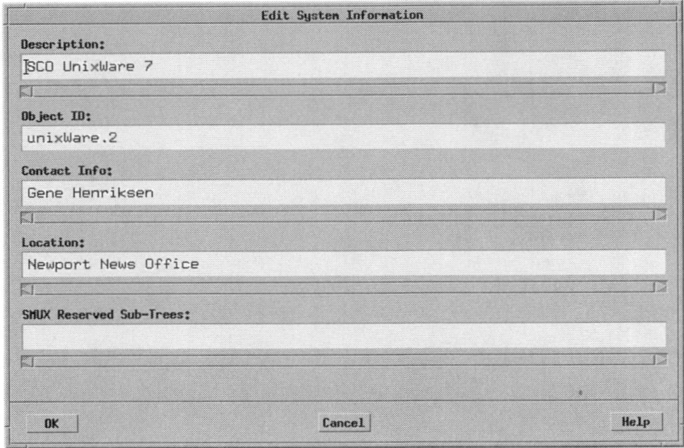

FIGURE 6.25 *The Edit System Information window.*

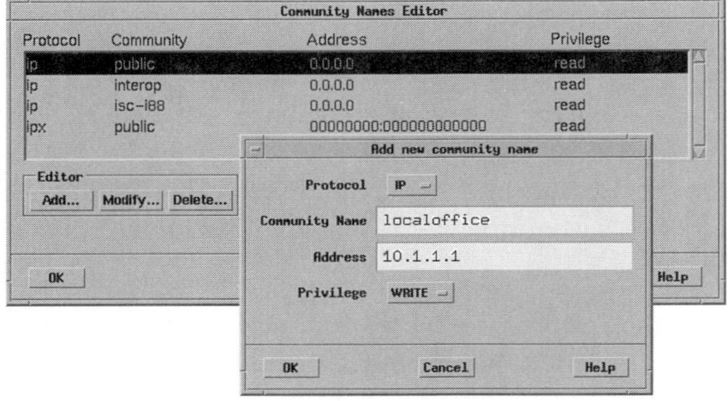

FIGURE 6.26 *Creating a new community.*

The SNMP agent is responsible for reporting information when queried by the SNMP management system. The SNMP agent may not be able to directly access the information. An example is routing information. The gated daemon maintains the routing information. When gated starts, it registers with the SNMP agent. By registering, gated becomes a SMUX (SNMP Multiplexing Protocol) peer. When the SNMP agent requires information on routing, it notifies gated, which in turn provides the information. In Figure 6.28, gated is listed with an object ID. This object is a predefined Management Information Base (MIB). The information gated reports will conform to the object ID. Using this method, organizations can define their own MIBs and create their own reporting functions.

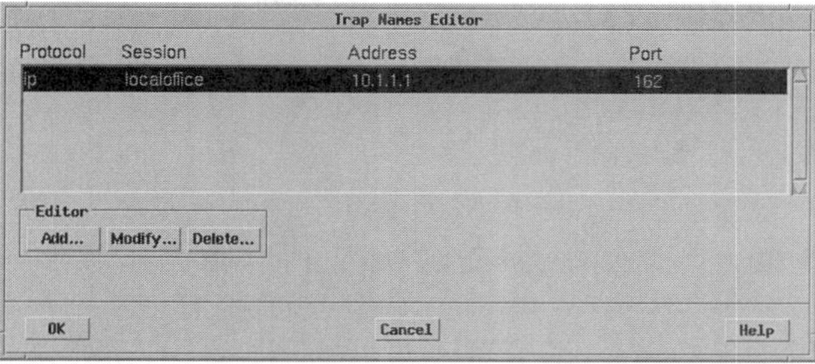

FIGURE 6.27 *The SNMP Trap Names Editor.*

FIGURE 6.28 *The Peer Names Editor.*

Lightweight Directory Access Protocol

Lightweight Directory Access Protocol (LDAP) is a distributed directory system. Just as DNS is a means of distributing the responsibility for maintaining the host name to IP address resolution that allows the Internet to function, LDAP provides a method of distributed responsibility for maintaining a directory of people and resources. UnixWare 7 has the tools to create an LDAP database. The LDAP Manager, in the Networking menu, allows adding LDAP daemons.

Domain Name System

Before creating a DNS configuration, you should have a good understanding of DNS and the information required to make it work.

To create the DNS configuration on UnixWare 7, you can manually create the files in the /etc/inet directory and the /etc/inet/named.d directory. The DNS Manager provides an easy method of creating the configuration files.

Tip

You do not need to use the DNS Manager to make your system a DNS client. Instead, use the Client Manager to create a DNS client.

Creating a Zone

To start, select SCOadmin, Networking, DNS Manager. When the DNS window appears, select Zones, Add to display the Add Zone window shown in the upper-left corner of Figure 6.29. If the server you are creating is a Caching Only server, this is the only step required. Enter the Zone name. Enter the networks for which this zone is responsible. You must enter a minimum of one network. Click the Name servers button and enter the name server IP addresses. For Secondary and Stub servers, the configuration is now complete. Click the Start of Authority button to get to the window in the lower-right corner of Figure 6.29.

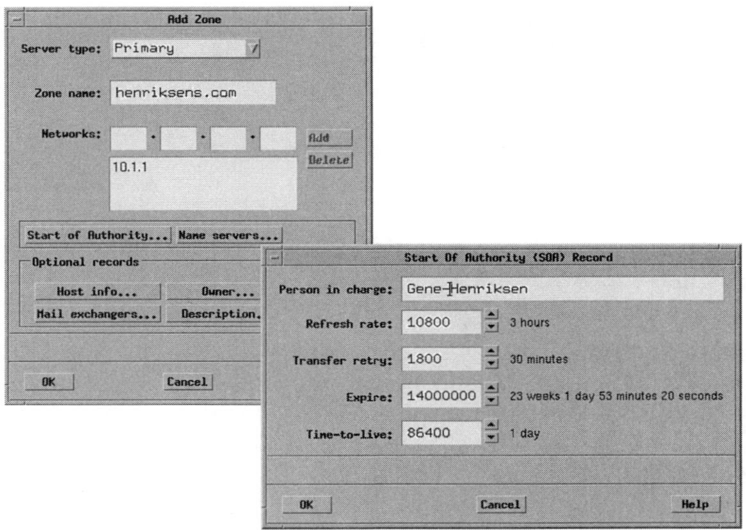

FIGURE 6.29 *Adding a DNS zone.*

The Start of Authority requires a name for the person in charge. You may not use space-separated fields. Click the OK button on Start of Authority and then on Add Zone. Exiting the DNS Manager will now create the records for the DNS zone. The files created are in the /etc/inet directory:

```
db.1.1.10
db.henriksens.com
db.local
```

The files created are based on the domain name and the network.

Adding Hosts to the Zone

To create entries for the hosts in the zone, from the DNS Manager select View, Records. You may import records from /etc/hosts or enter them manually. Figure 6.30 illustrates adding a host manually with aliases.

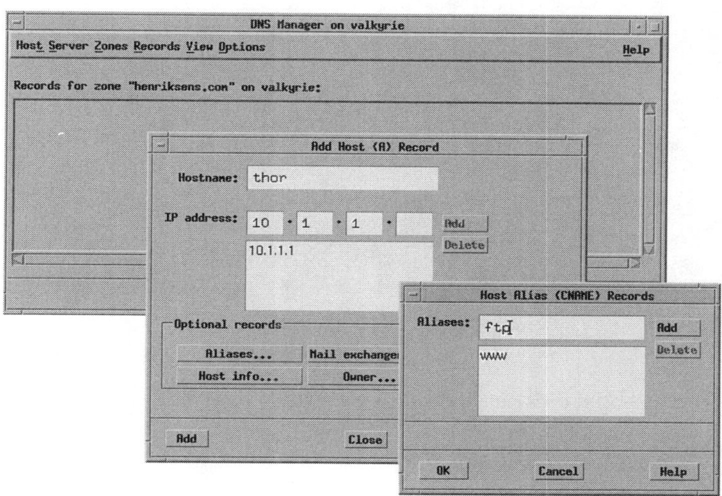

FIGURE 6.30 *Adding a DNS host record.*

Testing the Configuration

After the host name records have been entered, the DNS configuration can be tested. In the Options menu in the DNS Manager is the Test Configuration option. Enter a host name or an IP address and click the Query button. If you have configured the system correctly, you will get a result as shown in Figure 6.31. If it fails, you will get a `Host not found` message.

Configuring Server Options

The DNS Manager Server menu has the following configuration options:

- *Forwarders*—Designates the servers to forward requests to. Selecting the Yes option will stop the DNS server from attempting to contact root servers. This is suitable for firewalls.
- *Preferred*—Sets the order for returning host names where host names correspond to multiple IP addresses.

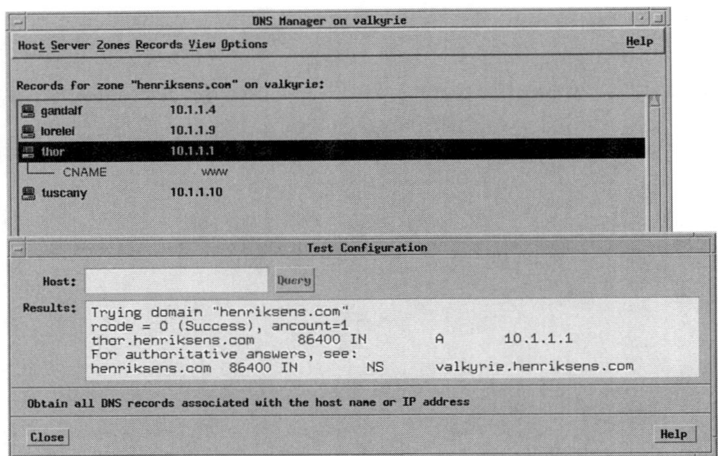

FIGURE 6.31 *Testing the DNS configuration.*

- *Bad Servers*—Specifies servers that should not be used.
- *Requesters*—Specifies hosts or networks allowed to request zone transfers.
- *Limits*—Configures limits on simultaneous zone transfers and maximum virtual memory that may be used by a nameserver.
- *Options*—Allows configuring advanced server options: recursion, fetch glue, and query log.

OpenServer 5 Tip

In the OpenServer 5 /etc/resolv.conf file, the `hostresorder` *parameter allowed setting the order in which host names were resolved by service (hosts file, DNS, NIS, and so on). This is now accomplished through the Client Manager, Services, Name Resolution Order.*

CHAPTER 7

WAN Network Configuration

- WAN interfaces
  Learn how different physical media can be used for wide area networking.
- Serial communications configuration
  Learn how to configure the UUCP files to support PPP.
- Point-to-Point Protocol
  Learn how to configure PPP on UnixWare 7. See how PPP uses bundles and links to create PPP communications.

WAN Interfaces

LANs can be interconnected over long distances to create *wide area networks (WANs)*. WAN connections may be slower than LAN connections. High-speed WAN connections can be very expensive.

WAN connections can run over a variety of physical media. Most connections will involve connecting through a telephone company using dial-up, leased lines, ISDN, ATM, and X.25. It is possible to use satellites to send signals from one location to another. Satellite communications is a good solution in some parts of the world with undeveloped telephone infrastructures.

Your needs and budget, as well as the services available in your area, will determine the logical choices for your organization.

The most basic WAN connection involves a modem using the public telephone system. With a modem on each end, speeds of up to 33,600 baud can be reached.

With special connections at one end, such as those used by an ISP, 56K modems can reach a maximum of 53K. In the United States, the Federal Communications Commission limits the maximum to 53K. The operating costs for a modem connection is dependent on the distance and length of call. While not suitable for heavy traffic, a dial-up connection may be adequate for mobile workers or email transfer. Some applications, such as character-based UNIX applications, may also run with adequate performance over these connections. Telephone line transmission quality may reduce connection speeds to 24K or less.

Integrated Services Digital Network (ISDN), available from the local telephone company, provides a high-speed, point-to-point connection. ISDN consists of one or more lines running speeds of 64KB/sec. These lines may be combined to provide speeds in multiples of 64KB/sec. Each 64KB/sec channel is charged separately for the connection time. In addition to the usage charges, a fixed monthly rate is charged, like it is with any telephone line. The setup time for an ISDN connection is less than a second, whereas dial-up modems may take 30 seconds to negotiate a connection.

Author's Note

For example, as of September 1998, Bell Atlantic offers ISDN service from a monthly rate of approximately $40 to $50, depending on location. Charges for connection time range from a high of 2 cents per minute (per 64KB/sec channel) down to high-volume discount pricing of 0.4 cent per minute with a minimum of 140 hours.

UnixWare 7 can use ISDN connections in three different ways:

- As an external ISDN router that is connected to the LAN
- As an external ISDN adapter, or *ISDN TA*, that connects to a serial port
- As an internal ISDN adapter board (PCI or ISA, for example)

Data connections over ISDN lines are made using a WAN protocol. Point-to-Point Protocol (PPP) is the most commonly used WAN protocol over ISDN.

Leased lines can include very high-speed lines for internetworking. The Internet uses high-speed leased lines to interconnect the backbone systems that carry the majority of traffic. Leased lines range from 64KB/sec to 274MB/sec. Leased lines may be used with PPP or *Serial Line Interface Protocol (SLIP)*. Leased lines are point-to-point lines with full-time connection.

Other technologies, such as *Digital Subscriber Line (DSL)*, frame relay, and cable modems, can be used by UnixWare 7 if they are connected to the LAN.

UnixWare 7 does not directly support adapters for these technologies. These LAN connections appear to UnixWare 7 as any other routed network.

Table 7.1 shows a comparison of the various network transfer speeds.

TABLE 7.1 COMPARISON OF NETWORK TRANSFER SPEEDS

Type of Connection	Transfer Rate in Bits per Second	Time to Transfer a 10MB file
Modem–9600 baud	9,600	2.42 hours
Modem–28,200 baud	28,800	48.54 minutes
Frame Relay	56,000	24.96 minutes
ISDN	64,000	21.85 minutes
Leased Line–T1	1,500,000	55.92 seconds
Leased Line–T2	6,300,000	13.31 seconds
Leased Line–T3	45,000,000	1.86 seconds
Leased Line–T4	274,000,000	.30 seconds
Ethernet–10 MB/sec	10,475,760	8.0 seconds
Ethernet–100 MB/sec	104,757,600	0.8 seconds

The authors would like to credit Tony Nelson of Open Learning Center for the information contained in this table.

Serial Communication Configuration

PPP and SLIP both use the connection server and ttymon as does UUCP. Serial communications for UUCP is configured with text files located in /etc/uucp. The /usr/lib/uucp directory contains symbolic links to the files in /etc/uucp for compatibility with OpenServer 5. /usr/lib/uucp also contains other files used in UUCP. The logs and transfers are kept in /var/spool/uucp. For compatibility with OpenServer 5, /usr/spool is a link to /var/spool.

The main files used in configuring UUCP and PPP/SLIP are

- *Devices*—the ports used for dialing other systems
- *Systems*—other systems' names and phone numbers
- *Permissions*—controls placed on remote systems accessing the local system (UUCP only)

Creating a dial-out UUCP system requires configuring the Devices and Systems files. To control access by remote systems connecting to a local system, the Permissions file is used to limit access to directories and commands. When a UUCP connection can be made to a remote system, a PPP or SLIP configuration can be made with the assurance that the underlying communications will work.

Creating a Dial-Out UUCP Configuration

To create a dial-out configuration, you need to modify two files:

/etc/uucp/Systems

/etc/uucp/Devices

The Systems file can be configured manually or through the Dial-Out Manager. The Devices file can be edited manually or through the Modem Manager.

Configuring the Devices

To use a modem you must configure both the serial port and the modem. These can both be configured through the Network Configuration Manager or from the Hardware menu where both the Serial and Modem Managers appear. Before a modem can be configured, though, you must configure the serial port. From the Network Configuration Manager, select Hardware, Add New WAN Device, Serial Port. Figure 7.1 illustrates the Network Configuration Manager menu path.

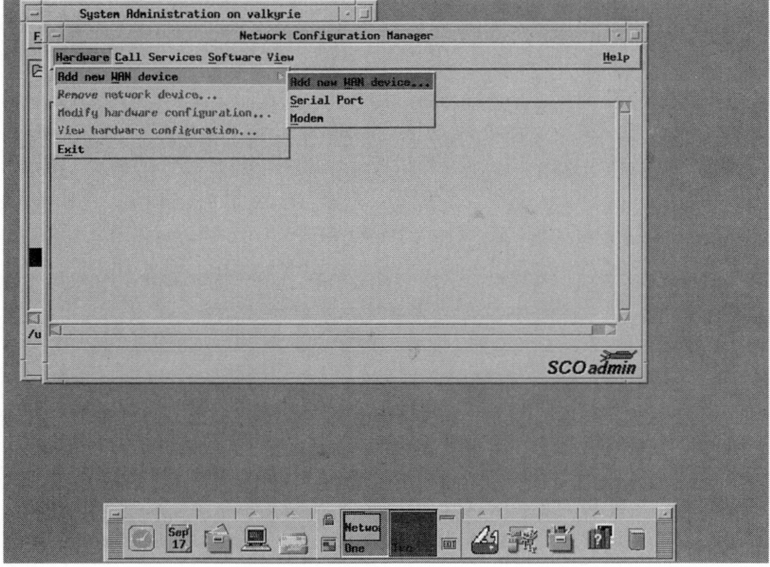

FIGURE 7.1 *Adding a serial port through the Network Configuration Manager.*

When in the Serial Manager, the system will detect the standard COM ports and allow you to configure them as Software Flow Control, Hardware Flow Control, Terminal, or Modem Port. Figure 7.2 illustrates the port modification window. On outgoing ports, the Port Settings button is grayed out.

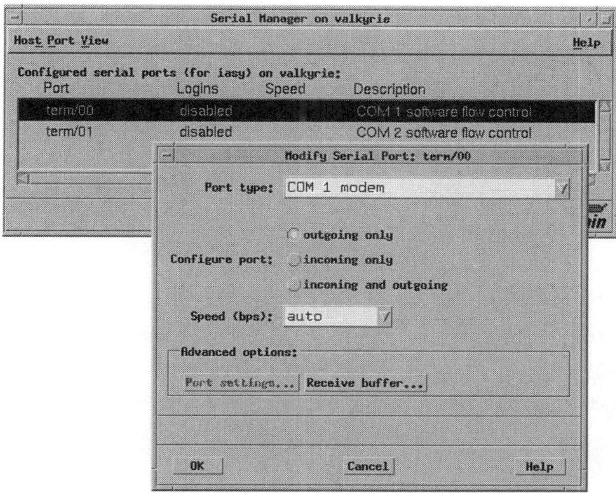

FIGURE 7.2 *Modifying a serial port for outgoing only.*

Configuring the Modems

After the serial ports are configured, the modems may be configured. The Modem Manager is available from the Hardware menu in SCOadmin or from choosing Network Configuration Manager, Hardware, Add New WAN Device, Modem. Figure 7.3 illustrates adding a modem. From the Modem Add option in the Modem Manager, you can choose Automatic Detection or Manual Configuration.

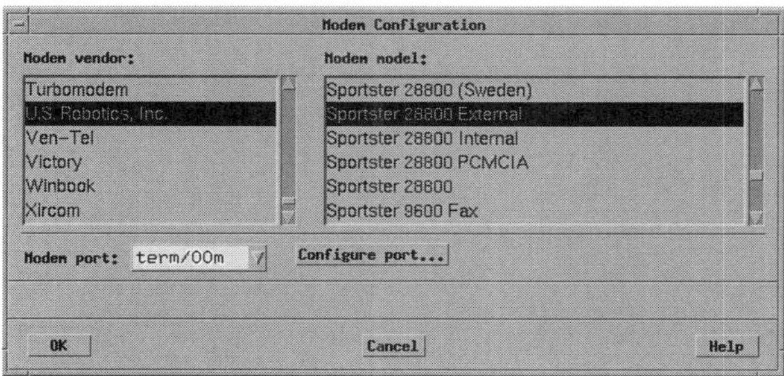

FIGURE 7.3 *Configuring a modem.*

Author's Note

Automatic Detection failed for my U.S. Robotics Sportster 56K modem. Only the modems listed in the /etc/uucp/Detect file are auto-detected. This list should grow with each release of UnixWare 7.

To manually configure the modem, select the modem vendor from the left column and the model from the right column. Select the port for the modem. Click OK. Figure 7.4 illustrates the Modem Manager after a modem is configured. As a result of the modem configuration, the /etc/uucp/Devices file had the following two lines added:

```
Direct term/00m,M - 57600 direct
ACU term/00m,M - Any Sportster_28800_External
```

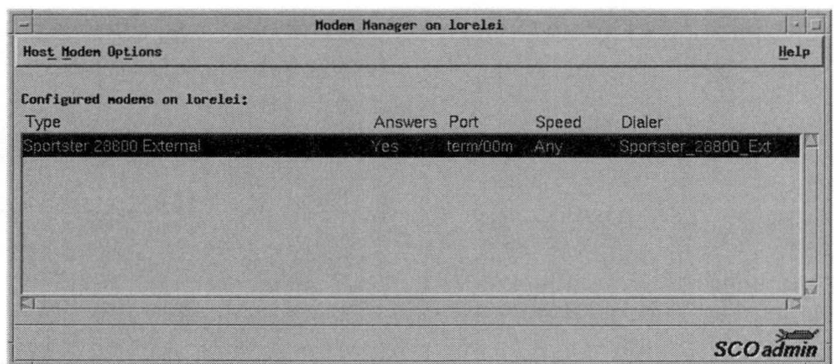

FIGURE 7.4 *The Modem Manager after configuration of a modem.*

OpenServer 5 Tip

There is no `-x` *option to set the debug level on* `cu`. *The* `-d` *option sets the debug.*

You may now verify the operation of the port by using the `cu` command to connect to the modem:

```
# cu -l term/00m
Connected
at
OK
ati4
U.S. Robotics 56K FAX EXT Settings...

   B0   E1   F1   M1   Q0   V1   X4   Y0
   BAUD=57600   PARITY=N   WORDLEN=8
   DIAL=TONE     ON HOOK    CID=0

   &A3   &B1   &C1   &D2   &G0   &H1   &I0   &K1
   &M4   &N0   &P0   &R2   &S0   &T5   &U0   &Y1

   S00=000  S01=000  S02=043  S03=013  S04=010  S05=008  S06=002
   S07=060  S08=002  S09=006  S10=014  S11=070  S12=050  S13=000
   S15=000  S16=000  S18=000  S19=000  S21=010  S22=017  S23=019
   S25=005  S27=000  S28=008  S29=020  S30=000  S31=128  S32=002
   S33=000  S34=000  S35=000  S36=014  S38=000  S39=000  S40=001
```

```
    S41=000   S42=000

    LAST DIALED #:

OK
```

To exit the cu session, press the tilde (~) followed by a dot (.). You should see the local system node name displayed after the tilde; if not, repeat the process.

Configuring Remote Systems

After the modem is configured and tested, you can configure the remote systems you will contact. You can edit the /etc/uucp/Systems file directly or use the Dialup Systems Manager. Figure 7.5 illustrates adding a new system to the Dialup System Manager.

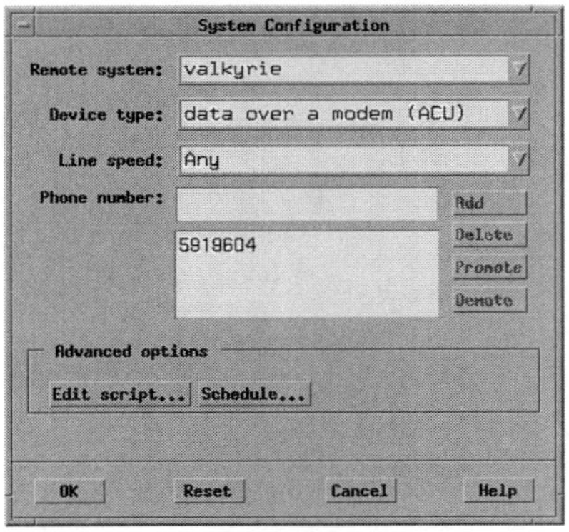

FIGURE 7.5 *Configuring a new system for the Systems file.*

The Edit script button allows configuring the chat script for the login process. The Schedule button allows setting schedules for contacting the remote system. When the OK button is clicked, the /etc/uucp/Systems file is updated. With the information shown in Figure 7.5, the following entry was placed at the end of the Systems file:

```
valkyrie Any ACU Any 5919604
```

After the system has been added to the Dialup Systems Manager, the display will appear as shown in Figure 7.6. To see the information in the second line under each system name, select Expand All from the Options menu. The Devices Available window is displayed by highlighting the desired system and selecting System, Show Device.

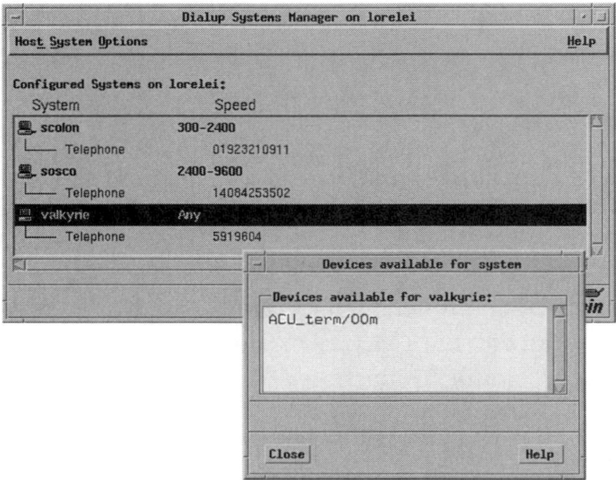

FIGURE 7.6 *The Dialup Systems Manager showing the telephone numbers.*

The Options menu offers a Test Connection with sub-options of `cu` and `uutry`. If you do not have jobs in the uucp queue for the remote system, `uutry` will not work. The `cu` option will attempt to contact the remote system. Figure 7.7 shows part of the debug script for contacting a system. Debug is turned on with the Options button.

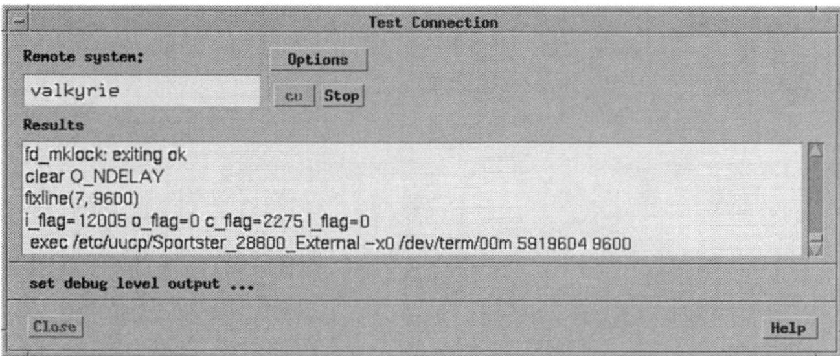

FIGURE 7.7 *Testing a connection.*

The same test performed in the Test Connection can be run from the command line with

```
cu -x valkyrie
```

The `x` option instructs `cu` to use the chat scripts that have been configured for the remote system. This will test the chat script correctness.

Add the `-d` option for debug mode:

```
cu -d valkyrie
```

Creating a Dial-In UUCP Configuration

To create a dial-in connection, use the Serial Manager to set up the port. On the dial-in port, select Incoming Only in the port configuration. Set the speed for a value greater than the maximum speed of the modem. This will prevent the data from the modem from overrunning the serial port capability.

Use the Modem Manager to set up the modem for the port. If the port is an incoming port, the Modem Manager will display Yes under the Answers column.

Use the Dialin Services Manager to assign different dial-in services to different ports. The Dialin Services Manager is in the Networking menu. In Figure 7.8 the acu type has two entries. The first entry is being changed in the Service Configuration window to use COM1, term/00m, for a login service /usr/bin/shserv. The COM2 port, term/01m, is configured as a PPP port.

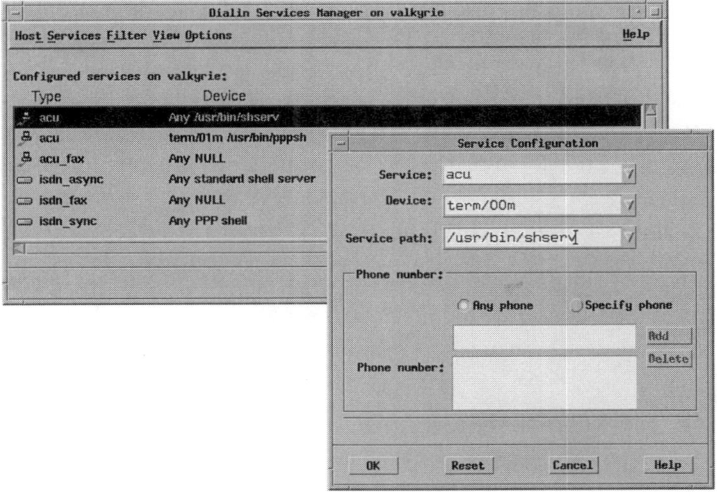

FIGURE 7.8 *Testing a connection.*

Tip

term/00m is actually /dev/term/00m. The m designation is for modem control. See Chapter 10, "Configuration of Serial Ports and Terminal Devices," for more information on serial ports.

After the appropriate service is configured, you should be able to connect to the dial-out port with the `cu` command and dial into the newly configured dial-in port.

Warning

Do not configure ports as bidirectional. SCO has reported a problem in Technical Article TA109580 with attempting to use a port for dial-in and dial-out. The port will not work in either direction. This should be fixed in a future release. See the SCO Web pages, `www.sco.com/ta`*, and use the search for TA number to find this TA.*

To create an entry for an unsupported modem, see SCO's Web site. Technical Article TA109390 explains how to create your own modem entries.

Point-to-Point Protocol (PPP)

PPP provides TCP/IP connections over telephone lines and is the primary method most people use to connect to the Internet in the United States. PPP connections can be made both outbound and inbound. The PPP Manager will be used to configure PPP connections. The PPP Internet Connection Manager can also be used for outgoing links.

UnixWare 7 PPP uses the concept of devices assigned to *link groups*. Link groups may consist of one or more devices of the same type. You cannot mix modems, serial lines, and ISDN adapters in the same link group. Link groups use the *Link Control Protocol* to configure the connections between the two ends of the PPP link. Because UnixWare 7 PPP must use a device from a link group, even if only a single modem is available for PPP, it must be in a link group.

UnixWare 7 defines a configured connection as a *bundle*. The bundle includes all of the information about the connection, the protocol, and the links that may be used. There are three types of bundles:

- Incoming
- Outgoing
- Bidirectional

Because of the differences in configuration between incoming and outgoing, bidirectional is seldom used.

Bundles also specify the compression to be used. The *Compression Control Protocol (CCP)* is recommended only if the medium does not provide compression, such as that provided by many modems.

Outbound PPP Configuration

To configure PPP Outgoing links, select SCOadmin, Networking, Network Configuration Manager, View, WAN, Software, Configure PPP Outgoing Link. The first window to appear in adding a PPP connection is shown in Figure 7.9. This is the Internet Connection Manager.

- The provider name is used to identify the link. It may be your ISP name or the name of a remote system that provides you a PPP connection. It is the name used to bring up the connection using pppattach.
- The remote system name is used in the /etc/uucp/Systems to identify the system to be contacted.
- Telephone numbers are added to the /etc/uucp/Systems entry. Multiple telephone numbers may be listed and are used in the order listed.
- The How to Connect area enables you to choose between On Demand or Use pppattach. If you select On Demand, any attempt to contact the remote system or other systems routed through it, such as pinging it, will bring up the connection. Use pppattach if you want the connection brought up manually.

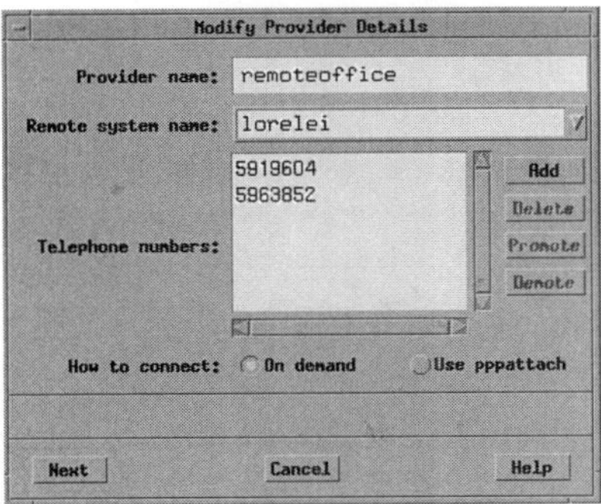

FIGURE 7.9 *Adding details for the remote provider.*

Author's Note

The titles of the windows will use either Add or Modify depending on whether this is the first time you are creating the new connection or modifying it. Any of these windows may be re-entered by selecting Provider, Modify, and selecting the desired topic.

PPP Authentication

PPP authentication can use CHAP, PAP, or a UNIX login. Select the appropriate buttons at the top of the window shown in Figure 7.10 and enter the password for the ones selected. If dialing into an ISP or other service provider, have it provide the details of authentication.

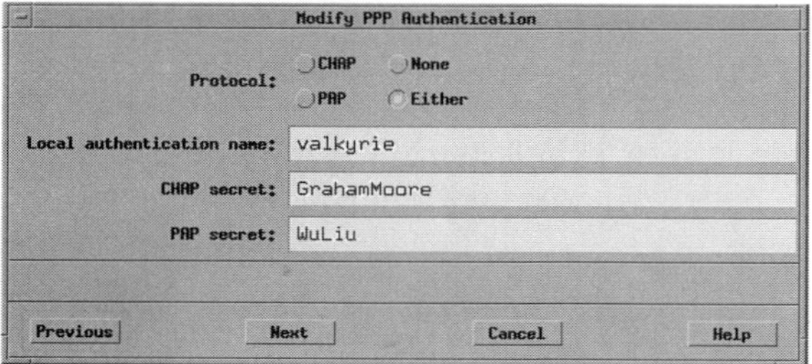

FIGURE 7.10 *Selecting PPP authentication.*

CHAP and PAP

CHAP (Challenge-Handshake Authentication Protocol) and PAP (Password Authentication Protocol) both have a place in securing PPP connections. PAP is the older of the two and has the disadvantage of sending a name and clear text password for authentication. Sending the password as clear text can lead to a security compromise. CHAP sends a name and encrypted password. While CHAP would appear to be more secure, names and passwords are stored on both systems in clear text form. Having the clear text stored on both systems offers an opportunity for breach of security.

PAP passwords can be made more secure than CHAP through the use of token cards, such as Enigma's SafeWord or Security Dynamics' SecurID. These devices send one-time passwords that are worthless if intercepted.

To reduce security problems, use different passwords for dial-in and dial-out. Use different passwords for each system to be authenticated. If using both PAP and CHAP, do not use the same password for both.

The Login Script

Both UUCP and PPP use the same login scripts. The login script's function is to look for the login prompt, reply with an account name, look for the password prompt, and send the password. A default login script is supplied with a prompt for the account and password.

In the example shown in Figure 7.11, the login script sends a carriage return to jog the remote system into sending a login. The system then expects to see the string `in:`, which is the end of the login prompt. The entire login prompt is not looked for in case the system sends a lowercase first letter and the system dialing in expects an uppercase, or vice versa. The dialing system then sends the account name, in this example `ranjit`, and waits for the end of the password prompt, `sword:`. When the dialing system receives the password prompt, it sends the password. In this case the password is `deshpande`.

To see the prompts from the remote system, use `cu` to connect to the remote PPP system and view the prompts.

After the login has occurred, the PPP implementation (pppd on UNIX) on the remote system communicates with PPP on the dialing system to set up the network link.

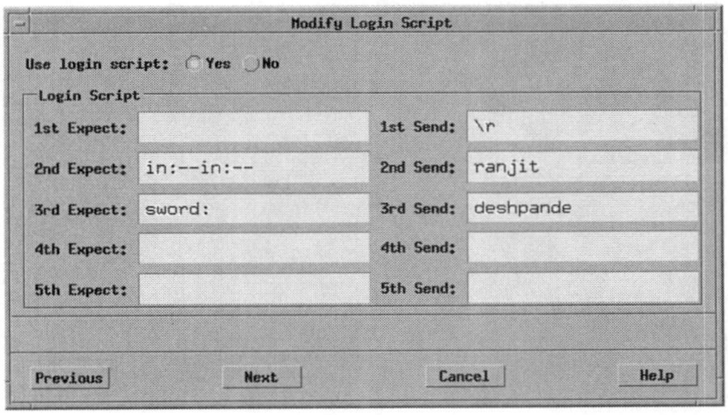

FIGURE 7.11 *Creating the login script.*

The Network Protocol

UnixWare 7 currently supports only TCP/IP over PPP. The network protocol parameters are set up for the connection as shown in Figure 7.12. Since PPP connections may not be dedicated links, the IP addresses may be reused by multiple connections. One system or the other must assign a pair of addresses that will be on the same network. These can be assigned by DHCP.

- *Local address assigned by*—Specifies whether the local or remote system sets the IP address for the local system during a PPP link.
- *Local IP address/host name*—The IP address or host name to be used on the local side of the link.
- *Remote address assigned by*—Specifies whether the local or remote system sets the IP address for the remote side of the PPP link.
- *Remote IP address/host name*—Specifies the IP address or host name to be used on the remote side of the link.
- *Use as default route*—Decide here if you want this PPP connection to be used as the default route. See Chapter 8, "Browsers and Intranets," for an explanation of routing.

- *Local host acts as gateway*—Specifies whether this system will forward packets between this link and other network interfaces. See Chapter 8 for more information on routing.
- *Act as proxy for ARP*—If a system using the same network portion of the IP address as the local subnet is connected via PPP, it cannot see or be seen by ARP on the local subnet. It has no ARP address if connecting via modem. In this case, the PPP can respond to ARP requests for the remote system, thus allowing it to become a member of the subnet.

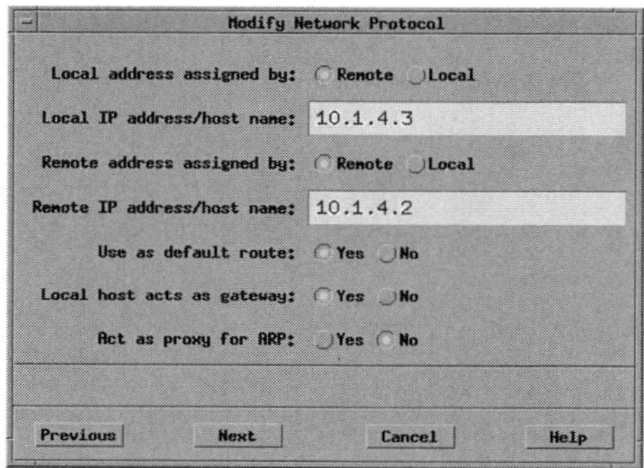

FIGURE 7.12 *Setting the network protocol configuration.*

Adding Name Servers

To use name servers, enter the local domain name, the domain search order, and the name servers in the order to be searched. After domains and name servers have been added, you can reorder them with the Promote and Demote buttons (see Figure 7.13).

Selecting Devices for PPP

The devices to be used can be either modems or ISDN lines. Although ISDN Async is an option, it is not currently supported.

Flow control may be Hardware, Software, or None, as shown in Figure 7.14. Hardware flow control is recommended.

Multilink provides the ability to connect several modems or lines into a single logical link. To use this, both ends of the connection must support multilink. To disable multilink, enter `1`. Multilink is often used to connect multiple ISDN channels to create a high-speed interface. Packets of data are split up and sent in parallel sets across the multiple links. When the packets arrive at the remote end, they are reassembled. Failure of a single fragment to arrive results in retransmission of the packet, not the fragment. For dial-up connections, multilink is not recommended unless line quality is very high. Noise on the phone lines could result in one modem reconfiguring for a lower speed, causing fragment-reassembly problems.

The modems configured with Modem Manager will be available for selection.

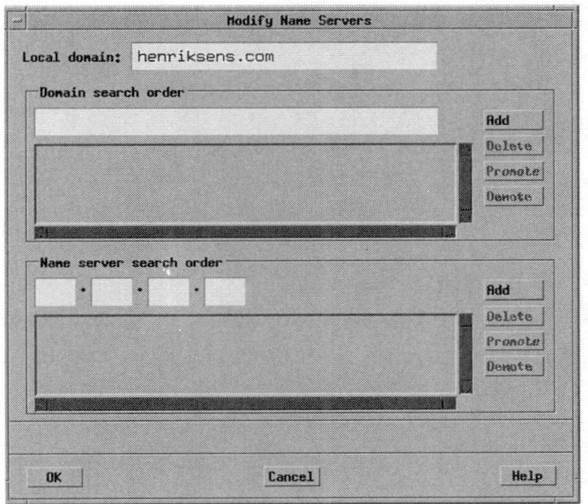

FIGURE 7.13 *Selecting the name servers.*

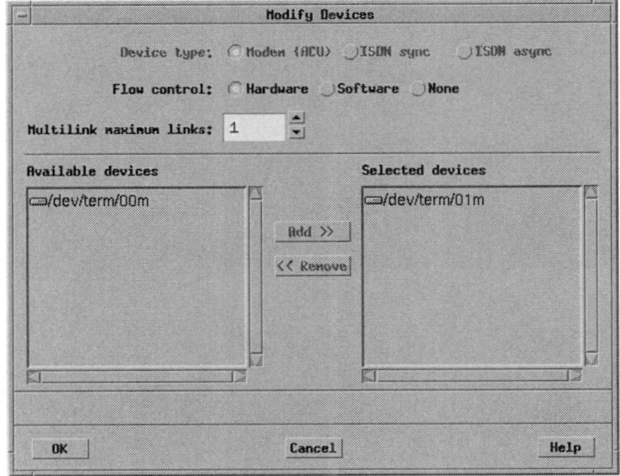

FIGURE 7.14 *Selecting the devices.*

After the configuration is complete, the PPP Internet Connection Manager will list the outgoing configuration you created. Figure 7.15 illustrates the window upon completion.

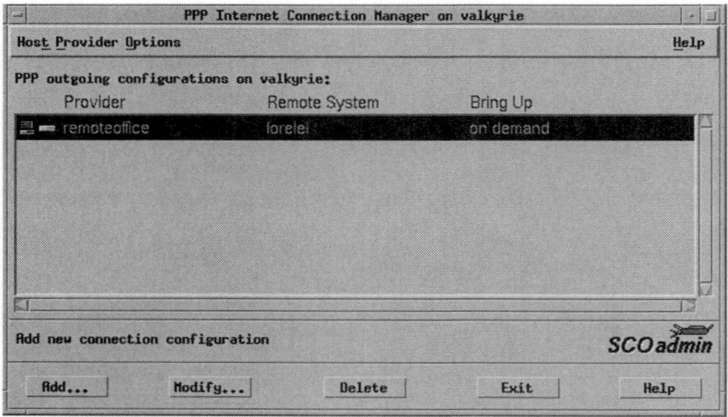

FIGURE 7.15 *The PPP Internet Connection Manager after configuration.*

After the configuration is completed, the following entry is added to the /etc/default/Systems file. Note that the password is stored in clear text form. This may be considered a security risk at your site. Be certain to keep the permissions on these files correct. The installed permissions allow reading only by user uucp and group uucp.

```
lorelei Any ACU Any 5919604:5963852 "" \r in:--in:-- ranjit sword:
➥deshpande
```

In addition, the /etc/ppp.d/.pppcfg file is updated. The information below is only a part of the .pppcfg file.

```
version SCO PPP 7.0v1.0 for Unixware 7.0
global bundle {
        type = bundle
        requirepap = disabled
        requirechap = disabled
        authname = valkyrie
        peerauthname =
        authtmout = 60
        mrru = 1500
        ssn = enabled
        ed = enabled
}
auth pap_lorelei {
        protocol = pap
        name = lorelei
        peersecret = WuLiu
        localsecret =
}
auth chap_lorelei {
        protocol = chap
        name = lorelei
        peersecret = GrahamMoore
        localsecret =
```

Incoming PPP Interface

The PPP incoming interface is created through the Network Configuration Manager. From the Network Configuration Manager select View, and then select Software, Configure PPP. The PPP Manager will start showing information on any configured PPP connections.

Adding a Link Group

To add a new Link group, select View, Link groups, and then select Edit, Add, Link group. The Add Link Group window is shown in Figure 7.16. Enter a name for the group. Select the link type. Hardware that is not configured is grayed out, in this case the two ISDN options. Select the hardware to be used. Select the flow control. With modems, hardware flow control is available. If the wiring of a direct connection does not include the hardware flow control connections, software flow control may be the best option.

Enter the telephone number for the modem, if applicable.

The Link Protocols button is used to specify which protocol will be used for the link. At the present time only the LCP protocol is available. The Advanced button contains three additional parameters:

- *Estimate of single link bandwidth*—Speed in bits per second.
- *Modules pushed before use*—Stream modules must be pushed onto the device before it can be used by PPP. The default is `asyh`.
- *Modules popped before use*—Stream modules must be popped from the device before it can be used for PPP. The defaults are `ttcompat` and `ldterm`.

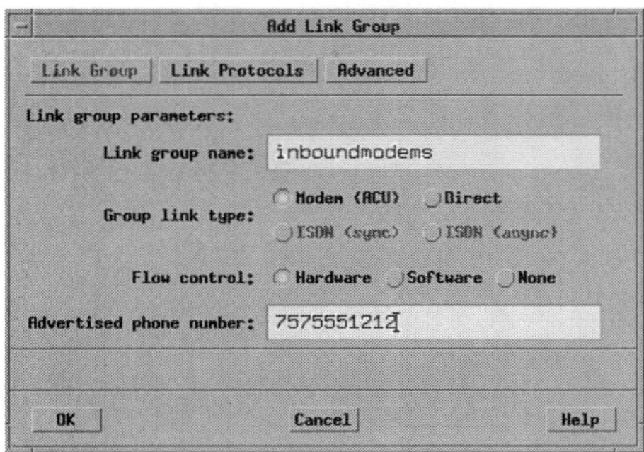

FIGURE 7.16 *Adding a link group.*

After the link group has been created, click OK, and the Add Links window will appear. After the initial configuration is complete, you can return to the

Add Links window by selecting Edit, Add, Links. The available links will be shown in the left window; select the desired links and click Add. Figure 7.17 illustrates adding a link.

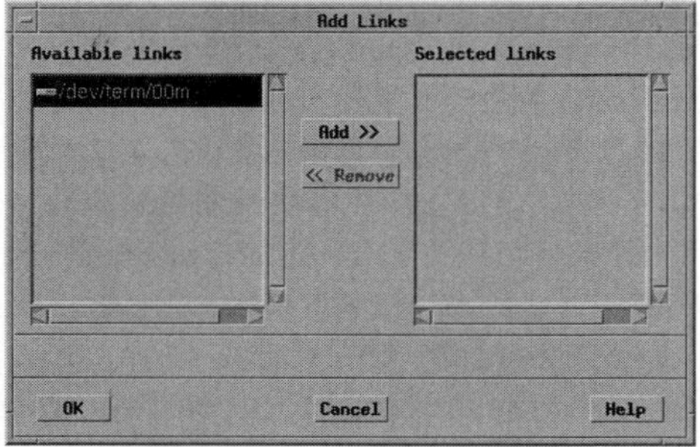

FIGURE 7.17 *Adding a link.*

Adding a Bundle

Now that the links have been created, the bundle can be created to use the links. From the PPP Manager, select View, Bundles. Select Edit, Add, Bundles.

Figure 7.18 illustrates adding a bundle. The Bundle name field is the same as the Provider name field in the PPP Internet Connection Manager. Select either Incoming or Outgoing.

If you use this method to establish outgoing connections, you can choose a Remote System Name from the pull-down list or click Edit to start the Dialup Systems Manager to add a new system to the /etc/uucp/Systems file. The method of initiating links field is the same as in the Internet Connection Manager.

The option to Use Auto-Detected PPP Session is linked to the options below it. Selecting Yes or No determines which authentication methods are available.

When auto-detect is set to Yes,

- It is answered by ppp.
- Specify either Caller ID telephone number or an Authentication ID for PAP/CHAP.

When auto-detect is set to No,

- User will log in at normal UNIX login and password prompt, so you must enter a login user name.
- Optionally, you may specify a Caller ID or Authentication ID.

Author's Note

For caller ID you must have a modem that supports caller ID and the drivers for it. It may be a separately chargeable item.

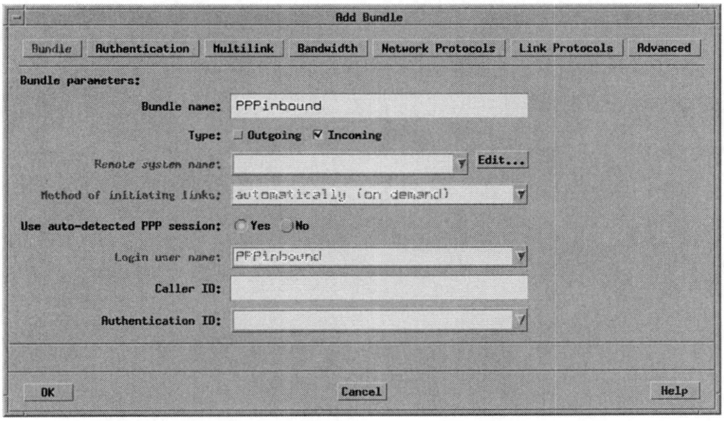

FIGURE 7.18 *Adding a bundle.*

Other buttons on the Add Bundle window allow additional parameters to be set:

- *Authentication*—configure PAP and CHAP
- *Multilink*—configure multilink PPP
- *Bandwidth*—parameters for bandwidth on demand
- *Network Protocols*—configure compression
- *Link Protocols*—currently only one is supported
- *Advanced*—inactivity timeouts

Modifying the IP Protocol Parameters for a Bundle

When you click OK on the Add Bundle window, the Modify IP Network Protocol window appears. The settings here echo the ones for the outgoing connection.

- *Local and Remote address assignment*—Four choices are in the drop-down list (for the first two options, you must enter an IP address):
    - By Local and Remote Can Override—The local system can set the address, but the remote can override it.

  - By Local and Remote Cannot Override—The local sets the address, and it cannot be overridden by a remote system.
  - By Remote—The remote system will assign the local address.
  - Use Address Allocation Server—Dynamic assignments are made. You must enter the name of an address allocation pool. The Edit button starts the Address Allocation Manager.

- *Use as Default Route*—If Yes, the incoming PPP route will be the default route. This is not normally set to Yes.
- *Act as a Gateway*—If set to Yes, allows the system to forward packets between the interfaces, which may be LAN and WAN in any combination.
- *Act as Proxy for ARP*—If set to Yes, will act as a proxy only if the remote and local systems use the same network address.
- *Network Mask*—Enter the network mask for the connection.

Other options across the top of the window allow setting Van Jacobsen compression, DNS server, packet filters, and advanced IP parameters. Packet filters are covered in Chapter 22, "Security." Figure 7.19 illustrates the Modify IP Network Protocol window.

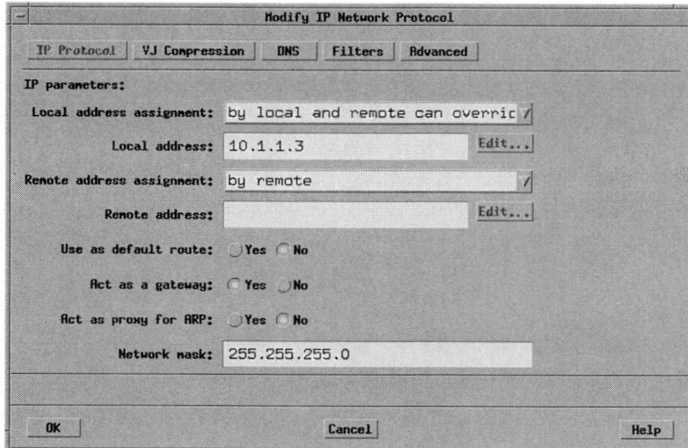

FIGURE 7.19 *Modifying the IP protocol parameters.*

Click OK at the bottom left of the Modify IP Network Protocol dialog box. As you can see from Figure 7.17, the Add Links window adds links to the bundle. Select the devices that the bundle will use. Click OK.

When you have completed the bundle, the PPP Manager window will appear, as shown in Figure 7.20.

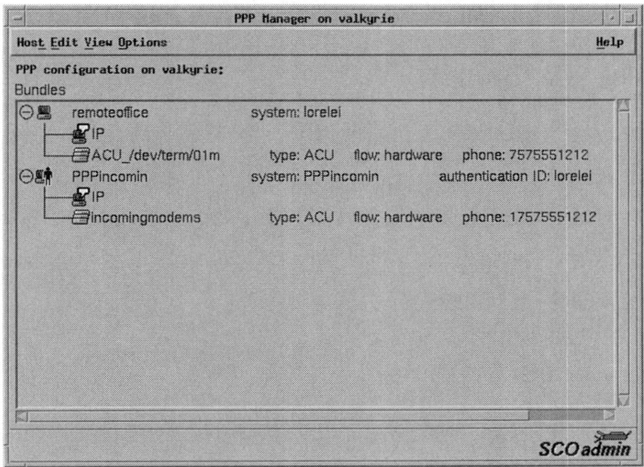

FIGURE 7.20 *The PPP Manager with configured bundles.*

Troubleshooting PPP

When the PPP configuration is complete, you can use `ifconfig -a` to see the configuration. Whether the configuration will appear depends on the configuration and whether the link is active.

- Manual outgoing interfaces can be seen after the connection is established.
- Auto-outgoing interfaces can be seen as soon as configuration is complete.
- Incoming bundles have interfaces when a connection is established.
- Bidirectional bundles interfaces depend on whether they are brought up manually or automatically.

```
Ifconfig -a
ppp0: flags=71<UP,POINTOPOINT,WANTIOCTLS,RUNNING> mtu 1500
      inet 10.1.4.3 --> 10.1.4.2 netmask ffffff00
perf. params: recv size: 4096; send size: 8192; full-size frames: 1
```

Start PPP logging and check the logs. Four levels of debugging output are available: None, Low, Med, and High. To turn on high-level debugging for a bundle named pppincoming, use

```
#ppptalk debug high bundle pppincoming
```

To turn on medium-level debugging for the link named modem1, use

```
#ppptalk debug med link modem1
```

The default log for debugging is /var/adm/log/ppp.log. See the man pages for options on changing the log name.

Check the routing between the PPP hosts and their local networks. See Chapter 8 for more on routing.

Reset `ppp`, stop the ppp daemon, and restart it. If you suspect a problem with a bundle or link, reset it.

```
#ppptalk reset bundle pppincoming
#ppptalk reset link modem1
```

To stop the ppp daemon, use

```
#ppptalk stop
```

To start the ppp daemon, use

```
#/usr/sbin/pppd
```

The `pppstatus` command can be used to display information on the current status of a bundle. The information includes the IP addresses, packet counts, link status, and other pertinent information.

The connection server can be run in debug mode to log messages. See the man pages for `cs` (1Mbnu). The debug log will be written to /var/spool/logs/cs.log.

Be certain the underlying modem and telephone connections are working as described previously in this chapter.

CHAPTER 8

Browsers and Intranets

- Routing
  Learn how to communicate between different networks.
- HTTP services
  Find out how to manage Web servers on your system.
- ftp server configuration
  Learn how to configure ftp services on your system.
- Network Time Protocol (NTP)
  Find out how to synchronize the clocks of the hosts on your network.

Routing

Communicating between different networks requires a router. A *router* is a system with multiple NICs that forwards packets from one network to another.

To configure a router in UnixWare 7, you need at least two NICs: One configured with an address in one network, and the other with an address in another network. Figure 8.1 shows a sample network topography, with three networks connected through two UnixWare 7 routers.

The three networks are 10.1.1, 10.1.2, and 10.1.3. Both routers, lorelei and valkyrie, have a NIC configured on the 10.1.1 network; and each has a second NIC, with lorelei configured on the 10.1.2 network and valkyrie on the 10.1.3 network.

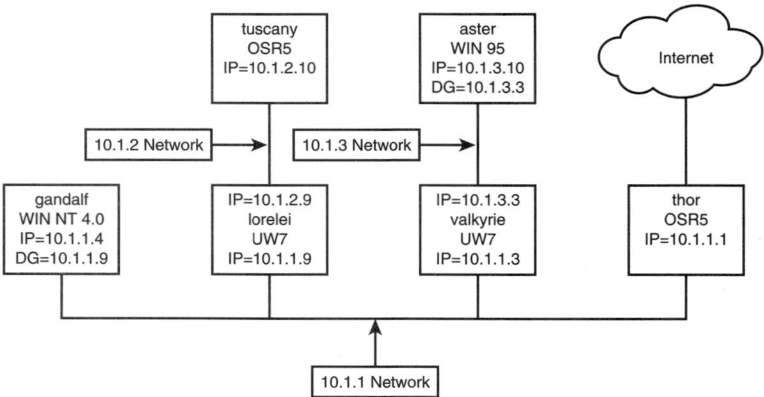

FIGURE 8.1 *Sample network topography.*

Tuscany can reach aster without any further configuration. Thor can reach tuscany and aster. However, systems running Windows (NT or 95) will need to have a default gateway configured to reach other networks. The ability of the UNIX machines to find the other networks without specifying a default gateway is accomplished through broadcasts by the routers. These router broadcasts notify the systems on their networks of other networks to which the routers have access.

Implementing Routing on UnixWare 7

In order to set the system to route packets between the networks, two kernel parameters, `ipforwarding` and `ipsendredirects`, must be set. These can be set automatically through the Network Configuration Manager by selecting TCP/IP under any configured NIC, then selecting Protocol, Modify Protocol Configuration. Clicking the Advanced options button produces the window shown in Figure 8.2. Click Yes for the Act as router? option.

Advanced Configuration

Act as router? Yes No

Pseudo ttys 32

Frame format Ethernet-II

Administrator for this system

Location of this system

OK Cancel Help

FIGURE 8.2 *Setting a system to act as a router.*

These parameters can also be set on the command line, with the `inconfig` command. This updates the /etc/inet/inet.dfl file. The syntax of the command is

```
#inconfig ipforwarding 1
#inconfig ipsendredirects 1
```

ipforwarding

The `ipforwarding` parameter instructs the router to pass packets between networks when appropriate. If this is set to `0`, systems on one network cannot access systems on other networks without first logging in to the router. This feature can be used to limit access to a network because only users who have an account on the router will be able to access other networks.

ipsendredirects

The `ipsendredirects` parameter specifies that redirects should be sent if forwarding out the same interface. In other words, if a packet is sent to a router that knows of a more direct route to the destination, the router notifies the sender of the more direct route. This redirect is sent in the form of an Internet Control Message Protocol (ICMP) packet. This should be set to `1` whenever `ipforwarding` is set to `1`.

Warning

The /etc/inet/inet.dfl file should not be edited manually.

Routing and IP Aliasing

IP aliasing, discussed later in this chapter, does not function the same as a second interface for routing purposes. Each system that needs to use the IP alias to reach another network will need to have a route explicitly established from its network to the alias. For example, if system A (10.1.1.104) has an alias that puts it on another network (10.1.2.104), a system on the 10.1.1 network will need to specify a route to network 10.1.2 through 10.1.1.104 in order to reach systems on 10.1.2. Specifying a route to host 10.1.2.104 through 10.1.1.104 will allow access to 10.1.2.104 itself, but not other systems on 10.1.2.

Routing Tables

To display the routing table, use the `netstat` command with the `-r` option. Systems identified in the /etc/hosts file will appear with the symbolic name in the default listing. A sample routing table is shown below:

```
# netstat -r
Routing tables
Destination      Gateway                Flags   Refs    Use     Interface
default          thor.henriksens.com    UGS     0       0       net0
```

continues

```
10/24              thor.henriksens.com       UG      0      0      net0
10.1.1/24          kingsley.henriksen.com    UC      1      0      net0
kingsley.henriks   localhost                 UGHS    26     44     lo0
10.1.2/24          thor.henriksens.com       UG      0      0      net0
localhost          localhost                 UH      2      1489   lo0
224/8              kingsley.henriksen.com    UGS     1      4      net0
```

Author's Note

The /24 indicates the number of bits in the netmask.

To show routing information with numerical IP addresses rather than symbolic names, add the -n option. This can be useful when tracking down network problems that may be related to symbolic naming. The following is a sample numerical routing table:

```
# netstat -rn
Routing tables
Destination     Gateway       Flags   Refs     Use     Interface
default         10.1.1.1      UGS     0        0       net0
10/24           10.1.1.1      UG      0        0       net0
10.1.1/24       10.1.1.104    UC      1        0       net0
10.1.1.104      127.0.0.1     UGHS    26       44      lo0
10.1.2/24       10.1.1.1      UG      0        0       net0
127.0.0.1       127.0.0.1     UH      2        1489    lo0
224/8           10.1.1.104    UGS     1        4       net0
```

Like individual hosts, networks can also be identified symbolically. The /etc/networks file is similar to /etc/hosts, except that the address given is that of an entire network or subnet. By default, the file exists with a single entry for loopback. The following is a sample /etc/networks file:

```
# cat /etc/networks
#ident  "@(#)networks   1.3"
#ident "$Header: /sms/sinixV5.4es/rcs/s19-full/usr/src/cmd/cmd-inet/etc/networks
,v 1.1 91/02/28 16:30:43 ccs Exp $"

#
# Internet networks
#
loopback          127
main              10.1.1
development       10.1.2
test              10.1.3
```

With the preceding /etc/networks file in place, the netstat -r output now appears as

```
# netstat -r
Routing tables
Destination        Gateway                   Flags   Refs   Use    Interface
default            thor.henriksens.com       UGS     0      0      net0
```

```
10/24             thor.henriksens.com      UG      0      0      net0
main/24           kingsley.henriksen.com   UC      1      0      net0
kingsley.henriks  localhost                UGHS    26     44     lo0
development/24    thor.henriksens.com      UG      0      0      net0
localhost         localhost                UH      2      1489   lo0
224/8             kingsley.henriksen.com   UGS     1      4      net0
```

The entries in /etc/networks are used for convenience in identifying networks by name and need not match the entries on other systems.

Routing Daemons

Routing daemons allow routes to be determined automatically. This is especially useful if the network changes frequently because the changes in routing are handled by the daemons. However, network traffic and CPU usage are both increased by using routing daemons rather than static or default routes.

UnixWare 7 provides the following routing daemons:

- routed
- gated
- mrouted

routed

The routed daemon starts by default on UnixWare 7 (unless the gated daemon has been configured) and usually does not need any configuration. Routing information is updated based on what routed learns from other routers on the network to which the machine running routed is directly connected.

The protocols implemented by routed are

- Routing Information Protocol (RIP) versions 1 and 2
- Internet Router Discovery Protocol (IRDP)

The routed daemon reads the /etc/inet/gateways file, if present, and installs the routes defined there into the kernel's routing table. The normal communication between routers will find routes and keep them up-to-date. An entry may be needed in the gateways file if

- Your router does not support broadcasting.
- Routers on the network are running incompatible protocols.
- Routes exist that may not be discovered by routed (a PPP connection to a machine that is not running a routing daemon will not be visible to other routers).

The following is a sample line from /etc/inet/gateways:

```
net 0.0.0.0 gateway 10.1.1.2 metric 1 passive
```

This sample line establishes 10.1.1.2 as the default gateway (through the 0.0.0.0 notation). The number specified after the `metric` designation represents the number of hops required to reach the gateway. See the manual pages on routed for more on the format of entries in /etc/inet/gateways.

gated

The gated daemon requires more configuration than routed, but offers more flexibility. For instance, use gated if

- Your UnixWare 7 system is acting as a router to an autonomous system (a set of routers and networks under the same administration).
- You want to perform load balancing between routers (in a situation where hosts can choose between different routers to reach the same destination).

The gated daemon can run one or more of these routing protocols:

- Routing Information Protocol (RIP)
- Internet Router Discovery Protocol (IRDP)
- Exterior Gateway Protocol (EGP)
- Border Gateway Protocol (BGP)
- Open Shortest Path First (OSPF)

OSPF has the ability to perform dynamic load balancing. This means that if multiple routes exist to a given host or network, each with the same distance (hops), OSPF will divide the load equally over the available routes. This is especially important on large intranets.

OSPF also allows administrators to specify that different types of IP packets should take different routes. Voice and video packets, for example, could be routed via a 100MB/sec connection, while other data takes a 10MB/sec route. Because of these features, OSPF scales well.

mrouted

The mrouted daemon can be run with either routed or gated and only needs to be configured if both of the following are true:

- You are running multicast programs that need to communicate on different networks.

- One or more of the routers between the server and client programs are not forwarding multicast packets.

Multicast addressing allows data to be sent from a server program to multiple client programs. For example, RealAudio can use multicasting to send data to multiple RealAudio players at the same time.

If both conditions exist, then mrouted should be configured on two hosts: One on the network reachable via multicast by the multicast server, and one on the network reachable via multicast by the multicast clients.

The mrouted daemon is configured through the /etc/inet/mrouted.conf file. This file exists by default, but contains no active entries. mrouted uses tunnels to support multicasting between subnets that are separated by routers that cannot understand multicasting. A *tunnel* is a virtual point-to-point link between two routers using mrouted anywhere on an internet. mrouted encapsulates the multicast IP packets so that they can travel along the tunnel and appear to intermediate routers as normal unicast datagrams. Add `tunnel` commands, as needed, in the format of

```
tunnel <local-address> <remote-address>
```

See the man page on mrouted for more information.

Configuring Routes

Routes can be manually configured using the `route` command. See the manual pages for a complete list of arguments and options. When a route is added using the `route` command, it stays in the routing table until the next reboot.

For example, to temporarily add a default route of 10.1.1.3, use

```
#route add default 10.1.1.3
```

To permanently add a route on a system not running the routed daemon, add an entry in the /etc/inet/config file. The following sample line exists in the file:

```
#4c:/usr/sbin/route::n::add default router_placeholder:
```

To create a route to network 10.1.3 through 10.1.1.3, use

```
4c:/usr/sbin/route::y::add -net 10.1.3 10.1.1.3:
```

To create a default route of 10.1.1.1, modify the line to read

```
4c:/usr/sbin/route::y::add default 10.1.1.1:
```

Default Route

If a particular router will be used to access multiple networks, it can be configured as the route to each of those networks or it can be used as the default route. This configuration must be performed on all machines using the router, unless they are running a routing daemon. The routed daemon comes up by default on UnixWare 7.

For example, suppose a system has access to several routers: 10.1.1.1, 10.1.1.2, and 10.1.1.3. 10.1.1.2 offers access to the 10.1.2 network. 10.1.1.3 offers access to the 10.1.3 network. 10.1.1.1 should be used to reach any other networks. Perhaps it is connected to the Internet. (Refer to Figure 8.1 for an illustration of this scenario.)

Configure individual routes for networks 10.1.2 and 10.1.3 through the appropriate routers, and configure 10.1.1.1 as the default route. Any request for networks other than 10.1.1, 10.1.2, and 10.1.3 will be sent to 10.1.1.1.

Alternatively, configure the routes for 10.1.2 and 10.1.3 on 10.1.1.1. This way, 10.1.1.1 can be set as the default route and will be able to handle requests to 10.1.2 and 10.1.3, as well as any that may be added later.

Troubleshooting Routing

To troubleshoot routing problems, you first want to verify that the host can see other hosts on its local network. Secondly, you want to check that it can reach remote networks. There are two primary tools for troubleshooting routing: `ping` and `traceroute`.

ping

The `ping` command can be used to verify that routes are working between two hosts. If the ping doesn't work, try the following:

- *ping `localhost`*—Verifies that the local protocol stack is working.
- *ping the broadcast address of the NIC*—Verifies that NIC is working (see Chapter 6, "LAN Network Configuration," for information on testing a NIC using the Network Configuration Manager).

Author's Note

You could test the NIC by pinging any system on the same network as the system being tested. However, this could be misleading if the system you chose to ping happened to be down at the time. Pinging the broadcast address will get a response as long as at least one UNIX system on the network is up and running. Windows computers do not respond to a broadcast ping.

- *ping the IP address of the router on the same network as the system being tested*—Verifies that the router is receiving your packets.

- *ping the remote IP address of the router*—Verifies that the router on your network is forwarding packets (if this does not work, and the router is running UnixWare 7, check the IP protocol stack on the router by pinging `localhost`, and verify that the `ipforwarding` kernel parameter is set to `1` on the router).

For example, given the systems shown in Figure 8.3, to troubleshoot connectivity on kingsley, use the following commands:

```
ping localhost

ping 10.1.1.255

ping 10.1.1.9

ping 10.1.2.9
```

If all of these tests are successful and the problem has not been resolved, use the `traceroute` command.

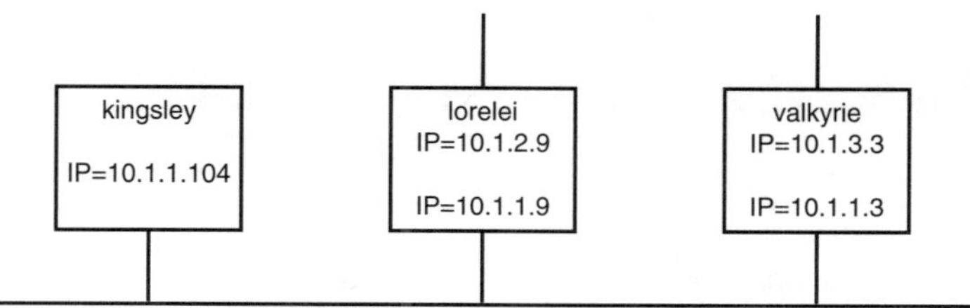

FIGURE 8.3 *Troubleshooting with ping.*

traceroute

The `traceroute` command will tell you at what point a route is broken. The following code is the result of a `traceroute` command run on kingsley (10.1.1.104). It shows the router (valkyrie) that is used to reach the specified host machine, which is on another network.

```
# traceroute 10.1.3.10
traceroute to 10.1.3.10 (10.1.3.10), 30 hops max, 80 byte packets
 1   valkyrie.henriksens.com (10.1.1.3)  0 ms  0 ms  0 ms
 2   10.1.3.10 (10.1.3.10)  10 ms  10 ms  0 ms
```

Warning

For UnixWare Release 7.0.1 systems, a PTF is in the works to address a problem that causes `traceroute` to be unable to locate any systems.

IP Aliasing

A single system with a single NIC can be associated with multiple IP addresses through the use of *IP aliasing*. Additional IP addresses are assigned to the existing network interface. Here is the result of an `ifconfig -a` on a system before aliases are added:

```
# ifconfig -a
lo0: flags=4049<UP,LOOPBACK,RUNNING,MULTICAST> mtu 16384
        inet 127.0.0.1 netmask ff000000
        perf. params: recv size: 4096; send size: 8192; full-size frames: 1
net0: flags=4043<UP,BROADCAST,RUNNING,MULTICAST> mtu 1500
        inet 10.1.1.104 netmask ffffff00 broadcast 10.1.1.255
        perf. params: recv size: 4096; send size: 8192; full-size frames: 1
        ether 00:60:08:9b:8c:0d
```

To add an alias, use the `ifconfig` command followed by the name of the interface, `alias`, and the IP address to be aliased. To add two aliases, for example, one as 10.1.1.204 and one as 10.1.2.204, to the net0 interface, use:

```
# ifconfig net0 alias 10.1.1.204 netmask 255.255.255.0
# ifconfig net0 alias 10.1.2.204 netmask 255.255.255.0
```

Author's Note

If the netmask is not specified, it defaults to the appropriate mask for the address's network class. For instance, for the 10.1.1.204 alias, which is a Class A address, the netmask defaults to 255.0.0.0.

After these commands have been issued, an `ifconfig -a` will show the aliased addresses:

```
# ifconfig -a
lo0: flags=4049<UP,LOOPBACK,RUNNING,MULTICAST> mtu 16384
        inet 127.0.0.1 netmask ff000000
        perf. params: recv size: 4096; send size: 8192; full-size frames: 1
net0: flags=4043<UP,BROADCAST,RUNNING,MULTICAST> mtu 1500
        inet 10.1.1.104 netmask ffffff00 broadcast 10.1.1.255
        perf. params: recv size: 4096; send size: 8192; full-size frames: 1
        ether 00:60:08:9b:8c:0d
        (alias) inet 10.1.1.204 netmask ffffff00 broadcast 10.1.1.255
        (alias) inet 10.1.2.204 netmask ffffff00 broadcast 10.1.2.255
```

If an alias is created in a separate network, as is the preceding 10.1.2.204 alias, routing will have to be configured.

Aliases can be removed using `ifconfig` as well. To remove the 10.1.2.204 alias, use

```
# ifconfig net0 -alias 10.1.2.204
```

Aliases created by using `ifconfig` on the command line exist for the current session only. Permanent aliasing can be accomplished in one of two ways:

- Entries may be created in the /etc/rc2.d/S70ipaliases file. This file does not exist by default. Create a shell script containing the `ifconfig` commands needed. For example, the following script will make the preceding aliases permanent:

```
# cat /etc/rc2.d/S70ipaliases
echo "Creating IP aliases:"
echo "\t10.1.1.204"
ifconfig net0 alias 10.1.1.204 netmask 255.255.255.0
echo "\t10.1.2.104"
ifconfig net0 alias 10.1.2.204 netmask 255.255.255.0
```

- Additions for the aliases can be made to the /etc/inet/config file. To create the same aliases in this fashion, append the following lines to /etc/inet/config:

```
4e:/usr/sbin/ifconfig::y::net0 alias 10.1.1.204 netmask 255.255.255.0:
4e:/usr/sbin/ifconfig::y::net0 alias 10.1.2.204 netmask 255.255.255.0:
```

Virtual Domains

IP aliasing allows for the creation of *virtual domains*, which are essentially virtual host(s) residing on your computer. The same physical machine can be used to host several companies' Web servers, for instance.

There is no single graphical manager for the creation of virtual domains. To set up a virtual domain under UnixWare 7, create an IP alias, and then do the following:

1. Update /etc/hosts or the DNS server with the new entry (see Chapter 6 for more on DNS).
2. Enable the multihome mail channel using the Mail Manager.
3. Create email accounts using the Virtual Domain User Manager.
4. Create a new Web server for the virtual domain using the Netscape Server Admin Manager (see the Administration section under Netscape Server Administration later in this chapter).
5. If desired, create an anonymous ftp server for the virtual domain using the FTP Server Manager (see the section, "Anonymous ftp," later in this chapter).

HTTP Services

Web servers provide the information displayed by Web browsers. The *HyperText Transfer Protocol (HTTP)* is used for communication between Web servers and their clients (Web browsers). Several Web servers are available for the UnixWare platform. The Netscape FastTrack Server is included with most UnixWare 7 editions. The Netscape Enterprise Server is available from SCO as an optional product. Apache is available on the Skunkware CD. For more information on Apache, see `www.apache.org`.

By default, UnixWare 7 systems run only one Web server. It serves SCOhelp and manual pages, and it runs on port 457.

> *Warning*
>
> *When using Netscape Navigator, the button to save preferences is not easily accessed with the default screen resolution of 800×600. You can reach off-screen options by using the Tab key, but you will be unable to see them. To get the buttons to appear, set the resolution to 1,024×768 through SCOadmin, Hardware, Video Configuration Manager. Also, if you change the domain name in /etc/hosts but not in /etc/resolv.conf, Netscape will report an error.*

Netscape FastTrack Server

The Netscape FastTrack server is started using the `nsfast` command. Its syntax is

```
nsfast action servername
```

The *`action`* is one of the following:

- `start`, `stop`, or `restart`, which are one-time actions
- `enable` or `disable`, which configure whether the server is to start at boot time

The *`servername`* matches the suffix of a directory under the /usr/ns-home directory that has a prefix of httpd-. For instance, there is a directory named httpd-scohelphttp.

Web browsers contact port 80 by default. To start the Netscape FastTrack server on port 80 and have it start every time the system boots, use

```
#nsfast enable 80
```

When this Web server is running, you can use any browser to reach it from any system with network connectivity to the host. Figure 8.4 shows the default Web page for host kingsley.

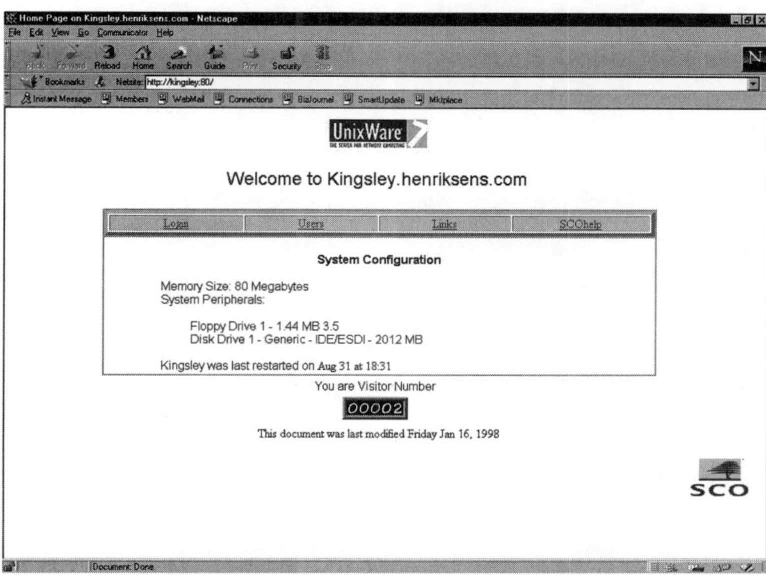

FIGURE 8.4 *Default port 80 Web server.*

Netscape Administration Server

Another Web server you might want to start is the *Netscape Administration Server*, which runs on port 620. It allows you to add, remove, and configure existing Web servers.

Stopping and Starting

To start the Netscape Administration Server through SCOadmin, select Netscape Server Admin. This will start the server if necessary, then start Netscape Navigator pointed to port 620 on your system.

The server can be started and stopped from the command line with the `/usr/ns-home/start-admin` and `/usr/ns-home/stop-admin` commands, respectively. After you have started the server this way, you can access it by starting a browser and pointing it to *`hostname`*`:620`, where *`hostname`* is the name of your system.

Administration

To access the Administration Server's home page, log in to the server with the username admin and the password assigned to root at the time of system installation.

The admin password does not change when the root password is changed. Figure 8.5 shows the Password window for Netscape Server Administration. See the section on Controlling Access for information on changing an unknown admin password.

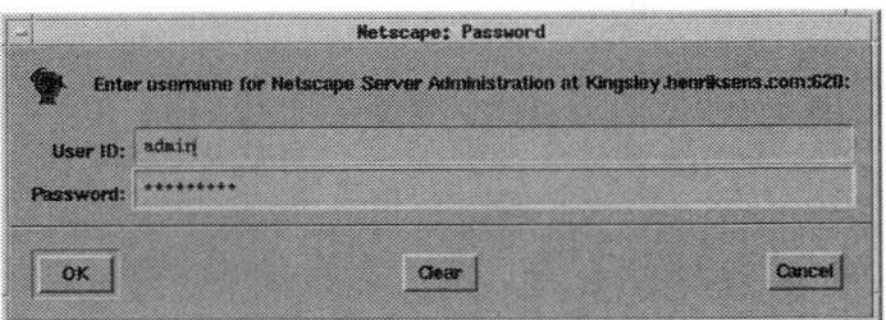

FIGURE 8.5 *Netscape Server Administration Password window.*

After the username and password have been successfully entered, the Netscape Server Selector window opens (see Figure 8.6). It has switches for the SCOhelp Web server, as well as the server running on port 80. Clicking these switches once toggles the run status of the servers between off and on.

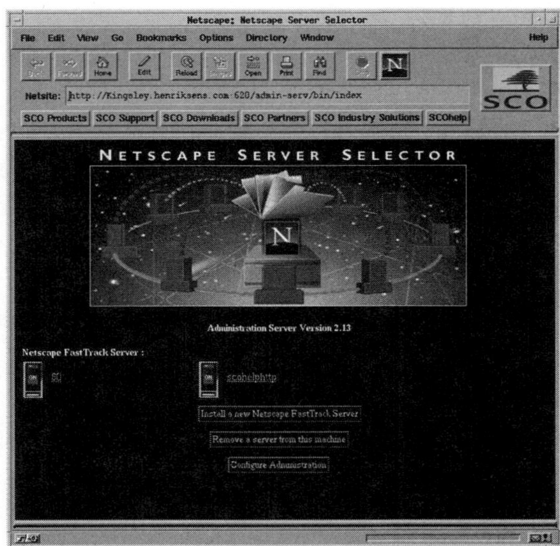

FIGURE 8.6 *Main server administration window.*

From the Netscape Server Selector window, Web servers can be added or removed. To add a Web server, select Install a New Netscape FastTrack Server. The window shown in Figure 8.7 is then opened. Installed Web servers can be removed by selecting Remove a server from this machine from the initial control screen.

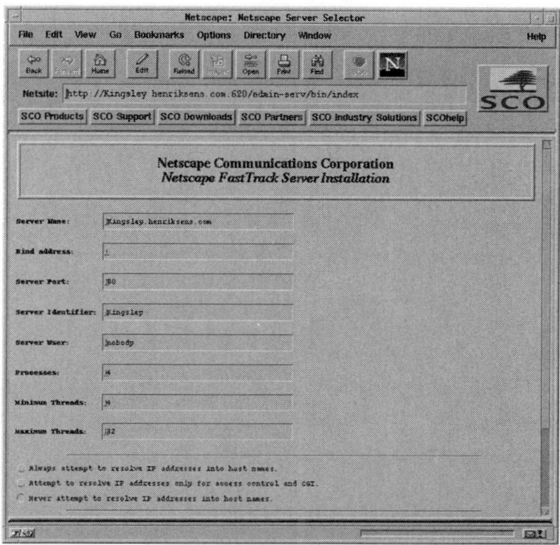

FIGURE 8.7 *Adding a Web server.*

Controlling Access

You can configure the Server Administration to control access. In Server Administration, select Configure Administration, then Access Control. This will open the window shown in Figure 8.8.

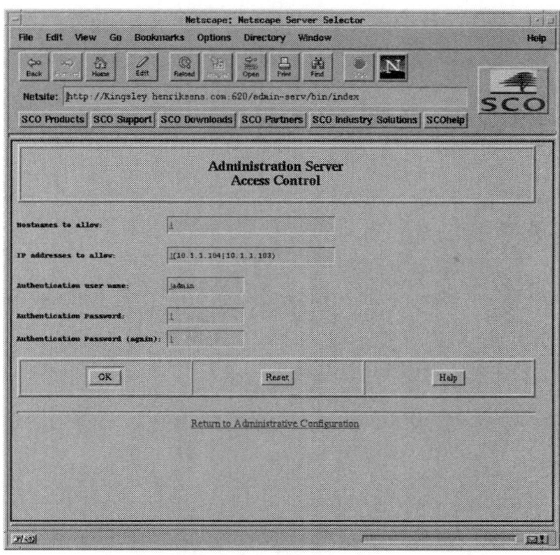

FIGURE 8.8 *Controlling access to the Server Administration.*

Here, you can specify the hosts that are allowed to run the Server Administration. The hosts should be identified by either name or IP address. Multiple host names or addresses should be separated with the pipe symbol (¦) and enclosed in parentheses. Remember to include the local system itself in the allow lists; otherwise, administration will not be possible from the console.

Author's Note

The closing parenthesis may appear as a pipe symbol in the graphical administration. It should be typed as a parenthesis regardless.

Access can also be managed by editing the /usr/ns-home/admserv/ ns-admin.conf file. The same conventions apply to listing multiple host names or IP addresses. This is also a good way to restore access to a host if it has been somehow corrupted. Here is a sample ns-admin.conf file:

```
# cat /usr/ns-home/admserv/ns-admin.conf
NetsiteRoot /usr/ns-home
Port 620
User root
ErrorLog /usr/ns-home/admserv/errors
AccessLog /usr/ns-home/admserv/access
PidLog /usr/ns-home/admserv/pid
ServerName Kingsley.henriksens.com
Backups 10
AdminUsers /usr/ns-home/admserv/admpw
Security off
Addresses (10.1.1.104¦10.1.1.103)
```

Troubleshooting Tip

If you change the host IP address using `netcfg`, it does not update the /usr/ns-home/admserv/ ns-admin.conf file. Therefore, the host itself is not authorized until you edit this file and restart the server.

You can also change the username and password in the Access Control window. If you have lost the password, you can edit the /usr/ns-home/ admserv/admpw file and delete everything following the colon after the username. This will allow you to log in without a password, then set a new one. Only root can edit this file.

Changes in Configuration

Configuration changes will not take effect until the server has been stopped and restarted.

If you have successfully made changes through the Administration Server itself, you will see a window such as the one in Figure 8.9. You then will be given the opportunity to shut down the server. To restart it, use the `/usr/ns-home/start-admin` command on the command line, or close the Netscape window and reselect Netscape Server Admin. This will start the server and open a Netscape Navigator window.

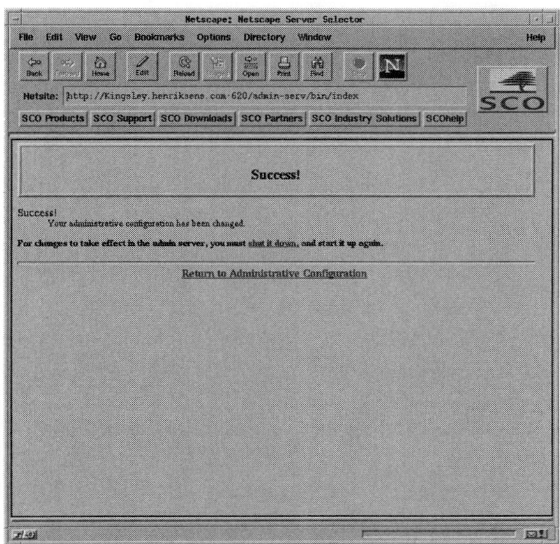

FIGURE 8.9 *Success!*

If you have made changes manually in the configuration files, you will need to stop the server with the `/usr/ns-home/stop-admin` command, then restart it with `/usr/ns-home/start-admin`.

ftp Server Configuration

FTP services are handled by *ftpd*, the ftp server daemon. The daemon can be configured either from the command line or through SCOadmin by selecting Networking, FTP Server Manager, which opens the window shown in Figure 8.10.

Enabling the ftp Server

The ftp server is enabled (that is, the ftpd daemon is running) by default. It can be enabled and disabled through the FTP Server Manager. If the ftp server is disabled, it can be enabled by selecting FTP, Server, Enable.

Disabling the ftp Server

Before the server can be disabled, the name and path of a shutdown file must be specified. To specify a shutdown file, such as /var/ftp/shutdown, select Options, General from the FTP Server Manager. The window shown in Figure 8.11 is displayed.

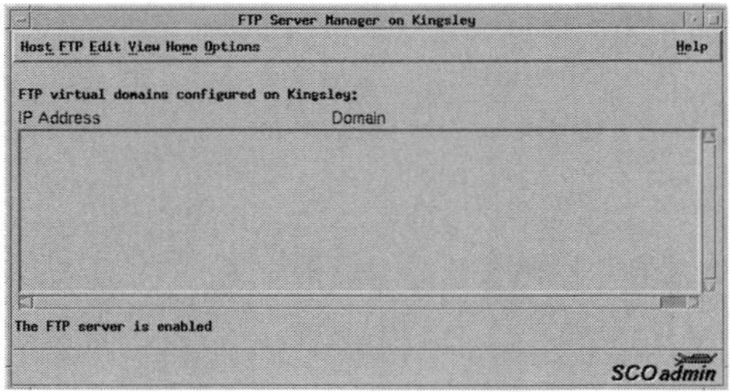

FIGURE 8.10 *Managing the ftp server.*

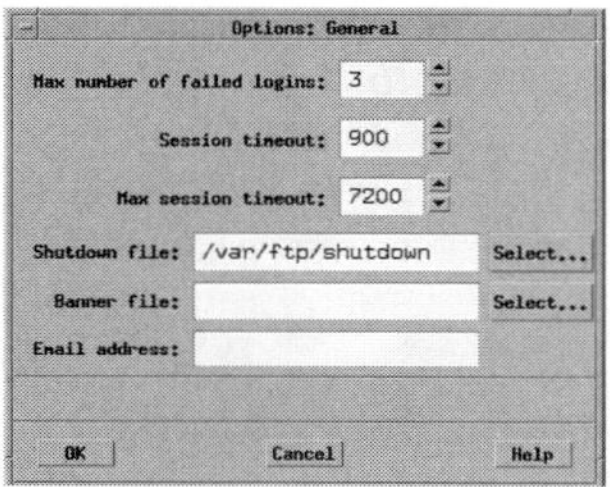

FIGURE 8.11 *Specifying a shutdown file.*

When the shutdown file has been set, the ftp server can be disabled by selecting FTP, Server, Disable. The window for disabling the ftp server is shown in Figure 8.12.

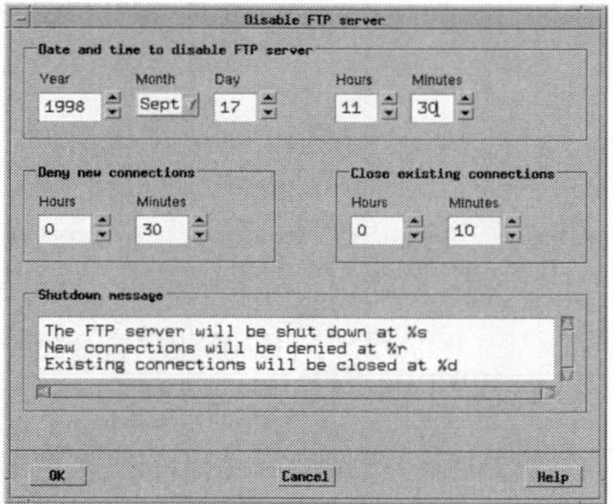

FIGURE 8.12 *Disabling the ftp server.*

You can specify the date and time the ftp server is to be shut down. You can also specify the point at which new connections will be denied access in terms of hours and minutes before the scheduled shutdown. The point at which existing connections will be closed is set in the same manner. In Figure 8.12, the ftp server is scheduled to shut down at 11:30 a.m.; new connections will be denied after 11:00 a.m. (11:30 – 30 minutes); and existing connections will be closed at 11:20 a.m. (11:30 – 10 minutes).

After the ftp server has been scheduled to shut down, a confirmation window will be displayed with the scheduled time, as well as a notice that the shutdown can be canceled by enabling the server.

Anonymous ftp

Configuring anonymous ftp allows Internet or intranet users to access files on the servers without having an account on the server. This is useful for distribution of documents, programs, and the like. To configure anonymous ftp for the primary domain, select FTP, Anonymous, Configure from the FTP Server Manager. The window displayed is shown in Figure 8.13.

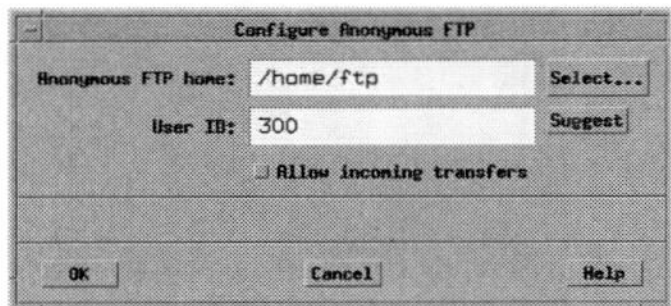

FIGURE 8.13 *Configuring anonymous ftp.*

You can specify both the home directory and user ID that should be associated with the anonymous ftp user, as well as whether to allow incoming transfers. Remember that allowing incoming transfers makes you susceptible to malicious attacks on your system (for example, filling the available disk space or storing pirated software).

After anonymous ftp has been configured, you will need to configure the home directory. From the FTP Server Manager, select Home, Anonymous FTP, Install. You will again be given the opportunity to specify whether to allow incoming transfers.

There are several options in the Home, Anonymous FTP menu in addition to Install:

- *Modify*—Allows you to change the Allow Incoming Transfers field.
- *Verify*—Checks that the ftp user is created correctly and that the home directory is created and correctly populated.
- *Correct*—Corrects errors found by Verify.
- *Remove*—Removes the ftp user's home directory, but not the user itself.

The availability of anonymous ftp can be controlled through the FTP Server Manager by selecting FTP, Anonymous, which offers the following selections:

- *Disable*—Makes anonymous ftp unusable.
- *Enable*—Makes anonymous ftp usable again.
- *Remove*—Removes anonymous ftp configuration, including both the ftp user and its home directory.

Anonymous ftp and Group Membership

UnixWare 7 offers the capability for anonymous users to change group membership during an ftp session. This allows specific areas within the anonymous ftp files to be protected by a password.

To enable this feature, you must do the following:

1. Set the Private option in the /etc/ftpaccess file to `yes`.
2. Create an entry in the /etc/ftpgroups file to map a pseudo group to a real group.
3. Change the group ownership of the files you wish to protect to the real group to which you mapped the pseudo group.

For example, to create a pseudo group, called accessgrp, mapped to the real group of sales, create an entry in /etc/ftpgroups containing the following:

```
accessgrp:xyz789abc123:sales
```

The string `xyz789abc123` represents an encrypted password. In order to get the encrypted password, use the `passwd` command to change the password on a user account to the desired group password. Then edit the /etc/shadow file to copy and paste the encrypted password into the /etc/ftpgroups file.

Tip

Remember that to copy and paste between files using vi, invoke vi on the command line with the name of the file to be copied from followed by the name of the file to be pasted to. You can then perform a yank on the desired text, which is stored in the buffer. Enter `:n` *to go to the next file, and paste the contents of the buffer.*

After you have created the proper entry in the /etc/ftpgroups file linking accessgrp to sales, change the group ownership of the files you wish to protect to sales. A user logged in as the ftp or anonymous user can assume membership in the pseudo group by entering the following:

```
site group accessgrp
site gpass password
```

For the rest of the current FTP session, the user will have access to files owned by the sales group.

FTP Classes

FTP classes are defined by the account type used and the IP address of the machine from which they are accessing FTP. The account types are

- *Real*—The account name and password entered at authentication time are found in /etc/passwd and /etc/shadow, and the user does not belong to a guest group.
- *Guest*—The account name entered at authentication time is a member of a guest group.
- *Anonymous*—The account name entered at authentication time is either *ftp* or *anonymous*.

Classes can be created through the FTP Server Manager by selecting View, Classes, Edit, Add. The window shown in Figure 8.14 is displayed.

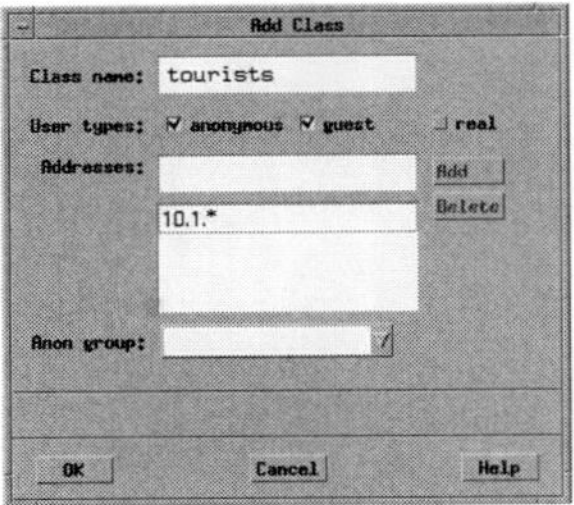

FIGURE 8.14 *Adding an FTP class.*

Class Limits

When classes have been defined, limits may be set on the number of users who are allowed simultaneous access, as well as what days and times access is permitted. Class limits are set through the FTP Server Manager by selecting View, Class Limits, Edit, Add. This opens the window shown in Figure 8.15.

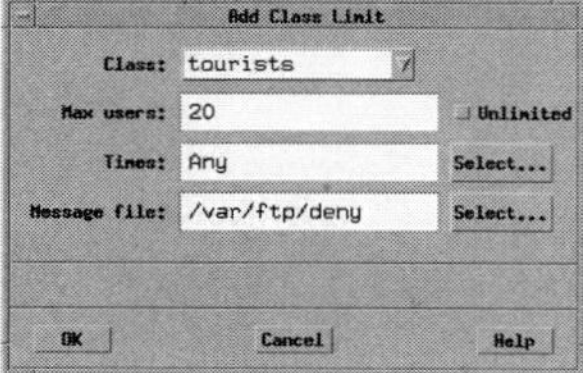

FIGURE 8.15 *Adding Class Limits.*

Select the class to limit; then, enter the maximum number of simultaneous users allowed from that class. Entering a `-1` has the same effect as selecting Unlimited. You can also specify a file containing the message to be displayed when access is denied. The default is to apply the limits to any time of the day, any day of the week. To specify particular date and time ranges, click the Select button next to the Times field. This will open the window shown in Figure 8.16.

Troubleshooting Tip

If you click Select and browse the directory structure to pick a file containing an access denied message, you may find that when you click to select the filename, it replaces the last directory name in the full path name rather than appending to it. You can manually edit the field to correct this problem.

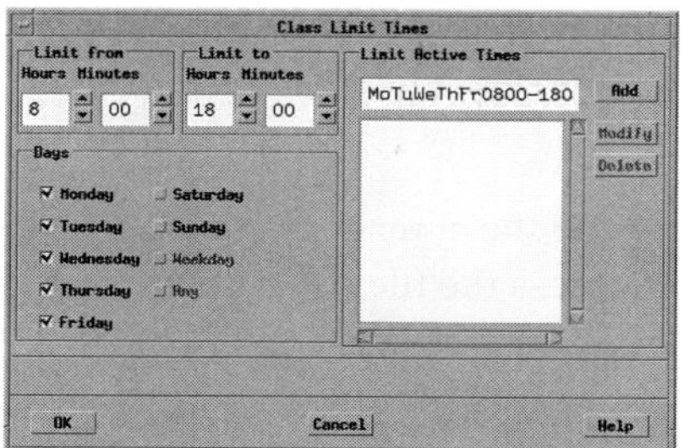

FIGURE 8.16 *Setting Class Limit Times.*

In this example, access is limited on weekdays, from 8:00 a.m. to 6:00 p.m.

Warning

If an ftp connection could be a member of more than one class, it is assigned to the first class listed. For this reason, you will need to either move, modify, or remove the "all" class (which encompasses all account types and IP addresses) before any connections are considered as members of other classes that you have defined. There is no capability for reordering classes through the FTP Server Manager, but the /etc/inet/ftpaccess file can be edited to accomplish reordering.

The configuration performed through the FTP Server Manager updates the /etc/ftpaccess file.

Username and Login Shell Restrictions

In addition to setting class limits, ftp access can be denied based on username or login shell. To deny ftp access to a specific user, enter the username in the ftp restricted users list, which is found in the /etc/ftpusers file. By default, root is denied ftp access. This prevents ftp users from being able to access or overwrite sensitive or critical files.

To deny access to users running particular login shells, you can remove the line listing that shell (for example, /bin/csh) from the /etc/shells file. Notice that the /etc/ftpusers file lists usernames to be denied, while the /etc/shells file lists login shells to be allowed.

FTP Conversions

Several types of conversions are available to ftp users by default. These include compression with `compress`, `GZIP`, and `ZIP`, and archiving directories with tar and cpio. These can also be used in combination with each other. To add other conversions, modify the /etc/ftpconversions file. See the manual page on `ftpconversions` for information on configuring this file.

The configured conversions can be used with the `ftp` commands. For instance, to get a file called *file* in compressed format, enter

```
get file.Z
```

This will cause the file to be compressed using the `compress` command, then transferred. The recipient must then uncompress the file. To uncompress a file called *file.Z*, use the following syntax:

```
#uncompress file.Z
```

The uncompressed file will be named *file*, and *file.Z* will no longer exist.

Similarly, to get a directory called *dir* in a compressed tar format, enter

```
get dir.tar.Z
```

This will cause the FTP daemon to send a compressed tar archive of the directory. The recipient must uncompress and extract the tarfile.

Other FTP Configuration

Additional FTP configuration may be performed by editing the /etc/ftpaccess file. See the manual pages for `ftpaccess` for more information. Also, flags can be set for the FTP daemon, ftpd. The manual pages for ftpd discuss these flags.

Network Time Protocol (NTP)

Hosts on a network may perform numerous functions involving time-oriented data (time-stamped logs, NFS, and so on). For this reason, it is important that the hosts all agree on the current date and time. An NFS backup of recently updated files will miss those files that the system performing the backup perceives to have modification dates in the future because of time synchronization problems with other hosts. Hosts on a network can be configured to exchange date and time information using the xntpd daemon, which uses NTP.

NTP Servers

There are hosts on the Internet that are used as reliable *time servers*. Some are synchronized with atomic clocks. The closer the host is in network hops to an atomic clock, the more reliable it is as a time server.

The term *stratum* is used to refer to a host's level of reliability. *Stratum 1 servers* are referred to as *primary servers*, and *stratum 2 servers* are called *secondary servers*. A server's local clock is set to stratum 3 by default, but it is recommended to set local clocks to stratum 10. The local clock should be used only if no configured time servers are reachable.

A local time server should be configured for every 100 hosts on an intranet. It should be configured to poll both a stratum 1 server and a stratum 2 server, in the event that the stratum 1 server is down. All other hosts on the intranet should poll the local time server, as well as their own local clock (127.127.1.1), in case the local time server is down.

Tip

Lists of primary and secondary public NTP servers are available at `www.eecis.udel.edu/~mills/ntp/servers.html`. *Recommendations and information on restrictions can also be found at this site.*

Managing Time Servers

To add a time server to a host through SCOadmin, select Networking, Client Manager, Services, Add, NTP client. The window shown in Figure 8.17 is displayed.

Author's Note

In order to enter time servers in the NTP Client Service Configuration window, you may first need to click Poll time servers for time, even if it is already selected.

Enter each time server the host will use. For a local time server, the servers entered here may be a primary and a secondary server, as well as the local clock. Other hosts on the intranet will enter the local time server and their own local clock. After the servers have been entered, click OK, then select Host, Exit to exit the Client Manager. This will update the /etc/inet/npd.conf file and start xntpd.

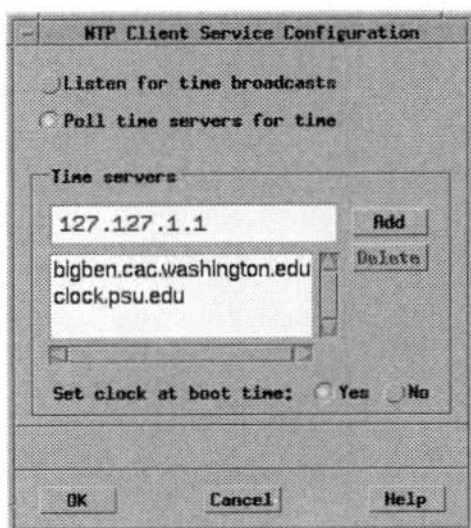

FIGURE 8.17 *Adding NTP servers.*

In order to change the stratum of the local clock to 10, add the following line to the /etc/inet/npd.conf file after the line listing the 127.127.1.1 server:

```
fudge 127.127.1.1 stratum 10
```

After entering the time servers shown in Figure 8.16, and adding the preceding line to change the stratum of the local clock, the /etc/inet/ntp.conf file would contain the following:

```
# ntp.conf


broadcastclient no
server bigben.cac.washington.edu
server clock.psu.edu
server 127.127.1.1
fudge 127.127.1.1 stratum 10
driftfile /etc/inet/ntp.drift
```

CHAPTER 9

NetWare

- **Connect to NetWare servers**
  UnixWare supports connections to Netware 3 and 4 servers for file and print services.
- **NetWare UNIX client**
  The UnixWare NetWare UNIX client allows UnixWare clients to access a NetWare file server. See how this is configured.
- **NetWare services**
  UnixWare can be a NetWare server to NetWare clients with an optional NetWare services package. See how this is installed.

NetWare on UnixWare 7

UnixWare 7 provides two types of NetWare-to-UnixWare 7 connectivity:

- NetWare UNIX Client (NUC)
- NetWare Services (NWS)

NUC is loaded by default with UnixWare 7. NUC provides an authorized UnixWare 7 user access to NetWare file systems using either NetWare 3 or NetWare 4 on the NetWare server. The NWS software package is an optional service. You will need a license from SCO to operate the software. It will install with a default license. The default license allows zero client connections. Unlike some other SCO optional software packages, there is no trial period with an unlicensed installation.

Author's Note

Attempting to connect from a NetWare client PC to a UnixWare 7 shared file system without licenses results in an `Access denied` *message when attempting to mount. Attempting to view the contents of the share produces a message stating that the share has been moved or removed. These error messages are logged in the /var/adm/log/osmlog file.*

If you are working with a large NetWare network, you will probably have access to a NetWare specialist. You will need to have some knowledge of NetWare Directory Services (NDS) and the tree and context in which you will be working.

NetWare UNIX Client (NUC)

NUC allows a UnixWare 7 user access to NetWare files. These file systems may be seen as a UNIX file system or a DOS file system. The SCOhelp references provide information on using the two methods of access. To use the UNIX file system approach, the NFS namespace must be loaded on the NetWare server.

On the UnixWare 7 side, you must have IPX/SPX loaded. IPX may be loaded as a separate protocol on a network interface card (NIC). It may also be loaded on TCP/IP to provide IPX packets tunneled through TCP/IP. Figure 9.1 illustrates adding the IPX protocol. IPX is required for UnixWare to access NetWare. If the NetWare server is using TCP/IP, the IPX protocol is tunneled through TCP much as NetBIOS is tunneled through TCP in the Windows/UnixWare environment. In this case, the NetWare server is running IPX, so IPX was loaded as a protocol rather than as a tunneled protocol.

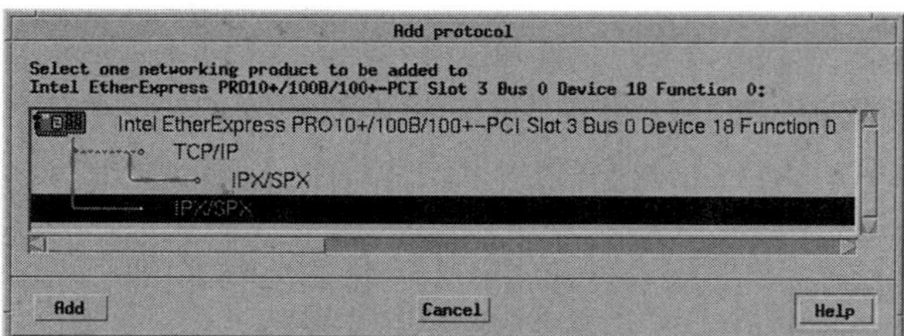

FIGURE 9.1 *Adding the IPX/SPX protocol to the NIC.*

Tip

If the IPX protocol is not available at boot, the NetWare shell is not started. You should reboot after configuring IPX. Several scripts in the /etc/rc2.d directory are used to start NetWare functionality. The commands to run are in the /etc/rc2.d directory:

```
sh S70Nnwip
sh S70Pnw start
sh S70Rnuc start
```

After IPX/SPX has been added and the system has been rebooted, you can log in as a NetWare user at the command line. To log in to a NetWare server, you will need a NetWare username and context. The login username will be the username and the context. For instance, if your user account is `mcnulty` and the context is `sco`, your username to be entered at the login would be `mcnulty.sco`. The following illustrates a NetWare login using the `nwlogin` command:

```
# nwlogin gingerw.nichols_family
Your current context is [Root]
Your current tree is: FAMILY_TREE
You are attached to server NICHOLS.
# lc /.NetWare/nichols/sys
doc          etc        mail        nichols       public vol$log.err
docview      login      netbasic    patches       tts$log.err
#
```

When the `nwlogin` is authenticated, the NetWare systems' shared directories are mounted on the /.Netware directory. Here are the entries from the `mount` command after the `nwlogin` was completed:

```
/.NetWare on /.NetWare read only on Tue Oct  6 15:17:28 1998
/.NetWare/nichols/sys on nichols:sys read/write on Tue Oct  6 15:24:40 1998
```

UnixWare users may now access the files on the NetWare server. In this case, the /.NetWare directory is mounted as read only.

Installation of NetWare Services (NWS)

The NWS package is included on the installation CD-ROM. To add this package to UnixWare, use `pkgadd` or the Application Installer. Prior to adding NWS, there are two entries in the NetWare folder of SCOadmin: NetWare Settings and NetWare Setup. After adding NWS, the number of entries increases by five. The new entries are

- Directory Services Install
- Directory Services Repair
- NetWare Licensing
- NetWare Server Status
- NetWare Volume Setup

If there is a NetWare server on the network, ensure that it is running before installing NWS. The IPX protocol should find the NetWare server and automatically pick up the same network number (see Figure 9.2).

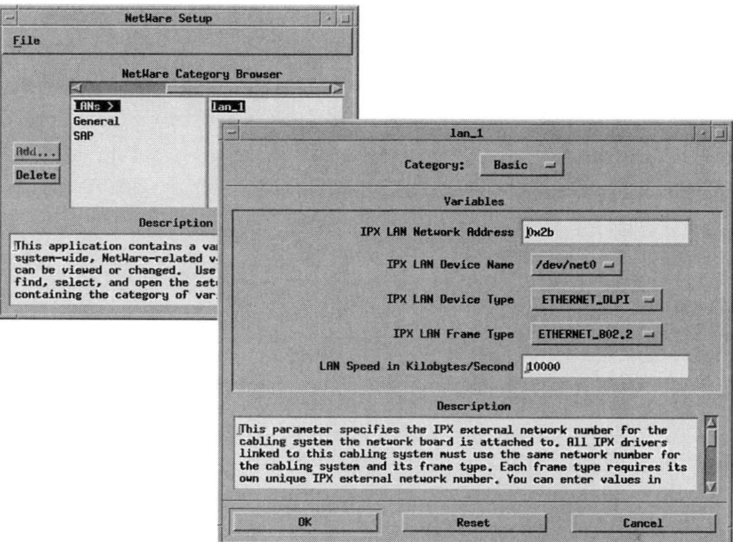

FIGURE 9.2 *The NetWare Setup after recognizing an existing NetWare LAN.*

Licensing

You may license the NWS package during or after installation. You may not use the package to connect to the UnixWare 7 system from a NetWare client even once without a license. The licensing window is shown in Figure 9.3.

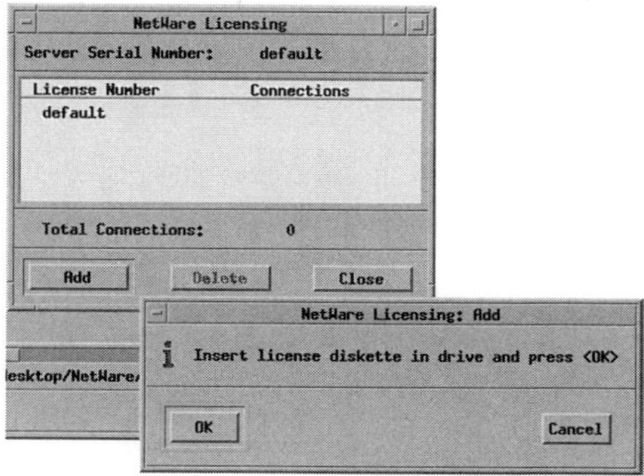

FIGURE 9.3 *The NetWare Licensing window.*

Loading the Software

Load the NWS package from the Application Installer or with `pkgadd`. The package consists of several components. The icon indicates this by showing two green boxes, instead of one. After the software is installed, you should reboot.

The new icons are now in the NetWare folder in SCOadmin.

Configuring NetWare

The configuration starts with installing directory services. Unless you have specific reasons not to do so, select the defaults in Directory Services. Figure 9.4 illustrates the Directory Services window.

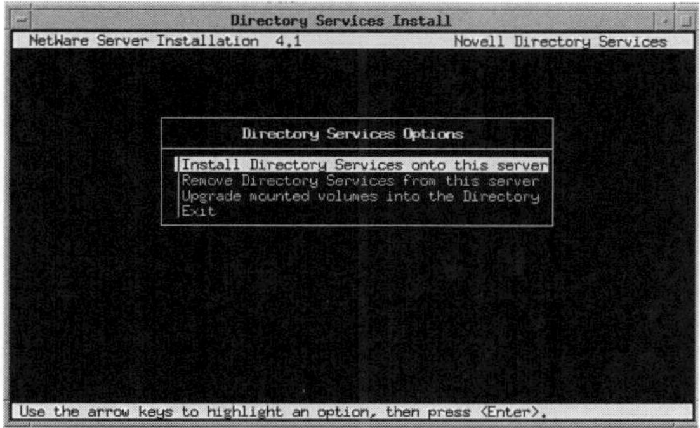

FIGURE 9.4 *The Directory Services installation window.*

Printing to a NetWare Printer from UnixWare 7

A UnixWare 7 printer that prints to a NetWare printer is created in the SCOadmin Printer Setup Manager. Select Printer, Add NetWare Printer.

Figure 9.5 illustrates the process of adding a NetWare printer. Enter a printer name and select the make and model of the printer. Click the Select button to the right of the NetWare Server box to pick a server from the list. When the server has been selected, click the Select button to the right of the NetWare Print Queue box to select from the available NetWare print queues.

Printing to a UnixWare 7 Printer from NetWare

To print from a NetWare printer queue to a UnixWare printer, create the printer as a normal UNIX printer. Highlight the UNIX printer and select Printer, Nprinter from the menu. The window shown in Figure 9.6 will appear. Fill in the NetWare Server, Print Server, and Print Queue text boxes. You may use the Select buttons to browse for each selection.

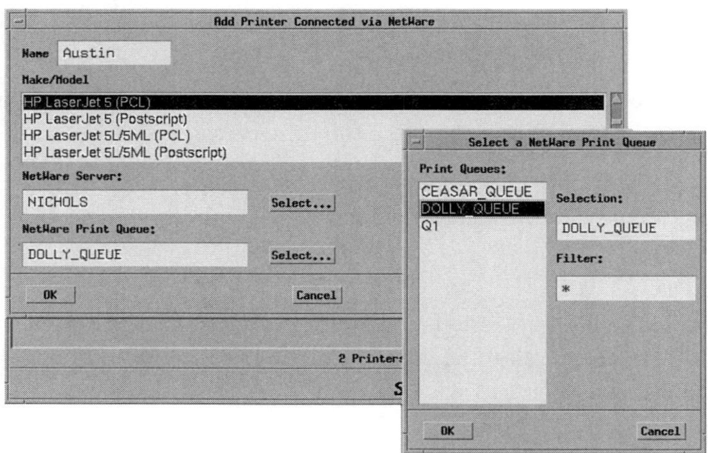

FIGURE 9.5 *Creating a UnixWare 7 printer that will print to NetWare.*

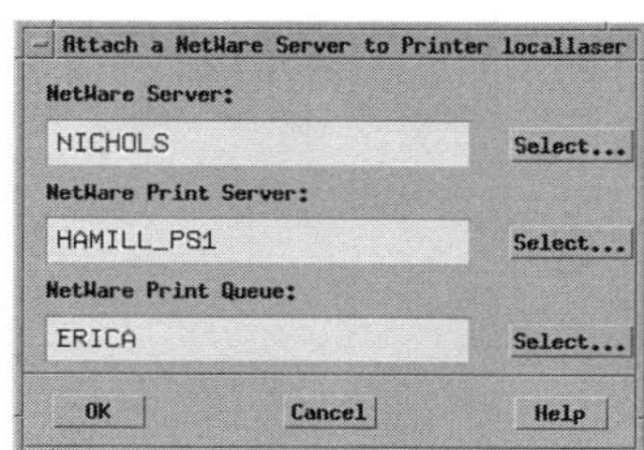

FIGURE 9.6 *Attaching a NetWare Server print queue to a local UNIX printer.*

CHAPTER 10

Configuration of Serial Ports and Terminal Devices

- Service Access Facility
  Learn how the Service Access Facility manages a range of services, including logins, network printing, and the inet daemon.
- Serial Manager
  Learn to use the Serial Manager to administer COM ports for use with terminals and other serial devices.
- Third-party serial port boards
  See how services are administered for a third-party serial board.

The Service Access Facility

UnixWare 7 uses the *Service Access Facility (SAF)* to deal with access to system services, whether through the console, serial connections, or network connections. The SAF consists of commands and daemons that administer these services.

With the large systems today, in which hundreds of serial ports may be enabled for login, running a getty process for each port creates excessive overhead in terms of processes. The SAF handles login ports in a fashion similar to the way inetd handles network requests: A single daemon process monitors a group of ports.

Getty processes are still available on UnixWare 7. However, SCO encourages system administrators to use the SAF capabilities and rely on getty only where software applications are looking for a getty process. Getty may not be supported in future releases of UnixWare 7.

The SAF architecture is a hierarchy of processes. A sample SAF diagram is shown in Figure 10.1.

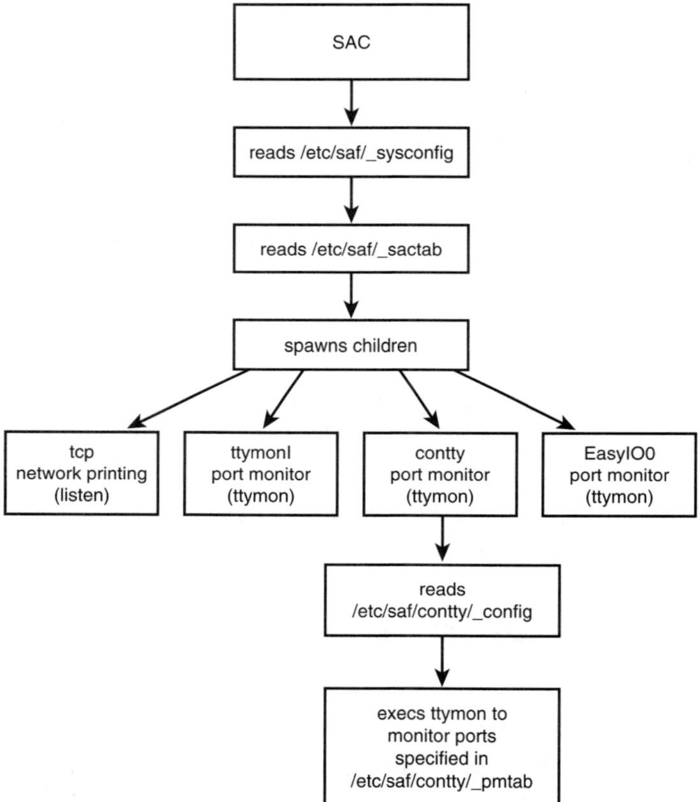

FIGURE 10.1 *The Service Access Facility.*

The Service Access Controller

The highest level of the SAF architecture is the *Service Access Controller (SAC)*. The SAC oversees all services and is the administrative point of control for port monitors. *Port monitor daemons* monitor ports assigned to them and control the services allowed on the ports. Port monitors are discussed in the following "Port Monitors" section.

The SAC program is started by `init` when the machine enters multi-user mode. It then reads the per-system configuration script found in /etc/saf/_sysconfig. The customizations to the SAC environment are made here and are inherited by the children of the SAC process.

Next, SAC reads the /etc/saf/_sactab to determine which port monitors are to be started. A sample _sactab is shown here:

```
# cat /etc/saf/_sactab
# VERSION=1
tcp:listen::3:/usr/lib/saf/listen -m inet/tcp0 tcp 2>/dev/null  #
inetd:inetd::0:/usr/sbin/inetd  #internet daemon
nbcots:listen::0:/usr/lib/saf/listen nbcots     #
contty:ttymon::0:/usr/lib/saf/ttymon    #
ttymon1:ttymon::0:/usr/lib/saf/ttymon   #
EasyIO0:ttymon::0:/usr/lib/saf/ttymon   #
```

The sample _sactab contains six entries with five colon delimited fields per entry. The first field contains the name of the port monitor, the second specifies the associated daemon, and the fifth is the command line to start the daemon. In the sample file, six port monitors will be started by SAC.

Port Monitors

A child process is spawned for each port monitor. Each child reads its configuration script, found in /etc/saf/<*pmtag*>/_config, where *pmtag* is the name given to the port monitor.

The child process then starts the port monitor daemon specified in the _sactab entry. In the sample, three port monitors use the ttymon daemon:

- contty (for console logins)
- ttymon1 (for serial ports)
- EasyIO0 (for a third-party serial port board)

The port monitor daemon will monitor ports specified in the port monitor's _pmtab, also found in the /etc/saf/<*pmtag*> directory specific to each port monitor. In the example shown in Figure 10.1, the contty port monitor looks for its configuration information in /etc/saf/contty/_config. It then `execs` the ttymon daemon to monitor the ports listed in /etc/saf/contty/_pmtab. The default _pmtab for the contty port monitor is

```
# cat /etc/saf/contty/_pmtab
# VERSION=2
2:u::reserved:reserved:login:/dev/vt02:::/usr/bin/shserv::console::Login
➥(vt02)\: :::::#
3:u::reserved:reserved:login:/dev/vt03:::/usr/bin/shserv::console::Login
```

```
➥(vt03)\: :::::#
4:u::reserved:reserved:login:/dev/vt04:::/usr/bin/shserv::console::Login
➥(vt04)\: :::::#
5:u::reserved:reserved:login:/dev/vt05:::/usr/bin/shserv::console::Login
➥(vt05)\: :::::#
6:u::reserved:reserved:login:/dev/vt06:::/usr/bin/shserv::console::Login
➥(vt06)\: :::::#
7:u::reserved:reserved:login:/dev/vt07:::/usr/bin/shserv::console::Login
➥(vt07)\: :::::#
8:u::reserved:reserved:login:/dev/vt08:::/usr/bin/shserv::console::Login
➥(vt08)\: :::::#
```

Note

This output has more than 80 columns per line. Each new line begins with a service tag; that is, `2`, `3`, `4`, *and so on.*

In this _pmtab setup, service is monitored on seven virtual terminals available at the console. The first field represents the service tag associated with a given port. For a service to be uniquely identified, both the pmtag and service tag (svctag) are needed. _pmtab also contains information about the authentication scheme to be used, the associated device name, and port monitor specific information.

Tip

In the preceding listing, /dev/vt01 does not appear, nor does /dev/console. These devices are not under the control of the contty port monitor. The console login is handled by an individual instance of ttymon, which is started by `init` *from /etc/inittab, and is set for respawn. It is not under the control of the SAC process. The login for /dev/vt01 (desktop) is started from the /etc/rc2.d/S99dtlogin script. If you wish to permanently disable the graphical login, rename the S99dtlogin script. To add a text login to /dev/vt01, add an entry to the contty port monitor. See the section on ttyadm for examples on adding services.*

sacadm

The `sacadm` command administers port monitors. `sacadm` performs the following functions:

- Add, remove, start, stop, enable, and disable port monitors.
- Install or replace a per-system configuration script (updates /etc/saf/_sysconfig).
- Install or replace a per-port monitor configuration script (updates /etc/saf/<*pmtag*>/_config).
- Print information about specific port monitors.

Port monitors exist in one of six states:

- STARTING and STOPPING are transitional states on the way to one of the other four states.
- An ENABLED port monitor is currently running.
- DISABLED indicates that the port monitor has been disabled.
- NOTRUNNING will appear when a port monitor has been stopped.
- FAILED indicates that the monitor has not been successfully started and has reached the maximum number of retries. (See the man page for the -n option for sacadm.)

See the sections "Stopping Port Monitors" and "Disabling Port Monitors" for differences between the NOTRUNNING and DISABLED states.

Listing Port Monitors

To show a list of currently configured port monitors, use the -l option with sacadm. It returns the pmtag, pmtype, flags, retry count, status, and command associated with each port monitor.

```
# sacadm -l
PMTAG          PMTYPE     FLGS RCNT STATUS     COMMAND
EasyIO0        ttymon     -    0    NOTRUNNING /usr/lib/saf/ttymon #
contty         ttymon     -    0    STARTING   /usr/lib/saf/ttymon #
inetd          inetd      -    0    ENABLED    /usr/sbin/inetd #internet
  daemon
nbcots         listen     -    0    ENABLED    /usr/lib/saf/listen
➥nbcots #
tcp            listen     -    3    DISABLED   /usr/lib/saf/listen -m
  inet/tcp0 tcp 2>/dev/null #
ttymon1        ttymon     -    0    ENABLED    /usr/lib/saf/ttymon #
```

Note

*The preceding output has more than 80 columns per line. Each new line begins with the port monitor tag (*EasyIO0*,* contty*,* inetd*,* nbcots*,* tcp*, and* ttymon1*). The EasyIO0 port monitor, used in several examples, is not a part of UnixWare 7, but rather a third-party add-on.*

Adding Port Monitors

To add a port monitor, use sacadm with the -a flag. When adding a port monitor, you must specify the pmtag, the type (ttymon, listen), the command to execute when starting the port monitor, and the port monitor version.

The standard run command for `ttymon` is /usr/lib/saf/ttymon. The ttymon version number may be obtained by executing `ttyadm -V`.

To add a port monitor of type `ttymon` with a pmtag of `contty`, use the following command:

```
# sacadm -a -p contty -t ttymon -c /usr/lib/saf/ttymon -v `ttyadm -V`
```

Tip

Using the ` character around a command causes the command to be executed and the output of the command substituted in the original command line. In this case, the `` `ttyadm -V` `` *returned a* 2.

Removing Port Monitors

To remove a port monitor, use the `-r` option. You must specify the port monitor by its pmtag, with the `-p` option. It will no longer appear in the `sacadm -l` listing, nor in the /etc/saf/_sactab. Its directory in /etc/saf will remain intact unless another port monitor of the same name is added, at which time the files are overwritten. To remove the contty port monitor added in the preceding command, use

```
# sacadm -r -p contty
```

Starting Port Monitors

To start a port monitor, use the `-s` option. Its status will show as `STARTING`, then `ENABLED`, after the startup is complete. When a port monitor starts, it reads its _pmtab file to determine which ports to monitor. To start the contty port monitor, use

```
# sacadm -s -p contty
```

Stopping Port Monitors

To stop a port monitor, use the `-k` option. Its status will be reported as `NOTRUNNING`. Services associated with the stopped port monitor will no longer be available. Because the ttymon handles logins only, a user currently logged in on a port administered by the stopped monitor will not be affected until the user logs out. At that point, no new login prompt will be displayed.

After a port monitor has been stopped, it must be restarted with the `-s` option to `sacadm` in order to restore services to the ports under its control. To stop the contty port monitor, use

```
# sacadm -k -p contty
```

Enabling Port Monitors

To enable a port monitor, use the `-e` option to `sacadm`. Enabling a port monitor does not cause it to re-read the _pmtab. To enable the contty port monitor, use

```
# sacadm -e -p contty
```

Disabling Port Monitors

To disable a port monitor, use the `-d` option to sacadm. This will cause the status to be displayed as `DISABLED`. Services handled by the given port monitor will stop immediately. As with stopping, disabling a port monitor will not affect users logged in on ports handled by the disabled monitor until they log out. At that point, no login prompt will be displayed. See the "`ttyadm`" section for information on setting a message to be displayed to a port when either the port itself or the monitor for that port is disabled.

Remember that disabling and re-enabling a port monitor does not cause the _pmtab to be re-read. Thus, if changes have been made to the services associated with a port monitor, it must be stopped and restarted for the changes to take effect.

To disable the contty port monitor, use

```
# sacadm -d -p contty
```

pmadm

The `pmadm` command administers individual port monitors. It performs the following functions:

- Add, remove, enable, and disable individual services.
- Add or delete authentication scheme and user ID information.
- Install or replace a per-service configuration script (/etc/saf/<*pmtag*>/<*svctag*>).

Listing Services

The `pmadm` command with the `-l` option lists all port monitors and services configured. To list the services associated with an individual port monitor, use the `-p` option and the pmtag. For instance, the following command will list all services for the contty port monitor:

```
# pmadm -l -p contty
PMTAG       PMTYPE     SVCTAG    FLGS   ID    SCHEME      <PMSPECIFIC>
contty      ttymon     2         u      -     login       /dev/vt02 - -
  /usr/bin/shserv - console - Login (vt02):  - - - -  #
contty      ttymon     3         u      -     login       /dev/vt03 - -
  /usr/bin/shserv - console - Login (vt03):  - - - -  #
contty      ttymon     4         u      -     login       /dev/vt04 - -
  /usr/bin/shserv - console - Login (vt04):  - - - -  #
contty      ttymon     5         u      -     login       /dev/vt05 - -
  /usr/bin/shserv - console - Login (vt05):  - - - -  #
contty      ttymon     6         u      -     login       /dev/vt06 - -
  /usr/bin/shserv - console - Login (vt06):  - - - -  #
contty      ttymon     7         u      -     login       /dev/vt07 - -
  /usr/bin/shserv - console - Login (vt07):  - - - -  #
contty      ttymon     8         u      -     login       /dev/vt08 - -
  /usr/bin/shserv - console - Login (vt08):  - - - -  #
```

Note

Each line in the preceding output is more than 80 columns long. The individual lines begin with the port monitor tag, in this case `contty`.

To uniquely identify a service, you must use both the pmtag assigned to the port manager and the svctag assigned to the service.

Adding a Service

To add a new service to a port monitor, use the `-a` option to pmadm. A service tag, port monitor specific information (specific to `ttymon` or `listen`, for instance), and the port monitor version number are required fields. By default, a new service is enabled upon creation. See the section on `ttyadm` for an example of adding a new service.

Removing a Service

Use the `-r` option to remove a service from a port monitor. This removes the associated entry from the /etc/saf/<*pmtag*>/_pmtab. If the monitor is currently running, the service will continue until the monitor is stopped and restarted, at which point it re-reads the _pmtab. To remove the login prompt from vt08, which is a part of the contty port monitor and has a svctag of `8`, run

```
# pmadm -r -p contty -s 8
```

Enabling a Service

To enable a service, use `pmadm` with the `-e` flag. If the port monitor specified is enabled, the newly enabled service is immediately available. To enable the login prompt for vt08, use

```
# pmadm -e -p contty -s 8
```

Disabling a Service

To disable a service, use the `-d` flag. The service is not stopped until the associated port monitor has been stopped and restarted with the `-k` and `-s` options to `sacadm`. Disabling and re-enabling the port monitor with the `-d` and `-e` options to `sacadm` will not cause the disabling of the service. See the "`ttyadm`" section for help on setting a message to be sent when a service is disabled. To disable the login prompt for vt08, run

```
# pmadm -d -p contty -s 8
```

OpenServer 5 Tip

Using the `-e` and `-d` options with `pmadm` for ports using `ttymon` is similar to using `enable` and `disable` with a device name for ports using getty. In UnixWare 7, the `enable` and `disable` commands are used exclusively with the print service.

ttyadm

The SAF requires each port monitor to provide a command that can be used to format and output data that can then be passed to the `pmadm` and `sacadm` commands. The two most commonly used port monitors are `ttymon` (to monitor login ports) and `listen` (to monitor network requests). The `pm`-specific commands for each are `ttyadm` and `nlsadmin`, respectively.

The `ttyadm` command is the front end for the ttymon daemon. It can be used to control many aspects of a service, including the setting of the bidirectional port flag (`-b`), the starting label in the /etc/ttydefs file for baud rate searches (`-l`), and the inactive (`disabled`) message (`-i`). It can also be used with the `-V` option to report the current version number.

Remember that `ttyadm` merely formats the information for use with `pmadm` or `sacadm`, and does not effect the change itself.

Because the `pmadm` command does not support an update capability for the basic information associated with a service, the service must be removed and readded to the port monitor to change any aspects other than the scheme and user ID associated with the service. (See the man pages for `pmadm` for more on the scheme and user ID settings.)

The command line required for adding a service can become quite lengthy and complex. Therefore, it is helpful to write scripts to perform these functions. As an example, the command

```
# pmadm -a -p ttymon1 -s term00 -S login -fu -v `ttyadm -V` \
-m "`ttyadm -d /dev/term/00 -l auto -s /usr/bin/shserv \
-p \"Serial Port Login: \" -i \"Service Disabled\"`"
```

starts a service with the following characteristics:

- Is associated with the ttymon1 port monitor
- Has a service tag of `term00`
- Uses the login scheme
- Creates a `utmp` entry
- Is associated with device /dev/term/00 (first serial port)
- Invokes /usr/bin/shserv
- Uses autobaud (automatic detection of baud rate)
- Gives a login prompt of `Serial Port Login:`
- Displays an inactive message of `Service Disabled`

The `\` at the end of each of the first two lines indicates to the shell that the command is being continued on subsequent lines. There can be no spaces after the `\`.

Another example of using `ttyadm` in concert with `pmadm` is the following script, which adds four additional virtual terminals to UnixWare 7. This results in 11 text login prompts, as in OpenServer 5.

```
for i in  09 10 11 12
do
pmadm -a -p contty -s $i -S login -fu -v `ttyadm -V` \
-m ì`ttyadm -d /dev/vt$i -l console -s /usr/bin/shserv \
-p \"Login (vt$i): \"`"
done
```

This adds four services, with tags `09`, `10`, `11`, and `12`, to the contty port monitor. It specifies a login scheme for authentication; that a `utmp` entry should be created; devices /dev/vt09 through /dev/vt12; the label “console” from the /etc/ttydefs file; that /usr/bin/shserv is the service to be invoked; and that the login prompt should be

```
Login (vt$i):
```

where `$i` is from `09` to `12`.

OpenServer 5 Tip

The console multiscreens in UnixWare 7 are named /dev/vt##, as opposed to the /dev/tty## found in OpenServer. Also, when scologin is disabled in OpenServer 5, a character login prompt appears in its place. In UnixWare 7, you must explicitly add `vt01` *to a port monitor's list; for instance, to the list of ports monitored by* `contty`.

/etc/ttydefs

The /etc/ttydefs file is used by `ttymon` to define the speed and terminal settings for a tty port. Each entry contains five colon-delimited fields. These fields contain

- tty label
- initial flags
- final flags
- autobaud
- next label

The `tty` label is used by `ttyadm` with the `-l` option to specify a starting point for baud rate searches.

The individual flags in the next two fields are separated by spaces. The initial flags are applied after the default flags (see the man page for `ttydefs` for the defaults) and remain in effect during the authentication sequence. The final flags are applied just before invoking the port's service.

If the autobaud field contains an `A`, `ttymon` will auto-detect the baud rate.

The final field contains the next label to try.

A partial /etc/ttydefs file is shown below:

```
# Auto baud rate, auto size/parity (good for direct lines)
auto: sane imaxbel iexten echoctl echoke -tabs cs8 -parenb ::A: 9600

# Fixed baud rate, default size/parity with hunt sequence
115200: 115200 sane imaxbel iexten echoctl echoke -tabs ::: 57600
57600: 57600 sane imaxbel iexten echoctl echoke -tabs ::: 38400
38400: 38400 sane imaxbel iexten echoctl echoke -tabs ::: 19200
19200: 19200 sane imaxbel iexten echoctl echoke -tabs ::: 9600
9600: 9600 sane imaxbel iexten echoctl echoke -tabs ::: 4800
4800: 4800 sane imaxbel iexten echoctl echoke -tabs ::: 2400
2400: 2400 sane imaxbel iexten echoctl echoke -tabs ::: 1200
1200: 1200 sane imaxbel iexten echoctl echoke -tabs ::: 300
300: 300 sane imaxbel iexten echoctl echoke -tabs ::: 115200
```

OpenServer 5 Tip

The /etc/ttydefs file replaces the /etc/gettydefs file as the reference file for labels indicating baud rate and flow control information. The single character labels (`m`, `n`, `o`, and so on) no longer appear. The login prompt to be displayed is not part of the entry in /etc/ttydefs. It is set with the `-p` option to `ttyadm`. Also, the `sane` command to restore terminal defaults no longer affects size or parity.

sttydefs

The `sttydefs` command is used to maintain the /etc/ttydefs file. `sttydefs` with the `-l` option displays the contents of the /etc/ttydefs file and can be run by any user on the system. If a label is specified, only the record matching that label is displayed. Here is an example of the output for a single label:

```
# sttydefs -l 115200
UX:sttydefs: INFO:
--------------------------------------------------------------
115200: 115200 sane imaxbel iexten echoctl echoke -tabs ::: 57600
--------------------------------------------------------------

UX:sttydefs: INFO: ttylabel:     115200
UX:sttydefs: INFO: Initial flags:        115200 sane imaxbel iexten
echoctl echoke -tabs
UX:sttydefs: INFO: Final flags:
UX:sttydefs: INFO: autobaud:
UX:sttydefs: INFO: nextlabel:   57600
```

`sttydefs` can be used with the `-a` option to add a label or with the `-r` option to remove a label. See the man pages on `sttydefs` for details on maintaining the /etc/ttydefs file.

Serial Manager

Two standard COM ports are usually installed on a system. There can be up to four. The device names used for these ports are as follows:

/dev/term/00	COM1
/dev/term/01	COM2
/dev/term/02	COM3
/dev/term/03	COM4

In addition, a character may be added to the device name to indicate the type of flow control used on the port.

/dev/term/##	Software flow control
/dev/term/##h	Hardware flow control
/dev/term/##s	Software flow control

/dev/term/##m	Modem (no flow control)
/dev/term/##t	Terminal (no initial flow control)

The first four serial devices can still be accessed using the more traditional UnixWare device names of /dev/tty00 through /dev/tty03. This is also true of the device names that specify flow control (dev/tty01h=/dev/term/01h).

The Serial Manager provides a painless method of configuring standard COM ports (see Figure 10.2). It handles the `sacadm`, `ttyadm`, and `pmadm` commands. It is reached from the SCOadmin Manager through Hardware, Serial Manager.

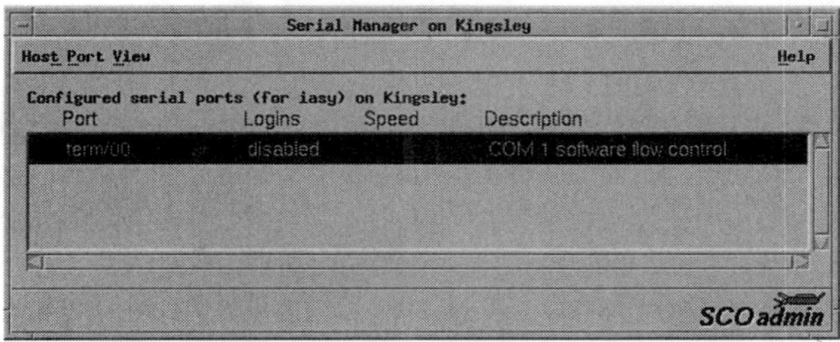

FIGURE 10.2 *The Serial COM Port Manager.*

Configuring COM Ports

To configure a serial port, click once to highlight the desired port, then select Port, Modify. You can also double-click the port. This brings up the Modify Serial Port window, as shown in Figure 10.3.

The port type offers four options:

- Software flow control
- Hardware flow control
- Terminal
- Modem

The type selected will determine the device name used. (See the serial port naming conventions at the beginning of this section.)

The port can be configured as outgoing, incoming, or both. Setting a modem port for both incoming and outgoing allows the modem to be used for dialin as well as for outgoing cu, uucp, SLIP, and PPP connections.

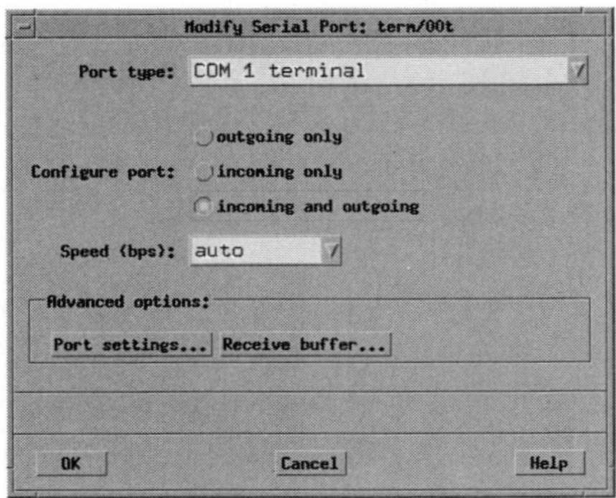

FIGURE 10.3 *Modifying a serial port.*

The baud rate can either be explicitly set or left to Auto for cycling through available baud rates. SCO recommends using the Auto setting for terminals. The Auto setting should not be used for incoming or bidirectional lines using *smartmodems* (modems that can simultaneously communicate at different speeds on the line and the port). With these modems, set the speed to the highest baud rate supported by the modem. Be sure to use the same speed for outgoing cu connections that ttymon is using for incoming connections. Otherwise, the modem will be left using the speed set by cu.

Author's Note

The Auto setting works nicely for terminals set up to and including 19200. For terminals at 38400, it is necessary to press the Break key repeatedly before each login to get the speed properly set. Explicitly setting the port to 38400 avoids the need for cycling through speeds, which may be more comfortable for an end user.

Stallion EasyIO: A Third-Party Serial Port Board

To add more serial ports to a system, a third-party serial port board is often used. Serial port boards and their drivers are not provided by SCO, but are available from other vendors. Each will have its own specific installation methods.

An example of a third-party COM port board is the EasyIO, of the Stallion family of boards. The EasyIO is an intelligent board, and drivers are included with the product. As a result, the ports do not appear in the Serial Manager as COM ports. The ports are administered through software provided with the product.

Loading the Software and Drivers

To install the software and drivers, use `pkgadd` (see Chapter 13, "Software Installation") and install all packages. After the package has been added, run easyadm from the command line. The Administration utility is shown in Figure 10.4. Configuration for the board itself should be performed before the board is physically installed.

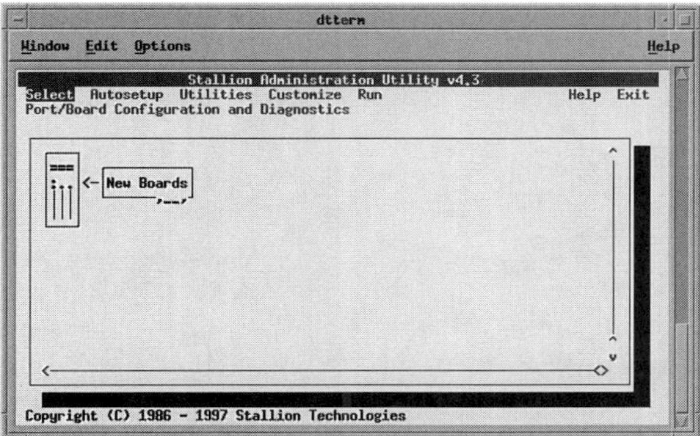

FIGURE 10.4 *Administration utility for Stallion EasyIO.*

Configuring a New Board

To configure a new board, choose Select, New Boards. Stallion recommends installing new boards in single-user mode. Select the board being installed from the list provided, as shown in Figure 10.5. Recommended settings are given for the configuration information. Other choices can be displayed by pressing F3.

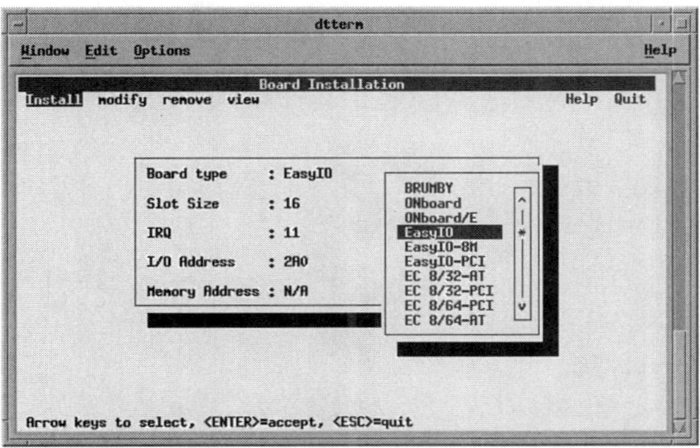

FIGURE 10.5 *Installing a new EasyIO board.*

After the settings have been entered, a representation of the board is shown with the selected configuration settings. This illustration varies for different boards and shows the proper dip switch settings, as shown in Figure 10.6.

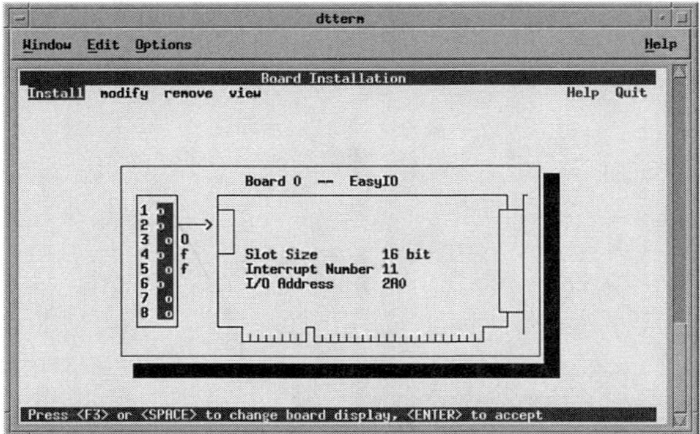

FIGURE 10.6 *Recommended board switch settings.*

After the settings have been entered and the dip switches on the actual board set as indicated in the diagram, you can exit the Administration utility. It will ask you whether to commit the changes and rebuild the kernel, or exit and lose the changes. After the kernel has been rebuilt, shut down and power the machine off to install the board. When the machine is rebooted, re-enter the `easyadm` utility to configure the ports.

Configuring the Ports

From the main menu, choose Select, then highlight the ports associated with the new board and press Enter (see Figure 10.7).

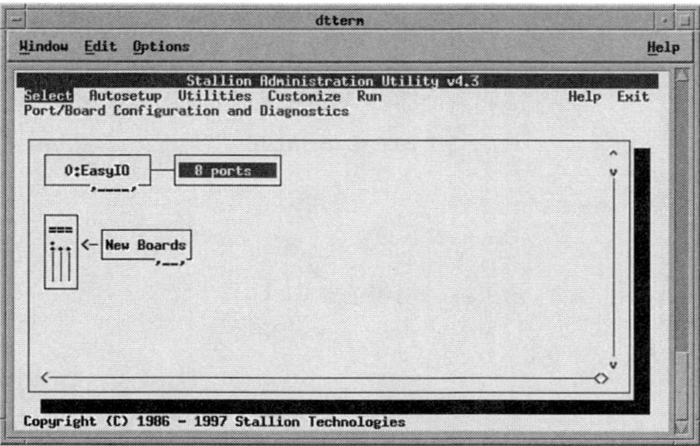

FIGURE 10.7 *Configuring ports.*

After selecting the group of ports, you enter the Panel Configuration (shown in Figure 10.8). Choose Select, then highlight the port to configure. This takes you to the Port Configuration screen.

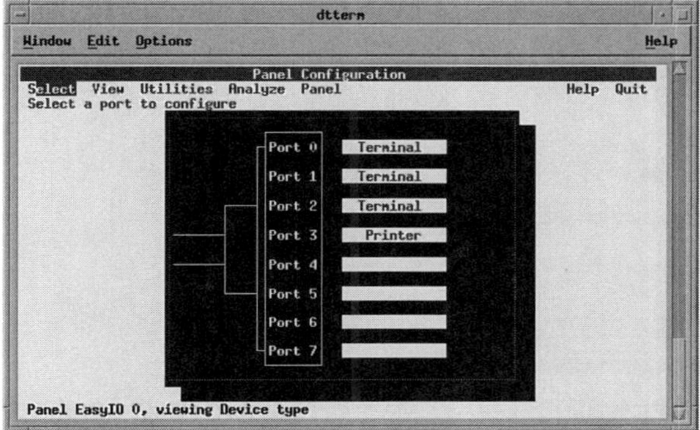

FIGURE 10.8 *Selecting a port for configuration.*

To add a new device to the port, select Configure. A drop-down box lists the following selections:

- Terminal
- Printer
- Modem
- UUCP Link
- Session
- Attached printer
- Other

The selections Session and Attached printer are available only after an initial device has been added to the port.

Printer Configuration

To configure a printer, first select Printer from the list. This brings up the window shown in Figure 10.9. Specify whether this is a UNIX printer (available through the print service) or a raw device.

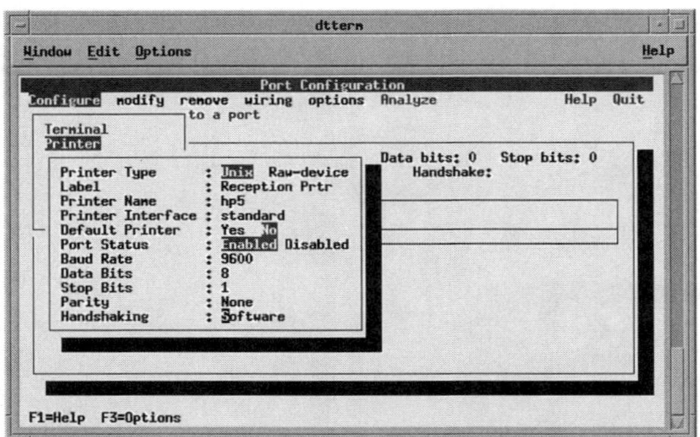

FIGURE 10.9 *Configuring a printer.*

A label may be entered for easy identification within the Stallion Administration software. To see these labels, rather than device types, on the Panel Configuration screen shown in Figure 10.8, go to that screen and choose View, Labels.

The printer name entered is the name to be used by the UNIX print service. The interface to be used is entered here. You can also specify whether the new printer should be used as the system default, as well as whether the printer should be enabled or disabled initially.

Communications parameters are also entered here. A baud rate of 9600, with 8 data bits, 1 stop bit, no parity, and software handshaking (XON/XOF) should work well for standard serial printers.

Terminal Configuration

Specifying a terminal for the selected port opens the window shown in Figure 10.10. The terminal type is set here. As with printers, an optional label may be entered for use within the Stallion Administration software.

You can specify whether the port should be Enabled or Disabled, as well as whether the baud rate should be Stable or Cycling. Choosing Cycling causes different baud rates to be tried by pressing the Break key on the terminal.

The Hotkey specification is used to configure multiple sessions for the terminal. After the terminal itself has been configured, go back to Configure and select Sessions.

The parameters for serial communications are set here as well. The speed should match the speed of the terminal being used. As with printers, a typical serial terminal configuration might be set to 8 data bits, 1 stop bit, no parity, and software handshaking (XON/XOFF), with the Hangup on DCD drop set to No. The port settings should match the setup on the terminal being used.

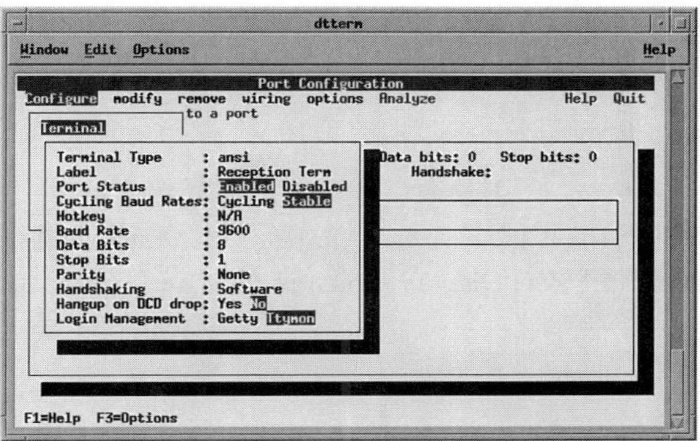

FIGURE 10.10 *Configuring a terminal.*

As mentioned earlier in the chapter, while `ttymon` is the preferred method of login management, getty capabilities are included for compatibility with applications that expect a getty process. This configuration screen allows you to select getty management.

The Stallion software handles creating the new port monitor, which in this case is tagged `EasyIO0`. It also enters the services for each port configured for use with a terminal. Following is the result of a `pmadm -l` command showing a configuration with terminals using `ttymon` login management on ports 0, 1, and 5:

```
# pmadm -l -p EasyIO0
PMTAG      PMTYPE    SVCTAG     FLGS ID   SCHEME     <PMSPECIFIC>
EasyIO0    ttymon    tty0a00    u         -          login  /dev/tty0a00
➥ h - /usr/bin/shserv - Easyadm1 ldterm login:  - - - -  #
EasyIO0    ttymon    tty0a01    u         -          login  /dev/tty0a01
➥ h - /usr/bin/shserv - Easyadm1 ldterm login:  - - - -  #
EasyIO0    ttymon    tty0a05    u         -          login  /dev/tty0a05
➥ h - /usr/bin/shserv - Easyadm1 ldterm login:  - - - -  #
```

If you specified getty login management, a file with the getty process set to respawn is created in the /etc/conf/init.d directory. Also, the getty process is started on the port immediately. Following are a process listing and configuration file that resulted from configuring the terminal on port 2 for getty login:

```
# ps -ef ¦ grep getty
root  1950     1   TS   80   0 11:05:56 tty0a02  0:00 /etc/getty tty0a02
Easyadm0
```

continues

```
# cat /etc/conf/init.d/atamod
apE::sysinit:/sbin/autopush -f /etc/ap/easyio.ap
EKum:23:respawn:/etc/getty tty0a02 Easyadm0
```

If getty processes are used for login, the `pmadm` and `sacadm` commands have no effect on the login. Disabling or stopping the EasyIO0 port monitor would prevent logins only on the ports using `ttymon`.

Monitoring Ports

Individual ports can be monitored by selecting Analyze, Monitor from the Port Configuration screen. A sample Port Display screen is shown in Figure 10.11.

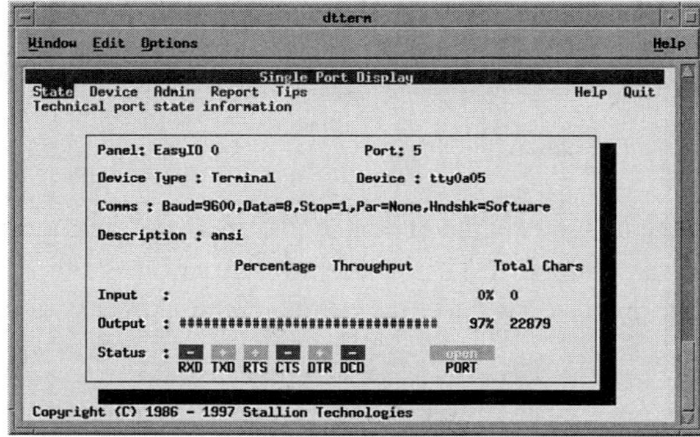

FIGURE 10.11 *Monitoring a port.*

CHAPTER 11

Printer Configuration

- The Print Service
  Learn how the UnixWare 7 Print Service works. The commands look familiar, but there are differences in the implementation.
- Controlling print jobs
  Learn about the Print Job Manager and how to use it.
- Parallel and serial ports
  Learn how to configure parallel and serial printers. Learn about printing to HP JetDirect network printers and how to use the features of these printers through your own print scripts.

The UnixWare 7 Print Service

The UnixWare 7 print subsystem will be familiar to administrators and users migrating from OpenServer 5 and UnixWare 2. Some differences occur in the locations of files and the way the system works. The `lpstat`, `lpsched`, `lpshut`, `accept`, `reject`, `enable`, and `disable` commands are all there, though.

> *OpenServer 5 Tip*
>
> *The /var/spool/lp/admins/lp directory is a link to /etc/lp. Because /etc/lp requires less typing, it is easier to* `cd` *to /etc/lp/interfaces than to /var/spool/lp/admins/lp/interfaces.*

Print Request Issuing

When a print request is issued using the `lp` command, the request is sent to lpsched. If the printer is rejecting requests, an error message is immediately displayed. If the printer is accepting requests, the print request is placed into the /var/spool/lp/tmp/<machine_name> directory. The filename of the information is the request ID with an extension, `-0`. The following listing shows the file named 17-0, the control information for print request ID 17.

```
C 1
D oki400
F /etc/hosts
O locale=C flist='/etc/hosts:506'
P 20
t simple
U root
s   0000
```

To decipher the preceding list:

> `C` is the number of copies to be printed, which is one in this case.
>
> `D` is the printer.
>
> `F` is the path to the filename. If the file was printed with the `-c` (make a copy) option to lp, then a file 17-1 would be in the directory and the `F` data would point to it.
>
> `O` contains the locale, the file list, and size (506 characters). The locale affects how information on the banner page will be formatted, such as the date.
>
> `P` is the priority (default is 20).
>
> `t` is the print job type (PCL, simple, PS). The filtering of the print job is affected by the print job type.
>
> `U` is the user who submitted the request.
>
> `s` is the outcome.

After the print job has completed, the information is moved to the /var/lp/logs/requests.1 file.

From the spool directory, the request is sent to the interface script, which initializes the device and sends the request to the device. For every printer created, a subdirectory exists in the /etc/lp/printers directory. The configuration for the printer is kept in the /etc/lp/printers/<printer_name>/configuration file. Two such files follow, one for a local printer and one for remote.

For a remote printer on a system named thor with an HP Laser using PCL, use

```
Banner: on:Always
Content types: pcl
Printer type: hplaserjet
Remote: thor!hp5si
```

```
Range: 3,8
Form feed: on
```

For a local parallel port printer, use

```
Banner: on
Content types: simple
Device: /dev/lp
Interface: /usr/lib/lp/model/standard
Printer type: oki-ol400
Modules: default
Form feed: on
```

After the print job has been spooled, lpsched will invoke the interface script in /etc/lp/interfaces that is named for the printer. Unlike in OpenServer 5, most printers, except PostScript, use a standard interface in UnixWare 7. In OpenServer 5, it was easy to modify the interface script for HP Lasers, Epsons, and the like; here the interface script is always the same. The controls for the printer are in the `terminfo` definitions. In /usr/share/lib/terminfo are source files and the directories holding the compiled `terminfo` entries for each printer.

> *Tip*
>
> *If you need to modify a `terminfo` entry, use infocmp(1M) to decompile the entry, use an editor to change the entry, and use tic(1M) to recompile it.*

Print Banners

Banners are set through administration to `on` or `on:Always`. The `on` setting allows users to override on the `print` command line with `-o nobanner`. The `on:Always` setting requires banners. To stop banners, edit the interface script and search for the line

```
nobanner="no"
```

and change it to

```
nobanner="yes"
```

> *Author's Note*
>
> *I always used the capability of OpenServer 5's HP Laser script to allow 66 text lines per page. This was commented out by default in the script. I have not been able to duplicate this through the UnixWare 7 controls. The `-o length=66` sets page length, not the number of text lines. I tried copying the OpenServer 5 Laser script to UnixWare 7, but each attempt to print resulted in a printer error. See the section "Using Scripts to Control Printing to HP" at the end of this chapter to see a workaround.*

Printer Creation

When printers are created, the entries in the /etc/lp/printers and /etc/lp/interfaces are created. Printers that print to a network printer on another host will not have an entry in the /etc/lp/interfaces directory. Their pointer to the remote system is contained in the configuration file in the /etc/lp/printers/<printer_name> directory, as was shown for the printer on thor:

```
remote: thor!hp5si
```

When configuring HP network printers, two entries are made in the /etc/lp/interfaces directory. The first is named for the printer as normal. However, this is not the true interface script. This script, when used with the HP Laser network printer configuration tools supplied with UnixWare 7, is a control script to get the print request through the actual interface and to the network printer. The actual interface script is in the /etc/lp/interfaces/model.orig directory. If the printer is named hp4000, there will be two files for the printer:

```
/etc/lp/interfaces/hp4000 /etc/lp/interfaces/model.orig/hp4000
```

UnixWare 7 supports lpd printing; however, there is no reference to /etc/printcap in the documentation for BSD style printing. The /etc/printcap and `lpd` command have been replaced by a sacadm port monitor that listens for the incoming requests. Use the `pmadm -l -p tcp` command to see the entries for ListenBSD and ListenS5.

Printer Setup Manager

The Printer Setup Manager is used to configure and control printers. Access to the Printer Setup Manager is through the SCOadmin GUI. Figure 11.1 shows the manager in the default, new-install state. The printer lmxnul is placed there during the installation of VisionFS.

The menus across the top of the window include the following functions:

Host	Open Host Open Host Group Exit
Printer	Add Local Printer Add TCP/IP Printer Add NetWare Printer (Make a local printer accessible to NetWare. Only if you installed NetWare support.) Copy Properties Make Default Control

	Set User Access
	Set Remote Access
	Nprinter (Printing to a NetWare que. Only if you installed NetWare support.)
	Delete
Server	Start
	Halt
View	Set Auto Refresh
	Refresh Now
Options	Point Help
	Toolbar
	Customize Toolbar

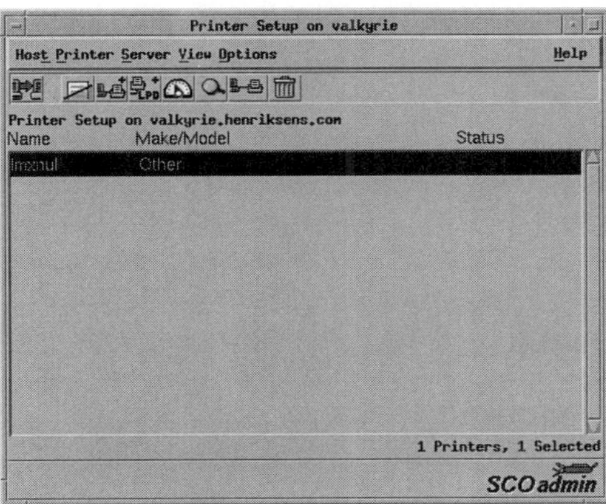

FIGURE 11.1 *The Printer Setup Manager.*

Add Local Printer

Adding a local printer requires a printer connected to a local parallel or serial port. From the Printer menu, click Add Local Printer. The window shown in Figure 11.2 appears. Enter a name for the printer. Select the Make/Model by scrolling through the list. Many more printer types are available with UnixWare 7 than were available with OpenServer 5 or UnixWare 2.

Select the connection type: Serial or Parallel. If the printer is parallel, select the connection port. If your printer port is LPT3, click Other and enter the device name. Note that the printer devices are not referred to as /dev/lp0 and /dev/lp1, but as LPT1 and LPT2. For serial printers, the window changes to provide choices of COM1 and COM2 plus Other. Also a Serial Configuration window appears, as shown in Figure 11.3, to allow setting the serial communication parameters of baud rate, parity, stop bits, and character size. For serial printers, the majority of problems are created by serial communications parameters.

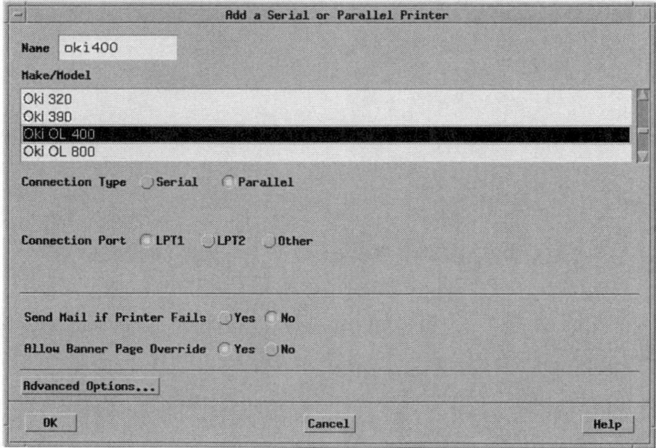

FIGURE 11.2 *Adding a local printer.*

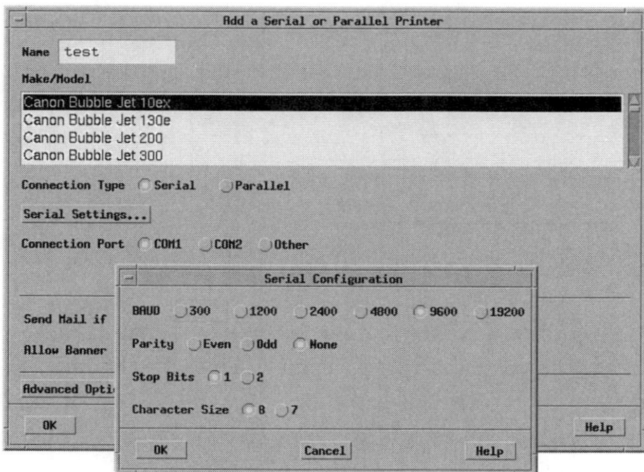

FIGURE 11.3 *Serial communications parameters.*

Select whether you desire mail sent when print jobs fail. Select to allow banner page overrides.

Tip

The banner page override does not prevent banners. It allows users to override the printing of banners by specifying the `-o nobanner` *option in the lp* `print` *command.*

The Advanced Options include Page Width, Page Length, Character Pitch, and Line Pitch. These work only with dot-matrix printers. These settings can be made from the command line with the `lpadmin` command.

Select OK to create the printer.

While adding a local parallel printer to a port where the printer is not connected or is turned off, you will receive an error message. This message warns that the system cannot communicate with the printer.

Add TCP/IP Printer

Network printing is everywhere in today's networks. Use the Add TCP/IP Printer window to create a networked printer. Figure 11.4 illustrates adding a TCP/IP printer.

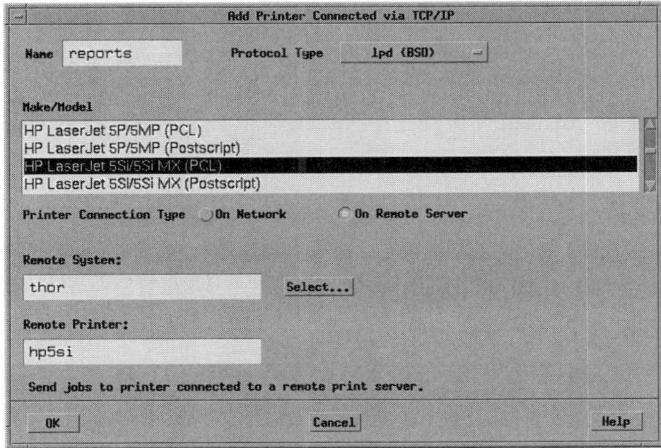

FIGURE 11.4 *Add a TCP/IP printer.*

Enter a printer name and select the Make and Model. The Protocol Type defaults to lpd, which is Berkeley Systems (BSD) style printing. The other option is System V, which is used with network printers, such as the Hewlett-Packard lasers with Jet Direct cards.

If the printer is connected to a remote UNIX (or other operating system that supports LPR/LPD), select On Remote Server. Enter the remote server name or click on Select to view available names from the name server or /etc/hosts file.

Enter the name of the printer on the remote computer. Click OK to create the printer.

For a network printer, select On Network and enter the remote printer name. The host name must be resolvable to an IP address.

Add NetWare Printer

To add a NetWare printer, enter the following:

- Printer name
- Make and model
- NetWare server name
- NetWare print queue

This will create a local printer that will print to a remote NetWare printer. See Chapter 9, "Services for NetWare," for more information on NetWare services.

Copy

To create a new printer that is similar to another printer, highlight the printer on the Printer Setup window and select Copy. Enter the new printer name. Change the make and model, connection type, and other parameters as required. An example of copying the printer created in Figure 11.2 is shown in Figure 11.5.

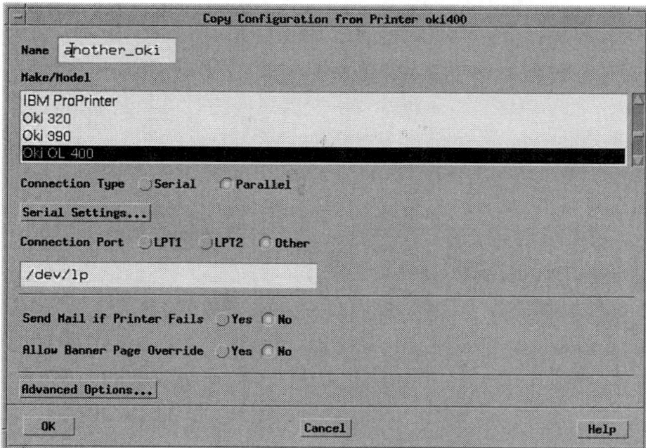

FIGURE 11.5 *Copying a printer.*

Properties

Select a printer, and select Properties from the Printer menu. The window shown is similar to the one used to create a printer. You may not change the name of a printer. On local printers you may change the port, but not the type (parallel or serial) to which they are connected.

Make Default

To make a printer the default for the system, highlight the printer and select Make Default from the Printer menu. The Status column of the Printer Setup will have the word `Default` to the right of the default printer.

Control

The Control option contains the enabled/disabled and accept/reject status of the printer. Figure 11.6 shows the window for Control Printer Job Submittal on Printer.

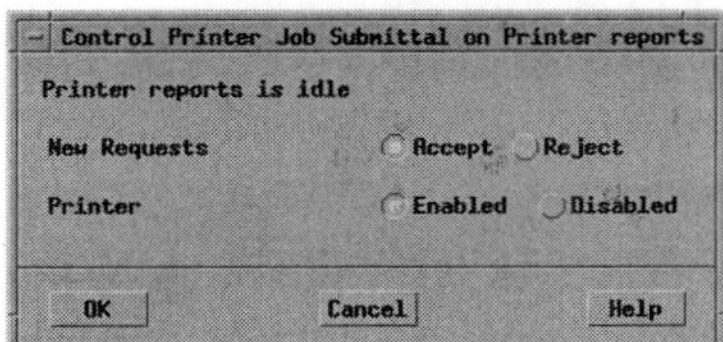

FIGURE 11.6 *The Control Printer Job Submittal window.*

Disabling a printer allows it to accept new jobs, but not print them. This is useful to temporarily stop a printer while adding toner and paper or while clearing a paper jam. Enabling a printer will restart jobs flowing to the printer. Enabling is also a way to restart a printer that had a fault.

Rejecting new requests will disallow any new print jobs from being queued for the printer. This is useful for printers that will be down for a longer period. Existing print jobs will continue to print. To stop them, you need to disable the printer.

When new printers are created, the printers are set to begin accepting new requests and are enabled to begin printing.

Set User Access

Access to the printer by local users can be restricted by the user. Figure 11.7 illustrates the process of denying access to a printer. The Allow List defaults to all accounts on the system. Highlight accounts and click Deny to add them to the Deny List. To return a denied account to the Allow List, highlight the name in the Deny List and click Allow.

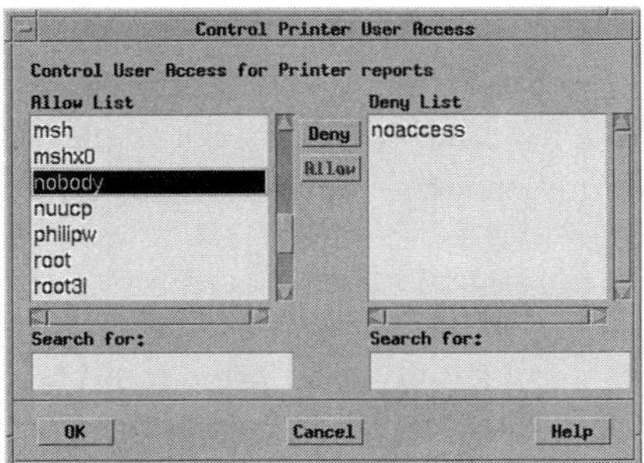

FIGURE 11.7 *The Control Printer User Access window.*

Control Printer Host Access

The Control Printer Host Access window allows the administrator to control remote access to a printer. Select the Access Mode (Allow or Deny) at the top of the window. Select host names from the Host List and click Add to add them to the list. Figure 11.8 illustrates this procedure.

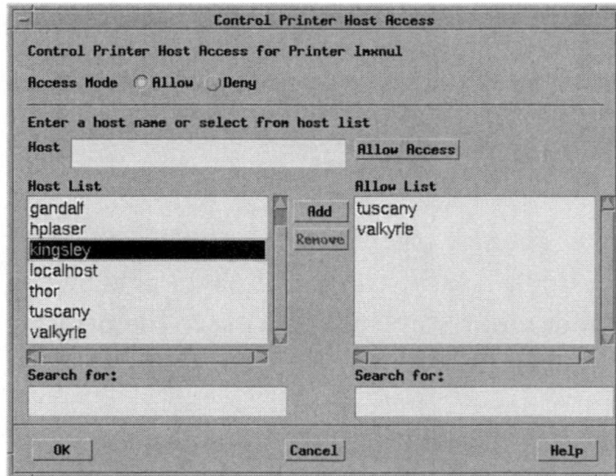

FIGURE 11.8 *The Control Printer Host Access window.*

When the hosts are allowed access, the files /etc/lp/printers/<printername>/users.allow and /etc/lp/printers/<printername>/users.deny are created.

Warning

A problem can occur when printing from one UnixWare 7 system to another using /etc/hosts files for host name to IP address resolution. The order of the Fully Qualified Domain Names (FQDN) and aliases in the /etc/hosts file on the printer host is significant. The users.allow and users.deny files use the host name, not the FQDN. The connections for remote printing are made by lpNet using the first name on the line with the IP address. If the FQDN occurs before the host name, a comparison of the names fails. The connections are logged in to /var/lp/logs/lpNet. If you cannot print to the host, check the log to see how the names are being logged compared to the names in the users.allow file. The order on the client system is not important.

The best solution to this problem: Edit the users.allow file and change the host names to FQDN. It is possible to reverse the order of the names in the /etc/hosts file to list the node name first and FQDN second. Although this fixes this problem, other network problems may appear. The problem is a bug in the Printer Setup Manager.

Below are two lines from the lpNet log. The order of FQDN and host name was switched, and the lp service stopped and restarted between these events. In the first line, the FQDN occurred before the host name. The second line shows the effect with the positions reversed.

```
08/04/98 08:59 c  1437 lorelei.henriksens.com lpd exiting, status=0
08/04/98 09:07 c  1458 lorelei lpd starting (passive)
```

Nprinter

To allow remote NetWare users print access to a local UnixWare printer, highlight the printer and select Nprinter from the Printer menu. Enter the name of the NetWare Server that contains the print servers that can route print requests to your local printer. You may need to log in to the server to accomplish this. Enter the NetWare Print Server or use the Select button to choose. Enter the NetWare Print Queue.

For more information on NetWare services, see Chapter 9.

Delete

Use this option to delete a printer. Highlight the printer and select Delete. The printer will not be deleted if print jobs are in the queue. To delete all jobs in the queue, use the Print Job Manager.

Server Start

Starts the print service if it has been halted.

Server Halt

This option halts the print service.

Command Line Print Service Control

The GUI presents an easy-to-use interface; but behind it the command line programs do the work. Those command line programs are available to the administrator for interactive use or shell scripting.

lpstat

The `lpstat` command is indispensable for checking on the status of one or more printers. The man pages for `lpstat` do not list the `-v` option, which lists the devices for each printer, but it works. A new option for OpenServer 5 users is `-R`. To list all print jobs in the queue ranked by priority, use the `-R`.

lp

The lp command spools print jobs to the printer queues. The lpr command is present in the /usr/ucb directory. The lp command is preferred; lpr is present for BSD compatibility. Also in the /usr/ucb directory are the lpq, lpc, lprm, and lptest commands.

lpadmin

The lpadmin command is used to create and control printers. Printers created with lpadmin are set to rejecting requests and disabled. You will need to run the accept and enable commands before they can be used.

To create an HP laser named hp1 attached to the parallel port using PCL with a printer interface of standard, use lpadmin as shown here:

```
lpadmin -p hp1 -T hplaser -I pcl -m standard -v /dev/lp0
accept hp1
enable hp1
```

To remove a printer, use the -x option. The print queue for the printer must be empty prior to attempting to remove the printer.

To make a printer the default for the system, use the -d option:

```
lpadmin -d hp1
```

To add a remote printer, use the -s *<server name>*. For a remote computer, you should also include the remote printer name:

```
lpadmin -p localhp -s lorelei!hplaser
```

When adding a remote printer, you must use the lpsystem command to register the remote system with the print service.

lpsystem

The lpsystem command defines communications parameters for remote print servers. The information is stored in the /etc/lp/Systems file. While this file can be edited with a text editor, it is recommended that you use the lpsystem command.

Three types of remote connections are supported:

- s5 (System V Release 4)
- bsd (SunOS)
- nuc (NetWare UNIX client)

The default is s5.

To add a new bsd connection, use

```
lpsystem -t bsd servername
```

Other options to the `lpsystem` command allow specifying a retry time and timeout. The *retry time* specifies the time to wait before attempting to re-establish an abnormally terminated connection. The *timeout* is the time to maintain a connection with no traffic.

The /etc/lp/Systems file contains lines specifying the parameters:

```
+:x:-:s5:-:10:2:-:-:Allow all System V connections
*:x:-:bsd:-:10:2:-:-:Allow all BSD connections
```

The + sign is used as a wildcard for s5 connections, and the * is the wildcard for bsd connections. To list the information for a system, use `lpsystem -l` *<system name>*:

```
# lpsystem -l thor
System:                      thor
Type:                        bsd
Connection timeout:          10 minutes
Retry failed connections:    after 2 minutes
Comment:                     none
```

To remove a connection, use the `-r` *<system name>* option. There can be no printers assigned to the system being removed.

The only reason given to edit the /etc/lp/Systems file is to support the ability on bsd connections of a root user on a remote system to remove jobs for any client on the server. To turn on this option, edit the file and replace the dash in the fifth field with a letter `t` (for *trusted*).

If you need a SunOS system to send print requests to UnixWare 7, the SunOS system will send them on port 515. You will need to configure this with `sacadm` and `nlsadmin`. Use the `-A` option to `lpsystem` to get the address you need to complete the configuration.

Other commands used in managing printers are:

- `enable` *<printer name>*—Allows spooled jobs to be sent to the printer.
- `disable` *<printer name>*—Stops print jobs from being sent to the printer. This is useful when performing maintenance on the printer, such as replacing ribbons, toner, or paper.
- `accept` *<printer name>*—Allows jobs to be spooled to the printer queue.
- `reject` *<printer name>*—Stops new print jobs from being spooled to the printer queue.

lpsched

To start the print service, run /usr/lib/lpsched. This is not normally necessary. /usr/lib/lpsched is a symbolic link to /usr/lib/lp/lpsched.

lpshut

To stop the print service, run /usr/lib/lpshut. This is not normally necessary.

Controlling Print Jobs

After the printers have been established, the users begin to send print requests to the queues. Unfortunately, printers seem to be among the problem-prone components due to the mechanical nature of printing. Managing the print jobs in the queues can be time consuming. The print jobs can be managed by the Print Job Manager in SCOadmin or from the command line.

Print Job Manager

The Print Job Manager provides a convenient way to manage print jobs from a graphical interface. The initial view of the Print Job Manager is shown in Figure 11.9. The jobs currently queued are shown.

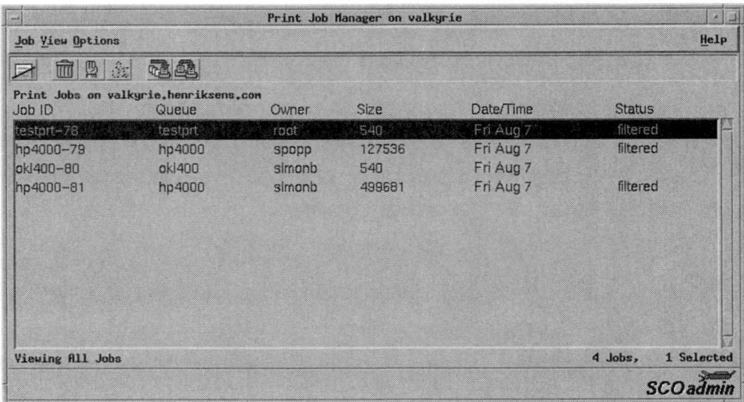

FIGURE 11.9 *The Print Job Manager.*

The Job Menu

The Job menu provides the actions that can be performed on print jobs. Figure 11.10 shows the Job menu. By default, the highlighted job is the one that will be acted upon.

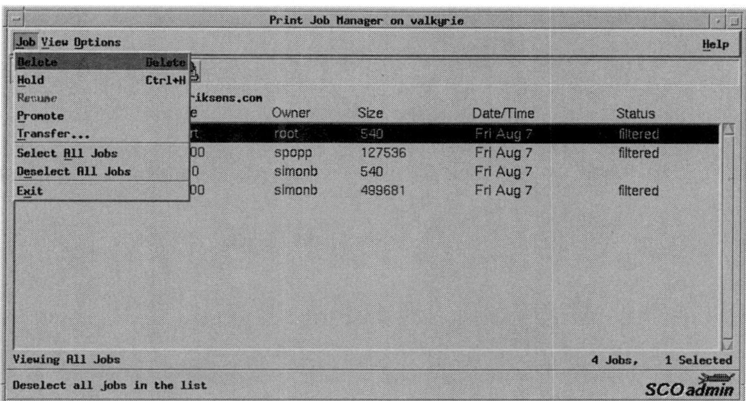

FIGURE 11.10 *The Job menu.*

Deleting Print Jobs

To delete a print job, highlight the job and select Delete from the menu. A window appears asking

```
Delete selected print job(s)?
```

Click OK to delete the job.

Holding a Print Job

To put a print job on hold, highlight the print job and select the Hold option. The job status will change to `Held`. When a Held job is highlighted, the Resume option becomes available in the menu.

Promoting a Print Job

To promote a print job to a higher priority and have it processed ahead of other jobs in the queue, highlight the print job and select Promote. The print queue will be reordered with the promoted job at the top.

Transfer a Print Job to Another Printer

To transfer a print job to another printer, highlight the print job and select Transfer. The window shown in Figure 11.11 appears. This window allows the selection of another printer. After transfer, the Job IDs remain the same, but the print queues will change.

To transfer all print jobs to another printer, choose Select All Jobs from the menu and then select Transfer.

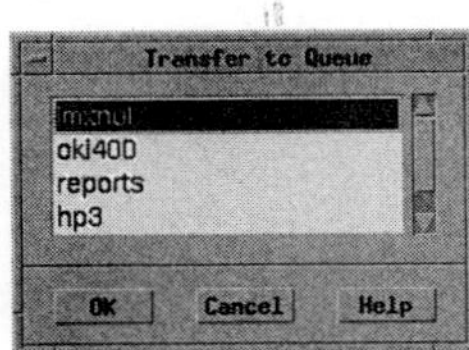

FIGURE 11.11 *Transferring a print job.*

The View Menu

The View menu allows the selection of the range of jobs to be displayed: all, by user, or by print queue.

The Set Auto Refresh option allows auto refresh to be turned off or on and the time interval for refresh to be set.

The Refresh Now option will refresh the status.

The Options Menu

The Options menu allows Point Help to be toggled on or off. The toolbar can be toggled on or off. The toolbar can be customized by adding or deleting icons.

Command Line Print Job Control

Print jobs can be controlled better from the command line than from the GUI. A good example is resuming a stopped printer job at a specific page, assuming a print filter is being used that can handle the page number requests:

```
lp -i <request-id> -H resume -P 10-
```

The `-P 10-` instructs the spooler to begin reprinting at page 10. The trailing dash on the `10` indicates to print through the end of file.

The `lp` command has many options for controlling the print jobs. The man pages provide just over seven pages of output on `lp` and its options.

The `cancel` command can be used to cancel one or more print requests. To cancel all print jobs for one user, use

```
cancel -u login-id
```

The `cancel` command will cancel the current job on the printer if executed as

```
cancel printer-name
```

Print jobs can be moved to other printers with the `lpmove` command.

```
lpmove request-id printer-name
```

will move a request to another printer.

```
lpmove printer1 printer2
```

will move all requests from *printer1* to *printer2*, and *printer1* will reject further print requests.

Parallel Ports

Printers attached to parallel ports are simple to configure in comparison to serial ports. Use the Device Configuration Utility to see if the parallel port is recognized.

```
                          UnixWare Device Configuration Utility
+----------------------- Hardware Device Configuration -----------------------+
¦          Device Name       IRQ    IOStart     IOEnd    MemStart    MemEnd     DMA  ¦
¦=    ===================    ===    =======     =====    ========    ========   ===  ¦
¦Y    Parallel Port          7      378         37f      -           -          -
```

If the parallel port is not recognized, check for possible conflicts with other devices.

UnixWare 7 can support two parallel ports. There are three general configurations for parallel ports:

Address	0x378	0x278	0x3bc
IRQ	7	5	7
Device Name	/dev/lp /dev/lp0	/dev/lp2	/dev/lp1

Most commonly, the first parallel port is 0x378. Some Compaq computers use 0x3bc as the primary. Occasionally, parallel ports are configurable as to the IRQ and the address. Take a few minutes to verify your configuration. With Compaq, use the System Partition utilities to provide the information if you are unsure.

Some printers, particularly new ones, require IEEE 1284 cables for two-way communication. Do not select longer parallel cables than required. Parallel transmission is more limited in distance than serial transmission.

If attaching a new laser-style printer, particularly a low-priced version, check first for UNIX compatibility. Some small printers require Windows software to control them and will not respond otherwise. These often do not have an emulation, such as HPIII, to use in the absence of the software. Such printers as the Okidata 4W are Windows-only printers.

Check the connectivity of the printer by redirecting output through the parallel port to the printer:

```
date > /dev/lp
```

If the date does not print on the printer, you have a connection problem.

Author's Note

If the printer prints letters that are occasionally incorrect, check to see if they are consistently wrong. For instance, if the incorrect value is always off by the same amount in the ASCII chart, there may be a broken wire carrying one of the bits to the printer. To check this, look at the misprinted characters. If there is always the same distance in the chart between the letter that should have printed and the letter that actually printed, then the wire(s) with those bits may have broken. I had a client who moved a printer and the result was `FALLS CHURCH` *printed as* `FADDS C@URC@`*. There was a difference of eight positions in the ASCII chart for both letters. Someone had jammed the printer cable against the wall, breaking the wire.*

Serial Ports

Serial ports may be smart ports, supplied with their own drivers by companies like Stallion and DigiBoard. See Chapter 10, "Configuration of Serial Ports and Terminal Devices," for more details on serial ports. The COM1 and COM2 ports that usually come installed on an Intel-based computer will appear in the Device Configuration Utility (DCU), as shown here:

```
                         UnixWare Device Configuration Utility
+----------------------- Hardware Device Configuration -----------------------+
¦        Device Name          IRQ    IOStart    IOEnd    MemStart    MemEnd    DMA  ¦
¦=    ===================     ===    =======    =====    ========    ========  ===  ¦
¦Y    COM Port                4      3f8        3ff      -           -         -    ¦
¦Y    COM Port                3      2f8        2ff      -           -         -    ¦
```

The ports for COM1 are represented in the /dev directory for OpenServer 5 compatibility as:

```
crw-rw-rw-    1 root     root      3,  3 May 15 15:09 tty1A
crw-rw-rw-    1 root     root      3,  2 May 15 15:09 tty1a
```

They have counterparts in the /dev/term directory:

```
crw-rw-rw-    1 root     root      3,  0 May 15 15:09 term/00
crw-rw-rw-    1 root     root      3,  1 May 15 15:09 term/00h
crw-rw-rw-    1 root     root      3,  3 May 15 15:09 term/00m
crw-rw-rw-    1 root     root      3,  0 May 15 15:09 term/00s
crw-rw-rw-    1 root     root      3,  2 May 15 15:09 term/00t
```

If your background is OpenServer, the tty1a and tty1A devices will act the same as OpenServer 5 devices. The term/00t is the same as tty1a. These should be used for software flow control, (XON/XOFF). The /term/00t can be used with a three-wire serial connection.

The tty1A device is the same as term/00h. Use these nodes for hardware flow control (RTS/CTS).

Test the serial printer in the same way as the parallel printer: Send data directly to the device. See Chapter 10 on configuring serial ports. With serial printers, you must take into consideration baud rate, parity, and word length in bits.

If the printer double-spaces the output, set the `-onlcr` option of the `stty` command in the interface script. This will stop the conversion of newlines to carriage-return/newlines. If the printer produces stair-step output down the page, the printer is set for printing DOS documents. Set the `onlcr` option of the `stty` command in the interface script to convert newlines to carriage return/newlines.

HP JetDirect Interface

There are two basic methods of configuring HP network printers. This is true for the external JetDirect Print Server devices as well as the internal cards on printers.

One method is to configure the IP address, netmask, and other parameters directly into the device. This configuration may be through the Control Panel on the printer, through the menu interface, or with telnet, depending on the device. If you need to telnet into an HP JetDirect print server, you will find the hardware or MAC address on the label for the device. The address will be six hexadecimal number pairs, such as: 00:60:B0:BA:6C:9A. To telnet into the device, use `arp` to create a static mapping from the MAC address to an IP address:

```
arp -s <ip address> <MAC address>
```

or

```
arp -s <hostname> <MAC address>
```

If you use the host name, it must appear in the /etc/hosts file. The MAC address should be colon separated. Once the `arp` command has been run, ping the host. If you can ping the host, telnet into the host and configure the IP parameters: IP address, netmask, and default gateway.

The other method is to configure the device as a bootp client. The default configuration for the HP device is to broadcast a request for a bootp server to discover its IP address.

The HP Network Configuration Script

UnixWare 7 provides the HP Network Printer (hpnp) utilities to configure the bootp server on UnixWare. The first step in using the hpnp utilities is to `cd` to /usr/lib/hpnp and run `hpnpinstall`. This will add support to the /etc/inetd.conf and /etc/services for the bootp protocol. The execution of `hpnpinstall` follows:

```
#hpnpinstall

                 HP Network Printer Configuration


Do you want to install or remove network printing (i/r/q)? [q]: i

Appending bootps entry to /etc/inetd.conf
Signalled inetd to re-read /etc/inetd.conf
You now need to run /usr/lib/hpnp/hpnpcfg to configure your printers.
Installation complete.
```

Author's Note

In spite of the preceding message about inetd being signalled to re-read the configuration file, I found that I had to reboot to get the bootp protocol working.

If the HP device does not have the MAC address printed on it (most printers do not), use the menu to print a configuration page. The JetDirect Print Servers generally have a button that will print a status sheet on an attached printer. The status sheet will include the MAC address and usually will show the IP address as 0.0.0.0. Before you can configure a printer for bootp, you must have the MAC address. You should also know the IP address and netmask you want to assign to the printer.

To start the configuration of the HP printer, run /usr/lib/hpnp/hpnpcfg.

```
#hpnpcfg
HP NETWORK PRINTER CONFIGURATION TASKS
                         MAIN MENU

        1) Verify installation of software
        2) Configure a printer with BOOTP/TFTP
        3) Verify BOOTP/TFTP configuration
        4) Verify network printer connectivity
        5) Verify network printer operation
        6) Add printer to spooler
        7) Remove printer BOOTP/TFTP configuration
        8) Remove printer from spooler

             ?) Help             q) Quit
```

```
Please enter selection:
```

Select option 1 to verify the software is correctly installed.

Author's Note

When I selected option 1, I received the following message:

```
The tftp service is not configured on this system.  Add the tftp
service to /etc/inetd.conf and create the tftp home directory
if it does not exist.  Signal inetd to read the /etc/inetd.conf
change. See the tftpd(1M) and inetd.conf(4) man pages for
details.

Press the return key to return to the main menu ...
```

To get the tftp service configured, find the following line in the /etc/inetd.conf file and remove the # from the left side.

```
#tftp     dgram    udp     wait     root     /usr/sbin/in.tcpd
in.tftpd -s /tftpboot
```

OpenServer 5 Tip

In OpenServer 5, to signal inetd to re-read its configuration file, you would use `kill -1` *similar to the following steps:*

```
ps -ef ¦grep inetd

kill -1 <PID_of_inetd>
```

The process is different on UnixWare 7 and is detailed in the /etc/inetd.conf file:

```
sacadm -k -p inetd
sacadm -s -p inetd
```

Troubleshooting Tip

I had to reboot to get the changes to take effect.

Configuring bootp for the HP Printer

To configure the bootp parameters for the HP printer, select option 2 from the hpnpcfg menu.

```
Enter peripheral's LAN hardware address: 0060B0BA6C9A

Enter the network peripheral name: hp4000

Enter IP address: 10.1.1.50

Add hp4000 to /etc/hosts? (y/n/q default=y):
```

```
Peripheral name and IP address have been added to /etc/hosts.
If your /etc/hosts file is updated automatically from a master
source, add the name and IP address to your master source after
the configuration is complete.

Enter subnet mask using dot notation (optional): 255.255.255.0

Enter default gateway name or address (optional):

Enter syslog server name or address (optional):

Enter idle timeout in seconds (default=90):

Do you want to limit printer access to certain hosts or
networks of hosts with an access list? (y/n/q default=n):

Do you want to configure SNMP related parameters? (y/n/q default=n):

Adding the following BOOTP entry to /etc/bootptab:

hp4000:\
         :ht=ether:\
         :ha=0060b0ba6c9a:\
         :sm=255.255.255.0:\
         :hn:\
         :ip=10.1.1.50:\
         :vm=rfc1048:

-------------------------------------------------------------

The printer BOOTP/TFTP configuration is complete.  Complete menu
item 3 to test the BOOTP/TFTP configuration before powering on your
printer.
```

Tip

Menu item 3 is not implemented. Ignore it.

If you turned on your printer to print a test page, turn it off, then turn it back on. Use option 4 to test the configuration. Option 4 pings the printer. If the printer does not respond, print a configuration page. Check the IP address to see if one was assigned. If an IP address was not assigned, the bootp server was not working. After three attempts, I rebooted the server. It worked after that.

If the printer responds, select option 5 to print a test page.

Configuring the HP Printer

To add the printer to the UnixWare print service, select option 6. The printer could also be added by using the Printer Setup Manager and selecting Add Network Printer with the connection on the network.

The questions and answer session is shown below. The term *lp spooler destination name* is what you want the local printer named. The *network peripheral name* is the host name in the /etc/hosts file for the printer. You need to know the printer type before starting this option; there is no help listing. Look in the file /usr/lib/scoadmin/printer/model.stz to locate all defined printer models. The context-type can be simple, PCL, or PS.

```
Enter the lp spooler destination name: hp4000

Enter the network peripheral name (default=hp4000):

Enter printer type: (default=unknown) hplaserjet

Enter context-type for printer (default=simple) PCL

Enter the spooler class for the peripheral to join (optional):

Will this be the default printer? (y/n/q default=n)

Ready to shut down the spooling system, configure the new destination,
and start the spooling system again.  When the spooling system is shut
down all printing will stop.  Any print requests that are currently
printing will be reprinted in their entirety when the spooling system
is restarted.

OK to continue? (y/n/q default=y)
```

You should now be able to print to the printer.

Configuring an HP as a Local Printer

In addition to printing over the network as previously described, it is possible to treat the printer as though it were connected to the local system through a pseudo-tty. The /usr/lib/hpnp directory is the location for the utility to set up this relationship. Use `hpnptyd` as follows:

```
/usr/lib/hpnp/hpnptyd -m /dev/ptypn -x host
```

where *n* is the pseudo-tty and *host* is the name of the printer. This will start a daemon process that redirects data sent to the pseudo-tty to the network printer. This will not automatically restart after a reboot. To make this permanent, add it to a startup script.

After you have the daemon running, use `lpadmin` or the Printer Setup Manager to create the printer.

The printer created in this manner can accept print requests from remote systems. See the `lpadmin`, `lpusers`, and `lpsystem` command sections earlier in the chapter for more information.

Using Scripts to Control Printing to HP

Application software does not always provide the capability to include the options to the `lp` command. Printing to a laser printer in landscape mode requires an option at print time, as does 66 text lines per page or compressed fonts.

A workaround for these limitations can be found in making an executable script that sets the options required and sends the file on to the print system. The file that follows has many options not currently in use. Uncomment the desired options, place the script in a directory as an executable, and use it instead of `lp`. The script will build a file with the desired HP PCL codes and forward the original wrapped in PCL commands to the lp system. This script is set to print 66 text lines per 8.5-by-11 page.

For applications that require several possible combinations, create scripts for each scenario and make them appear as printers in the application. All of the scripts can send their output to the same print queue, if necessary.

```
#-----------------------------------------------------------
#           For use with PCL 5 compliant HP Laser printers
#
#
# This script will que print jobs in a directory below /usr/tmp
# named by the printer name. It will then use lp to print the job.
#
# For example:
# If your printer name is hp3, the directory where hp3's print jobs
# will be queued is /usr/tmp/hp3
#
# Use the printer queue name here.
printer="hp3"
copies=1
# Determine if the temp directory exists, if not create it
if [ -d /usr/tmp/$printer ]
   then
      continue
   else
      mkdir /usr/tmp/$printer
      chmod 777 /usr/tmp/$printer
fi
#
```

```
# Build the file to be printed starting with the printer control codes
#
# Reset printer to default state
echo "\033%-12345X@PJL enter language=pcl" > /usr/tmp/$printer/$$_$copies
# Reset printer - pcl reset code
echo "\033E\c" >> /usr/tmp/$printer/$$_$copies
# Set line termination mode
echo "\033&k2G\c" >> /usr/tmp/$printer/$$_$copies
# Set landscape mode
#echo "\033&l1O\c" >> /usr/tmp/$printer/$$_$copies
# Set reverse landscape mode
#echo "\033&l3O\c" >> /usr/tmp/$printer/$$_$copies
# Set portrait mode
#echo "\033&l0O\c" >> /usr/tmp/$printer/$$_$copies
# Set reverse portrait mode
#echo "\033&l2O\c" >> /usr/tmp/$printer/$$_$copies
# Duplex commands
# Simplex - single sided copies
#echo "\033&l0S\c" >> /usr/tmp/$printer/$$_$copies
# Duplex - Long-Edge Binding
#echo "\033&l1S\c" >> /usr/tmp/$printer/$$_$copies
# Duplex - Short-Edge Binding
#echo "\033&l2S\c" >> /usr/tmp/$printer/$$_$copies
# Font Selection
# Set symbol set
#echo "\033(8U\c" >> /usr/tmp/$printer/$$_$copies
# Set fixed spacing
#echo "\033(s0P\c" >> /usr/tmp/$printer/$$_$copies
# Set point size
#echo "\033(s8.5V\c" >> /usr/tmp/$printer/$$_$copies
# Set style to upright solid
#echo "\033(s0S\c" >> /usr/tmp/$printer/$$_$copies
# Set stroke weight to medium
#echo "\033(s0B\c" >> /usr/tmp/$printer/$$_$copies
# Set primary pitch landscape mode
#echo "\033(s13H\c" >> /usr/tmp/$printer/$$_$copies
# Set primary pitch portrait mode
# echo "\033(s16.6H\c" >> /usr/tmp/$printer/$$_$copies
# Set VMI (vertical motion index) landscape mode
#echo "\033&l5.45C\c" >> /usr/tmp/$printer/$$_$copies
# Set VMI (vertical motion index) portrait mode
# echo "\033&l7.20C\c" >> /usr/tmp/$printer/$$_$copies
# Set lineprinter type
#echo "\033(s0T\c" >> /usr/tmp/$printer/$$_$copies
# Set text length and page length
echo "\033&l66p2e7.6c66F\c" >> /usr/tmp/$printer/$$_$copies
# Allow left margin adjustment - change 0L to 2L, 4L etc
#echo "\033&a3L\c" >> /usr/tmp/$printer/$$_$copies
# Use sed for CR->LF conversion - non AIX systems
#sed -e "s/$//g" $1 >> /usr/tmp/$printer/$$_$copies
# Put the file to be printed in the tmp file
cat $1 >> /usr/tmp/$printer/$$_$copies
```

```
# COBOL reports only. Fixes the cr-lf-eof problem in Cobol reports
#echo "" >> /usr/tmp/$printer/$$_$copies
# Reset the printer at end of job
### NOTE: make sure the last command string does NOT end in "\c"
echo "\033E\c" >> /usr/tmp/$printer/$$_$copies
# Print the file
lp -s -c -d $printer  /usr/tmp/$printer/$$_$copies
# Give lp a chance
sleep 3
# Clean up
rm /usr/tmp/$printer/$$_$copies
exit 0
#
# End of interface file
#
```

Author's Note

I have used the preceding scripts to create portrait 66-lines-per-page, portrait-compressed, and landscape 66-lines-per-page print drivers for software that does not support a long `lp` *command. Create the driver in /bin as hp4, hp4l, hp4w, and so on so that the command line becomes /bin/hp4 <filename>. This provides additional capabilities to software not designed for print line options.*

CHAPTER 12

Removable Media

- Tapes
  Learn how to add and access tape drives.
- CD-ROMs
  Learn how to add CD-ROM drives and mount CD-ROMs.
- Diskettes
  Find out how to access diskette drives and handle DOS floppies now that the DOS commands are no longer part of UnixWare 7.
- Backups
  Learn about several backup methods, both command-line and graphical.
- Sound cards
  Discover how to configure and test sound cards.
- Plug and Play
  Find out about using Plug and Play in UnixWare 7.

Adding Storage Devices

Adding storage devices is a simple operation with UnixWare 7 (provided, of course, that you have wisely chosen from the list of approved hardware). New storage hardware is recognized and device nodes are created at startup. Supported devices require no configuration, aside from hardware concerns such as SCSI IDs and termination or master/slave jumpers when using IDE.

To see the list of currently recognized devices, use `sdiconfig -l`.

The output for a system with a SCSI controller will look similar to

```
# sdiconfig -l
0:0,7,0: HBA       : (amd,1) AMD SCSI
  0,0,0: DISK      : SEAGATE ST52160N         0344
  0,2,0: TAPE      : ARCHIVE Python 25501-XXX6500
```

The results are very similar with an IDE controller, as shown here:

```
# sdiconfig -l
0:0,7,0: HBA       : (ide,1) Generic ESDI/IDE/ATA
  0,0,0: DISK      : Generic IDE/ESDI          1.00
```

Tapes

UnixWare 7 supports a wide variety of tape devices and two types of tape controllers for 1/4-inch cartridge tapes: SCSI and QIC-02. Installation varies slightly between SCSI and non-SCSI devices. Regardless of the type of drive, the UnixWare 7 tape driver treats the drive as a SCSI.

SCSI Tape Install

To add a SCSI tape drive, you may need to set the SCSI ID and ensure that the SCSI bus is properly terminated. See the SCSI tutorial in Chapter 2, "Hardware Configuration," for more on SCSI configuration, and follow the tape manufacturer's instructions.

After the device is physically configured, it is ready to be physically added to the system. Shut down the system, attach the new tape drive to the host adapter, and boot the system. You should then be able to access the tape drive.

Hot adding of any SCSI device uses the `sdiadd` command. See Chapter 19, "Storage Devices, Filesystems, and Permissions," for details on using `sdiadd`.

Non-SCSI Tape Install

To install a non-SCSI tape, you will first need to install the device driver software. After the software is installed, shut down the system and install the tape controller. The recommended controller settings for a QIC-02 or non-ATAPI IDE are

- IRQ 5
- I/O base address 300
- DMA channel 1

After the tape controller is installed, physically attach the tape drive to the controller and boot the system.

Tape Drive Names

A tape drive uses device names in the /dev/rmt directory; they are numbered sequentially as drives are added, with the first being 1. The device name used to access the tape specifies how the tape is to be handled. These include

- *ctape#*—Non-retensioning, rewinding device
- *ntape#*—Non-retensioning, non-rewinding device
- *rtape#*—Retensioning, rewinding device
- *nrtape#*—Retensioning, non-rewinding device
- *utape#*—Unload on close device

To add a package from the first tape drive, for example, use

```
#pkgadd -dctape1
```

In addition, the tape can be accessed using the SCSI nomenclature. For instance, a device on controller 1 with a target ID of 2 can be accessed with /dev/rmt/c1b0t2l0 and its variations for tape control (n, r, nr, and u).

To extract data from a tar archive in the first tape drive, for example, use

```
#tar xvf /dev/rmt/c1b0t2l0
```

The /dev/rmt/c0s0 syntax, as found in UnixWare 2, is still provided.

Tape Drivers

The mass storage target driver that supports tape controllers in UnixWare 7 is st01.

Non-SCSI tape controllers require either the ictha HBA (found on the UnixWare 7 Installation CD-ROM, which can be installed through the SCOadmin Application Installer) or a vendor-supplied device driver developed for use with UnixWare 7.

In early editions of UnixWare 7, there have been problems with installing the ictha HBA during system installation. It is recommended that the system be installed with the minimum required hardware, adding such peripherals as tape drives after installation.

Tape Commands

Two main commands can be used to control tape devices. They are `tapecntl` and `tape`.

tapecntl

`tapecntl` sends commands to the sub-device /dev/rmt/ntape# and defaults to ntape1 if not specified. Remember that some options might not be supported by some tape devices or device drivers. Options to `tapecntl` include

- *-e*—Erase the tape.
- *-r*—Reset the tape device.
- *-t*—Retension the tape.
- *-w*—Rewind the tape.

The default mode for I/O is a fixed block of 512 bytes. See the `tapecntl` man page for a complete list of options.

tape

The `tape` command can be used to perform some of the same functions as `tapecntl` and is provided for backward compatibility with OpenServer 5. If no device is specified, it defaults to the device named in /etc/default/tape. For example, to specify the first cartridge tape as the default for the `tape` command, create the following entry in /etc/default/tape:

```
device = /dev/rmt/ctape1
```

The following commands can be used with `tape` to effect the same results as the `tapecntl` flags previously listed:

- *erase*—Erase the tape.
- *reset*—Reset the tape device.
- *reten*—Retension the tape.
- *rewind*—Rewind the tape.
- *rfm*—Wind tape forward to the next file mark.

CD-ROMs

CD-ROM devices can be added to configured IDE or SCSI controllers.

CD-ROM Installation

As with installing tape devices, you should first verify that the SCSI host adapter or IDE controller you intend to attach to the device is configured. You can use the `sdiconfig` command for this purpose.

After configuring the CD-ROM drive (setting the ID and termination with a SCSI device), shut down the system, physically attach the device, and boot the system.

As noted in the section on tape drives, hot adding of any SCSI device uses the `sdiadd` command. See Chapter 19 for details on using `sdiadd`.

Tip

For ATAPI CD-ROM, a slave CD-ROM device is not supported without a master device on the same controller.

CD-ROM Device Names

The device names for CD-ROM drives are /dev/cdrom/cdrom# (block device) and /dev/rcdrom/cdrom# (character or raw device); and they are named sequentially, beginning with 1. The block device is also accessible as /dev/cdrom/c#b#t#l#, as shown here:

```
brw-rw-rw-    2 root     sys      110,   0 Sep 19 11:30 c1b0t5l0
brw-rw-rw-    2 root     sys      110,   0 Sep 19 11:30 cdrom1
```

Both cdrom1 and c1b0t5l0 share the same major and minor device numbers (110, 0). See Chapter 19 for a complete explanation of SCSI nomenclature.

CD-ROM Drivers

The mass storage target driver that supports CD-ROMs in UnixWare 7 is sc01.

UnixWare 7 supports both SCSI and IDE CD-ROMs. The IDE device driver supports IDE Advanced Technology Attachment (ATA) and ATA Packet Interface (ATAPI).

Troubleshooting Tip

There are some known problems with ATAPI IDE CD-ROMs. Check the Late News *Web site (accessible from* `doc.sco.com`*) for a list of models known to have difficulties, as well as those known to work. If you have a CD-ROM drive that is known to have problems, check the SCO Support Web site to see whether a downloadable supplement is available to add support for your device. A new IDE HBA to address issues with CD-ROM devices will be available in PTF7050, which is on the way for UnixWare 7.*

Mounting CD-ROMs

To mount the file system contained on the CD-ROM, use the `mount` command with the `-F cdfs` option to specify the file system type. A CD-ROM must be mounted as read-only. This can be specified with either one of the following two options:

`-r`

`-o ro`

The standard options that apply to the `mount` command may be used as well as some options specific to CD-ROMs. These specific options are used in conjunction with the `-o` option. See the man pages for `mount_cdfs` for a complete option list.

Author's Note

UnixWare 7 is less forgiving than OpenServer in the `mount` command syntax. You must specify the file system type and to mount read-only, or the mount will fail. For example, to mount a CD-ROM in /mnt, use

```
#mount -F cdfs -r /dev/cdrom/cdrom1 /mnt
```

Diskettes

To access a diskette, you must know the correct device file to use for the specific diskette (density and drive). If you need to transfer data to a diskette, it must first be formatted.

Diskette Device Names

Diskettes are accessed through device files that reside in the /dev/dsk (block device interface) and /dev/rdsk (raw device interface) directories. Using the block device provides faster access, whereas the raw device offers more flexibility through more direct access. For instance, the `format` command uses the raw device.

The device name specifies whether the floppy drive to be accessed is drive 0 (`f0`) or drive 1 (`f1`). The device name specifies the density after the drive specification. The floppy drives' densities are described in Table 12.1.

TABLE 12.1 FLOPPY DRIVE DENSITIES

Drive Specification	Density
3e	3.5" extra high density (2.88MB)
3h	3.5" high density (1.44MB)
3d	3.5" double density (720KB)
5h	5.25" high density (1.2MB)
5d16	5.25" double density, 16 sectors per track (320KB)
5d9	5.25" double density, 9 sectors per track (360KB)
5d8	5.25" double density, 8 sectors per track (320KB)
5d4	5.25" double density, 4 sectors per track (320KB)

A `t` appended to the device name specifies the entire disk and is used with the `format` command. A trailing `u` specifies the entire disk, except for track 0 of cylinder 0, and applies only to `5d8`. A device file without a trailing `t` or `u` refers to the entire disk except for cylinder 0. Thus, the raw device for a 1.44MB 3.5" diskette in floppy drive 0 is /dev/rdsk/f03h.

The /dev/fd0 and /dev/fd1 device nodes still exist for backward compatibility with OpenServer. They are linked to devices in /dev/dsk, such as `f03ht`.

Formatting a Diskette

Use the `format` command to format a diskette in preparation for transferring data to it. For instance, to format the 1.44MB 3.5" diskette in floppy drive 0, use

```
#format /dev/rdsk/f03ht
```

The `format` command can be used with the `-v` option to display the formatting information.

If you do not know the device name, you can use the `devattr` command with the `-v` option, followed by the device's alias (diskette1). The `fmtcmd` attribute contains the command to format the specified device.

```
# devattr -v diskette1 ¦ grep fmtcmd
fmtcmd='/usr/sbin/format -v /dev/rdsk/f03ht'
```

DOS Diskettes

The `dosdir`, `doscp`, `dosrm`, and similar commands do not appear in UnixWare 7 starting with 7.0.1 due to licensing issues. See the `mtools` section in this chapter for information on commands that replace the functionality of the `dos*` commands.

Mounting DOS Diskettes

You can still mount DOS diskettes as file systems with the `mount` command. To mount a DOS-formatted floppy in drive 0 to the /mnt directory, for instance, use

```
#mount -F dosfs /dev/fd0 /mnt
```

It can then be accessed with the same commands as any other file system.

mtools (DOS Command Equivalents)

The `mtools` package on the Skunkware CD-ROM can be installed using the Application Installer to add utilities for DOS diskettes. It installs in the /usr/local/bin directory. You will need to add this directory to your `PATH` variable to access the `mtools` commands. Running the `mtools` command itself lists the supported commands, as follows:

```
# mtools
Supported commands:
mattrib, mbadblocks, mcd, mcopy, mdel, mdeltree, mdir, mformat
minfo, mlabel, mmd, mmount, mpartition, mrd, mread, mmove
mren, mtoolstest, mtype, mwrite, mzip
```

On the whole, `mtools` commands behave as you would expect from the DOS versions. The commands are named with a leading `m` followed by the DOS command. `mlabel` creates a label on the diskette, `mrd` removes a directory, and so on. `mtools` commands use UNIX-style pattern matching for filenames, rather than DOS-style. For instance, use `*` to match all files, rather than `*.*`.

As in SCO OpenServer, you can address the first floppy drive as a: and the second as b:. Remember to use forward slashes in the pathname, rather than a DOS-style backslash, unless you use quotes around the backslash.

To change or add to the default drive mappings, create the /usr/local/etc/mtools.conf file. This file does not exist by default. The /etc/default/msdos file is not used by `mtools`. The format is *`drive=device`*. To define the m drive as the first floppy, for example, add the line

```
m=/dev/dsk/f03ht
```

The default drive mappings include

- a=/dev/fd0
- b=/dev/fd1
- c=/dev/hd0d (no longer valid; this would map to the DOS partition on the primary hard drive in OpenServer)

Your current location within the DOS file structure is saved in $home/.mcwd. Entering the commands

```
#mcd a:
#mmd newdir
#mcd newdir
```

will result in the creation of a directory, newdir, on the DOS A: floppy and will change the working directory to newdir. Executing an `mdir` without specifying a directory does a dir of the new directory. This recording of the current location persists after a logout for a period of six hours. Logging back in during the lifetime of .mcwd and placing a different DOS floppy in the drive, which does not have a directory called newdir, results in an error message when executing `mdir` without any arguments. You can use `mcd a:/` to orient yourself in the top directory level of the new floppy.

If a `.logout` script is used for your login, it is recommended that the $home/.mcwd file be removed in that script.

Note

`mcd` *does not affect your current UNIX working directory.*

You can use the mcopy command to copy files onto the floppy. You must, however, specify the destination in the a: format, such as

```
#mcopy /etc/motd a:/newdir
```

Entering the following

```
#mcopy /etc/motd .
```

will not create a file in the current DOS directory. Rather, it will create a file in the current UNIX directory.

To correctly translate UNIX text files to DOS, and vice versa, use the -t option to mcopy. Failure to use the -t will result in UNIX text files appearing as a single line in DOS and DOS files having an extra newline character (^M) in UNIX. Both dtox (DOS to UNIX) and xtod (UNIX to DOS) are available for after-the-fact conversion, if needed.

Author's Note

For a complete description of the capabilities of mtools*, see the man pages. To access the man pages for* mtools*, edit /etc/default/man and add /usr/local/man to the* MANPATH *variable.*

Removable Hard Drives

Removable hard drives offer the convenience and flexibility of other removable media, but have the advantages of an additional hard drive. Specifically, entire file systems can be created and swapped around on a system to suit the needs at a given time.

The drive itself should be recognized at boot time. Check for recognition with sdiconfig -l. See Chapter 19 for instructions on creating new file systems.

Author's Note

We added a SCSI Syquest SyJet 1.5GB removable hard drive and created two file systems on it: one vxfs and one ufs. We then moved the device to another host with a different SCSI controller and were able to mount the file systems with no problem. This does not guarantee that it will work between all SCSI controllers.

Backups

Several commands can be used to back up files and file systems. You can also use the compress and uncompress commands to reduce the space needed on backup media. If backing up a single file, use compress on the file itself. If backing up multiple files, you can create a tar format archive in a single file, then compress the archive file before writing it to the backup media. See the tar command as discussed in the sections that follow for creating a tar format file.

The following sections discuss the use of the pax, tar, cpio, dd, ufsdump, and vxdump commands, as well as the graphical backup functionality of ARCserve.

Backup Issues

When backing up directories that contain symbolically linked files, the default behavior is to back up the link only, not the data to which it points. You can override this default with the L option for both tar and cpio. The downside is that the data is restored in the file that previously contained the link, and the link is broken.

To back up the data and preserve the link, be sure to back up both the directory containing the link as well as the directory containing the data. In this case, the L option is not used because the default behavior will produce the desired result.

A symbolically linked file will appear in a long listing (ls -l) with an l before the file's mode and a -> after the filename, followed by the filename to which the link points. The following is a listing of a symbolically linked file:

```
# ls -l /lib/cron
lrwxrwxrwx     1 root      sys               11 May 12 11:32 /lib/cron ->
➥/etc/cron.d
```

Another issue to consider when creating a backup plan is the use of *incremental backups*. The objective of incremental backups is to archive only those files that have changed since the last backup. The benefit is that less time and space are required to create the backup. The drawback is that several backups may need to be restored in the proper order to restore a complete file system, which increases the chance of data loss due to media failure.

Author's Note

Where time and storage space permit, I prefer full backups to incremental backups. This is simply because of the increased risk of data loss when you must rely on a series of backups to be restored.

pax

For moving archives from one operating system to another, pax (portable archive interchange) will read cpio and tar archives. pax can also be used to copy directory structures. pax has been modified to support archives greater than 2GB. pax uses the -r option to read an archive and the -w option to write an archive. To read a tape archive and report the names without copying the files (the equivalent of tar tv or cpio -itv), use

```
#pax -rv -f /dev/rmt/ctape1
```

The -k option may be used to specify not to overwrite existing files. The -u option specifies ignoring files that have a less recent modification date than the file to be overwritten.

tar

The tar command can be used to archive data to diskettes, tapes, or files. The default device for tar, as well as references to other devices usable by tar, can be found in /etc/default/tar. The following is a standard /etc/default/tar file:

```
# cat /etc/default/tar
#ident  "@(#)tar:tar.dfl        1.1.3.6"
#ident "$Header: /sms/sinixV5.4es/rcs/s19-full/usr/src/cmd/tar/tar.dfl,
➥v 1.1 91/
02/28 20:11:52 ccs Exp $"
#           device              block   size    tape
archive0=/dev/rdsk/f0q15dt      15      1200    n
archive1=/dev/rdsk/f1q15dt      15      1200    n
archive2=/dev/rdsk/f05ht        15      1200    n
archive3=/dev/rdsk/f15ht        15      1200    n
archive4=/dev/rdsk/f03dt        18      720     n
archive5=/dev/rdsk/f13dt        18      720     n
archive6=/dev/rdsk/f03ht        18      1440    n
archive7=/dev/rdsk/f13ht        18      1440    n
archive8=/dev/rmt/c0s0          20      0       y
#archive9=/dev/null #reserved
#
# The default device in the absence of a numeric or "-f device" argument
archive=/dev/rdsk/f0t           15      1200    n
```

tar is capable of archiving subdirectories within 17 levels of subnesting. It is easy to use and has the ability to override absolute pathnames, even if that is how the archive was created.

There are, however, several disadvantages to tar. Specifically:

- Although usable in specifying files to archive, filename expansion is not supported for extracting data (that is, exact filenames must be specified).
- It may be difficult to transfer data to platforms other than UnixWare 7 when the archive spans media.
- Currently, the tar man page does not specify that tar can handle large files (larger than 2GB).

The three most commonly used options with tar are

- *cv*—Copy files, listing filenames as they are copied.
- *tv*—View the contents of the archive.
- *xv*—Extract files, listing filenames as they are extracted.

In addition, numbers can be used to specify the media as listed in /etc/default/tar. For instance, to archive all files in the current directory to the primary tape drive (archive8), use

```
#tar cv8 *
```

Using the `f` option specifies a file or device to be used for the archive. For example, to list the files in an archive called /home/msh/tarball, use

```
#tar tvf /home/msh/tarball
```

Remember that the `L` option instructs `tar` to back up the data associated with symbolically linked files rather than the links themselves. For instance, to archive the /etc directory storing data rather than links, use

```
# tar cvL8 /etc
```

Using the `A` option results in overriding absolute pathnames. To restore /etc/hosts, archived in the /home/msh/tarball file, into the /tmp directory, use

```
#cd /tmp
#tar xvAf /home/msh/tarball /etc/hosts
```

Tip

In the past, `tar` *would not archive empty files and directories. Device files could not be backed up with* `tar`*. In UnixWare 7,* `tar` *handles empty files and directories with no problem, and it will back up device files successfully.*

See the man page for `tar` for a complete list of options.

cpio

The `cpio` command can be used to archive data files, but is also designed to archive entire file systems. While the syntax is more cumbersome than `tar`, it does not have some of the limitations. Specifically:

- It allows filename expansion for extraction.
- It is more portable with other platforms because it offers an ASCII header option (`-c`).
- The `cpio` man page states that it can handle large files (greater than 2GB).

As with `tar`, `cpio` can override absolute pathnames when extracting data even if absolute pathnames were used when the archive was created.

In addition, `cpio` accepts filenames to be archived from standard input. Other commands, such as `find`, can be used to pipe filenames to `cpio`.

The following are some commonly used options to `cpio`:

- *-vocBL -O device*—Create an archive on the specified device.
- *-Bitv -I device*—Examine contents of an archive on the specified device.
- *-vicdumB -I device*—Extract files from an archive on the specified device.

As with `tar`, the `v` option specifies that the requested operation is to be performed in a "verbose" fashion (listing the filenames). Also as with `tar`, the `L` option specifies that when symbolically linked files are encountered, the data itself—rather than the link—is to be archived.

To archive the entire contents of the /stand filesystem to a tape using absolute pathnames, use

```
#find /stand ¦ cpio -vocBL -O /dev/rmt/ctape1
```

To perform the same backup using relative pathnames, use

```
#cd /stand
#find . ¦ cpio -vocBL -O /dev/rmt/ctape1
```

To restore the backup just created into the current directory, use

```
#cpio -vicdumB -I /dev/rmt/ctape1
```

The `-O` and `-I` options can be replaced with command line redirection. Using this syntax, the previous examples become

```
#find . ¦ cpio -vocBL > /dev/rmt/ctape1
#cpio -vicdumB < /dev/rmt/ctape1
```

See the `cpio` man page for a complete listing of options.

dd

The `dd` command allows block-by-block transfer of data, as opposed to transferring files. This can be useful for duplicating media. For example, `dd` is used for copying images from /info/images on the UnixWare 7 Installation CD to create install and/or network installation diskettes (see Chapter 4, "Installation of UnixWare 7"). It can also be used to control the exact placement on destination media, as well as for skipping records on input or converting between ASCII and EBCDIC. See the man pages for more on `dd`.

ufsdump

The `ufsdump` command performs incremental backups of ufs filesystems. You can back up to a device or a data file. The backup destination should be specified with the `f` option, followed by the device file or regular file to which to write. For instance, to backup a ufs filesystem mounted at /ufsarea to a file in the /home filesystem called ufsdata, use

```
#ufsdump f /home/ufsdata /ufsarea
```

Author's Note

If you are backing up to a device, you must specify the device file in the command line. It will not use a default, as stated in the man pages.

The filesystem to be backed up can be specified either by the device or mount-point. See the man pages for `ufsdump` for a complete list of options, including the incremental dump level (0–9). A dump level of 9 is assumed unless a dump level is explicitly stated.

Use the `ufsrestore` command to restore a backup created using `ufsdump`. The syntax to restore the entire backup contained in the file /home/ufsdata into the current directory is

```
#ufsrestore xf /home/ufsdata
```

vxdump

To perform incremental filesystem backups on a vxfs filesystem, use `vxdump`. You can use the same syntax for `vxdump` as for `ufsdump`. To back up a vxfs filesystem mounted at /vxarea to a file in the /home filesystem called vxdata, use

```
#vxdump f /home/vxdata /vxarea
```

A complete list of options to `vxdump` is available in the man pages.

To restore a backup created using `vxdump`, use the `vxrestore` command. For example, to do a complete restore of the preceding backup into the current directory, use

```
#vxrestore xf /home/vxdata
```

ARCserve/Open and ARCserve/Open Lite

ARCserve/Open Lite comes with the Base Edition of UnixWare 7. The full ARCserve/Open is licensed with all other editions.

The Lite version does not allow backups of systems other than the host, nor does it allow for scheduling repeated automatic backups.

Warning

ARCserve takes control of tape devices. To access your tape from the command line, you will need to use the `astop` *command to stop ARCserve. The* `astart` *command restarts ARCserve. If you fail to stop ARCserve before executing a command that attempts to access the tape device (*`tar`, `cpio`*), the command will hang.*

The script that starts ARCserve is /etc/rc2.d/S69ARCserve. If you do not want it to start automatically, you can rename or move this file.

Accessing ARCserve/Open

ARCserve/Open is accessed through SCOadmin, SCO ARCserve/Open Backup Manager. Selecting the ARCserve option brings up the window shown in Figure 12.1.

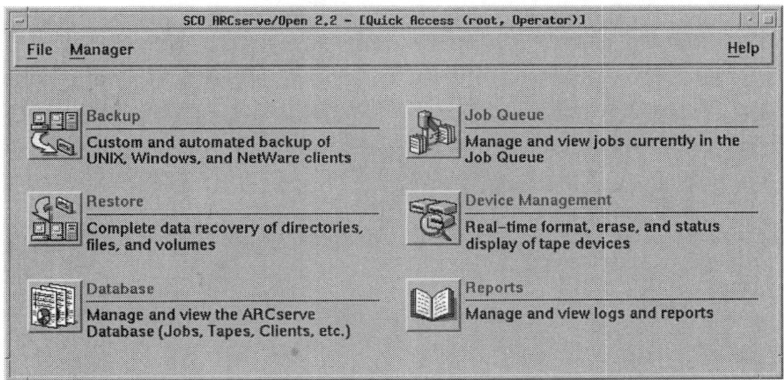

FIGURE 12.1 *ARCserve/Open main window.*

Creating Backups with ARCserve/Open

To use ARCserve to create backups, you must first have a backup device available. Select Device Management to view the configured devices. Tape drives are in a group called Mars by default. Figure 12.2 shows the Device Management window.

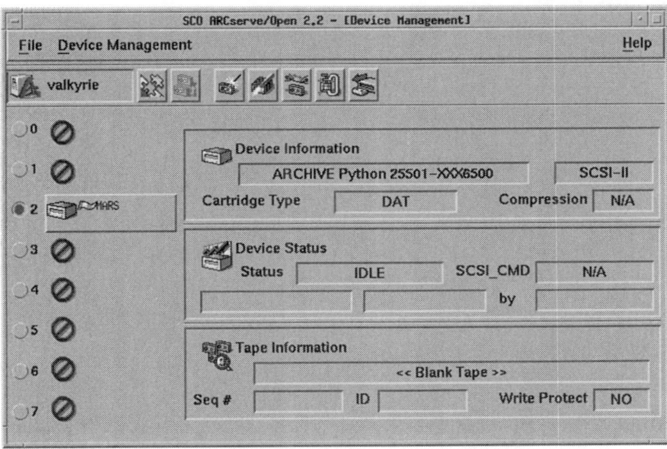

FIGURE 12.2 *Managing devices.*

Backup media are given names at the time of formatting. You can format a tape by clicking the wand icon above a tape; by pressing Shift+F; or by selecting Device Management, Format from the menu at the top of the window. You will be told the current name, sequence number, and ID number of the tape in the drive, then asked for the new name. You will refer to this name when selecting the media to which to back up. After a tape has been formatted, it is given an ID. Be sure to record the tape name and ID on the tape itself. This will save time when restoring data, as you will be told what tape holds the data you want. Figure 12.3 illustrates the Format window.

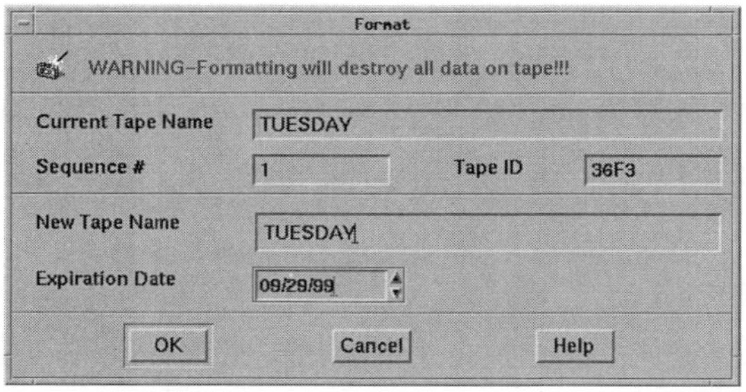

FIGURE 12.3 *Formatting a tape.*

To create a backup, click the Backup icon in the main ARCserve window. You can then specify what you wish to back up by host, filesystem, directory, and so on. You can select the entire system, one or several filesystems, as well as one or many directories and files. In Figure 12.4, only the /home filesystem is selected for backup.

You must specify the media. This can be done by clicking the desired Device Group (for example, MARS), or by clicking Destination, which opens the window shown in Figure 12.5. Several other options may be specified here, including timeout settings and tape options.

You can also specify backup options, such as verification to be performed, if any. The default is for no verification to be performed. You can also stop the backup history from being recorded in the database if you so desire (see Figure 12.6).

After you have specified the source and destination for the backup and selected the desired backup options, select Backup, Run from the Backup window. This opens the window shown in Figure 12.7.

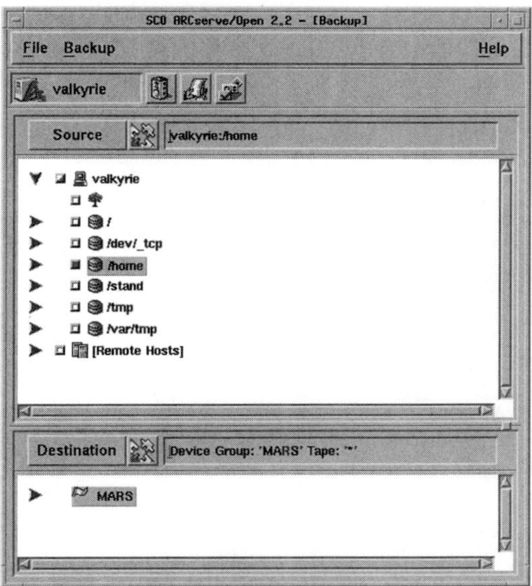

FIGURE 12.4 *Selecting files for backup.*

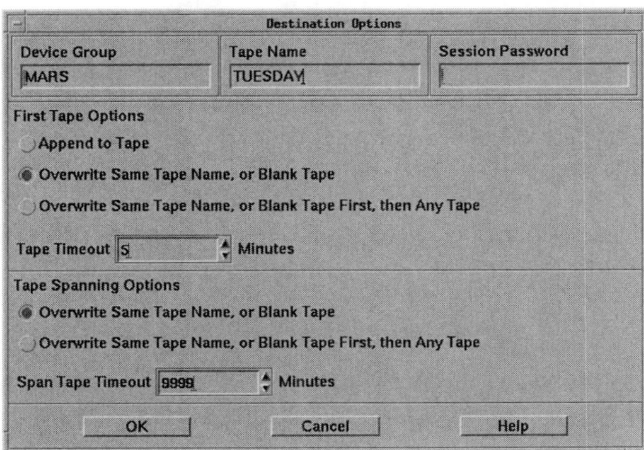

FIGURE 12.5 *Specifying the backup media.*

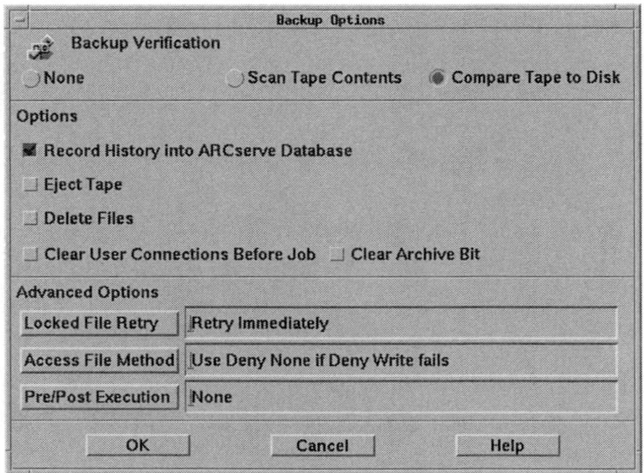

FIGURE 12.6 *Specifying backup options.*

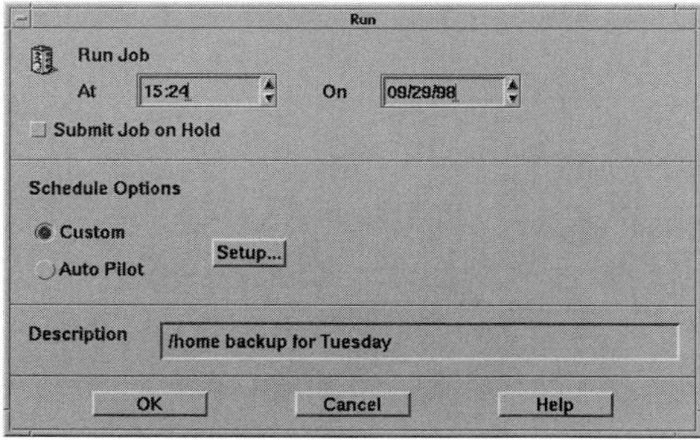

FIGURE 12.7 *Submitting a backup job.*

You will be given the opportunity to specify when the job is to run as well as whether it should be submitted to the job queue on hold. You can also modify the schedule options to create a regularly scheduled job. A description of the job may also be entered. When the options have been set to your satisfaction, click OK to submit the job.

You can view the job by clicking the Job Queue icon in the main ARCserve window. Figure 12.8 shows the Job Queue.

To monitor the progress of a job, click to highlight the desired job. You may then monitor the job by clicking the icon on the far right; pressing Shift+N; or selecting Job Queue, Monitor Job from the menu. This will open the window shown in Figure 12.9.

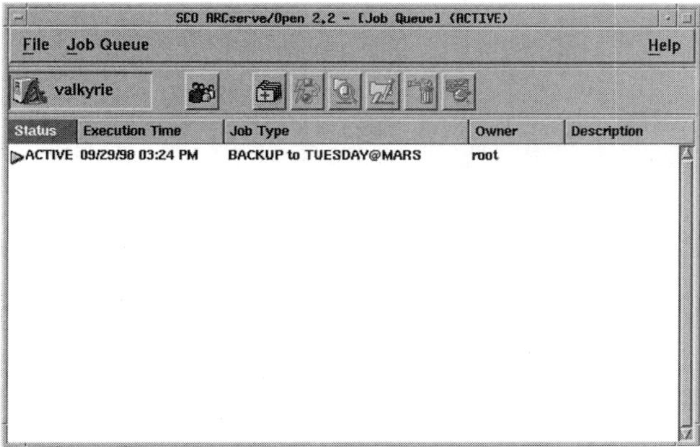

FIGURE 12.8 *Viewing the Job Queue.*

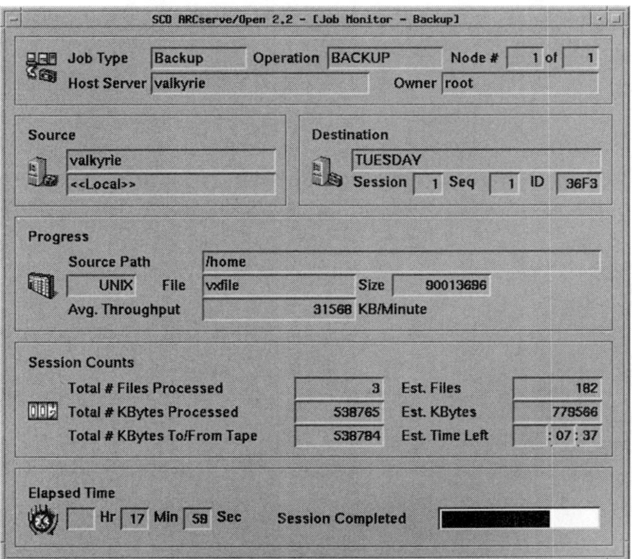

FIGURE 12.9 *Monitoring a backup.*

Restoring Data with ARCserve/Open

To restore data from a backup tape, click the Restore icon in the main ARCserve window. You can then specify which filesystems, directories, and/or files you wish to restore as well as the destination to which they should be restored (see Figure 12.10).

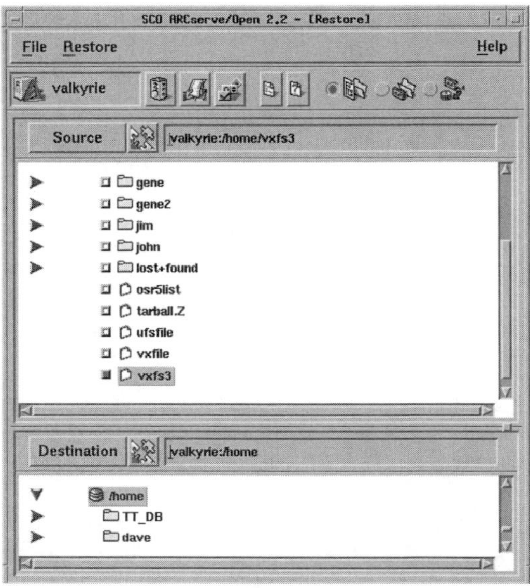

FIGURE 12.10 *Restoring data.*

After specifying the files to be restored, select Restore, Run from the menu. This will open a confirmation window and allow you to submit the job to the queue. A window will then open to tell you what media will be required to restore the specified file, as shown in Figure 12.11.

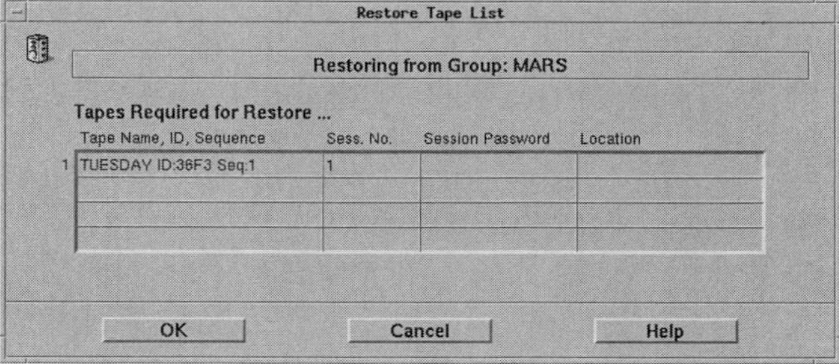

FIGURE 12.11 *Tapes required for data restoration.*

As with a backup, a data restore can be monitored by highlighting the desired job in the Job Queue window. You may then monitor the job by clicking the icon on the far right; pressing Shift+N; or selecting Job Queue, Monitor Job from the menu. This will open the window shown in Figure 12.12.

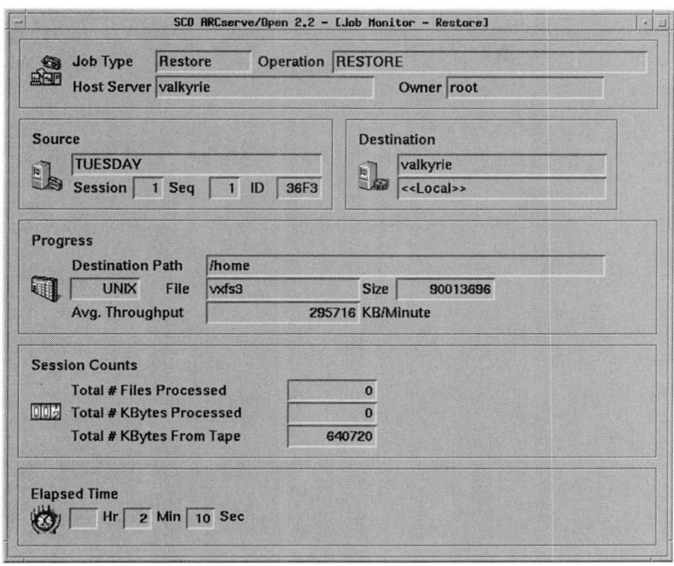

FIGURE 12.12 *Monitoring a restore.*

ARCserve/Open 6.0

ARCserve/Open 6.0 will be available in the near future. It will be accessed by a browser at port 6060. At the time of this writing, the installation instructions are as follows:

1. Remove any existing ARCserve packages with `pkgrm` (to check for installed packages, you can use `pkginfo | grep -i arc`).
2. Add the new package with `pkgadd`. Add the server first, then the manager.
3. Add the client package for UnixWare 7. Use `pkgadd` to add the UAGENT package.
4. Run `asetup`.

When you perform the setup, you will be asked for a domain name. This is for an ARCserve domain only. You should pick a primary host to maintain the ARCserve database. You will be given the opportunity to set the password for the ARCserve user, `arcroot`. If you do not change it, it has no password. Also, answer `y` to set equivalence for the root user of the primary host to `arcroot`.

After you have run `asetup`, you can start ARCserve with the `astart` command.

The ARCserve package will install by default in the /opt directory. It is accessed by pointing a browser to `hostname:6060` (see Figure 12.13).

FIGURE 12.13 *ARCserve accessed through a browser.*

Author's Note

In the Beta version of ARCserve/Open 6.0, some functions worked better from Netscape 4 running on a Windows PC than from the UnixWare 7 host.

Scheduling Automatic Backups

To create an automatic backup scheme, select the source, destination, and options in the same manner as you would for a one-time backup. When you submit the job to the queue, select Auto Pilot in the Schedule Options area, as shown in Figure 12.14.

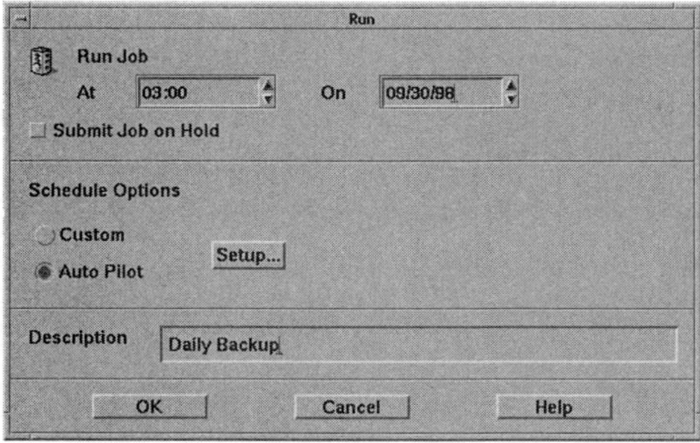

FIGURE 12.14 *Selecting Auto Pilot.*

After selecting Auto Pilot, click Setup. The window shown in Figure 12.15 will open to allow you to specify the details of your backup schedule.

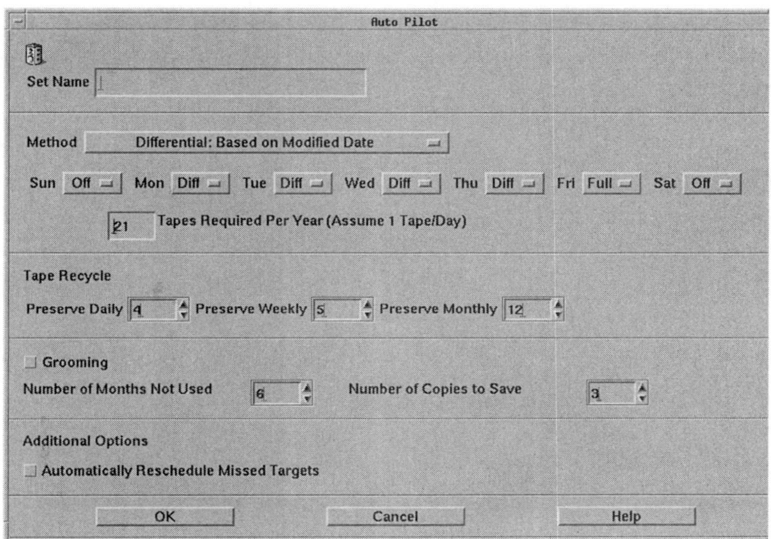

FIGURE 12.15 *Setting a backup schedule.*

When you have set this up, you need only insert the appropriate tapes at the appropriate times. A job will always exist in the job queue for the next scheduled backup.

Plug and Play

Plug-and-Play (PnP) configuration can be handled either by the operating system or the BIOS. UnixWare 7 provides a manager for PnP cards. It is accessed through SCOadmin, Hardware, PnP Configuration Manager. The manager provides a list of cards and devices detected, and allows you to either select settings or allow the BIOS to handle the configuration. Figure 12.16 shows the initial PnP Configuration Manager window.

You can enable or disable a setting in the BIOS for PnP OS. If it is enabled, the BIOS assumes that the operating system will handle the PnP cards. If it is disabled, the BIOS will try to assign what it considers the best settings. Because the BIOS is not aware of non-PnP cards, this may result in conflicts.

The recommended course of action varies based on whether there are non-PnP cards intermixed with the PnP ones. On a system without non-PnP ISA cards, the recommendation is to set the BIOS to PnP OS Disabled prior to running the PnP Configuration Manager. The BIOS will pick settings, which will be picked up by the PnP Configuration Manager as the current settings. Figure 12.17 shows the settings window with current settings displayed. To modify the settings, you can click the Good, Acceptable, or Sub-optimal selections and apply settings of your choosing.

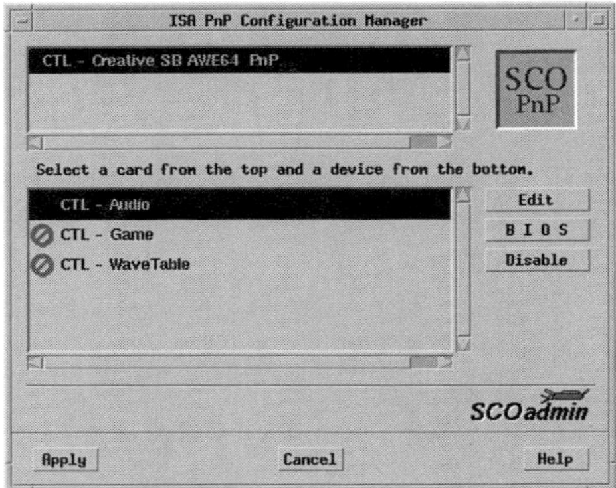

FIGURE 12.16 *The PnP Configuration Manager.*

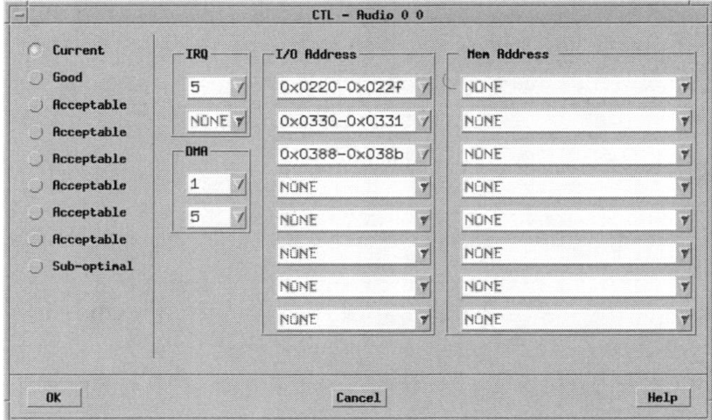

FIGURE 12.17 *Viewing the current settings.*

If these settings seem to work, save them through the PnP Manager, then set the BIOS to PnP OS Enabled.

On a system with non-PnP ISA cards, set the BIOS to PnP OS Enabled to prevent conflicts caused by the BIOS picking settings that are currently used by the non-PnP cards. When you run the PnP Configuration Manager, there will be no "current" settings for the PnP cards.

To further complicate matters, some cards have assigned settings that they use until configured by the PnP protocol. This can result in hardware conflicts, including the inability to boot if the conflict involves the boot device controller. To work through this problem, set the BIOS to PnP OS Disabled to allow the BIOS to resolve the conflict and allow booting. Getting the settings in the PnP Configuration Manager cooperating with the BIOS may involve some experimentation.

Sound Cards

To add a sound card, shut down the system, physically install the card, and restart the system. You can configure the card through SCOadmin, Audio Configuration Manager. For UnixWare 7.0.0, you need to download an audio package update at `ftp://ftp.sco.com/pub/drivers/UW700/audio`. The initial window of the Audio Configuration Manager is shown in Figure 12.18.

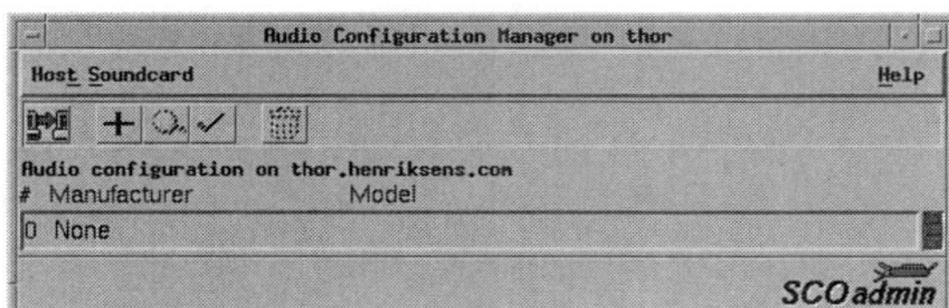

FIGURE 12.18 *Using the Audio Configuration Manager.*

To add a new sound card, either click the icon showing a plus sign or select Soundcard, Add from the menu. You will then be given the window shown in Figure 12.19, which allows you to specify the manufacturer and model to be installed or select Auto Detect.

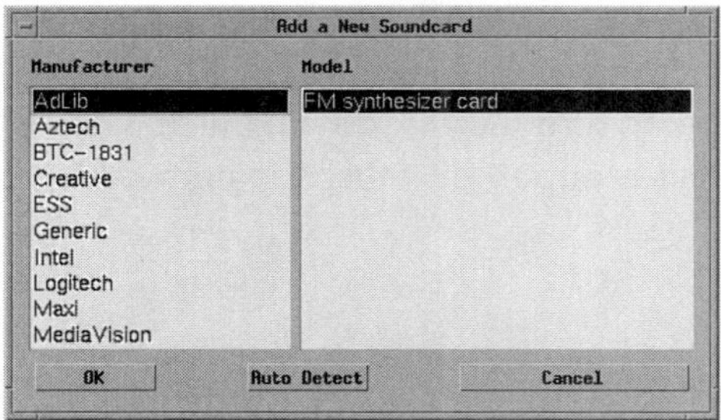

FIGURE 12.19 *Adding a sound card.*

Using the auto-detection will display the window shown in Figure 12.20. You then have the opportunity to choose between accepting the detected configuration and canceling the configuration.

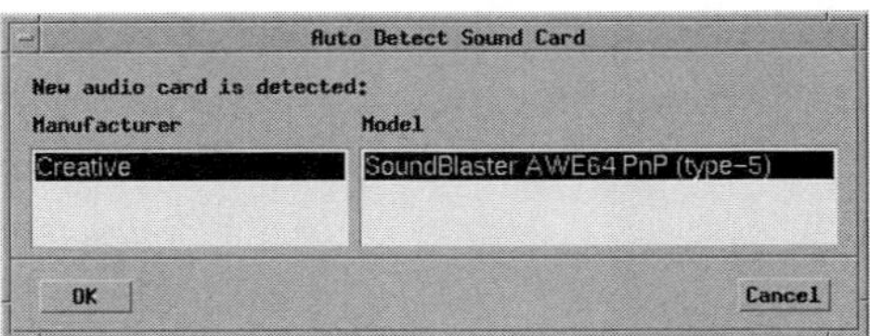

FIGURE 12.20 *Auto detection of a sound card.*

After accepting the manufacturer and model information, you are given the chance to modify the configuration. To accept the suggested configuration options, click OK (see Figure 12.21).

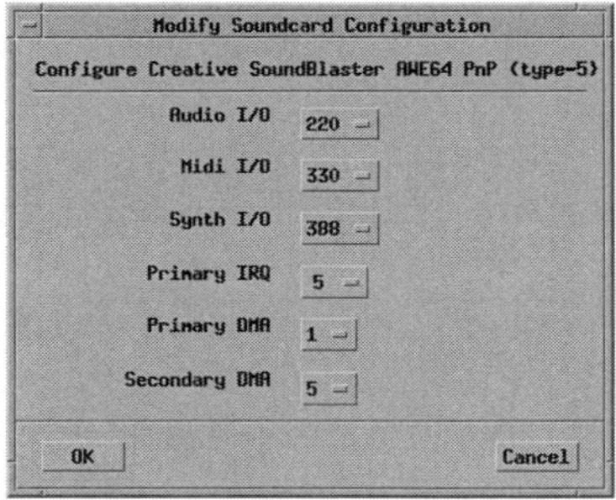

FIGURE 12.21 *Configuration of a sound card.*

When the configuration has been specified, you are given the opportunity to test the sound card by clicking Play Sound (see Figure 12.22). It will continue to send a snippet while you remember to turn the volume on, un-click the Mute button, and so on. When you can hear output, click the Stop button to cease the test sounds.

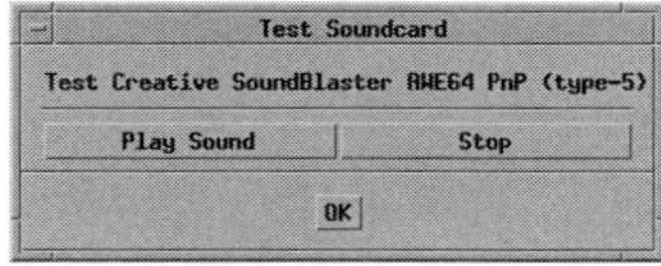

FIGURE 12.22 *Testing a new sound card.*

CHAPTER 13

Software Installation

- Software packages
  Understand what constitutes a software package and a set.
- The Application Installer
  Learn to use the Application Installer to install software.
- `pkgadd`
  Learn to use `pkgadd` and the related commands to manage software packages.
- Setting up an install server
  Learn how to set up an install server to enable installations of UnixWare 7 and software packages over your network.

UnixWare 7 Software Packages

The UnixWare 7 operating system and application software is divided into logical collections of files and executables that comprise independently installable units called *software packages*. Here is a partial listing of the `pkginfo` command listing packages on one of the install CD-ROMs:

```
# pkginfo -d cdrom1
application ARCserve        SCO ARCserve/Open from Cheyenne
application BASEdoc         UnixWare Documentation
application BASEman         UnixWare Manual Pages
```

Several packages may be assembled into a *set*. Sets are referred to as *Set Installation Packages*, or *SIPs*. The Internet Services package group is a SIP referred to as *BaseWeb*. The following list shows all sets installed on the system.

```
# pkginfo -c set
set          BaseWeb       Internet Services
set          UnixWare      Core Systems Services
set          afps          SCO Advanced File and Print Server
set          arcserve      Data Management Services
set          doc           Documentation Services
set          winsrvcs      Windows Integration Services
```

Each release of a package is known as an *instance* of the package. Each instance is described by a package identifier that has the following components:

`PKG`	The package abbreviation. This remains constant for all occurrences of a package.
`VERSION`	The software version.
`ARCH`	The software architecture.

A database of installed software is maintained in /var/sadm/install/contents. The database consists of entries for all files belonging to packages installed on the system.

Information in the file is similar to the following entry for the `pg` command.

```
/usr/bin/pg f sysutil 0555 bin bin 32832 47799 886526314 base
```

From this entry, you can determine the following information regarding /usr/bin/pg:

- It is a file (`f`).
- It is a member of the sysutil package.
- The permissions should be set to `0555`.
- It is owned by bin, group bin.
- The size of the file in characters is 32832.
- The result of running the `sum` command is 47799.
- The time of last modification is 886526314.
- The other package that contains this file is base.

Some entries, such as the `passwd` command, may belong to many other packages.

The /var/sadm/pkg directory has subdirectories for each package installed that include information on dependencies, pre-install, post-install, and remove scripts.

All of this information is maintained by the package add (`pkgadd`) and remove (`pkgrm`) utilities.

Package Management with the Application Installer

The Application Installer cannot be run in the non-graphical Charm mode. It must be run from the GUI. From the SCOadmin menu, select Software Management, Application Installer. The Application Installer window is split in two. The top half of the window displays applications available on removable media. The bottom half of the window shows the applications already installed. Figure 13.1 illustrates the Application Installer window.

The Install From box defaults to CD-ROM; click on the down arrow to select other removable media. The Update View icon on the right will catalog the available packages and display them. A pop-up window will ask you to wait while it catalogs the applications on the media. Other media include Tape, Floppy Disk (Disk_A, Disk_B), Network Install Server, and Other. The Other entry is used for packages that have been spooled to disk, but not installed. The default directory for Other is /var/spool/pkg.

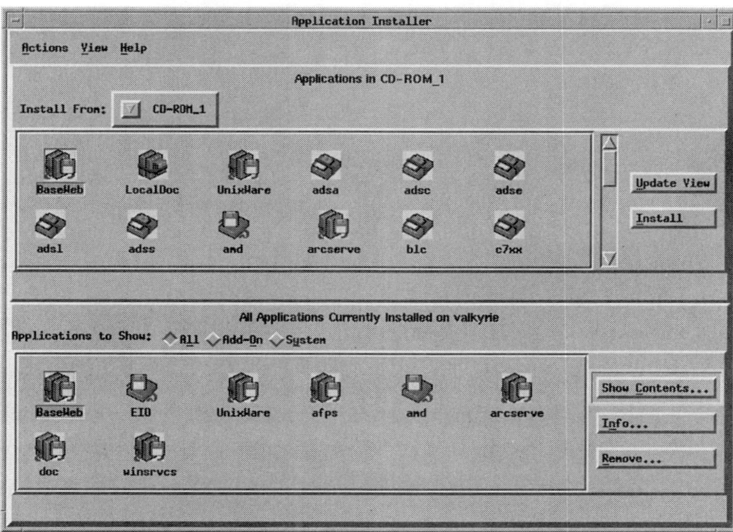

FIGURE 13.1 *The Application Installer.*

The icons that appear with two books and a diskette are sets. The icons with a single book and diskette are a package. If the red ribbon around the set has been cut, the package (or set) has been installed.

To install a package, highlight the icon and click the Install button on the right.

The bottom half of the Application Installer window contains installed software icons. Highlight an icon and click the Show Contents button to see the contents of a set or package. Figure 13.2 illustrates the window from Show Contents.

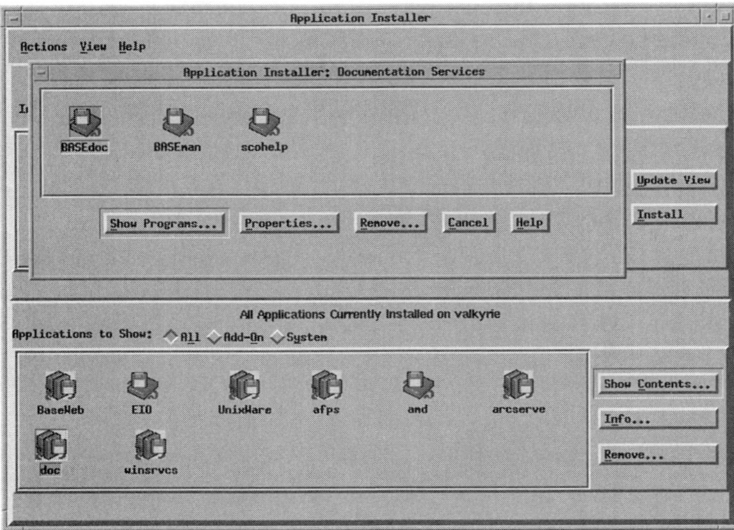

FIGURE 13.2 *The contents of a set.*

When the icon selected is a set, the packages that make up the set are shown. To see the programs that make up a package, click Show Programs. If the initial icon was a package, the programs are shown in the window. In Figure 13.2, the doc set has been selected. It is composed of BASEdoc, BASEman, and SCOhelp.

From Figure 13.2, a package within a set can be removed. To remove a package or set from the main window, highlight the icon and click the Remove icon. Packages may have *dependencies*, other packages that are required for them to operate. Normally you cannot remove a package that is required for another package to operate. The `-a` option to `pkgrm` ignores dependency requirements.

To see the properties of a package or set, select the icon in the bottom half of the window and click the Info button. The category will specify either application or set. For sets, to see the properties of single application packages, select Show Contents and then highlight the icon. Click Properties from the window shown in Figure 13.2.

The Info or Properties window (see Figure 13.3) displays the Application name, Version, and Architecture referred to earlier as the defining information for a set or package.

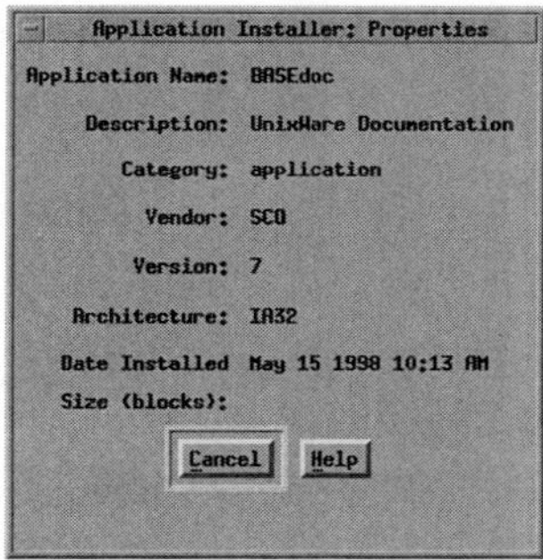

FIGURE 13.3 *The properties of a package.*

To install a package or set, select the icon in the top half of the window and click Install. A window like the one in Figure 13.4 will guide you through the installation. Likewise, to remove a package, select the package in the bottom half of the window and click Remove.

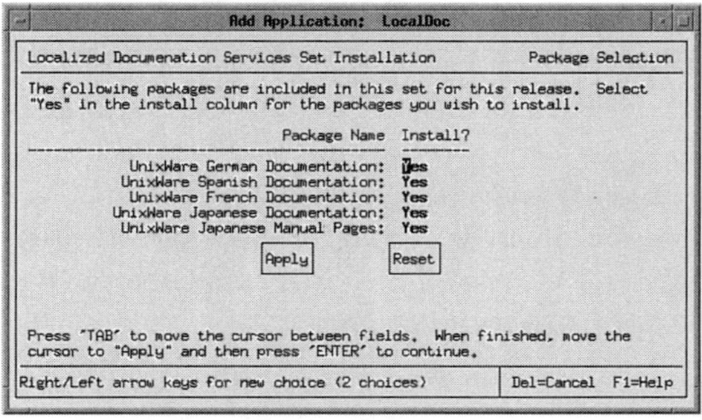

FIGURE 13.4 *Installing a package.*

If you are installing a SCO OpenServer package, check the SCO compatibility setting by clicking the Action-Options menu items, and check that the compatibility is set to 3.2.

Application icons can be copied to a user's applications window after the application has been installed. Figure 13.5 illustrates the process of copying the icons to a user's applications folders.

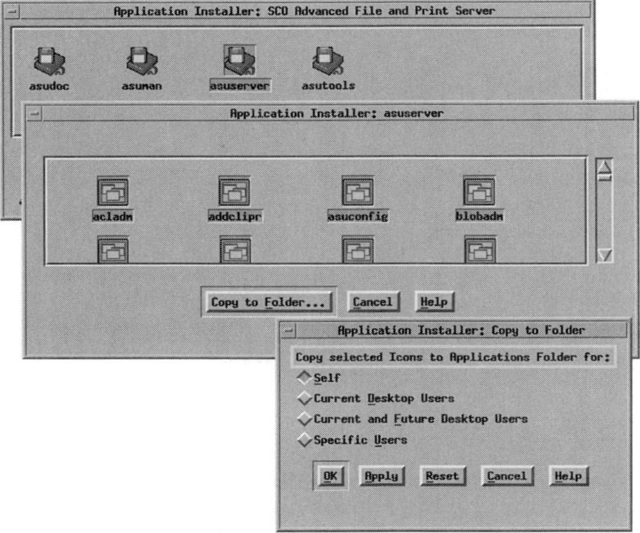

FIGURE 13.5 *Copying icons to folders.*

Package Management from the Command Line

From the command line, all the package management functions can be performed with more information available than through the GUI. In addition, packages can be spooled to the system without being installed. Packages may be stored on media in one of two formats. The *datastream format* contains a header record and a series of cpio archives. Datastream packages can be read from any raw device. The *filesystem format* appears in filesystem form. Package formats can be converted using the `pkgtrans` command.

Adding Packages with *pkgadd*

To add a package from a distribution medium, use the `pkgadd` command. An installation from diskette could be

```
pkgadd -d diskette1
```

The device, diskette1, must be specified as /dev/dsk/f0t or have an alias in the /etc/device.tab. Diskette1, ctape1, and cdrom1 are aliases that you may find in the device.tab.

If no package name is given in the command, a list of all packages available is displayed. The user can then enter the package name. The dialog for starting a `pkgadd` from diskette follows.

```
# pkgadd -d diskette1

Insert diskette into Floppy Drive 1.
Type [go] when ready,
  or [q] to quit: (default: go)

Installation in progress.  Do not remove the diskette.

The following packages are available:
  1  EIO      Stallion ATA 5
              (i386) 5.4.0

Select package(s) you wish to process (or 'all' to process
all packages). (default: all) [?,??,quit]:
```

If multiple packages were on the medium, you could type the names of the desired packages or accept the default of `all`.

Tip

If you need to duplicate package installs over a large number of systems, use `pkgask` to create answer or response files. This way, you can have the remote installation use the `-r` option with the response files.

In the /var/sadm/install/admin directory are two files: default and check. The default file has the settings used by `pkgadd`. To create a different set of default conditions, create a new file and specify that file to `pkgadd` with the `-a` *`filename`* option.

The format of the default file is

```
mail=root gene
instance=overwrite
partial=nocheck
runlevel=nocheck
idepend=quit
rdepend=quit
space=quit
setuid=nocheck
conflict=nocheck
action=nocheck
basedir=default
```

The pkgadd man pages describe the contents of the default file. In this example, mail is sent to root and the system owner, Gene. If another instance of the package exists, it will be overwritten. There is no check for conflicts, setuid programs, or appropriate run level for installation. By comparison, the file named /var/sadm/install/admin/check would ask the installer on all of the quit and nocheck items shown in the default file.

Spooling a Package

Using pkgadd, you can spool a package from the distribution media and place it in a spool directory. From the spool directory it may be installed later or shared out to other systems for network installs. To spool a package, use

```
pkgadd -s <spooldir> -d <device> pkgname
```

You may receive the following error message:

```
# pkgadd -d cdrom1 -s ttajava

Insert CD into SCSI CD-Rom Drive 1.
Type [go] when ready,
  or [q] to quit: (default: go)
UX:pkgadd: ERROR: unable to transfer package to file system format
    use the -s option to transfer package in datastream format
UX:mailx: WARNING: No message !?!
```

The error message suggests that you use the package transfer command with the -s option to use a datastream format. In the pkgtrans command, the two devices are listed in order as source and target. The desired package is listed at the end. Here is the result of trying that method:

```
# pkgtrans -s cdrom1 /var/spool/pkg ttajava

Insert CD into SCSI CD-Rom Drive 1.
Type [go] when ready,
  or [q] to quit: (default: go)
UX:pkgtrans: ERROR: unable to complete package transfer
    - invalid or unknown device </var/spool/pkg>
```

The -s option did not work in this case. Run the command without the -s:

```
# pkgtrans cdrom1 /var/spool/pkg ttajava

Insert CD into SCSI CD-Rom Drive 1.
Type [go] when ready,
or [q] to quit: (default: go)
Transferring <ttajava> package instance to
        </var/spool/pkg> in file system format
# lc /var/spool/pkg/ttajava
install  pkginfo  pkgmap   reloc
```

After the successful completion, you can list the contents of the package under the new package directory.

You may now run pkgadd with no options and it will locate the packages in the /var/spool/pkg directory.

Removing Packages with *pkgrm*

The pkgrm command will remove installed or spooled packages. If the package name is a SIP, all the packages that are members of the SIP and the SIP information will be removed.

```
pkgrm package_name
```

You may also remove spooled packages with the -s option to pkgrm.

```
pkgrm -s spooled_pkg_name
```

Viewing Information with *pkginfo*

To view information on packages, use the pkginfo command. Several options are available. If the package name is listed, the information is about that package only.

```
# pkginfo -x BASEman
BASEman          UnixWare Manual Pages
                  (IA32) 7

# pkginfo -l BASEman
   PKGINST:  BASEman
      NAME:  UnixWare Manual Pages
  CATEGORY:  application
      ARCH:  IA32
   VERSION:  7
    VENDOR:  SCO
   SETINST:  doc
   SETNAME:  Documentation Services
      DESC:  UnixWare runtime and developer manual pages
    PSTAMP:  UW7 01/14/97
  INSTDATE:  May 15 1998 09:45 AM
    STATUS:  completely installed
     FILES:  5032 installed pathnames
               10 shared pathnames
              179 directories
             53682 blocks used (approx)
```

Displaying Information with *displaypkg*

The displaypkg command displays a list of installed packages with no information other than the package name.

```
# displaypkg

        The following software packages have been installed:

SCO ARCserve/Open from Cheyenne Documentation
SCO ARCserve/Open from Cheyenne
UnixWare Documentation
UnixWare Manual Pages
Netscape FastTrack Server Documentation
```

Checking the Accuracy of Packages

After a package is spooled or installed, the accuracy can be checked with the `pkgchk` command. Use `-d` to point to the spool directory; it does not use a default of /var/spool/pkg. The `-v` option is for verbose reporting.

Warning

In early versions of UnixWare 7, `pkgchk` has been reported for listing discrepancies in error.

```
# pkgchk -d /var/spool/pkg -v ttajava
## checking spooled package <ttajava>
$INSTDIR/java/admin-du.cab
$INSTDIR/java/admin-ns-install.jar
$INSTDIR/java/admin-s.jar
$INSTDIR/java/admin.cab
$INSTDIR/java/asad-du.cab
$INSTDIR/java/asad-ns-install.jar
$INSTDIR/java/asad-s.jar
$INSTDIR/java/asad.cab
depend
pkginfo
postinstall
postremove
preremove
request
```

When `pkgchk` is run, it can detect problems with checksum, size, permissions, and ownership. It can fix problems in permissions and ownership. Problems in size and checksum can be repaired only by restoring or re-installing the package.

Installing Packages That Do Not Conform to *pkgadd*

Software written to the SCO OpenServer custom installation specifications can be installed with `custom`. The SCO custom+ format is not supported. The information on the files will not be included with the `pkgadd` compatible information, but will be placed in the /etc/perms directory. The `fixperm` command is available for checking files and permissions on those packages.

For pre-release 4 UNIX Systems Labs style software packages, the `installpkg` and `removepkg` commands are available.

Other software may require the use of `cpio` or `tar` to extract the data into the install directory or a temporary directory from which it will be installed.

Setting Up an Install Server

A UnixWare 7 system can be used as an install server for installing the operating system over the network (see Chapter 4, "Installation of UnixWare 7," for details on installation) and for installing software packages to remote systems.

To create an install server, select Install Server from the SCOadmin Software Management menu. From the Network Install Server Setup window, select Actions, Disable. Then select the Package menu.

The two available options under the Package menu are Load System and Load Add-On Package. To load the operating system packages, select Load System. Figure 13.6 illustrates the Load System window. Select the device from the drop-down list at the top of the window (default is CD-ROM 1, if available). Select the language (default is the C locale). Current versions have a problem that require the locale to be C. Click the Update View button to see the image files. If you do not want to load the packages onto the hard drive, click Leave on Device. For operating system install servers, all packages need to be copied to disk.

Click OK to register these for the install server. When complete, click the button in the upper-left corner and select Close.

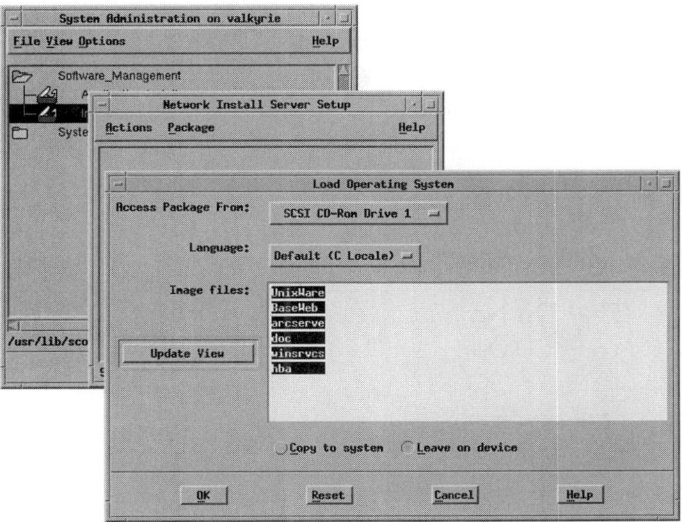

FIGURE 13.6 *Loading the operating system packages.*

To load additional packages from the media, select Load Add-On Package. In Figure 13.7, the Load Add-On Package window is open with the Network Install Server Setup window behind it showing the packages loaded from the Load System operation. If the packages are on a different device, select the new device. Click Update View.

Highlight each package you want to have loaded. To leave the packages on the media rather than copying to disk, select Leave on Device. Click OK. To exit, click the button in the upper-left and select Close.

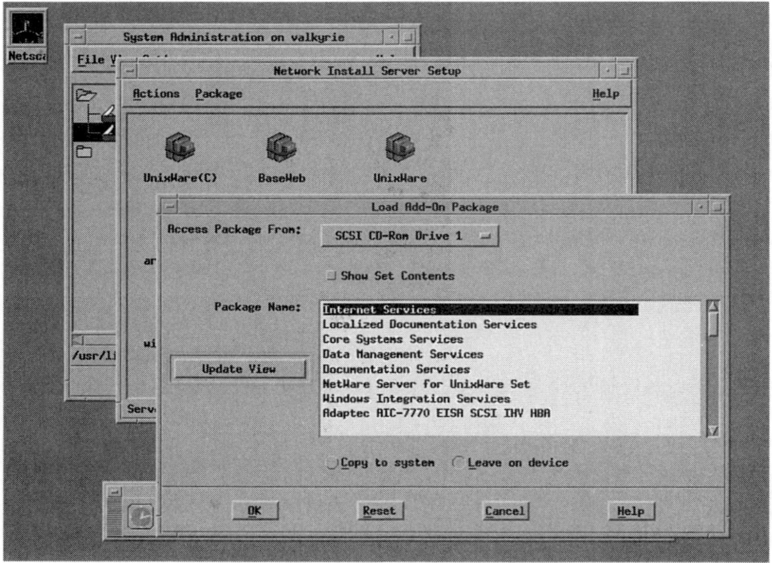

FIGURE 13.7 *Selecting packages for the install server.*

Warning

If you go through the routines more than once and try to re-add the same packages, you will get an error as shown in Figure 13.8.

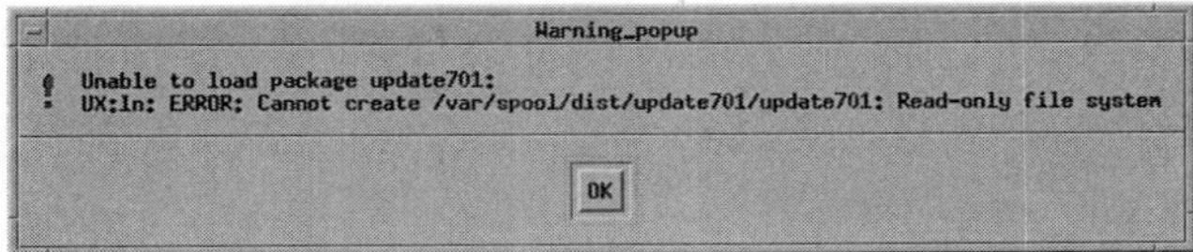

FIGURE 13.8 *Error message when trying to re-add a loaded package.*

The reason for the error is that the CD-ROM is mounted on /installr. The process of adding a package to the installable set is to create a link from /var/spool/dist to the appropriate directory on the CD-ROM. When the link is made, the software tries to create the new link in the CD-ROM, which is read-only.

When all of the packages are loaded, click Actions, Enable in the Network Install Server Setup window. Figure 13.9 illustrates an install server with packages ready to be installed.

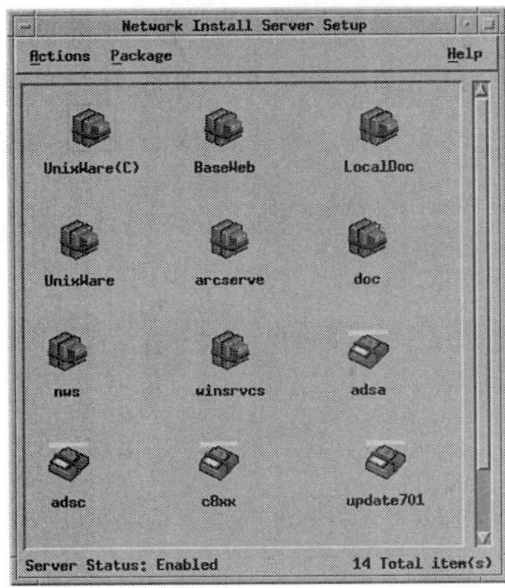

FIGURE 13.9 *The install server packages with the server enabled.*

From a remote system, run SCOadmin and select Software Management. Select the Application Installer option. Enter the name or IP address of the install server and click Update View. Figure 13.10 illustrates a system ready to install applications from a remote system.

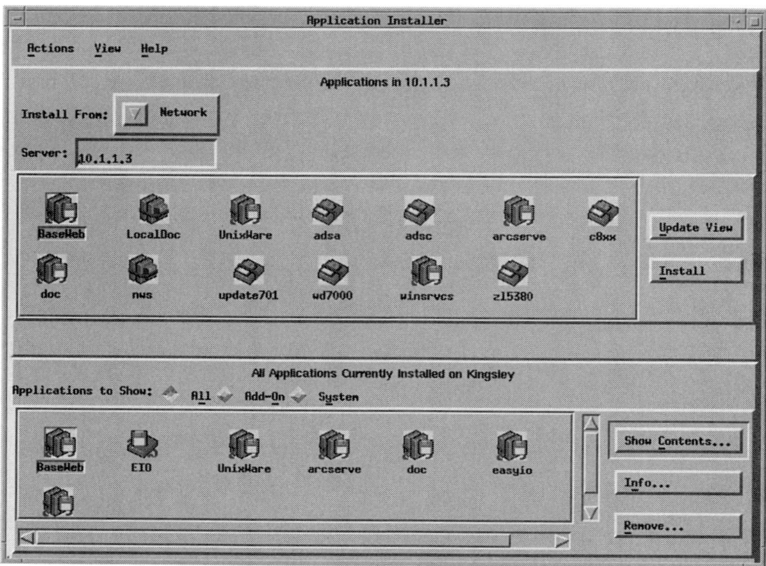

FIGURE 13.10 *The install server packages as seen from a remote system.*

CHAPTER 14

Wrapping Up the Install

- Registering the system
  Register your system with SCO to stop messages about unregistered software on your system.
- Emergency recovery disks
  Learn how to create and test ERDs.
- Emergency recovery tapes
  Two types of tapes can be created. Understand both types and learn how to create them.
- Building the indexes for SCOhelp
  SCOhelp needs search indexes. Learn how to create them.
- System log book
  You have heard it before, but log books can be crucial to recovery.

Registering the System with SCO

After the system has been installed and rebooted, the mouse configured, software installed, printers operational, and user accounts set up, a couple of final tasks need to be completed. The installation is not complete until you have registered the system, created emergency recovery media, set up the indexing for SCOhelp, and created a System log book. This chapter will show you how to handle these tasks.

To help prevent software theft, SCO implemented a software registration procedure. Registration of software helps SCO notify users of software upgrades and new products. Reinstalling generally creates a new SCO System ID and may require re-registering. To register your system, you need to have the license information and the SCO System ID. The System ID is displayed in the License Manager. To use the License Manager, from SCOadmin select License Manager. Highlight the license you want to register and double-click the license, or select License, Register. Note in the Register License window (shown in Figure 14.1) that both the license number and the SCO System ID are displayed.

Warning

In version 7.0.0 of UnixWare 7, deferring the license procedure at install will result in no System ID being generated. As a result, the system cannot be licensed.

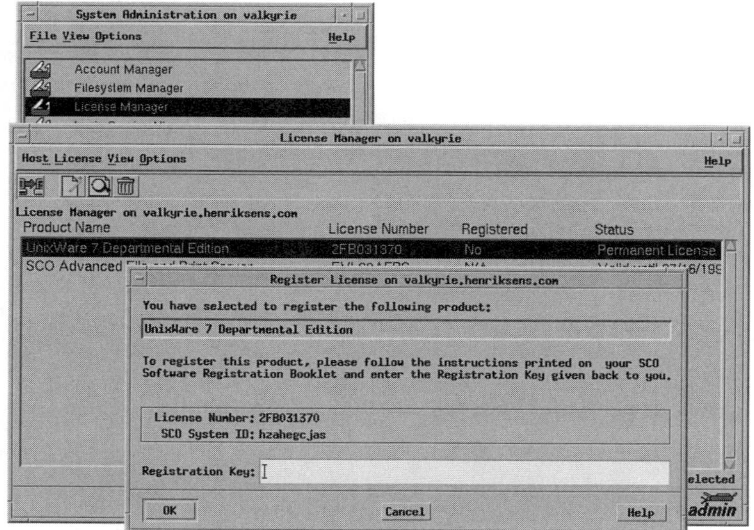

FIGURE 14.1 *The License Manager and Register License windows opened for registration.*

SCO Web Registration

When you have the SCO System ID, you can proceed with registration. SCO has provided several methods of registration. By far the quickest is registering on the Web. On the SCO Web site (`www.sco.com`) at the bottom of the page is a blue icon labeled Register. Figure 14.2 illustrates the Web page. When registering on the Web, print out the Web page for reference when your registration key is displayed. File the registration page with your System log book. In some instances, if the Web browser cache is not turned off, you may not get anything when you print. You may also request an email confirmation of your registration.

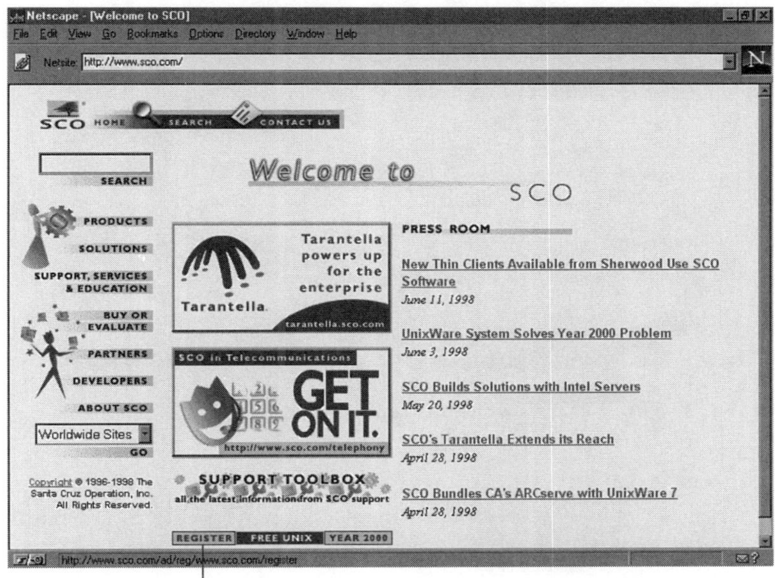

FIGURE 14.2 *The SCO Web page with the Register icon at the bottom of the page.*

Non-Web Registration

For other methods of registration, see the instructions on the Web at `www.sco.com/products/prodreg.htm` or the SCO Software Registration booklet that comes with the media. These provide information on registering by email, fax, Web, and postal service mail.

The Web page shown in Figure 14.3 is the current Web information page on registration.

Web sites are known to change, so referenced addresses may change. Until you complete the registration, you will continue to get messages stating that unregistered software exists on the system.

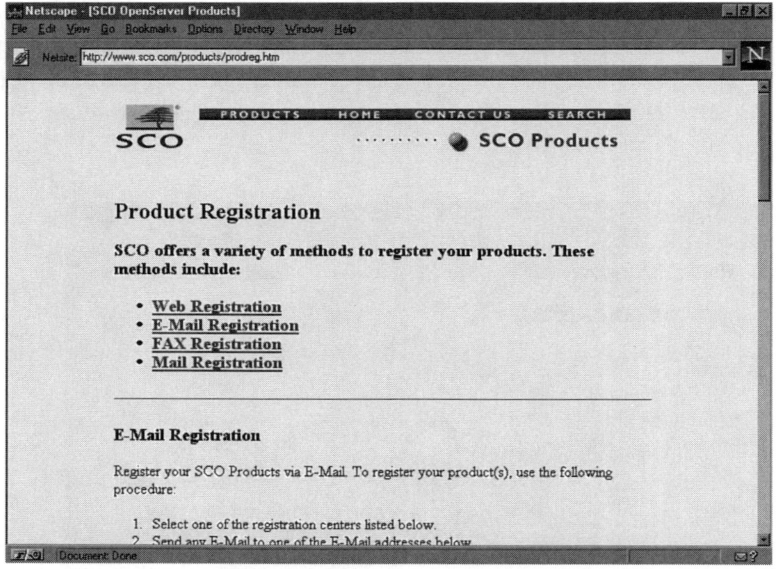

FIGURE 14.3 *The SCO registration instructions Web page.*

SCOhelp on Registration

If Web access is not available, look for instructions in SCOhelp. The path to the information is: Installation and Licensing, Licensing and registering SCO Products, Registering products.

Re-Registering After Hardware Replacement

If you have to reinstall on a new hard drive or different system, you will need to re-register. Because you have already registered, the Web site will provide a list of reasons for re-registration, such as installing a new system. The SCO System ID is unique and is generated at installation.

The Copy Protection Daemon

To prevent illegal copies of UnixWare from being installed on the same network, all systems running UnixWare 7 will broadcast their serial numbers at boot time and every 24 hours. All UnixWare 7 systems listen for these broadcasts and compare the serial numbers to their own list of serial numbers. If a system receives a broadcast from another system with a duplicate number, it displays a message to the console and writes it to the /var/adm/syslog. The message will identify the system with duplicate licenses.

The Copy Protection Daemon (sco_cpd) is started during boot and runs continuously. The Policy Manager daemon (ifor_pmd) watches for killing or tampering with sco_cpd. If ifor_pmd detects a problem with sco_cpd, it writes a message to /var/adm/syslog and to /dev/console. No new optional services licenses will be granted until the daemon is restarted or the system is rebooted.

The UnixWare 7 Emergency Recovery Diskettes

UnixWare 7, like UnixWare 2, uses the `emergency_disk` and `emergency_rec` commands to create emergency recovery media. The diskettes do not resemble the OpenServer 5 "boot and root" floppy disks. UnixWare 7 uses these diskettes to boot a mini-kernel into a memfs (memory file system) so the system is running entirely in memory.

Chapter 23, "Emergency Recovery," covers the recovery process with the emergency disks and tapes. You may want to read that chapter to get a better idea of how the disks and tapes will be used.

Author's Note

If you have never worked with the emergency disks and tapes and can afford the time, I would strongly recommend creating the emergency disks and tapes and restoring the system on which they were made. Performing an emergency restore will increase your confidence level in the process and the media as well. You will feel much better performing an actual emergency recovery if you have practiced on one. Make two sets of disks and tapes and store one set offsite.

At a minimum, you should boot the system from the emergency diskettes to make sure they work.

Creating the Diskettes

To create the emergency diskettes, you will need two formatted diskettes. Format high density 3.5" diskettes with the following command:

```
format -v /dev/rdsk/f03ht
```

If the first diskette is not formatted, the emergency_disk script will prompt the user to enter `f` to format the diskette.

The creation of the emergency diskettes involves two scripts, prep_flop and cut_flop in the /usr/lib/drf directory.

The creation of the diskettes requires 30MB of disk space. The default directory is in /usr. Check the available file space. If 30MB is not free in the filesystem containing /usr, you will need to specify the work directory with the `-d` option. To create the diskettes, run

```
emergency_disk [-d directory] disk_drive
```

For example, to create an emergency set using `/home` for the work area and using the primary diskette drive:

```
emergency_disk -d /home disk1
```

A temporary log file, /tmp/drf_*PID*.log, will be created during the process, where *PID* is the process ID of the emergency_disk process. If the process ends with a failure, check the log for additional information.

The dialog for the process will be similar to

```
#emergency_disk -d /home disk1
Please insert a floppy disk and press <ENTER>
This will take some time. Please wait ...
Examining symbol tables of various loadable modules
Saving symlist ...
Stripping various files.
(A number of lines involving removing white space from files appear)
Copying /home/work_3335/.drf_mach/stand/unix.nostrip into
/home/work_3335/.drf_mach/stand/unix
Making file system images
16 blocks
(Several more lines of display)
Done with boot floppy.
Insert SECOND boot floppy into disk1 drive and press
    <ENTER>   to write floppy
    f         to format and write floppy
    s         to skip
    d         to change output device, or
    q         to quit
(Here the user should press ENTER after inserting the second formatted
disk)
Creating second boot floppy image
(several lines of output containing the number of blocks written)
Done with SECOND boot floppy.
/usr/lib/drf/prep_flop: Done
Creation of the Emergency Recovery boot floppy was successful.
```

The process of creating the diskettes takes about 15 minutes. You should create two sets. Test both sets. Store them in different locations—preferably one should be offsite.

The diskettes should be labeled with the system name and date. These should be re-created if the disk layout, tape drive, or HBA changes.

If you are interested in how the diskettes are created, review the /sbin/emergency_disk script and the prep_flop and cut_flop scripts in the /usr/lib/drf directory.

Author's Note

The diskettes created are system specific. Each system needs its own set of diskettes. My experience is that systems booted from diskettes not created on that specific system or an identical system will not boot.

Warning

Two problems can occur in creating and using the emergency recovery diskettes. The first problem will appear during the creation of the diskettes when the locale has been set to other than the default, such as en_US:

```
ERROR --mkfs of ramdisk filesystem failed.
UX:memfs sbfmkfs: Error: cannot open /etc/dcu.d/locale/en_US/txtstrings
```

The problem is that there is no en_US directory in the /etc/dcu.d/locale and /usr/lib/drf/locale directories. To work around the problem, create the following symbolic links:

```
#ln -s /etc/dcu,d/locale/C /etc/dcu.d/locale/en_US
#ln -s /usr/lib/drf/locale/C /usr/lib/drf/locale/en_US
```

If you used other than U.S. English, your error messages will indicate a different directory than en_US.

The second problem occurs when booting from the diskette. Instead of getting the menu, you will see a VT0> prompt. The problem is caused in certain versions by a copyright notice in the first 10 lines of /usr/lib/drf/locale/C/txtstr. Remove the lines and re-create the diskettes. After the change the size of the txtstr file should be 6996 bytes. Run sum -r to verify the correct version.

```
#sum -r txtstr
14937       14 txtstr
```

After modification, the first line of the file should be:

```
#ident "@(#)drf:cmd/txtstr.c 1.13.2.1"
```

Creating the Tapes

The emergency tapes can be created in two formats:

- The default format is cpio.
- The second format is a `dd` copy of the primary hard drive.

Both tapes create a small cpio archive at the front of the tape containing information on the disk drive layout. This information is used in restoring a disk. For this reason, each UnixWare 7 system needs its own emergency tapes.

The default tape has two cpio archives:

- The first is the disk layout information.
- The second is the data from the UNIX partition and a system partition, if it exists.

If a UNIX partition exists on the second hard drive, the /usr, /home, and /home2 filesystems will be copied if they exist. If NetWare Services is installed, it will also back up the SYS: volume of the NetWare Server and any master NDS partitions.

The `-e` option specifies a `dd` copy of the primary disk. A small cpio archive containing the disk parameters for recovery is written to the tape, and then the primary disk is copied to the tape using `dd`. This tape will copy all partitions, UNIX and non-UNIX. The `-e` option does not copy anything from the secondary hard disk.

Upon recovery, all of the operating systems should work as they had when the tape was created. The `dd` tape can be used for single disk systems if the tape drive capacity is large enough to contain the entire disk plus the small cpio archive. The `dd` command will not prompt for additional volumes.

Author's Note

If creating a `dd` tape, I strongly recommend creating a cpio tape also. Since `dd` copies byte-for-byte, replacing the disk drive with a different disk could create problems in restoring a `dd` tape.

To create the emergency recovery tapes, the system must be in single user mode. The command syntax is

```
emergency_rec [-e] tapedrive
```

where *tapedrive* is a system tape drive, such as ctape1. The `-e` option specifies the `dd` option.

The dialog for the creation of the default tape is similar to

```
#emergency_rec ctape1
Place a tape in ctape1 and press <ENTER> or enter [q/Q] to abort:
(press ENTER)
copying the hard disk(s) to tape, please wait ...
908480 blocks
Creation of the Emergency Recovery Tape was successful
```

When using the `-e` option, the main difference in the dialog is

```
Copying the primary disk to tape, please wait...
```

If an error occurs, a message will appear, such as:

```
WARNING: Disk Driver: HA 0 TC 0 LU 0 CHECK CONDITION 0x6DD0E002
A "MEDIUM ERROR" condition has been detected
.
.
.
Creation of the Emergency Recovery Tape was NOT successful
```

Emergency recovery tapes should be created whenever changes are made to the operating system. These tapes are not a replacement for daily backups, however.

The SCOhelp Indexes

When the system is initially installed, a mail message is sent to root to build the SCOhelp indexes. The message will look like this:

```
Run this command (in the background or scheduled with an at(1) job at a
convenient time).
/usr/man/bin/config_search -f
```

With the number of login screens available at the console, switch to another screen and run the command; it can take up to 30 minutes to run depending on the number of documentation packages installed. If this command is not run, searching in SCOhelp either will not work or will return incomplete results. If the search indexes are not fully configured, SCOhelp will remind you to run the command when you attempt to run a search through SCOhelp.

Author's Note

If you installed your system with an incorrect domain name and attempted to correct it by changing the entries in the /etc/hosts file, SCOhelp will not work. Netscape looks in the /etc/resolv.conf file for the domain name. The domain name will be there whether or not you implement DNS. The problem appears to be in the `ping` *command used by Netscape. A patch, PTF7102, is being worked on to fix this problem.*

The System Log Book

The *System log book* is an administrative task that often does not get done, particularly in small businesses. The log book serves an important function in two areas:

- Researching previously seen problems
- Restoring the system

The System log book should contain information on all software installed, license numbers, activation keys, version numbers, and other appropriate information, such as options used at install.

If you lose your SCO license number information, SCO is hesitant about handing out new licensing information to avoid giving away licenses. If you have the license information, media packs are inexpensive to replace, about $69 on SCO's Web site for free UnixWare 7.

Author's Note

SCO generally will charge for replacement licenses, although there once was a case where proof of purchase was used to get a new license number by a company whose licenses had been misplaced. Do not count on free replacement.

The System log book should also contain information on the hardware in the system: drive sizes, SCSI IDs, controller models, tape drive model, memory size, and so on. Unfortunately for those of us who have been accustomed to OpenServer's /etc/hwconfig program, the DCU is as close as we can get to the information currently. Use `resmgr` to print out the configuration.

The System log book should contain information on problems that have occurred and how they were resolved. How many times have you had to try to remember how a particular problem was resolved several years ago? The new system administrator inheriting responsibility for a system will thank you for creating a well-documented System log book.

PART III

Maintaining the System

CHAPTER 15

System Administration

- System management
  Several miscellaneous system managers that do not fall into other chapters are discussed here. Learn how to manage systems remotely.
- Producing an exhaustive system configuration report
  UnixWare 7 has a utility from the beta development that produces an HTML document with comprehensive system information; learn how to run it.
- Changing the system name
  There is more to changing the system name than you may expect. Learn how to catch all the occurrences of the system name.

System Management

Many of the graphical administration tools have been discussed throughout this book. Some do not fall into operation categories, such as networking or file system management. Those remaining tools are included in this chapter along with some other general system administration.

Remote Administration

Remote administration is possible from the command line through `telnet` and `rlogin`. Remote administration is also possible using the GUI. To enhance the ability to use remote administration while maintaining security, UnixWare 7 offers the ability to allow a system administrator to designate the remote systems and users that will be allowed to remotely administer the local system.

The SCOadmin managers that do not support remote administration are

- Print Job Manager
- Device Configuration Utility
- Plug and Play Manager
- Video Configuration Manager
- SCOadmin Setup Wizard
- All of the NetWare managers
- Intranet Manager
- Network Configuration Manager
- Application Installer
- Install Server
- System Monitor
- The System Tuner

The Setup Wizard

Remote administration is configured through the SCOadmin *Setup Wizard*. The Setup Wizard provides an easy method of configuring both system owners and remote systems authorized to manage the local system. Start the Setup Wizard from the main SCOadmin menu. Figure 15.1 illustrates the initial window.

FIGURE 15.1 *The SCOadmin Setup Wizard initial window.*

After the initial window, another window of instructions is provided describing the steps to be performed. The third window presents a single question: Do you want the local system to be administered by one or by multiple remote systems? If you select multiple administration hosts, the window illustrated in Figure 15.2 will be displayed. If you select one remote administrative host, a window with only one place for a host name will appear.

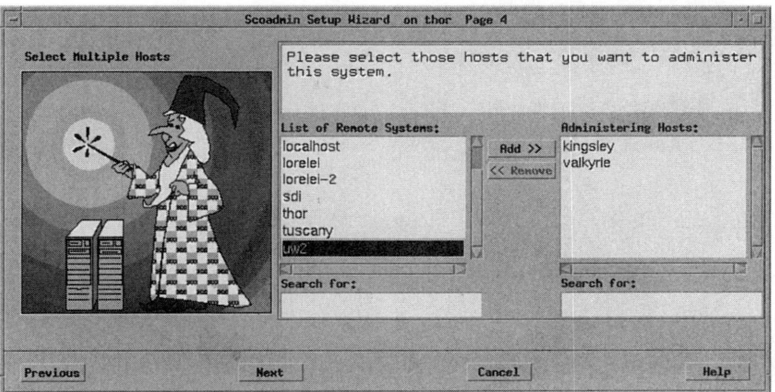

FIGURE 15.2 *Selecting the remote hosts allowed to manage the local system.*

After you have selected the hosts to manage the local system, the next window allows assigning additional system owners (see Figure 15.3). The root user and all active user accounts will not appear in the list of possible accounts. System owners can also be assigned from the command line with the `/usr/lib/scoadmin/account/make-owner` command and from the Account Manager. See the man pages for make-owner (1M) for more information.

Warning

System owner authorizations confer considerable powers to a user account; use caution in creating system owners. Remote login without a password is enabled by the .rhosts files. These should be used carefully because of security considerations.

The final window to appear is a recap of the selections made in the previous windows (see Figure 15.4). Click the Confirm button to finish. When the wizard closes, the settings have been made. To allow remote administration, the local system owner has a $HOME/.rhosts file created (or updated if it already exists). The entries for the system owner, gene, are shown below based on the entries made in the Setup Wizard:

```
kingsley gene
valkyrie gene
```

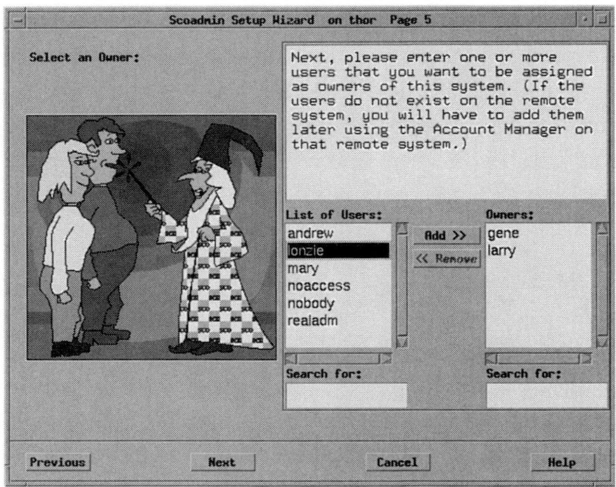

FIGURE 15.3 *Choosing system owners.*

Having created these local files also requires that the user, gene, be a system owner on both of the remote systems, which in this example are kingsley and valkyrie. gene has been given the system owner privileges on the local system.

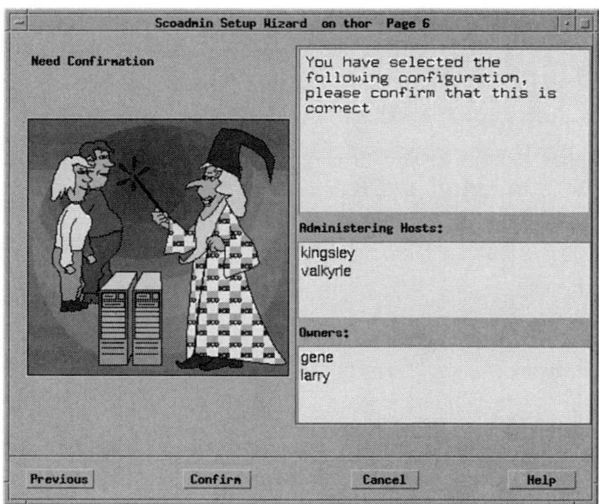

FIGURE 15.4 *The final Setup Wizard window.*

Creating Host Groups for Remote Administration

After the systems are configured for remote administration, the systems can be administered one at a time or in a group. To administer the systems in a group, you need to create a *host group*.

To create the host group, start a SCOadmin manager, such as the Accounts Manager. From the Host menu select Open Host Group. The list of managers that support host group administration is short:

- Accounts Manager
- File System Manager
- Printer Setup Manager
- System Defaults Manager

From the Open Host Group window shown in the upper-left corner of Figure 15.5, select a master host and the managed hosts. The selection window is shown in the lower-right corner of Figure 15.5. When you have selected the hosts to be managed, you may want to save the host group. It is not saved by default. Click the Read button and select Write. A window titled `Open File` will appear with the home directory of your current login. Enter the name of the file you wish to create for the host group. Click OK. You may have one host group per file, but you may have multiple files.

There are three levels of prompts available. The three levels are

- *On Error*—This is the default level. Prompts will appear when an operation fails on a remote host. You will be prompted if you want to skip to the next host in the group.
- *Never*—You will never be prompted to move to the next host.
- *Always*—After each operation completes, you will be prompted to skip to the next host.

After you have created host groups, you may use them by clicking the Read button; select Read and enter the name of the file with the desired host group. In Figure 15.6, the host group named acct_hostgroup is selected.

Warning

When you perform an operation on a host group, it takes effect on all hosts in the group. For instance, if you create a printer on the parallel port for a host group, a printer will be created on each host in the group. Be certain you want the action to take effect on all hosts.

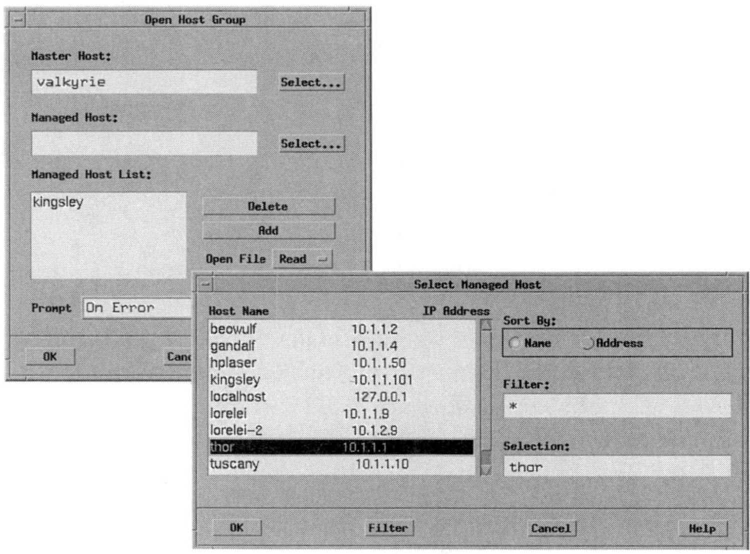

FIGURE 15.5 *Creating a host group.*

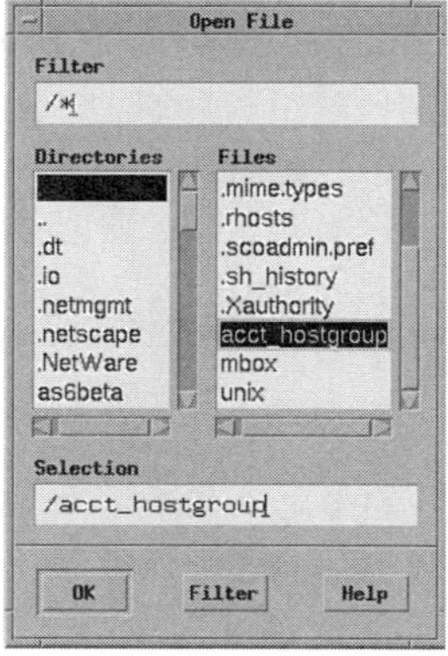

FIGURE 15.6 *Selecting a host group to open.*

Author's Note

The user interface for setting up hosts' groups is not typical of the interfaces SCO has implemented in the other managers. There are several points to keep in mind while using the host group's creation and modification:

- *When adding a managed host, it is not clear that you are updating the window below until you've added a few hosts.*
- *It's very unclear as to what the Read/Write button does.*

- *It's not possible to back out of the Write phase without attempting to write something—there's no Cancel button. The file written out is an ASCII text file with the master host name on the first line and the other hosts listed on additional lines.*

If remote administration is not working, try the following:

- Use `rlogin` from the master system to a managed system. If you cannot `rlogin` without a password, check the .rhosts file on the managed system for your account.
- Log in to the managed system and run the manager. If you cannot run the manager, your local privileges are not set correctly.

International Settings Manager

The International Settings Manager can be reached by selecting SCOadmin, System, International Settings Manager. The initial window displays the current settings for the system. Under the Settings menu option, the Modify option allows setting the Locale, Keyboard, and Code Set. Figure 15.7 illustrates the International Settings Manager.

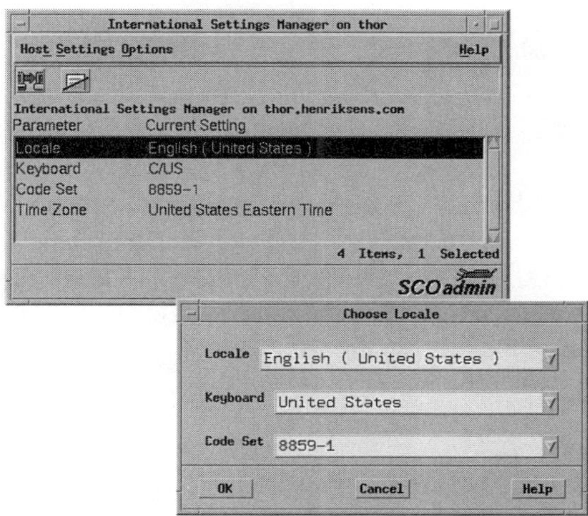

FIGURE 15.7 *Changing the International Settings.*

The International Settings Manager changes files in /etc/default. The locale can be set on a systemwide basis here.

System Defaults Manager

The *System Defaults Manager* provides a single point from which many of the system defaults can be reviewed or modified. Some of these files are in the

/etc/default directory. Several of these defaults are single entries. To modify the defaults, double-click the name of the defaults or single-click and select Defaults, Modify. Figure 15.8 shows part of the list of defaults files available. To the right of many of the names is the man page reference.

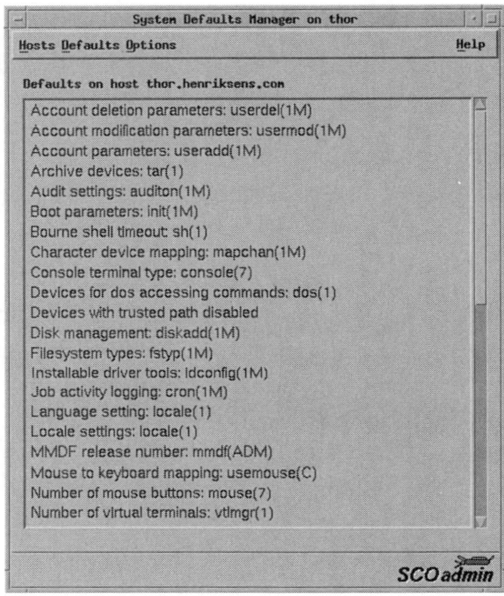

FIGURE 15.8 *The Systems Defaults Manager.*

When you modify the defaults, the file is brought into the desktop editor. You may use arrow keys to move around the window, the Delete key to delete the character under the cursor, and the Backspace key to delete the character to the left of the cursor. To enter new characters, type them in. There is no insert mode and command mode as in the vi editor. Figure 15.9 illustrates modifying the /etc/default/tar file.

System Information Manager

The *System Information Manager* is a one-screen report of basic system information. Select SCOadmin, System, System Information. Figure 15.10 illustrates the information.

System Logs Manager

The *Systems Logs Manager* shows only two logs in the list when the system is installed. To make this tool more valuable, you may add more logs to it. Figure 15.11 illustrates the System Logs Manager. From the main window you can determine the size of the logs.

```
Modify tar
#ident  "@(#)tar:tar.dfl        1.1.3.6"
#ident "$Header: /sms/sinixV5.4es/rcs/s19-full/usr/src/cmd/tar/tar.dfl,v 1.1 91/
#           device              block    size   tape
archive0=/dev/rdsk/f0q15dt      15       1200    n
archive1=/dev/rdsk/f1q15dt      15       1200    n
archive2=/dev/rdsk/f05ht        15       1200    n
archive3=/dev/rdsk/f15ht        15       1200    n
archive4=/dev/rdsk/f03dt        18       720     n
archive5=/dev/rdsk/f13dt        18       720     n
archive6=/dev/rdsk/f03ht        18       1440    n
archive7=/dev/rdsk/f13ht        18       1440    n
archive8=/dev/rmt/c0s0          20       0       y
#archive9=/dev/null #reserved
#
# The default device in the absence of a numeric or "-f device" argument
archive=/dev/rdsk/f0t           15       1200    n

OK                              Cancel                               Help
```

FIGURE 15.9 *Modifying the /etc/default/tar defaults file.*

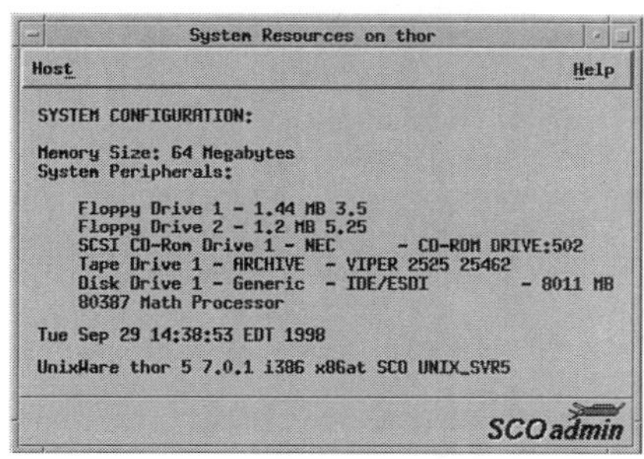

FIGURE 15.10 *The System Information Manager.*

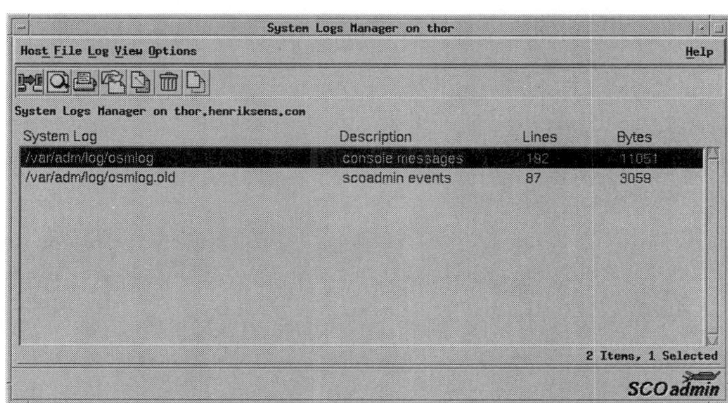

FIGURE 15.11 *Viewing the System Logs Manager.*

To add new logs to the list, select Log, Include Log. The window shown in the upper part of Figure 15.12 will appear. To browse for a log file, click Select. The window in the lower-half of Figure 15.12 will appear. Many of the log files are in the /var/adm and var/adm/log directory. As an example, you may want to include /var/adm/log/ppp.log.

You may also want to add application-specific logs for your installation. To clear entries from log files, select Log, Clear. Files may be dropped from the window with Log, Exclude. From the File menu option, you may view the contents of a file, save the contents of the file into another file, or print a file.

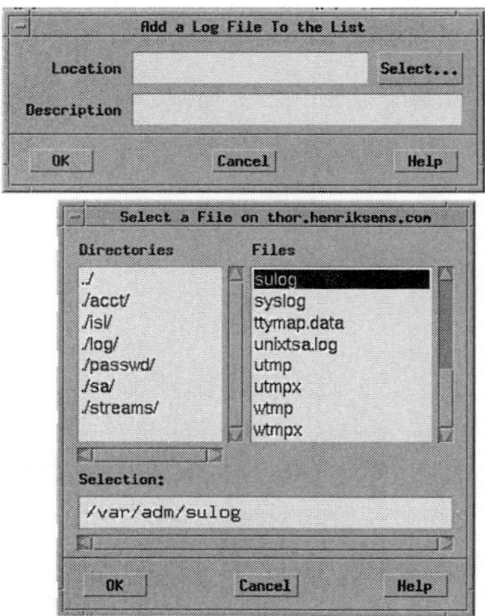

FIGURE 15.12 *Including a new log in the System Logs Manager.*

To clear other files that are not included here, you should use the `> filename` method. This is better than deleting and re-creating the file because the ownership and permissions are not changed. The following files will continually grow unless truncated:

/var/adm/wtmp	A history of all logins (linked to /etc/wtmp). This file may be empty under low security.
/var/adm/loginlog	A record of bad login attempts (see the man pages on loginlog(4)). This will appear only if created by an administrator.
/var/adm/sulog	A record of all su attempts.
/var/adm/osmlog	The operating system messages log.

System Time Manager

The *System Time Manager* allows setting the date and time, as shown in Figure 15.13. The time zone may also be changed through the Host, Change Time Zone or by clicking the time zone icon.

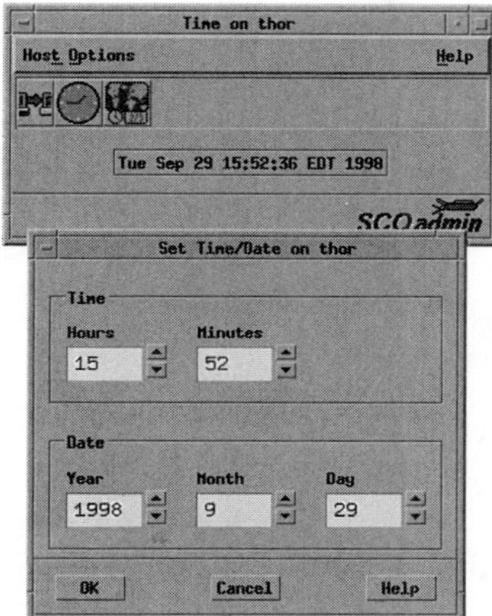

FIGURE 15.13 *Setting the date and time with the System Time Manager.*

Warning

If you test for Year 2000 problems on your system, you should not set the time forward and test, then set the time back. This can leave process running in a negative elapsed time. Files that are used by the operating system may have had their date of last access set to a future date and time. These changes can cause unexpected and undesirable behavior. You should either reinstall the operating system after such testing or restore a tape of the root file system to restore the date and time.

Video Configuration Manager

Under the Hardware menu option in SCOadmin is the *Video Configuration Manager*, shown in Figure 15.14. From the Video Configuration Manager, you can change the video adapter, the monitor, and the resolution.

Warning

Incorrectly setting the video can result in loss of all screen functionality. Setting an inappropriate refresh rate may damage the monitor. You may restore the video to standard VGA by telnetting into the system or booting to single-user mode and executing one of the following:

```
/usr/bin/X/setvideomode -stdvga

/usr/bin/X/setvideomode -default
```

The option to reset to default will restore the video setting to the initial installation video settings. Executing `setvideomode` *without options will display the current system video configuration. The /usr/bin/X11/VideoHelp command will report what the system thinks the video chipset is.*

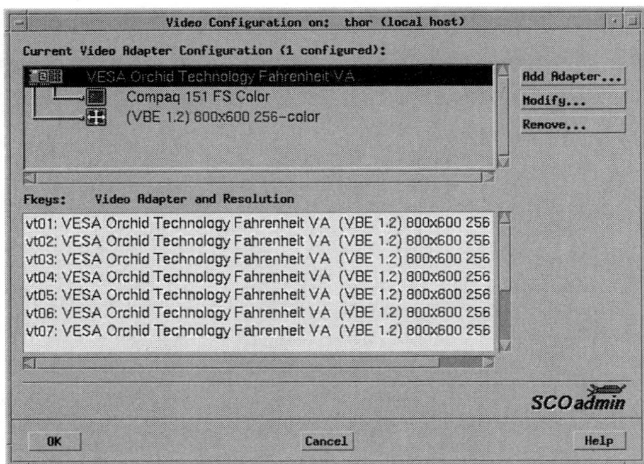

FIGURE 15.14 *The Video Configuration Manager.*

From the window shown in Figure 15.14, you may modify the monitor or resolutions settings. Click either the monitor or the resolution under the adapter and click the Modify button to bring up the Modify window shown in Figure 15.15. You may change the monitor type, the resolution, and the function key setup.

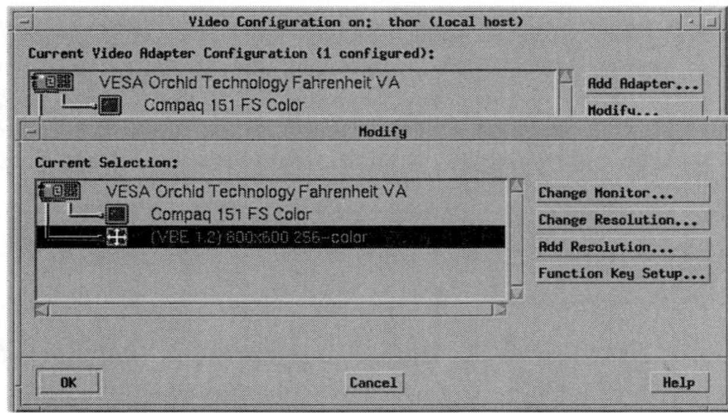

FIGURE 15.15 *Changing the monitor, resolution, or function key setup.*

Reports Manager

The *Reports Manager* has two categories of reports:

- Users
- System accounting

The user reports are presented in Chapter 17, "User Administration." The Reports Manager allows enabling and disabling of accounting and generating accounting reports. Reports on accounting are available on a daily or monthly basis. The Reports Manager is in the System folder in SCOadmin.

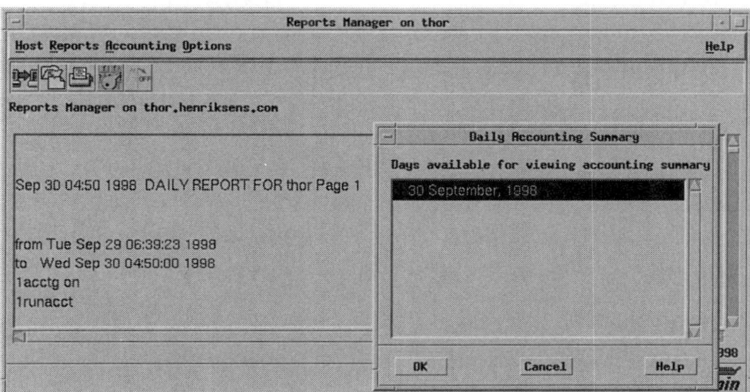

FIGURE 15.16 *Viewing the Daily Accounting report through the Reports Manager.*

Under the Reports menu is the File Security option. This option will provide details on any files that do not have the proper size or ownership based on the /etc/security/tcb/privs file.

```
UX:initprivs: WARNING: File "/usr/bin/talk" fails validation: entry
ignored
UX:initprivs: WARNING: 1 entry ignored in "/etc/security/tcb/privs"
```

Logging Options for SCOadmin

When using SCOadmin, the logging detail can be increased from the default error logging. Figure 15.17 illustrates the logging options. SCOhelp states the errors are logged to /var/adm/syslog, which is not completely correct. Some messages appear in both the /var/adm/syslog and the /var/adm/log/osmlog. One SCO technical staff person recommends watching both logs.

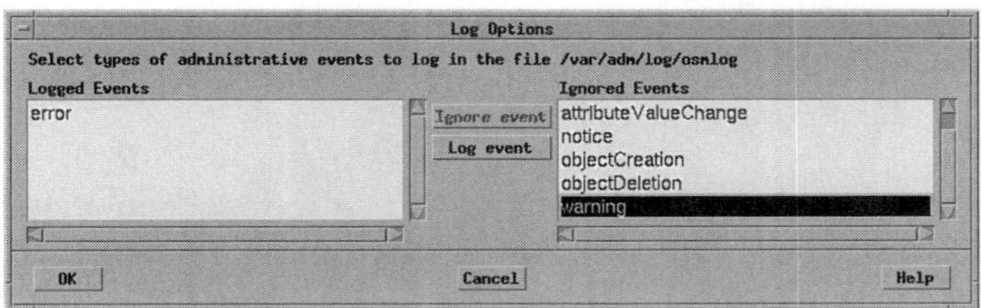

FIGURE 15.17 *Setting the logging options for SCOadmin.*

Producing an Exhaustive System Configuration Report

Many tools exist in UNIX to print information about a system. The most complete on UnixWare 7 is the *z35SysInfo script*. This was designed during the UnixWare 7 Beta program. It will send email to `gemhwinfo@sco.com` if your system is connected to the Internet. You may want to change the script to remove the email references or change the email address to root at your system. To run the script, execute the following from the command line:

```
# sh /usr/lib/X11/testtools/z35SysInfo
```

After it has been run, look in /tmp for a file named <*systemname*>.sysinfo.html. Use your browser to read it. The output is an excellent addition to your System administration logbook. Copy the file from /tmp if you want to save it. Remember that /tmp is a memfs and, therefore, temporary.

Figure 15.18 shows the first page of the listing with all the commands that were used to accumulate the information.

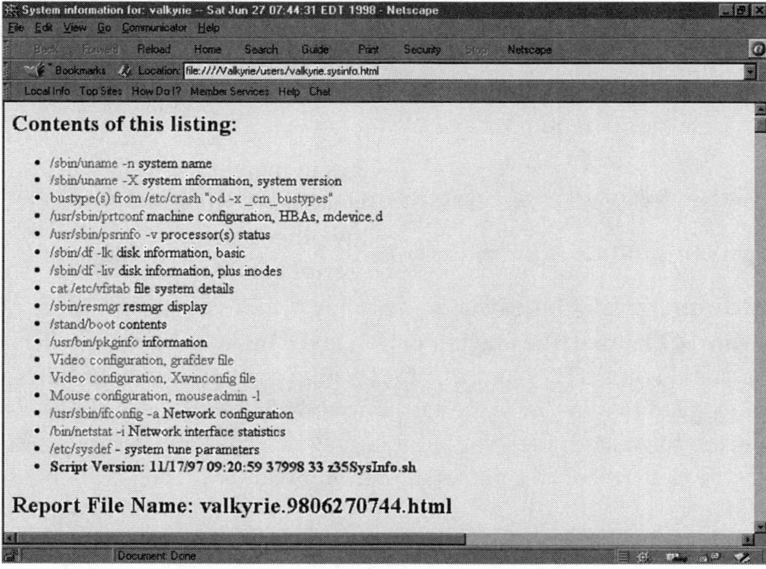

FIGURE 15.18 *The first page of the sysinfo listing.*

The listing contains one of the best listings of the hardware configuration available for UnixWare 7. Figure 15.19 illustrates the information from the Device Configuration Utility (DCU).

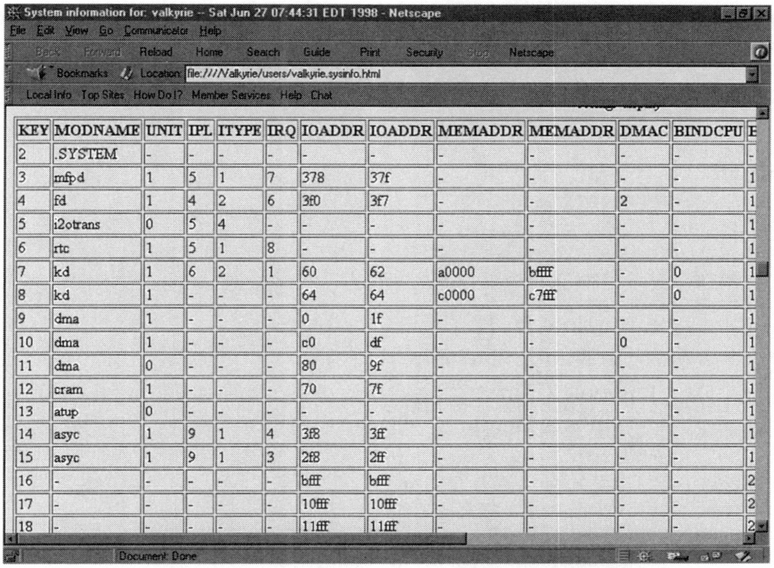

KEY	MODNAME	UNIT	IPL	ITYPE	IRQ	IOADDR	IOADDR	MEMADDR	MEMADDR	DMAC	BINDCPU	E
2	.SYSTEM	-	-	-	-	-	-	-	-	-	-	-
3	mfpd	1	5	1	7	378	37f	-	-	-	-	1
4	fd	1	4	2	6	3f0	3f7	-	-	2	-	1
5	i2otrans	0	5	4	-	-	-	-	-	-	-	1
6	rtc	1	5	1	8	-	-	-	-	-	-	1
7	kd	1	6	2	1	60	62	a0000	bffff	-	0	1
8	kd	1	-	-	-	64	64	c0000	c7fff	-	0	1
9	dma	1	-	-	-	0	1f	-	-	-	-	1
10	dma	1	-	-	-	c0	df	-	-	0	-	1
11	dma	0	-	-	-	80	9f	-	-	-	-	1
12	cram	1	-	-	-	70	7f	-	-	-	-	1
13	atup	0	-	-	-	-	-	-	-	-	-	1
14	asyc	1	9	1	4	3f8	3ff	-	-	-	-	1
15	asyc	1	9	1	3	2f8	2ff	-	-	-	-	1
16	-	-	-	-	-	bfff	bfff	-	-	-	-	2
17	-	-	-	-	-	10fff	10fff	-	-	-	-	2
18	-	-	-	-	-	11fff	11fff	-	-	-	-	2

FIGURE 15.19 *The DCU information in sysinfo.*

Changing the System Name

Changing the system name involves changes in many places. Depending on your configuration, the name change using `uname -S` will change the node name for basic purposes, but it misses many other places where the name is imbedded in files such as /etc/hosts. The script below will search through the file system in known locations to change all occurrences. This script is also designed to change the IP address.

Author's Note

If you find another location where the name change is missed, please send me an email.

```
#!/bin/sh
# script to change name and IP address of a UnixWare 7 system
# Andrew Merrill, The Computer Classroom
#
# you must reboot after running this script
#
# to use, set the four variables below to appropriate values

oldname=old-system-name
newname=new-system-name

oldip="old-ip-address"
newip="new-ip-address"
```

```
###########################################################################
# change system name from $oldname to $newname

/sbin/setuname -n $newname

for file in \
/etc/inet/hosts \
/etc/net/ticlts/hosts \
/etc/net/ticots/hosts \
/etc/net/ticotsord/hosts \
/etc/netware/.olduname \
/etc/netware/nwconfig \
/etc/nodename \
/usr/ns-home/admserv/httpd-80/magnus.conf \
/usr/ns-home/admserv/ns-admin.conf \
/usr/ns-home/cgi-bin/counters/conf/count.cfg \
/usr/ns-home/docs/include/hostname.inc \
/usr/ns-home/docs/include/nodename.inc \
/usr/ns-home/docs/include/scohelp.inc \
/usr/ns-home/docs/include/ttalogin.inc \
/usr/ns-home/httpd-80/config/magnus.conf \
/usr/ns-home/httpd-scohelphttp/config/magnus.conf \
/usr/vision/vfsprofile/current.prf \
/usr/vision/vfsprofile/factory.prf \
/var/adm/isl/ifile \
/var/adm/lastlog
do
    if cp $file $file\#
    then
        sed "s/$oldname/$newname/g" < $file\# > $file
    fi
done

for dir in \
/var/spool/lp/requests/$oldname \
/var/spool/lp/tmp/.net/requests/$oldname \
/var/spool/lp/tmp/.net/tmp/$oldname \
/var/spool/lp/tmp/$oldname
do
    mv $dir `echo $dir | sed "s/$oldname/$newname/"`
done

rm /var/spool/lp/temp
ln -s /var/spool/lp/tmp/$newname /var/spool/lp/temp

########################################################################
# change IP address from $oldip to $newip

for file in \
/etc/confnet.d/inet/interface \
/etc/inet/config \
/etc/inet/hosts \
```

```
/etc/inet/nb.conf \
/usr/ns-home/admserv/ns-admin.conf \
/var/adm/isl/ifile
do
    if cp $file $file\#
    then
        sed "s/$oldip/$newip/g" < $file\# > $file
    fi
done
```

CHAPTER 16

Starting and Stopping

- **Run levels**
  Learn how run levels control UnixWare 7. New to SCO OpenServer users is run level 3.
- **Startup**
  Learn how the startup routines work. Boot alternate copies of UnixWare 7 or other operating systems.
- **Shutdown**
  Learn how to shut down the system several different ways.

UnixWare 7 Run Levels

UNIX uses *run levels* to move from one state of operation to another. The run levels are passed to the `init` process, which initiates the run level changes and maintains the operations of the current run level. Starting and stopping UnixWare 7 is controlled by passing new run levels to `init`. `init` manages run levels and determines, based on the /etc/inittab, which processes should be run as the system changes run levels.

The run levels for UnixWare 7 include:

- `0`—Shut down. It is safe to turn off power.
- `1`—Administrative mode. All filesystems are mounted whether the system is brought up to run level `1` or down from multiuser to run level `1`.

OpenServer 5 Tip

In OpenServer 5, `init 1` dismounts all filesystems other than /stand and root. Another difference is that when leaving run level 1 for run level 3, the console remains logged in.

- 2—Multiuser. All filesystems are mounted; no network file sharing.
- 3—Multiuser with network file sharing. NFS daemons are started, and remote NFS filesystems are mounted. VisionFS shares are available. This is the default run level from boot.
- 4—Not used.
- 5—Shut down and display `Press any key to reboot.`
- 6—Shut down and reboot.
- S,s—Single-user mode. The case of S does not matter. The actions taken by run level S depend on whether the run level was initiated from `init` or `shutdown`. If run level S is entered from other than the system console, the system console is reassigned to the device executing the level change. When the system is rebooted, the console will still be on the reassigned device. If the reassigned console can be accessed upon reboot, a message will be sent to the physical console stating where the console has been reassigned. If the device cannot be accessed, the console assignment reverts to the physical console.
    - When moving to run level S from multiuser by use of `init`, all filesystems are left mounted. Many processes, including the lp scheduler, continue to run. For instance, it is possible to perform network operations such as telnet.
    - When moving to run level S from multiuser by the `shutdown` command, the only filesystems left mounted are root, /stand, /var, /dev/fd, and /proc.
    - When booted to run level S, the root, /stand, /var, /dev/fd, and /proc filesystems are mounted. No network programs are running.

  The S,s state is the only one that does not require a properly formatted inittab.
- Q,q—Instructs `init` to reread the inittab for changes. If you change the /etc/inittab, the only ways to have it take effect are to reboot or to use the `init Q` command.

- `a,b,c`—Pseudo-states that can be defined to run certain programs without changing the actual run level. A *pseudo-state* can be used for a process that needs to be restarted while the system is running, but needs to be restarted by `init`. This technique is used, for instance, to restart the daemons for PC Enterprise after reconfiguring the setup.

The remainder of this chapter focuses on how to move between run levels and what happens as run level changes occur.

Starting UnixWare 7

Starting UnixWare 7 can be as simple as turning on the power and walking away while the computer boots. It is when problems occur that the need to understand the boot process arises.

The Power-On Startup Test Sequence

When an Intel-based computer is powered up, the system's BIOS runs a series of *Power-on Self-Tests (POSTs)*. Usually, systems are set to boot from the primary hard drive. The system checks the fdisk table on the hard drive to locate the active system partition. Up until this point, the boot has been non-operating system specific. When the active partition is located, the system loads the partition boot code. In UnixWare 7, this information is located in the *boot slice*. See Chapter 19, "Storage Devices, Filesystems, and Permissions," for more information on the file system slices and their uses. After the partition boot code is loaded, the operating system load begins.

OpenServer 5 Tip

With OpenServer 5, the partition boot code loaded the boot program from /stand. This provided the `boot:` *prompt. With UnixWare 7, unless you intervene in the boot process, you will not see the boot prompt.*

The /stand Directory

The UnixWare 7 kernel and the files that control the boot process reside in the /stand filesystem. The /stand filesystem is a *bfs file system*, a very simple filesystem with no subdirectories and no special device files. Following are the contents of /stand:

```
bfs.blm     dcmp.blm    license       resmgr        stage3.blm
boot        hd.blm      logo.img      resmgr.sav    unix
bootmsgs    help.txt    platform.blm  smallfs.blm   unix.old
```

The files with the .blm suffix are boot-loadable modules. The stage3.blm is the UnixWare 7 boot program, the equivalent of OpenServer 5's /stand/boot. The boot file is not executable. It replaces the /etc/default/boot in OpenServer 5.

The contents of boot are

```
#ident  "@(#)stand:common/boot/conf/boot.hd     1.3"
#ident  "$Header: $"

BLM=hd.blm
files=resmgr,license
rootfs=vxfs
TZ_OFFSET=14400
```

Boot File Parameters

Additional parameters can be added to the boot file and can be set interactively at the boot prompt.

The following parameters are recognized by the boot process:

`BOOTPROG=`*`filename`*	*`filename`* is the program to load during boot. To boot from unix.old, use `BOOTPROG=unix.old`.
`BOOTDEV=`*`device`*	*`device`* is the name of the disk device from which the BOOTPROG is loaded. The format is `hd (unit[partition][,slice])` To boot DOS, enter `boot hd(0,dos)`, assuming there is a DOS partition on the primary disk.
`AUTOBOOT=YES¦NO¦num`	Indicates whether boot should load the kernel or enter an interactive boot session. The default is `num=5` seconds.
`TIMEOUT=`*`number`*	If set, specifies the number of seconds boot will wait for an interactive entry before autobooting.
`CONSOLE=`*`device`*	Overrides the default console device: `CONSOLE=kd(0)`. You can boot with the console redirected to COM1 or COM2. Check the /dev/term/* entries to determine which minor device you want to use. The format is `CONSOLE=iasy(`*`minordev, Bbaudrate`*`)` For example, to set the console to the /dev/term/00h device for hardware flow control at a baud rate of 38,400: `CONSOLE=iasy(5,B38400)`
`INITFILE=`*`filename`*	The `INITFILE` defaults to /etc/inittab. This is passed to `init` at boot time.

Tip

If you must experiment with changing the /etc/inittab file, make a copy that can be specified in the `INITFILE` *parameter at boot time for recovery in case you make a mistake. If /etc/inittab is missing, the system will display an error,* `Cannot start /etc/inittab`, *and use /etc/conf/init.d/kernel as the inittab.*

The following parameters are not recognized by the boot process, but are passed through to the kernel:

`INITSTATE=`*`runlevel`*	Set *`runlevel`* to the desired run level for booting; `INITSTATE=S` will boot into single user mode. This is handy for recovering the system if you have accidentally selected an incorrect video mode.
`DISABLE_CACHE=(YES/NO)`	When set to `YES`, this disables use of internal and external memory caches.
`ENABLE_4GB_MEM=(YES/NO)`	Setting this to `YES` will enable detection of memory over 4GB.
`ROOTFS=`*`fstype`*	Allows overriding the default root filesystem type built into the kernel. If set to blank, it will allow checking with all configured filesystem types.
`LUNSEARCH=(c:b,t,l)`	Defines devices that should not be searched beyond LUN 0. *LUN* is the Logical Unit Number of the device.

Refer to the man pages on `boot`(4) for more information.

The Bootmsgs File

All of the messages used during boot are stored in the bootmsgs file. Here is part of the bootmsgs file:

```
#ident  "@(#)stand:common/boot/conf/msgs/bootmsgs       1.5"
#ident  "$Header: $"
BOOTMSG1=Starting UnixWare...
BOOTMSG2=Bootstrap Command Processor\
Ready for boot commands... [? for help]\

TITLE=UnixWare 7, based on UNIX System V Release 5 from SCO
COPYRIGHT=Copyright  1976-1998 The Santa Cruz Operation, Inc. and its
suppliers.\
All Rights Reserved.\
\
```

```
RESTRICTED RIGHTS LEGEND:\
\
When licensed to a U.S., State, or Local Government, all Software produced\
by SCO is commercial computer software as defined in FAR 12.212, and has\
been developed exclusively at private expense.  All technical data, or SCO\
commercial computer software/documentation is subject to the provisions of\
FAR 12.211 - "Technical Data", and FAR 12.212 - "Computer Software"\
respectively, or clauses providing SCO equivalent protections in DFARS or\
other agency specific regulations.  Manufacturer: The Santa Cruz Operation,\
Inc., 400 Encinal Street, Santa Cruz, CA 95060.
AUTOMSG=Automatic Boot Procedure
```

The Help File

When booting, help can be obtained from the `[boot]` prompt by typing a question mark or **`help`**. The help information is stored in the help.txt file. Here is part of the help.txt file:

```
Available BOOT commands:
  ? -or- help -- Display this message
  boot [<filename>] -- Load and run specified program; default is BOOTPROG
  dir [<dev>] -- List all files in /stand directory; default device is
➥BOOTDEV
  logo -- Display the logo image until a key is pressed
  logo off -- Don't display logo
  show [-a ¦ <param>] -- Show boot parameter values
        -a -- Show all boot parameters, even messages
        <param> -- Show only the specified boot parameter
  <param>=<value> -- Set the value of a boot parameter
  <param>+=<value> -- Append the value to a boot parameter, inserting a
➥comma

Parameters that are recognized by BOOT:
  ALIGN=<num> -- Alignment requirement for FILES images
  AUTOBOOT=yes¦no¦<num> -- Minimum time (sec) to wait while loading BOOTPROG
  BLM=<filename>{,<filename>} -- Bootstrap Loadable Modules loaded into BOOT
  BOOTDEV=<dev> -- Device BOOTPROG is loaded from
  BOOTMSG1=<text> -- Message displayed when starting to boot
  BOOTMSG2=<text> -- Message displayed when entering interactive mode
  BOOTMSG3=<text> -- String displayed at beginning of command line
  BOOTMSG4=<text> -- String displayed when waiting to display more
  BOOTPROG=<filename> -- Filename of kernel or other program to load and run
```

The Resmgr File

The resmgr file maintains a copy of the Resource Manager database. This is a binary file. The previous copy is saved as resmgr.sav. The resmgr is read at boot time and contains details of device hardware and software configured on the system.

The Unix File

Two copies of the UnixWare 7 kernel, unix and unix.old, are kept in /stand. If experimenting with changes, it might be a wise idea to keep a known good copy, perhaps named unix.good.

OpenServer 5 Tip

Unlike OpenServer 5, UnixWare 7 does not keep copies of unix.safe and unix.install in /stand.

Getting to a Boot Prompt

When booting, you will never see the boot prompt unless you interrupt the boot process. Unlike OpenServer 5, UnixWare 7 does not display a boot prompt allowing you to boot to single user mode.

To interrupt the boot process, press the space bar or the Enter key when you see the UnixWare 7 logo. The logo will disappear and the Boot Command Processor will appear:

```
Boot Command Processor
Ready for boot commands... [? For help]
[boot]
```

The Boot Command Processor

From the boot prompt, you may set any of the parameters for the boot file discussed earlier. If you are having problems with booting, type the **dir** command to list the contents of the /stand directory.

Typing a **?** or **help** will display the help.txt file. When the parameters have been set, type **boot** to restart the boot process.

The show command will show all of the current boot settings. The boot settings determine the device for booting, the boot program, autoboot timeout, and boot message strings. To see the current settings plus the messages file, use show -a. The show command followed by a parameter name can be used to show single parameters:

```
[boot] show BOOTDEV
BOOTDEV=hd(0,2)
```

Booting to Single-User State

To get the system to single-user state, you must get to the boot prompt. At the boot prompt, type the following lines:

```
[boot] INITSTATE=S
[boot] boot
```

Enter the root password when prompted for single-user state. Perform the tasks. Enter a CTRL+D or type **exit**. When prompted for a run level, enter **3** for multiuser, networking mode.

```
# exit
ENTER RUN LEVEL (0-6,s or S): 3
```

Booting Another Kernel

To boot a kernel other than unix, bring the system to the boot prompt. Use the `dir` command to be sure the desired kernel exists in /stand. Set the `BOOTPROG` variable and reboot.

```
[boot] BOOTPROG=unix.good
[boot] go
```

Tip

`boot`, `b`, `go`, *and* `g` *are all synonyms. Use the one you prefer.*

Another method of booting a different version of UNIX is to type the following:

```
[boot] b unix.good
```

Booting Another Operating System

If you have loaded multiple operating systems, you may boot them from the Boot Command Processor. You must know the drive number and, optionally, the partition number and slice number. The format is

```
hd(drive_number[,partition][,slice])
```

If the partition is not defined, it defaults to the active partition, which should be UNIX if the system boots to UNIX without intervention. Other operating systems that may be specified are XENIX, DOS (DOS_12, DOS_16, DOS_32, DOS_EXT), NT, and OS2.

For instance, if the fdisk table shows a DOS and UNIX partition, you can start the DOS partition by using

```
boot hd(0,DOS)
```

Because it is possible to specify the slice number, there exists the possibility of creating backup, bootable root slices.

init and the inittab File

As the kernel is loaded, the `init` process is started. The role of `init` is to spawn processes. In a listing of processes, `init` has process ID 1. The configuration file for init is the /etc/inittab. The inittab file contains the actions for `init` to take when changing run levels.

The inittab is re-created when the kernel environment is rebuilt. Changes to the inittab are not permanent. Change the appropriate files in the /etc/conf directories to ensure that the changes are brought into newly created inittabs. If you make changes to inittab, signal `init` to reread the inittab by using the `init Q` command. The /etc/inittab is rebuilt automatically after a kernel rebuild, and the system reboots to use the new kernel and inittab. Some software will not require a kernel relink, but will make changes to the inittab. In these cases, `init Q` must be used.

The inittab file consists of lines containing four colon-separated data fields. The fields are

- *Label*—a unique identifier of up to four characters
- *Run-level*—the run-level at which `init` executes the entry
- *Action*—a keyword indicating the action `init` takes
- *Process*—the program that `init` will execute

The `action` keyword may be one of the following:

- *Sysinit*—Execute before accessing the console.
- *Initdefault*—Indicates the default system state.
- *Boot*—Process this entry only at the boot-time read of the inittab file.
- *Bootwait*—Process the entry the first time the system goes from single user to multiuser mode.
- *Wait*—Upon entering the run level that matches this entry, execute and wait for termination.
- *Once*—Upon entering the run level that matches this entry, execute but do not wait. If the process dies, do not restart it.
- *Respawn*—If the process does not exist, start it. If it dies, restart it. Generally used for terminal login sessions.
- *Off*—Do not process this entry.
- *Ondemand*—Same as `respawn`; used with run-levels `a`, `b`, and `c`.

- *Powerfail*—Execute when a power failure signal is received, but do not wait for it to complete.
- *Powerwait*—Execute when a power failure signal is received and wait for the process to terminate.

The following is the line from the inittab that sets the default state to 3, multi-user with networking:

```
is:3:initdefault:
```

The next line illustrates how a single entry can execute in multiple run levels. The processor administration tool manages systems with multiple processors. The psradm program is executed in run levels 1, 2, 3, and 4.

```
onl:1234:wait:/sbin/psradm -n -a
```

These next lines control the system's actions as run levels are switched from 0 through 6. Note that the programs to be run, with the exception of /sbin/uadmin, are shell scripts. The entries for these scripts in the /etc directory are symbolic links to these files. Of the scripts listed, only the r2 entry is executed in two run levels: 2 and 3.

```
r0:0:wait:/sbin/rc0 off >/dev/console 2>&1 </dev/console
r1:1:wait:/sbin/rc1 >/dev/console 2>&1 </dev/console
r2:23:wait:/sbin/rc2 >/dev/console 2>&1 </dev/console
r3:3:wait:/sbin/rc3  >/dev/console 2>&1 </dev/console
fw:5:wait:/sbin/uadmin 2 2 >/dev/console 2>&1 </dev/console
rb:6:wait:/sbin/uadmin 2 1 >/dev/console 2>&1 </dev/console
```

The console login is available at all levels.

```
co:12345:respawn:/usr/lib/saf/ttymon -g -p "Console Login: " -d /dev/
➥console -l console
```

To speed up the process of getting the logins to the users, some of the processes are delayed until the logins are started. The dinit script executes the startup scripts in /etc/dinit.d, which include uucp, lp, and cron.

```
d2:23:wait:/sbin/dinit >/dev/console 2>&1 </dev/console
```

The Startup Directories

When `init` reads the inittab, it runs scripts such as /sbin/rc2 to get to the appropriate run level. The rc2 script runs scripts located in the /etc/rc2.d directory. This also occurs with the following directories:

- /etc/rc0 and /etc/rc0.d
- /etc/rc1 and /etc/rc1.d

- /etc/rc3 and /etc/rc3.d
- /etc/dinit and /etc/dinit.d

OpenServer 5 Tip

There is an /etc/rc.d directory. Unlike OpenServer 5, this directory does not have the subdirectories numbered 0 through 9. Scripts in /etc/rc.d will be executed by /etc/rc2.d if they do not also exist in the /etc/init.d directory.

If you need to have an activity start at a particular run level, insert a script in the appropriate directory. The scripts should be placed in the /etc/init.d and then linked into the appropriate directory for the run level. For example, the file MOUNTFSYS exists in the /etc/init.d directory. The file /etc/rc2.d/S01MOUNTFSYS is a hard link to MOUNTFSYS. Files are executed in ASCII sorted sequence. S01MOUNTFSYS executes before S02PRESERVE.

The /etc/rc2.d Directory

The /etc/rc2.d directory contains the following list of scripts by default:

```
K20nfs          S42ls          S70unixtsa     S88ldap
S01MOUNTFSYS    S65loopback    S71ppp         S90sysinfo2html
S02PRESERVE     S69ARCserve    S73snmp        S93scohelphttp
S02audit        S69inet        S74netbios     S99dtlogin
S02mse          S70Nnwip       S75rpc         S99ms_srv
S05RMTMPFILES   S70Pnw         S79sr
S15mkdtab       S70Rnuc        S80nis
S15nd           S70pf          S81sendmail
```

Only files with an uppercase S or K are executed. The S files are executed for starting and the K files when stopping. To disable a script, rename it with a lowercase first letter. Do not remove scripts, you may need them later.

To add a user-defined routine for startup, you should carefully pick the position your file will occupy in the sort sequence. If your routine depends on NFS or VisionFS, it should be placed in the /etc/rc3.d directory. Normally, user-defined routines should go toward the end of the list. A commonly used entry is S89USRDEFINE.

When making user-defined entries, you should log error messages to a file because they may get lost in the boot messages. Test the script at the command line first to make sure that it does not hang up the system. If the commands being started will run for a long time, start them in the background:

```
command &
```

The /etc/dinit.d Directory

As a safe alternative, place your script in the /etc/dinit.d directory because those scripts start after the logins are generated. The following scripts are in the dinit.d directory:

```
S23ttymap        S70uucp      S80cs        S81np
S69keymaster     S75cron      S80lp        S85perf
```

The /etc/rc3.d Directory

The rc3.d directory brings the system to multiuser with network file sharing. A default installation with NFS and VisionFS will have the following entries:

```
S22nfs       s90visionfs
```

If you write a script that is dependent on remote access, place it after the scripts in this directory, such as S91USRDEFINE.

Kernel Rebuild on Boot

When changes are made that require a kernel rebuild, the rebuild is performed at reboot by default. If the system is shut down with a run level of 5 or 6, the rebuild is performed at shutdown rather than at boot.

At boot, messages will appear that the kernel will be relinked. Press Enter to start the rebuild. When complete, the system will reboot to use the new kernel. The old kernel is `/stand/unix.old`, and the newly linked kernel is `/stand/unix`.

To stop the system from automatically rebuilding the kernel on boot, set the `AUTOREBLD` flag to `NO`:

```
defadm idtools AUTOREBLD=NO
```

You will be required to confirm the rebuild. At the prompt, you are asked to press Enter to confirm the rebuild or press Esc to stop the rebuild. If Esc is pressed, the rebuild is scheduled for the next boot.

Stopping UnixWare 7

Shutdown is the orderly method of warning users and gracefully shutting down UnixWare 7. The only time you should turn off the power without shutting down the operating system is in an emergency or if the system has locked up and you cannot get enough control to shut down.

There are several methods of shutting down the system. SCOadmin offers a Shutdown Manager. The `shutdown` command can be run from the command line. The `init` command can be used to signal the `init` process to stop. For special purpose use there is `reboot` and `halt`, which are part of the BSD compatibility package. If `halt` and `reboot` are not in the /usr/ucb directory, add the bsdcompat package to the system from the install media.

The System Shutdown Manager

From the SCOadmin menu, select System, System Shutdown Manager. Figure 16.1 illustrates the System Shutdown Manager with a message typed in and five minutes until shutdown. If you set the time to zero minutes, you cannot type in a message.

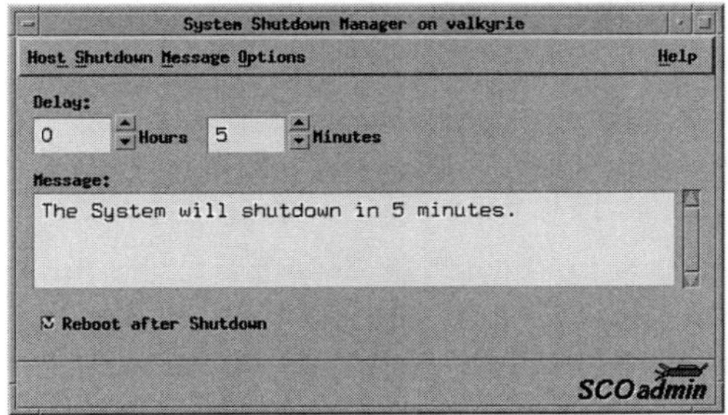

FIGURE 16.1 *The System Shutdown Manager.*

From the System Shutdown Manager, you can select the Host menu to shut down another host. The Shutdown menu allows you to begin the shutdown. From the Message menu, you can read in the message from a file or clear the message. When you select Shutdown, Begin Shutdown, a pop-up window appears asking `Shutdown system?`. Press OK to shut down or Cancel to quit.

When you have started the shutdown, the message you entered will appear on all logged-in terminals, as shown in Figure 16.2. If you need to stop the shutdown process, run `ps -ef` on the system. The `shutdown` command will appear in the listing. Shutdown can be killed by root.

> **Warning**
>
> *The `shutdown` command will appear in the process status listing as will a `sleep` command that is the timer for the shutdown. Do not kill the `sleep` command or the shutdown will begin immediately.*

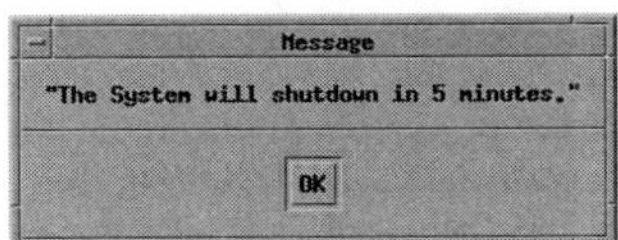

FIGURE 16.2 *Shutdown message displayed to users.*

The *shutdown* Command

UnixWare 7 can be shut down from the command line with the `shutdown` command. The format is

```
shutdown -g<grace> -i<level> -y
```

The grace period is the time in seconds to wait before starting the shutdown. The default is stored in /etc/default/shutdown.

> *OpenServer 5 Tip*
>
> *The grace period is not minutes!* `-g5` *will bring the system down in five seconds, not five minutes.*

The level for the `-i` option is the new run level. The default is `0`, shutdown. The `-y` option answers the question: `Do you want to continue?`

> *OpenServer 5 Tip*
>
> *There is no option to send a message with the reason for the shutdown. The* `-f` *option will return an error message. There is also no* `su` *option for shutting down to single user.*

Depending on the number of users logged in at the time shutdown is executed, the behavior may vary. If several users are logged in, there will be three messages. The grace period will be used between each of them. If the only user logged in is the one issuing the `shutdown` command, or if the grace period is zero, then no messages are issued.

Using *init* to Shut Down

Shutdown is a shell script wrapper around the `init` command. If you do not need to wait for messages, you may issue the `init` command directly with the new run level. For example,

```
# init 0
```

will start a shutdown. This will go through all the normal shutdown processes.

> *Tip*
>
> *There is no need to type the* `sync` *command before either the* `shutdown` *or* `init` *command. Many users with a background dating back to XENIX habitually type* **`sync;sync;shutdown`**. *When the disks are unmounted, a sync is performed to flush the buffer cache to disk before shutdown.*

Any of the run levels detailed earlier in this chapter can be used with either the `shutdown` or `init` command.

halt

The /usr/ucb directory has a `halt` command. `halt` writes out impending disk data and stops the processor. While the man pages state it is the equivalent of the `init 0` command, it does not display the announcements of the processes halting that `init 0` does. `halt` is a component of the bsdcompat package.

reboot

The `/usr/ucb/reboot` command performs a halt and multiuser reboot. One of the options to reboot is `-n`, which means "do not sync the disks."

Is the `-n` option safe? The man pages state for the `-n` option:

> Avoid the sync (1M). It can be used if a disk or the processor is on fire.

Reboot is a component of the bsdcompat package.

Ctrl+Alt+Delete

If the system parameters are set correctly, you may initiate a reboot with the Ctrl+Alt+Delete keystroke combination. This option will probably not be set on a server. When Novell first promoted UnixWare, they featured it as a desktop operating system where a quick reboot would not affect other users. To set this configuration, execute:

```
/etc/conf/bin/idtune -g CONSOLE_SECURITY
```

The output should be similar to:

```
0    1    0    3
```

The value in the first column is the current setting. The second column is the default. The third and fourth columns are the minimum and maximum.

This setting is used to set two capabilities. The first is Ctrl+Alt+Delete for rebooting. The second is to set Ctrl+Alt+P to panic the system. The value in the first column should be set as follows:

CONSOLE_SECURITY	Ctrl+Alt+Delete	Ctrl+Alt+P
0	Disabled	Disabled
1	Enabled	Disabled
2	Disabled	Enabled
3	Enabled	Enabled

If the output number in the first column was not set correctly, set it with

```
/etc/conf/idtune -f CONSOLE_SECURITY <new_value>
```

The *new_value* should be replaced by a number from 0 to 3. Then relink the kernel:

```
/etc/conf/bin/idbuild -B
```

Reboot to make the kernel effective. The Ctrl+Alt+Delete combination, when used by root or the system owner, will reboot the computer.

The Directories Used in Shutdown

Just as startup uses directories of scripts to create processes, shutdown closes down the processes. The scripts check to see if they were sent a `start` or `stop` argument and execute scripts accordingly.

The /etc/rc2.d directory contains a single file beginning with K. This is used when moving from run level 3 to run level 2 and stops NFS. The /etc/rc1.d directory is used to kill processes when going down to run level 1 and to start processes when moving up to run level 1.

```
K00ANNOUNCE  K20lp     K67snmp    K68sendmail   S01MOUNTFSYS
K10dtlogin   K40nfs    K68Nnuc    K69inet       S02mse
K19ms_srv    K40ppp    K68Pnw     K80nis        S42ls
K19np        K44ldap   K68Rnwip   K85nd
```

The /etc/rc0.d directory contains several scripts used to shut the system completely down. These scripts are responsible for the orderly shutdown of processes to avoid data loss.

```
K00ANNOUNCE   K10dtlogin   K20lp    K44ldap   K68Rnwip      K69inet
K02audit      K19ms_srv    K40nfs   K68Nnuc   K68netbios    K80nis
K02mse        K19np        K40ppp   K68Pnw    K68sendmail   K85nd
```

Shutting down the system properly will prevent loss of data in program buffers and will leave the system in the proper condition for a reboot.

CHAPTER 17

User Administration

- **User account properties**
  Learn about the properties you can control when setting up an account.
- **SCOadmin user management**
  Learn how to create and manage user accounts with the graphical user interface.
- **Command-line user management**
  Learn how to create and manage accounts from the command line.
- **User and password reporting**
  Learn how to run account and password reports.

User Accounts

Two methods of managing user accounts are available:

- Graphical
- Command line

Both methods are covered here. The two methods are not intermixed to allow the graphically oriented administrator to avoid the commands and filenames associated with the command line methods. Both methods may be interchanged by the administrator to suit the requirements of the moment.

The command-line oriented administrator and programmers will find all the commands and files in one section for reference purposes. The latter part of the chapter covers the files that control default configuration for users, the graphical access to the default configuration files, and user status reports, which are generated from the User Management GUI.

Each user requiring login access to a UnixWare 7 system must have a user account. The user accounts are maintained in the /etc/passwd file. Additional information is maintained in the security database located in the /etc/security directory. Topics on user administration related to security are discussed in Chapter 22, "Security."

Default options may be set for user administration. These are covered in both the graphical and command line sections. Setting defaults can speed the management of users and reduce the possibility of errors.

Login Shells

When users log in to a UnixWare 7 system, they run a *shell*. With UnixWare 7 there are a variety of shells for use depending on the user's needs:

- /sbin/sh—the only shell trusted for administration when the Enhanced Security utilities are installed; this is the default shell for the root and the system owner account
- /usr/bin/sh—the Bourne shell
- /u95/bin/sh—a version of the Korn shell that complies with the X/Open Interface Definitions, also known as ksh-93
- /usr/lib/rsh—a restricted shell with reduced functionality

OpenServer 5 Tip

/usr/bin/rsh is the remote shell, not a restricted shell like /bin/rsh in OpenServer 5.

- /usr/bin/jsh—a Bourne shell with job control capabilities
- /usr/bin/csh—a version of the C shell
- /usr/bin/ksh—a link to /u95/bin/sh
- /usr/bin/wksh—a windowing Korn shell
- /usr/bin/rksh—a restricted Korn shell
- /usr/bin/ksh88—a Korn shell

- bash—(Bourne Again shell) available on the SCO Skunkware CD
- /OpenServer/bin/sh—an OpenServer Bourne shell
- /OpenServer/bin/ksh—an OpenServer Korn shell
- /OpenServer/bin/csh—an OpenServer C shell

The selection of shell is dependent on the user's preferences and needs. For C programmers, consider the C shell. For security risks, select a restricted shell. For good shell scripting capability, select a Korn shell. Often users log in and are immediately presented with an application menu. These users have no knowledge of the shell that was run; the administrator can use a shell that suits the administrator and the application.

System Environment Login Files

When users log in, the environment scripts for their shells are executed. For Bourne and Korn shells, the /etc/profile and the .profile script in the user's home directory are executed. For users of the C shell, the /etc/cshrc is executed; then the .login file and .cshrc are executed in the home directory.

Tip

The Korn shells do not execute the .kshrc file by default when the user is created using the `useradd` *command. Check the .profile in the user's home directory to be sure the* `ENV` *variable is set to* `.kshrc`*:*

```
ENV=$HOME/.kshrc
export ENV
```

The /etc/profile and /etc/cshrc files set the time, terminal type, and perform other housekeeping functions. These environment files contain more than their OpenServer 5 counterparts. You should examine them with respect to your operating environment.

The .profile for the Korn shell is very short in comparison to its OpenServer counterpart. The file states that it is a default script, and the user is expected to edit it according to the user's needs.

To make changes for all users system wide, place the lines of script in the /etc/profile or /etc/cshrc depending on their login shells.

To change the .profile or .login for all newly created users, change the default scripts for the different shells before creating the user accounts.

Changing the scripts in the skeleton directory will ensure that each new account gets the correct script at creation time.

Warning

There are two directories for skeleton (.profile and .login) files: /etc/skel and /usr/lib/scoadmin/account/skel. The /etc/skel directory is used by the command line program useradd. The /usr/lib/scoadmin/account/skel directory is used by the graphical SCOadmin utility. In a future release, the two will be integrated. Check to see if both exist on your system. One solution to the problem is to set the default `SKELDIR` *in /etc/default/useradd to the directory used by SCOadmin. Another solution would be to create one directory as a link to the other.*

The problem with the two directories noted above had me doubting my ability to correctly create accounts. The .profile in /etc/skel has no active lines, while the one in the scoadmin directory does.

In the /usr/lib/scoadmin/account/skel directory is the .env file. The purpose of the file is to allow inclusion of environment variables that are not shell dependent in format. When I tested this feature, the variables I added were not included in the new user's .env and my additions were deleted from the copy in the skel directory. Changes to the .profile were copied over correctly.

The home Directory

The home directory defaults to the user's name in the /home directory, such as /home/tammym. The home directory contains the user's startup files. If users store files in their home directories, the home directory structure should be backed up regularly.

Warning

The home directory default is established in the /etc/default/useradd file for the command line useradd utility. For the SCOadmin GUI, the /usr/lib/scoadmin/account/accounts file holds the defaults.

If VisionFS, included with UnixWare 7 at no extra charge, is installed for PC-based users, they may use their home directory as a backup location for their PC-based files. If VisionFS is being used for this purpose, you will need to back up the directories and watch disk space. Chapter 19, "Storage Devices, Filesystems, and Permissions," contains information on user disk quotas.

Troubleshooting Tip

Make sure your PC users do not accidentally back up the entire C: drive to their home directory in order to save a few files. A quick way to have them back up critical files is to mount their home directory onto their PC. Create a batch file on the PC with a line such as:

```
XCOPY /E /S C:\"MY DOCUMENTS" F:
```

This will copy the contents of their MY DOCUMENTS directory to their F: drive, assuming that is the name of the local drive for their UNIX home directory. Create a shortcut on the desktop of the PC that executes the batch file. Change the icon to an appropriate one, such as the life raft. To back up, they double-click the life raft icon.

The Group Membership

Groups provide a way to manage users and provide access to system resources for them. Users may belong to multiple groups. The limit on the number of groups a user can belong to is set in NGROUPS_MAX. NGROUPS_MAX defaults to 16 groups and is a tunable parameter.

To change NGROUPS_MAX, in the SCOadmin GUI select System, System Tuner, Process Limit Parameters. The range for NGROUPS_MAX is 1 to 32. This limit is the maximum number of groups a user may belong to simultaneously. A user may use the `newgrp` command to become a member of a group to which he/she is not normally assigned.

The Locale

The locale specifies the language the user will see when using the system, such as the currency symbol, time and date representation, sort order, and the names of days and months. The C locale is the standard POSIX locale. Although C is the default, it should not be used unless you need a POSIX environment. For the United States, use the EN_US locale.

Graphical User Account Management

The SCOadmin graphical interface provides the administrator with an easy method of managing user accounts. This section will explore the Account Manager and its capabilities. To get to the Account Manager, start SCOadmin. Account Manager is the first manager on the list.

The Account Manager is shown in Figure 17.1. In the figure, the Status column has icons, which is not the default view. To get the status icons, select Options, Status.

The Status icons are shown in Table 17.1 along with the character representations when running SCOadmin in character mode. The superuser icon appears in color and the user icon appears in black.

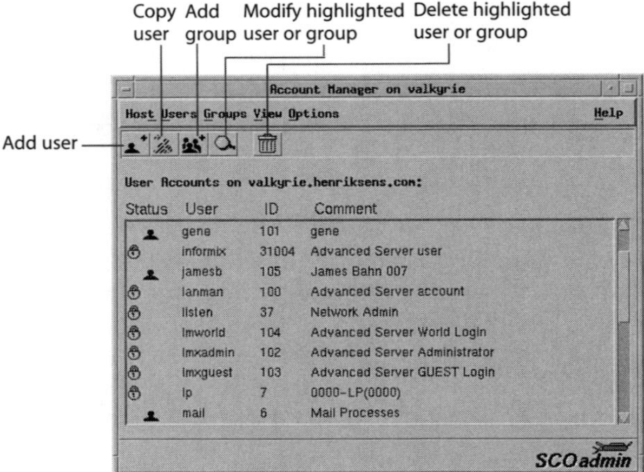

FIGURE 17.1 *The Account Manager.*

TABLE 17.1 THE STATUS ICONS

Description	Icon	Character
Distributed account		>
Group		G
Locked account		#
Account has no password		!
Pseudouser		P
Retired user		R
Superuser		S
User		none

User and Group Management Menus

To modify the users and groups, the Account Manager has a Users and Groups menu. To set the information being viewed to users or groups, use the View menu. In the Options menu, you can set user and group defaults. Each menu option is covered in detail in the following sections.

Adding a New User

To add a new user, click the Add User icon or select Users, Add New User. The New User window is shown in Figure 17.2.

A username in UnixWare 7 can be up to 254 characters in length. POSIX limits usernames to 32 characters.

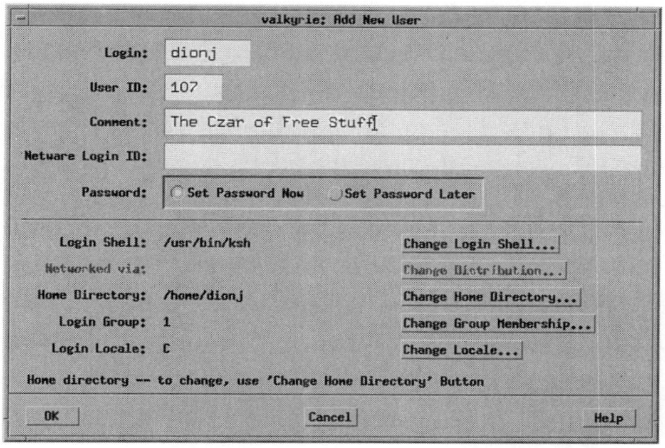

FIGURE 17.2 *Adding a new user.*

The GUI will accept a maximum of eight characters only. SCO recommends usernames of three to eight characters for compatibility with other UNIX systems. The information for login shell, home directory, group is filled in from the /usr/lib/scoadmin/account/accounts file. The locale is filled in automatically from the /etc/default/locale file.

Currently, Advanced File and Print Server is not integrated into the GUI, so you cannot select Advanced Server for the Distributed Via option.

Figure 17.3 illustrates selecting a login shell. The drop-down box lists all the available shells. The login shell may be changed at a later time. Be sure to check the login shell files if you change shells. This is particularly applicable when the move involves the C shell.

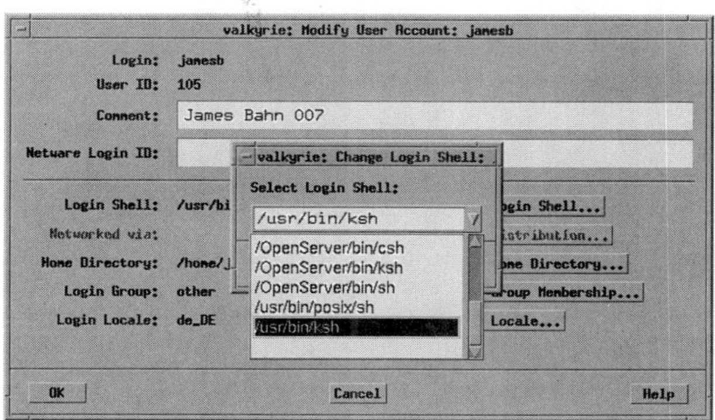

FIGURE 17.3 *Selecting a login shell.*

The home directory can be changed during creation of the account or later. Figure 17.4 shows the Change Home Directory window. If moving an existing user's home directory, click the Move Files from Old Home Directory check box to have the user's files transferred to the new directory. If the new home directory exists prior to the decision to move the user's home directory, a pop-up window will warn that the directory exists and cannot be created. You will not be able to move the home directory to a pre-existing directory.

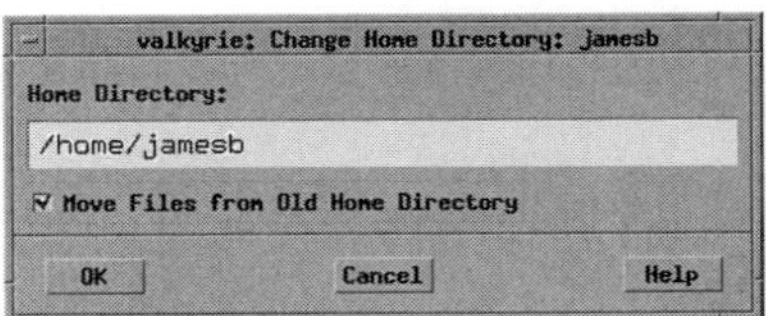

FIGURE 17.4 *Selecting a home directory.*

Changing Group Membership

Users can be members of multiple groups. Clicking on Change Group Membership brings up the Change Groups window shown in Figure 17.5. When looking in the /etc/group file, you will not find the users listed in the group for their Login Group. For example, if Other is the default login group and you add 10 users, none will show up in the /etc/group file under the Other group. Because the login group membership is part of the /etc/passwd file, it is redundant to list the users in that group in the /etc/group file. If a user is added to additional groups, the username will appear in those groups in the /etc/group file.

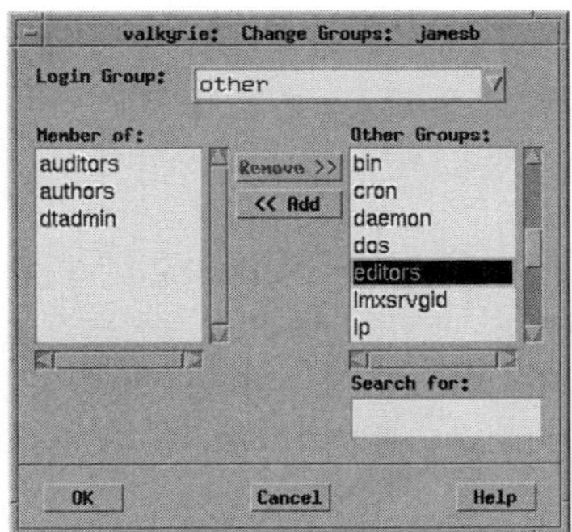

FIGURE 17.5 *Changing group membership.*

Changing Locale

Changing locale is shown in Figure 17.6. The Locale controls internationalization of commands, utilities, and applications. Using this option, the Locale can be set on a per user basis. The International Settings Manager allows setting the Locale for the system. The drop-down box will list all locales loaded on the system.

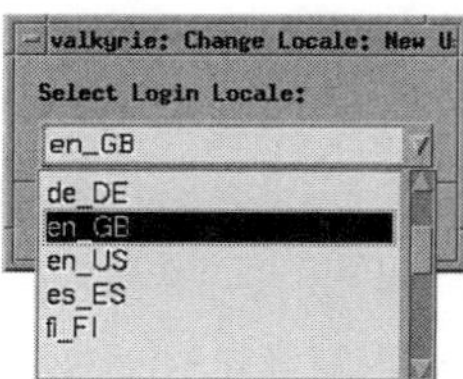

FIGURE 17.6 *Changing locale.*

Setting Passwords

The Set Password Now button is selected by default. Clicking the OK button will bring up the Set Password window, as shown in Figure 17.7. To create a user with no password, click the Remove Password button. To create a password, enter the password in both blocks to confirm the correct spelling and click OK. The Force Password Change allows you to create a user account and force the user to change passwords on the first login.

The same window is used to add or change a user's password. The only difference is the window title when displayed.

> *Tip*
>
> *When an account is locked, you must change the password to unlock it. There is no menu option to unlock accounts.*

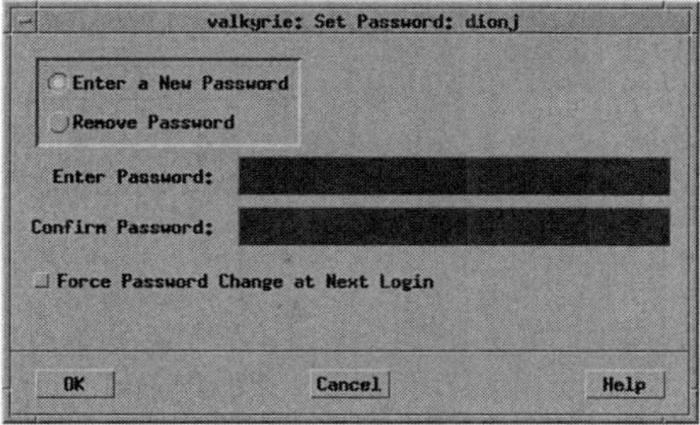

FIGURE 17.7 *Setting the password.*

Modify a User

To modify a user, double-click the username or highlight the user with a single click and select Users, Modify.

From the Modify window, you can change everything on the screen except the user ID and the login name. If you need to modify those, see the section later in this chapter on the `usermod` command.

Delete a User

To delete a user, highlight the user to be deleted and click the trash can icon, or select Users, Delete. In both cases, a window appears containing a message for confirmation of the delete:

```
This will remove the account: <account name>
```

Warning

Unlike OpenServer 5, UnixWare 7 will remove the user and the user's home directory. You are not asked to confirm the removal of the home directory or any files in it.

If you want to leave the home directory intact, use the `userdel` command. As an alternative to deletion, you can lock the account.

Copy a User

To copy a user, highlight the selected user, select Users, Copy Selected User or select the Copy User icon on the toolbar. The window used for adding a new user is presented. The only items that can be entered are the login name, user ID, comment, and NetWare Login ID. The remaining options are grayed out.

If you intend to copy users often and the setup required varies from one group to another, setting the defaults will not handle the defaults in all cases. Instead, set up template accounts. Name the template accounts with a special character so they will be at the top of the accounts list alphabetically. For instance, _sales, _support, _acctng, and so forth. When setting up the template account, click Set the Password Later to avoid having anyone use the account. By not setting the password, the account is locked.

Creating a new account becomes a matter of entering the name, comment, NetWare Login ID, and the home directory. The Login Shell, Networked Via, Login Group, and Locale should be set from the account being copied. Unfortunately, the settings made in the Expirations, Authorizations, and Remote Access do not copy.

Lock the Account

To lock an account, highlight the user and select Users, Lock. A confirmation window appears:

```
This will lock account: <account name>
```

Click on OK to lock. To unlock the account, change the password.

Change the Password

To change a user's password, highlight the user and select Users, Change Password. The password window shown in Figure 17.7 is displayed. Click OK when complete.

Set Expiration

To limit the lifetime of a password, set the expirations. Figure 17.8 shows the password controls. The Days Required between Changes is to prevent someone from changing to a required password, perhaps under supervision, and then running the password program to change the password back immediately. These settings are based on the defaults for the security level. For more about security, see Chapter 22.

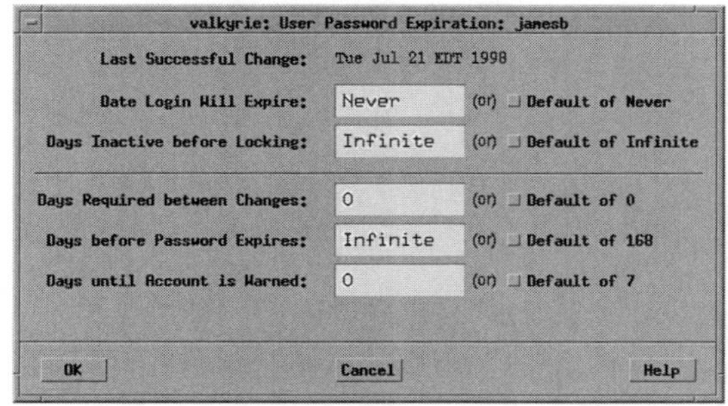

FIGURE 17.8 *Password expiration.*

Assign Authorizations

Authorizations provide the ability to assign administrative tasks to users without providing them with root access. To add a new authorization, click the authorization and click Add. To delete an authorization, click the authorized item and click Remove. Clicking the Account *<account name>* Has Owner Privileges will provide all authorizations to the account. Figure 17.9 illustrates the user authorizations.

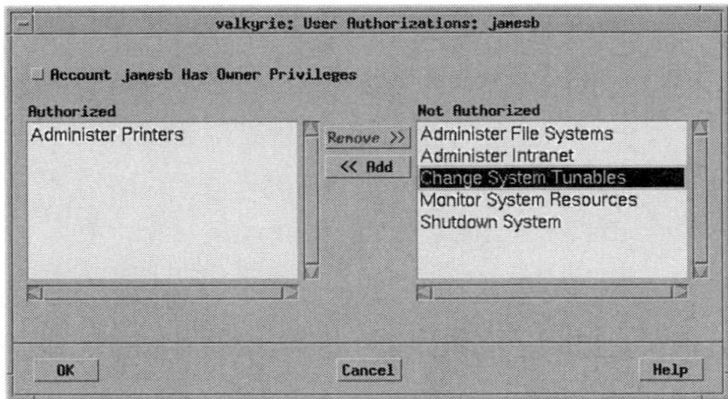

FIGURE 17.9 *Changing user authorizations.*

Grant Remote Access

Users on remote systems that need to rlogin back to the system on which the account is being created can be given permission to log in without a password by using trusted access. To restrict this activity to individual users, the .rhosts file is created in the user's home directory. The administrator can create this file from the graphical interface by selecting the Remote Access menu option, as shown in Figure 17.10.

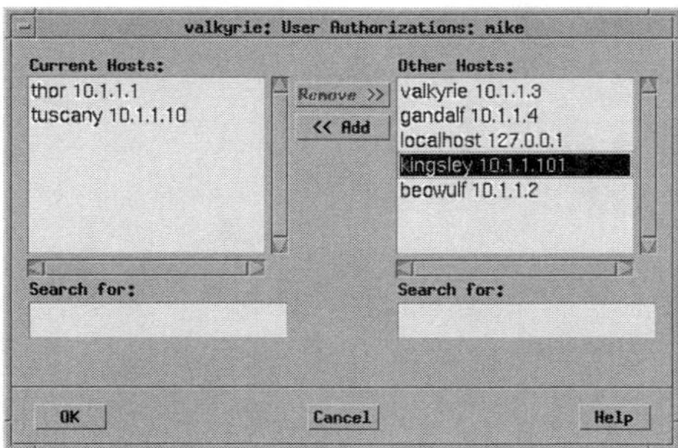

FIGURE 17.10 *Creating Remote Host Access to the local login.*

Add New Group

New groups are added by either double-clicking the Group Add icon on the toolbar or by selecting Group, Add New Group. Figure 17.11 illustrates the process of adding a new group. Select names from the Other Users box and click Add to enter them into the group.

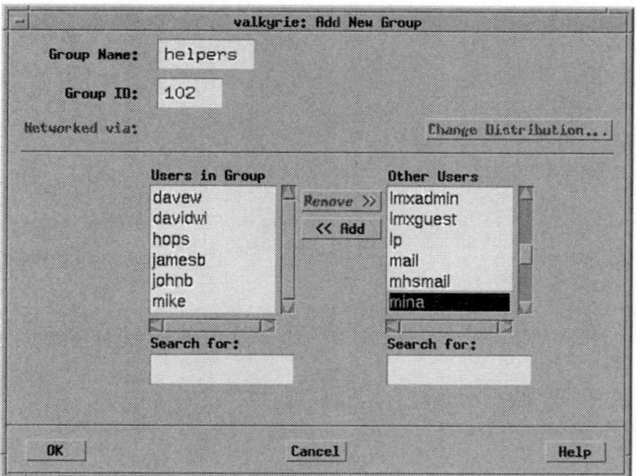

FIGURE 17.11 *Adding a new group.*

Modify Group

To modify a group, you must select View, Groups. The listing of usernames changes to a listing of groups. Double-click a group, or select Groups, Modify. The same window shown in Figure 17.11 is presented for modification of the group member users.

Delete Group

To delete a group, select Groups, Delete. If the Delete option is grayed out, select View, Groups. A warning window appears with the following message:

```
! This will remove the group: <group name>
Click OK to delete the group.
```

View by Users

To view users instead of groups, select View, Users. If viewing groups at the time, the Groups option is grayed out.

View by Group

To view groups instead of users, select View, Groups. If viewing users at the time, the Users option is grayed out.

User Defaults

You can change up to four user defaults. Select Options, User Defaults. The User Defaults window is shown in Figure 17.12. Changing the login shell is similar to changing the login shell for an individual user. A drop-down list of all shells is provided for selection.

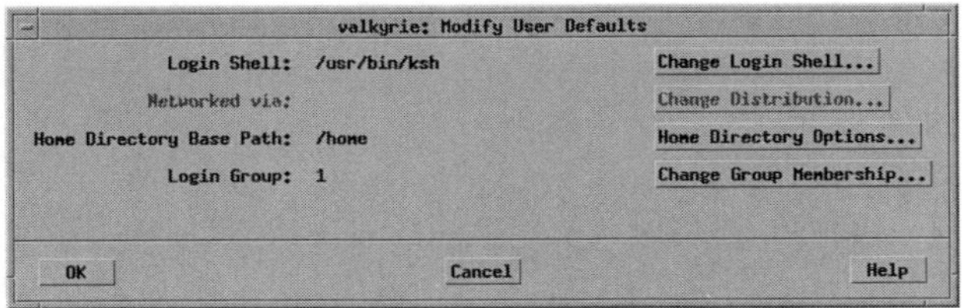

FIGURE 17.12 *Modifying user defaults.*

The Home Directory choice also includes permissions for the Home directory. Figure 17.13 illustrates the home directory to be created in /home with `rwxr-xr-x` permissions. These are the standard settings for traditional security.

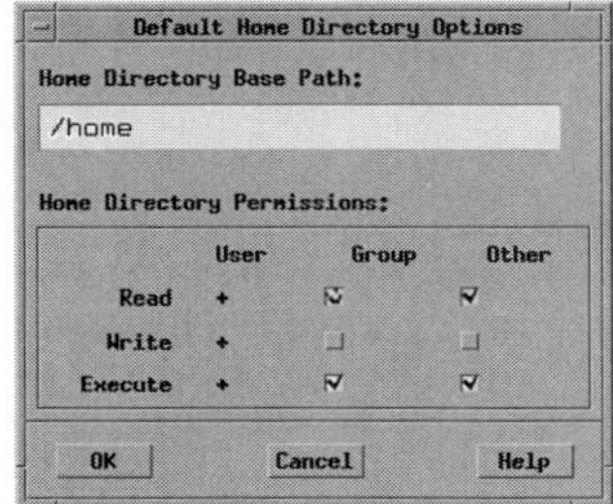

FIGURE 17.13 *Setting the default home directory path and permissions.*

The login group defaults to Other. This can be changed or additional groups may be added.

Warning

When the Change Default Groups window opens, it displays the login group ID, not the login group name. When OK is clicked, you will get a Create Group window, as shown in Figure 17.14, that states the login group does not exist and suggests that you create a group named 1. To avoid this, change the Login Group to Other or whichever group name you prefer. This will be fixed in a future version.

Group Defaults

Figure 17.15 illustrates the Modify Group Defaults window. The Minimum and Maximum Group IDs and the Networked Via are the only options.

Show Status

To show the status of users and groups, you must toggle the Status option by clicking it. Computing the status takes extra time so you may not want to use this if your user database is large.

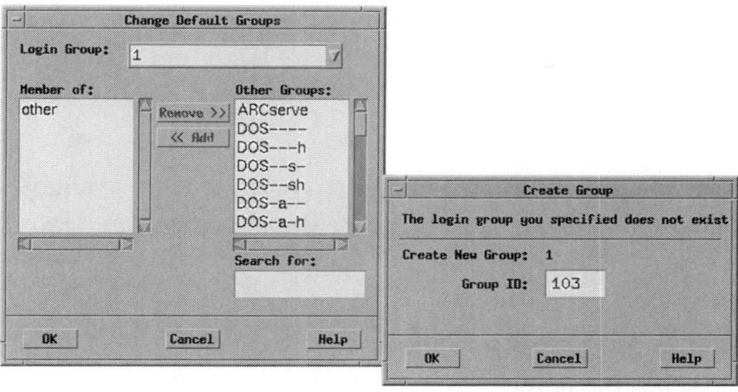

FIGURE 17.14 *Adding to or changing the default groups.*

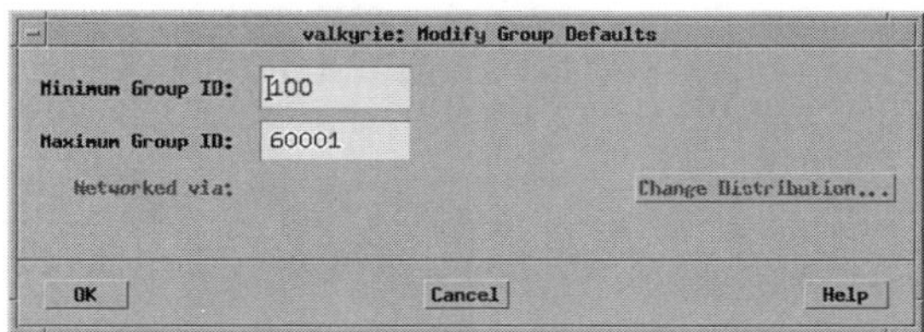

FIGURE 17.15 *Modify the group defaults.*

Point Help

Another toggle option, Point Help, provides one line of descriptive information. It is *context-sensitive*, meaning it provides a description for the option under the mouse pointer. Figure 17.2 has a Point Help of:

```
Home Directory --
```

To change, use the Change Home Directory option. In the figure, the mouse pointer was on the home directory (/home/dionj).

Toolbar

The Toolbar option hides or displays the toolbar with the icons. There is no option to add or delete icons on the toolbar.

Command-Line User Account Management

For shell scripting, command-line oriented administrators, and systems that may not support the graphical interface, the commands that are run from the GUI are available for use on the command line. Many more options are available on the command line than in the GUI.

If you want to remove a user while not deleting the user's home directory, use the command line. If you want to change the user's ID or login name, use the command line. The commands available will allow more flexibility over account parameters than will the GUI.

UnixWare 7 uses the same basic files to maintain users that are available in UnixWare 2 and OpenServer 5. The /etc/passwd, /etc/group and /etc/shadow files all exist on UnixWare 7.

Tip

Each of the commands discussed in this section has more information available in the man pages. You should refer to the man pages to get the complete list of options.

Several programs are available to list the users and parameters for their accounts. One of these programs is logins. This command did not exist on OpenServer 5.

The default execution of logins with no options provides a list of all users with the username, UID, group, group ID, and comment.

```
#logins
root            0       sys             3       0000-Admin(0000)
daemon          1       daemon          12      0000-Admin(0000)
...
mike            115     other           1       Mike Almond
johnb           116     other           1       John Boland
davidwi         117     other           1       David Wight
davew           118     other           1       Dave Williams
hops            119     other           1       Mike Hopkirk
andrewm         120     other           1       Andrew Malcolm
```

The logins program will accept 10 letter options and a group and user list. Selecting the `-x`, extended information, the `-a`, two password expiration fields, and selecting a user with the `-l` option yields the following output:

```
# logins -a -x -l andrewm
andrewm         120     other           1       Andrew Malcolm
                         /home/andrewm
                         /usr/bin/ksh
                         PS 072298 20 60 10
                         30 123198
```

The user, `andrewm`, has a user ID of 120 and belongs to group other, group ID 1. The user comment is `Andrew Malcolm`. The home directory is /home/andrewm, and the login shell is /usr/bin/ksh. The fourth line of output has `PS`, which signifies that the account is passworded; the last password change was 07/22/98. The minimum days between password changes is 20. The maximum life of a password is 60 days. The user will be warned 10 days before password expiration. The last line shows that the account will be locked after 30 days of inactivity and the account expires on December 31, 1998.

The users program will list all logged-in users in a compact linear format. The users program is not available on OpenServer 5.

```
/usr/ucb/users
mikea ranjitd martyg drangula
```

The output of users is similar to `who -q`. `who -q` will also include a line with the total number of users logged on.

```
who -q
mikea ranjitd martyg drangula
# users=4
```

The userls program provides additional user information.

```
#userls -a -l andrewm
pw_name=andrewm pw_uid=120 pw_gid=1 comment='Andrew Malcolm'
pw_dir=/home/andrewm pw_shell=/usr/bin/ksh groups={techs,editors}
```

Other options exist for these programs to create the output you may desire.

useradd

To create accounts from the command line, the `useradd` command has 16 options that can be supplied. The `useradd` command provides much more control over creating a user than the GUI. The defaults for `useradd` come from /etc/default/useradd.

```
#ident     "@(#)useradd.dfl     1.3"
#ident  "$Header: useradd.dfl 2.0 91/07/13 $"
SHELL=/usr/bin/ksh
HOMEDIR=/home
SKELDIR=/etc/skel
GROUPID=1
INACT=
EXPIRE=
DEFLVL=USER_LOGIN
AUDIT_MASK=id_auth,priv,process,cov_chan
HOME_MODE=755
```

```
useradd -u 201 -g 100 -s /usr/bin/csh -c "Kurt Gollhardt" -e "12/31/1998"
-m kurtg
```

The preceding `useradd` command will create a user named `kurtg` who uses the C shell, has an account expiration of 12/31/1998, has a UID of `201`, and has a login group of `100`. The comment in the /etc/passwd file is `Kurt Gollhardt`. The home directory, `-m` option, will be created in the default path. The account is locked until a password is provided. The administrator can quickly give the account a password with

```
password kurtg
```

userdel

Users can be deleted with the `userdel` command. There are two options to the `userdel` command other than the user name:

- The `-r` option will remove the user's home directory.
- The `-n` option is used to change the aging of the UID.

To immediately reuse the UID, specify `-n 0`. To never reuse the UID, specify `-n -1`. To reuse in 24 months, specify `-n 24`.

```
userdel -r -n 0 megm
```

The /etc/default/userdel file provides the default age for reusing the UID. The default setting is 12 months.

```
#ident    "@(#)userdel.dfl    1.2"
#ident  "$Header: userdel.dfl 2.0 91/07/13 $"
UIDAGE=12
```

Warning

If you have created users with the GUI and then deleted them with the `userdel` command, you may be leaving behind administration roles for the user. To avoid any security problems, execute `adminuser -d <login_name>` to delete any references to the user in the administrative roles. This is covered more thoroughly in Chapter 22.

usermod

The `usermod` command modifies existing accounts. The defaults file for `usermod` actions is /etc/default/usermod, shown below:

```
#ident    "@(#)usermod.dfl    1.2"

# This file contains the list of files/directories that usermod will
# search when the -U option is used.  The files/directories to be
# searched are specified by the $LOCAL_PATH and $REMOTE_PATH variables.
# These variables consist of complete path names separated by colons.
# The purpose of the search is to chown files currently belonging to
# the specified user to the new uid for that user.
#
# Only files/directories belonging to the specified user will be chown'd;
# other files/directories in the search path will be unchanged.  All
# files and directories under a specified directory are examined.
#
# If a pathname ends with "{login}",  "{login}" is translated by usermod
# to the logname of the user whose uid is being changed.  For example,
```

```
# the default value of MAILDIR is /var/mail/{login}.  For the command
# "usermod -u 123 -U foo", the result will be that the file /var/mail/foo
# will be chown'd to belong to uid 123 (and, of course, logname foo will
# have uid 123 as well).
#
# The files/directories specified by $LOCAL_PATH will not be followed
# to remote machines but the files/directories specified by $REMOTE_PATH
# will be followed to remote machines.  For example, if $HOMEPATH is in
# the list specified by $LOCAL_PATH and $HOMEPATH=/home/{login}, then
# for the command "usermod -u 123 -U foo", all files and directories
# belonging to logname foo under /home/foo and residing on the local
# machine will be chown'd to belong to uid 123 which will be foo's new
uid.

HOMEDIR=${HOMEDIR:=/home}
HOMEPATH=$HOMEDIR/{login}
MAILDIR=/var/mail/{login}
MAILFORWARD=/var/mail/:forward/{login}
UUCPDIR=/var/spool/uucppublic/receive/{login}
PRESERVEDIR=/var/preserve

LOCAL_PATH=$HOMEPATH:$MAILDIR:$MAILFORWARD:$UUCPDIR:$PRESERVEDIR
REMOTE_PATH=
```

If your installation uses directory paths for user files other than those shown in the /etc/default/usermod, you should modify the file to reflect your system usage.

Use `usermod` to change these user account characteristics:

Characteristic	Option
User ID	`-u`
User login name	`-l`
Login group	`-g`
Supplemental groups	`-G`
Home directory	`-d`
Login shell	`-s`
Comment in the password file	`-c`
Inactive days before account is locked	`-f`
Expiration date	`-e`
Audit mask	`-a`
Netware Directory Services authentication context	`-n`

When changing some characteristics, other options will aid in keeping everything neat.

- If the UID is being changed, the command will search directories in the /etc/default/usermod and change the old UID to the new UID (`-U`, used with `-u`).

```
usermod -u 1234 -U davew
```

- If a new home directory is specified, move the user's home directory to the new home directory (`-m`, used with `-d`).

```
usermod -d /home2/kathryna -m kathryna
```

The `-o` option allows changing a UID to an existing UID, effectively giving two users the same UID. This is not recommended for security purposes.

Author's Note

Here's a good example of using the `-o` option.

Problem: All users log in as user1 to use a specific software application. The .profile allows them to drop to the `$` prompt after exiting the application. They are then supposed to log out, but often do not. They are left in the application directory where a vengeful user could remove files. By changing the login script to `exec` the application (as opposed to running it), they will not be left at the `$` prompt. However, the administrator needs to be at the dollar prompt to execute updates to the software.

Solution: Create a new passworded user with a profile that leaves him in the proper directory with a dollar prompt for executing the commands for software updates. Give that account the same UID as the `user1` login. With the same UID, there are no permission problems and the data can be protected with 700 permissions.

Using `exec` with a command replaces the original command with the executed command. When used in the login, script like this:

```
exec menuprog
```

The login shell is replaced by the command `menuprog`. When the user exits `menuprog`, there is no login shell and a new login prompt appears.

Use of the `-o` option to change UIDs to the same number is shown below:

- The lines in the password file before the `usermod` command:

```
karenad:x:119:1:Karen Adams:/home/karenad:/usr/bin/ksh
gfd:x:300:100:George F Demarest:/home/gfd:/usr/bin/ksh

usermod -u 300 -U -o karenad
```

- The lines in the password file after the `usermod` command:

```
karenad:x:300:1:Karen Adams:/home/karenad:/usr/bin/ksh
gfd:x:300:100:George F Demarest:/home/gfd:/usr/bin/ksh
```

Because the `-U` option was used, the ownership of the home directory of Karen Adams was changed from UID 119 to UID 300. A listing of the /home directory now shows both the /home/karen and /home/gfd as owned by Karen. The ownership display occurs because the name associated with UID 300 is located by searching the /etc/passwd file from top to bottom. If Karen appears first, the operating system associates UID 300 with her account.

> **Warning**
>
> *Failure to use the `-U` option or not having the correct directories in the /etc/default/usermod will result in the administrator having to manually search for and change the ownership of the user's files.*

groupadd

The `groupadd` command will add groups to the /etc/group file. A new option for OpenServer users is the `-K`. The new option points to a path in which scripts named groupadd.pre and groupadd.post are located. These will be run before and after the addition. At the time of writing, the `-K` option was not functioning. It may be fixed by the time you read this. The `-o` option allows duplication of a group ID.

```
groupadd -g 999 test
```

groupdel

The `groupdel` command will delete a group. The command has no options; simply specify the group name.

```
groupdel test
```

groupmod

The `groupmod` command is used to modify the group name or ID. It also allows for duplication of group IDs with different group names.

```
groupmod -g <new group id> -n <new group name> group
```

```
groupmod -g 998 -n testers test
```

Changing System Defaults with *defadm*

The /etc/default directory contains a series of files with values for various system functions. The files can be changed with an editor, such as vi, or with the defadm utility.

To list all the files in the /etc/default directory, run `defadm` with no options. To list the values in one file, execute `defadm` with the name of the file:

```
# defadm useradd
SHELL=/usr/bin/ksh
HOMEDIR=/home
SKELDIR=/etc/skel
GROUPID=1
INACT=
```

```
EXPIRE=
DEFLVL=USER_LOGIN
AUDIT_MASK=id_auth,priv,process,cov_chan
HOME_MODE=755
```

To view the setting of a particular value, execute `defadm` for that file and value:

```
# defadm useradd SHELL
SHELL=/usr/bin/ksh
```

To change a setting, execute `defadm` with the new value.

```
# defadm useradd SHELL=/usr/bin/csh
# defadm useradd SHELL
SHELL=/usr/bin/csh
```

To delete a value from a file, use the `-d` option.

```
# defadm -d useradd EXPIRE
```

Changing System Defaults with the GUI

In addition to defadm and vi, you can configure system defaults through the GUI. Figure 17.16 illustrates the System Defaults Manager. It is reached from SCOadmin through the System folder.

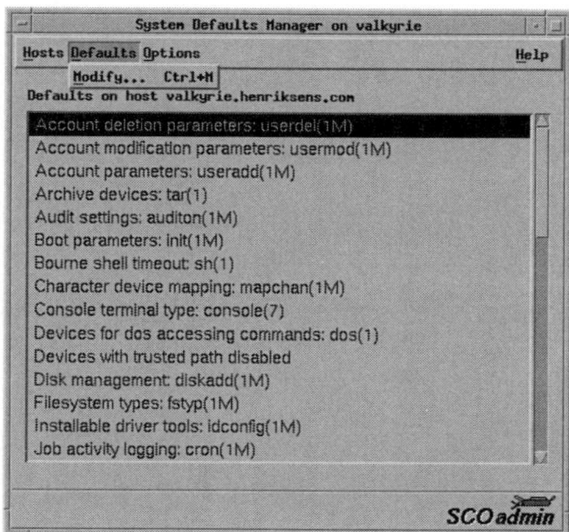

FIGURE 17.16 *Modify default settings files from the GUI.*

passwd

The file passwd exists as a command (/usr/bin/passwd), which is linked to /bin/passwd and a file (/etc/passwd).

The /etc/passwd file is a standard UNIX passwd file. If you decide not to use the GUI or the `useradd`, `usermod`, or `userdel` commands, you can edit the passwd file. You may need to use the `creatiadb` command after editing the passwd file to straighten out the security database. SCO does not recommend directly modifying the database files by hand.

The `passwd` command has several options. These options allow an administrator to examine the status of passwords and to lock accounts by creating an unusable password. Without options, `passwd` allows users to change their password.

The `-s` option allows the administrator to examine any account's password status or users to check their own status.

```
# passwd -s andrewm
andrewm  LK  07/22/98  20  60   10
```

The account `andrewm` is locked. The last password change was 07/22/1998. The minimum password life is 20 days, the maximum password life is 60 days, and andrewm will be notified 10 days before the password expires.

The `-l` option allows locking an account.

```
# passwd -l spopp
# grep spopp /etc/shadow
spopp:*LK*:10430::::::
```

Warning

There is a bug in `passwd -s` that causes it to show accounts as locked when they are not.

Other options to the `passwd` command allow forcing the user to change passwords at the next login and setting the maximum, minimum, and warning days for a user's passwords.

The /etc/shadow File

From an OpenServer 5 perspective, there are several new fields in the /etc/shadow file.

```
hiramc:IRgW8zeHPwhiM:10430:20:65:8:30:10591:
```

The line from the /etc/shadow file includes:

- Login name
- Encrypted password
- Date of last password change (this is the number of days since 1/1/1970)

- Minimum days between changes
- Maximum password life in days
- Days before expirations that warnings start
- Days of inactivity before account is locked
- Date of expiration for account (this is the number of days since 1/1/1970)

The /etc/default/login File

One of the files that can be modified by `defadm` is /etc/default/login. Variables in the login file determine

- Whether failed logins will be logged.
- Whether passwords are required.
- Whether root and other privileged users can log in from other than the console.
- The default umask for file creation.
- Other login-related features.

To log failures of logins after the `LOGFAILURES` number of attempts is exceeded, you must create the /var/adm/loginlog. The loginlog file does not exist by default. Create the file with read and write permission for the owner only. The owner must be root with the group of sys. To create the file, use the `touch` command while logged in as root:

```
touch /var/adm/loginlog
ls -l loginlog
-rw-r--r--    1 root     sys              210 Sep 14 15:56 loginlog
```

The following is a sample failure from the `loginlog`.

```
root:/dev/pts007:Mon Sep 14 15:56:15 1998
```

Two important parameters set in the login file are

- `PASSREQ`—When set to `YES`, all users must have a password. If a password is not in effect, they will be asked for one at the next opportunity provided by password aging.
- `MANDPASS`—If set to `YES`, all users are required to have a password. This overrides `PASSREQ`. Users with a null password are denied access.

The /etc/default/passwd File

You can control the password parameters for each user through the GUI (choose Account Manager, Users, Expirations) or through the option in `usermod`. For systemwide controls, you can set parameters in the /etc/default/passwd file.

By default, there is only one setting in the file:

```
PASSLENGTH=3
```

Other options include:

- `MINWEEKS`—Minimum number of weeks before a password can be changed. In a newly installed system, the value is `0`.
- `MAXWEEKS`—Maximum number of weeks a password can be unchanged. In a newly installed system, the value is `24`.
- `WARNWEEKS`—Number of weeks before a password expires that the user is to be warned. In a newly installed system, the value is `1`.
- `PASSLENGTH`—Minimum number of characters in a password. The `PASSLENGTH` values are `1`, `3`, `6`, or `8` according to your system security profile: 1=low, 3=traditional, 6=improved, and 8=high.

Note that the values here are in weeks while the values stored in /etc/shadow are in days.

Status Reporting

Reports of Password Status and User Login activity are available through the GUI. To run these reports from SCOadmin, select System, Reports Manager, Reports.

The reports for Password Status are

- By Users (see Figure 17.20)
- Systemwide

The reports that are available for user logins are

- By Users
- By Terminals
- By System
- Current Login Users (shown in Figure 17.20)
- By All Users

To start the reports, select Reports and either User Logins, shown in Figure 17.17, or Password Status.

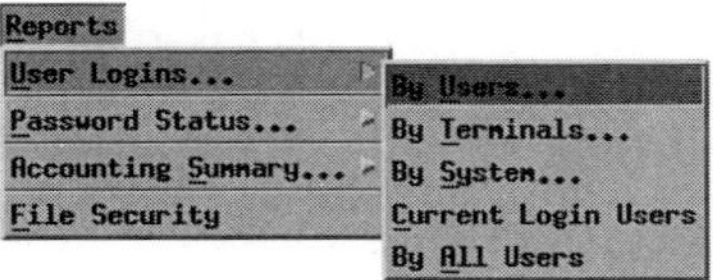

FIGURE 17.17 *The User Logins Reports options.*

To run the User Logins by Users, a selection window appears as shown in Figure 17.18. Highlight desired users on the left and click Add to add them to the list. The same format window is used to select terminals in the By Terminals report.

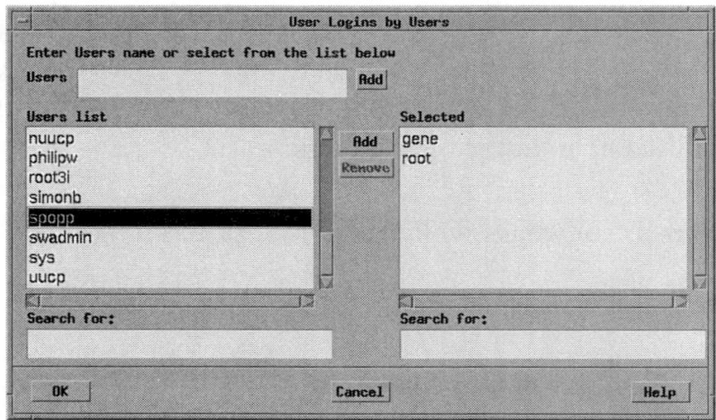

FIGURE 17.18 *Selecting users for the report.*

After the users have been selected, run the report by clicking OK. The report will appear as shown in Figure 17.19.

To run the Password Status report by user, the same selection window is presented. The report is shown in Figure 17.20.

With any of the reports in the Reports Manager, you may print the report to a printer, print the report to a file, or save the report as a file. Under the Host menu option, select Print Report, or Save Report As. The windows for these options are shown in Figures 17.21 and 17.22.

Reports Manager on valkyrie

Host Reports Accounting Options Help

Reports Manager on valkyrie.henriksens.com

Name	Terminals	Login Time	Status	Logout Time	Duration	System
philipw	vt12	14:09 07/23/98	RUNNING		00:04:40	
root	console	11:39 07/23/98	RUNNING		02:34:27	
root	dtremote	12:59 07/23/98	RUNNING		01:14:08	
root	pts006	11:27 07/23/98	RUNNING		02:46:37	
simonb	vt11	14:09 07/23/98	RUNNING		00:04:57	
spopp	vt09	14:08 07/23/98	RUNNING		00:05:09	

User Login Report of Current Login User(s)

SCOadmin

FIGURE 17.19 *The User Logins report of current users.*

Reports Manager on valkyrie

Host Reports Accounting Options Help

Reports Manager on valkyrie.henriksens.com

Name	Status	Changed On	Min.Days	Max.Days	Expiration	Warning
philipw	Unlocked	07/23/98	0	Infinite	Never expires	0 day
root	Unlocked	05/15/98	0	Infinite	Never expires	0 day
simonb	Unlocked	07/23/98	0	Infinite	Never expires	0 day
spopp	Unlocked	07/23/98	20	65 days	12/31/98	8 days

Password Status Report of User philipw,root,simonb,spopp

SCOadmin

FIGURE 17.20 *The User Logins Reports options.*

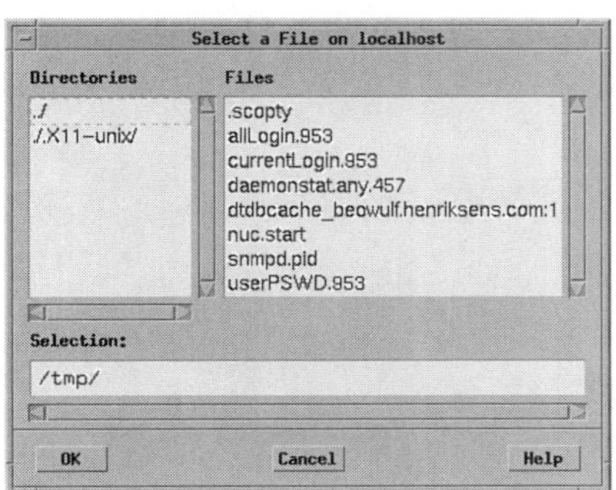

FIGURE 17.21 *Saving a report as a file.*

In Figure 17.22, when the Print To option is Printer, the printers are available for selection along with the print command. When the File Name option is selected, the printers are grayed out and the File Name box is available.

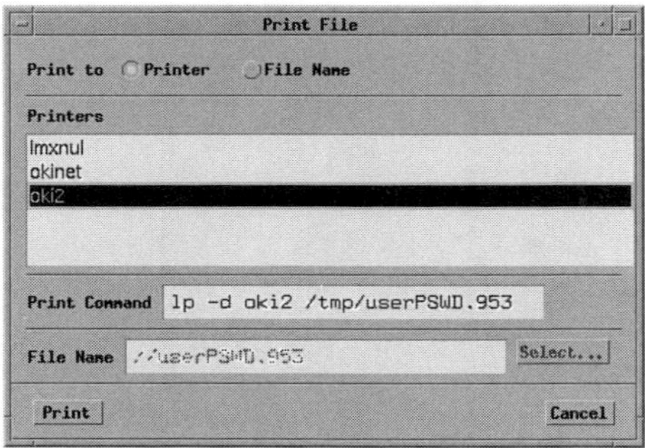

FIGURE 17.22 *Print a file to a printer or a file.*

CHAPTER 18

Process Management

- Processes
  Learn how processes are created and controlled. Learn about Light Weight Processes.
- Scheduling processes
  Learn how to schedule jobs with the graphical Task Scheduler.

Processes

A *process* is an instance of a program that is executing. Processes manage the system and handle the users' requests. Process management involves the creation, use, and stopping of processes.

The initial processes are spawned from the UNIX kernel file as it is loaded at boot time. Many of these processes do not have actual executable files residing on disk. New processes are created by existing processes through *system calls* to the operating system. These calls are generally the fork or exec calls.

Process Genealogy

Processes are created by existing processes. The new process is called the *child process* and the creating process is called the *parent process*. When the child process starts, the parent usually goes into a wait state. When the child process terminates, it sends a termination signal to the parent. The parent then continues operation.

Each process has a *process ID (PID)* assigned at process creation time. Each process is also associated with its parent's PID. The *parent's PID (PPID)* is used to track back up the genealogical tree.

Figure 18.1 illustrates the genealogy of a login. The login shell, PID 1234, was started by a ttymon (PPID 675). From the login shell, a new process, the application menu, was created to run the application menu. The login process is now in a wait state. The application menu (PID 1239) spawned a new process at the request of a user to run an application program. The menu then went into a wait state. The application program has PID 2345 with a PPID of 1239. Upon exiting the application program, a signal will be sent to the menu indicating that the child process has terminated and the menu will become active.

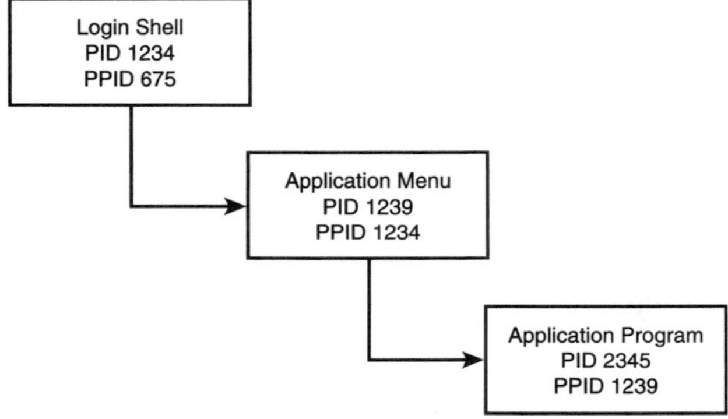

FIGURE 18.1 *Process genealogy.*

OpenServer 5 Tip

With the login processes now being handled by the Service Access Facility (see Chapter 10, "Configuration of Serial Ports and Terminal Devices"), the parent process of a login is not the init process, but a ttymon and a sac process. Init is the parent of the sac process. Init is the parent process of most user processes. Init has process ID 1.

The Process Status Command (*ps*)

The command to view processes and their current status is the `ps` command. There are several options to the `ps` command. Executed with no options, `ps` provides a short list of the processes of the user on the terminal being used to execute the command.

```
# ps
   PID  CLS PRI TTY       TIME COMD
  1358   TS  70 pts014    0:00 sh
  1500   TS  59 pts014    0:00 ps
```

From this listing, you can determine the process ID, the Class, the Priority, the terminal or TTY used, the CPU time consumed, and the command being run.

To get more information, you can specify the `-f` option for a full listing.

```
# ps -f
     UID   PID  PPID  CLS PRI  C    STIME TTY     TIME   COMD
    root  1358  1356   TS  70  0 12:01:55 pts014  0:00   -sh
    root  1522  1358   TS  59  0 13:42:32 pts014  0:00   ps -f
```

The listing now includes the User ID (root), the PPID, the system time when the command started, and more information on the command being run. Here the `sh` is preceded by a `-`, indicating that PID 1358 is a login shell. The next line indicates the option with which `ps` was run. The `C` column is an estimate of recent CPU usage. The `C` time is used by the scheduler to determine the priority for getting the process onto the CPU.

To get a list of all processes, use the `-e` (extended) option.

```
# ps -ef
     UID    PID   PPID   CLS   PRI   C     STIME TTY        TIME COMD
    root      0      0   SYS    79   0 08:07:10 ?          0:06 sysproc
    root      1      0    TS    70   0 08:07:10 ?          0:01 /sbin/init
    root     66     65    TS    80   0 08:07:24 ?          0:01 /etc/ifor_pmd
```

This listing was limited to only three lines for purposes of illustration. Here we have the same data columns; the number of processes has been expanded to include all processes on the system.

Other useful options include the ability to locate processes for a user or a terminal. The `-t` (terminal) option and `-u` (user) option can be very handy for troubleshooting.

```
# ps -u gene
   PID  CLS PRI TTY       TIME COMD
  1374   TS  80 vt12      0:00 ksh
/dev/pts014

# ps -t pts014
   PID  CLS PRI TTY       TIME COMD
  1358   TS  70 pts014    0:00 sh
  1578   TS  59 pts014    0:00 ps
```

Other options provide the ability to specify other criteria for selection and display. See the man pages on `ps` for more detailed information.

Tip

If you run the ps *command and get no output, you probably do not have the /proc and /processorfs filesystems mounted. List the contents of /proc; it should not be empty. If it is, check the /etc/vfstab. There should be entries for /proc and /processorfs that look like the following lines:*

```
/proc   -   /proc   proc   -   no   -   -
/processorfs   -   /system/processor   profs   -   yes   -
```

If these lines do not exist, add them to the vfstab.

Process Types

Processes can be divided into two major categories: system and user. Both system and user processes can be single- or multi-threaded. Multi-threaded processes run subprocesses that share the same process ID. In UnixWare 7, the subprocesses are called *Light Weight Processes*. When processes terminate, they are removed from the process table. Occasionally, a process may terminate and remain in the process table and is referred to as a *defunct process*.

Light Weight Processes

Light Weight Processes (LWPs) belonging to a process have several distinguishing characteristics. They

- Share the same process ID
- Share the same resources, including address space
- Make system calls and block I/O for resources
- Are scheduled independently

The major advantage of LWPs is that they can be scheduled in parallel on multiprocessor systems. Depending on how the software is written, this can speed up processing because LWPs for a single process perform multiple tasks simultaneously.

To see the LWPs, use the `-L` option to `ps` (in this case restricting the output to PID 0 (`-p0`):

```
# ps -L -p0
   PID   LWP   CLS  PRI  TTY   LTIME   COMD
     0     2   SYS   79    ?    0:00   sysproc
     0     3   SYS   79    ?    0:00   mod_noti
     0     4   SYS   79    ?    0:00   fsflush
     0     5   SYS   79    ?    0:00   bdelay
     0     6   SYS   79    ?    0:00   adtflush
     0     7   SYS   79    ?    0:00   strdaemo
```

This listing illustrates the LWPs numbered 2 through 7 for PID 0, sysproc.

Another way to see the LWPs is to `cd` to the /proc filesystem. Then `cd` to the PID of the process you want to examine. In that directory, you should find a subdirectory named lwp. The lwp directory contains the LWP IDs. In this case you select PID 0. `cd` to /proc/0/lwp and list the entries.

```
# pwd
/proc/0/lwp
# lc
10   12   14   16   18   2    21   23   25   27   29   30   32   34   36   5    7    9
11   13   15   17   19   20   22   24   26   28   3    31   33   35   4    6    8
```

System Processes (Daemons)

System processes are processes not started by users or associated with terminals. These processes perform work in the background and keep the system running. Often these processes are referred to as *daemon processes.*

Author's Note

When I attended SCO's training class for instructors, Charlie Simms, then SCO's chief instructor, pointed out that daemon is derived from the Greek, meaning "guiding spirit" or "guardian angel." It does not come from the Germanic word demon, meaning "evil spirit."

A system process can be distinguished in a `ps` listing by the `?` in the TTY column.

```
UID      PID    PPID  CLS   PRI  C    STIME      TTY    TIME COMD
root       0    0     SYS   79   0    08:07:10   ?      0:06 sysproc
root       1    0     TS    70   0    08:07:10   ?      0:01 /sbin/init
root      66    65    TS    80   0    08:07:24   ?      0:01 /etc/ifor_pmd
```

OpenServer 5 Tip

Several of the processes that had low PIDs in OpenServer 5 now appear as LWPs under sysproc.

User Processes

User processes are associated with specific user IDs and terminals. It is easy to separate these processes from system processes by specifying the user name or terminal ID in the `ps` command. To list all user processes, those processes that do not include the word `root` at the beginning of the line, execute the following:

```
ps -ef | grep -v "^    root"
```

The string at the end is a double quote, carat, four spaces, `root`, and a double quote. The carat specifies the beginning of the line. There are four spaces from the beginning to the letter `r` in `root`.

Defunct Processes

Defunct processes are caused by the parent process termination prior to the termination of the child process, or the parent process not waiting for the child's termination.

```
root    980    979              0                              0:00 <defunct>
```

Normally, defunct processes are not a problem. If the parent terminates, init will inherit the defunct process and remove it. The only resource being used by a defunct process is the process slot. If an abnormally large number of defunct processes was created, they could inhibit the creation of new processes. In that case, it would be necessary to reboot the system.

Process Priorities

Each process has an associated priority that determines its CPU scheduling. Process priorities range from 0 to 127, with 0 being the lowest priority. Some system processes cannot be killed with the `kill` command. These processes have priorities between 75 and 99 on UnixWare 7.

Unlike OpenServer 5, UnixWare 7 allows changing the priority class of processes at the command line. If you have developed an application that requires more execution control than that afforded by the normal time-sharing class, you may want to read the man pages on `priocntl(1)` and see the SCOhelp section on configuring the scheduler. Both subjects can be found in SCOhelp by searching for the term `priority class`.

The *nice* Command

The `nice` command allows running of an individual process with a different scheduling priority than usual. The `nice` value does not actually change the priority associated with the process, but `nice` values affect the algorithm that calculates process priorities.

User processes have a default `nice` value of 20. Increasing the `nice` value of a process results in that process getting less CPU priority. If the system is busy, the process will take longer to execute. The `nice` command can be used with an increment value between 1 and 19. The default value is 10, and values greater than 19 are treated as 19. The increment can be specified either in a `-##` syntax or with the `-n` option. For example, to run the `find` command with a `nice` increment of 15, use:

```
#nice -15 find / -name core
```

or

```
#nice -n 15 find / -name core
```

A root user can use the `nice` command to increase the priority of a process by specifying a negative increment value; for example, `--15` or `-n -15`.

The *renice* Command

To change the `nice` value of running processes, use the `renice` command. Using the `-p` flag allows you to specify processes by their process ID. Using the `-u` flag followed by user names or IDs will change the `nice` value for all processes running for the specified users. To increase the `nice` value for all processes for a user named Mina, use

```
renice 30 -u mina
```

Managing Processes

Managing processes can be performed through the command line utility `kill` or through the graphical Process Manager in SCOadmin. User logins can be viewed through the graphical Login Sessions Viewer or with the `who` and `w` commands. See the man pages for `who` and `w` if you are not familiar with them.

kill

One of the primary tools for managing processes is the `kill` command. The format of the `kill` command is

```
kill [-signal] PID
```

Several signals can be sent to processes. Some processes are written to trap signals and act accordingly. When the system begins a shutdown, it sends `kill` signals to processes to indicate that they should shut down in an orderly manner. When programs are hung and not responding or locked in a loop, other `kill` signals may be used.

Tip

Signals are a method of communicating with processes. Signals are sent to processes for many reasons to indicate that actions have been completed or actions should be taken. Signals can be sent to a process to instruct it to go to an end of a job, which is how users usually use signals.

- `kill` (with no signal) or `kill -15`

  Some programs are written to trap this signal, terminate their child processes, and perform an orderly shutdown of the process.

- `kill -1`

  Certain programs use this as a signal to re-read their configuration script.

- `kill -2` (same as pressing the Delete key)

  The `-2` signal terminates a process.

- `kill -3` (same as pressing Ctrl+\)

  More forceful than `kill -2`. Usually generates a core file containing a memory dump of the program. Core dumps are worthless to users unless they have tools for analyzing the core dumps. Core dumps generally should be removed.

- `kill -9`

  An untrappable signal that should terminate any user process without allowing it to shut down in an orderly manner.

OpenServer 5 Tip

Core dumps in OpenServer 5 were all named core. *In UnixWare 7, the names are core.xxxx, where xxxx is the PID of the program. Do not use the find command with core* to remove core files. There are many files that start with* core *that are part of the system files, such as /usr/include/sys/core.h; and some of the help files include* core *as part of their names.*

If a process is hung waiting for a hardware response, such as a tape drive that has quit responding, it is often necessary to reboot to stop the process.

Warning

When killing the processes all the way up the genealogy list to init, if you are using ttymon on the ports, you may kill sac and ttymon. Because sac is started by init, it will be respawned but ttymon will not. You will not see a login on the terminal until you restart the ttymon.

The Process Manager

The Process Manager is located in SCOadmin. It provides a graphical listing of the process table. Figure 18.2 illustrates the default view in Process Manager.

From the Process Manager, the Process menu provides several options:

- *Delete*—Deletes the selected process from the listing. This does not kill the process.
- *Priority*—Adjusts the priority (see Figure 18.3). This is another way to use the `renice` command.
- *Find*—Finds a process based on a pattern search. The wildcards ? and * may be used (? represents one character and * represents any number of characters).
- *Signal*—Sends a kill signal to a process (see Figure 18.4).

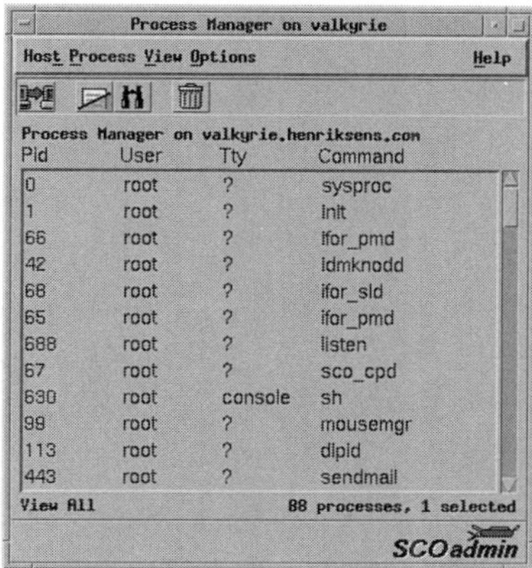

FIGURE 18.2 *The Process Manager.*

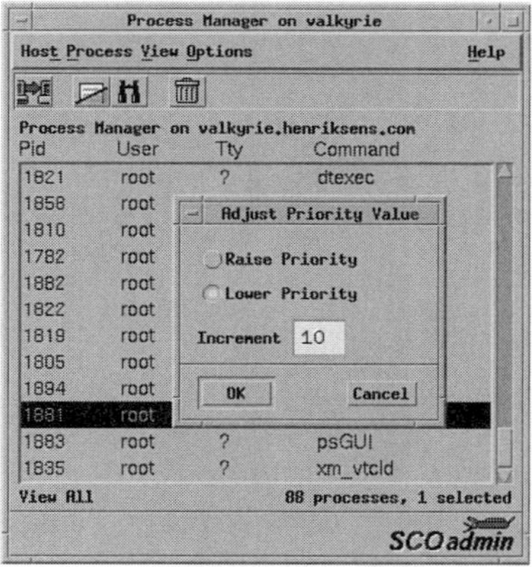

FIGURE 18.3 *Adjust a process priority.*

- *Find Attribute*—Searches based on a single attribute, such as PID or Command. The operators Greater Than, Less Than, and Equal To are available for the search (see Figure 18.5).

To adjust the priority value, use the Priority option. The window shown below the Priority option offers the opportunity to raise or lower process priorities.

To send a kill signal to a process, select the Signal option. From the window shown in Figure 18.4, select the signal from the drop-down box and press OK.

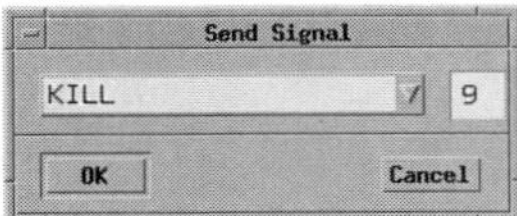

FIGURE 18.4 *Send a signal (kill) to a process.*

To search for a process or group of processes by searching for an attribute, select the Find Attribute option. Figure 18.5 illustrates Find Attribute. Any attributes displayed in the Process Manager's list can be used for the search. The display list can be modified as described later in the View option Attributes.

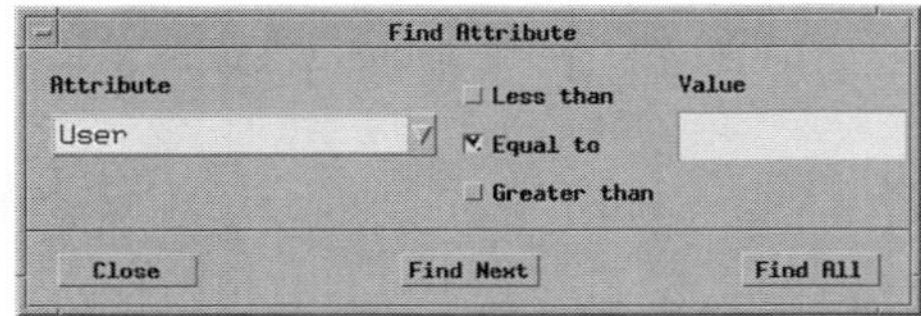

FIGURE 18.5 *Find a process based on an attribute.*

The View menu offers the following options:

- *All*—View all processes.
- *By User*—Select users to view (see Figure 18.6).
- *By Tty*—View processes for selected ttys.
- *By Pid*—View only selected processes.
- *Attributes*—Select columns for the listing (see Figure 18.7).
- *Attribute Filter*—Selection criteria within a column.
- *Sort*—Sort by criteria in increasing or decreasing order.
- *Set Auto Refresh*—Set time for auto refresh cycle.
- *Refresh Now*—Refresh the list.
- *Refresh Tracking*—Currently, the Refresh Tracking option has no functionality.

The default setting is to view all users. The three options to reduce the processes seen—By User, By Tty, and By Pid—all use the same type of selection window. Figure 18.6 shows the selection By User.

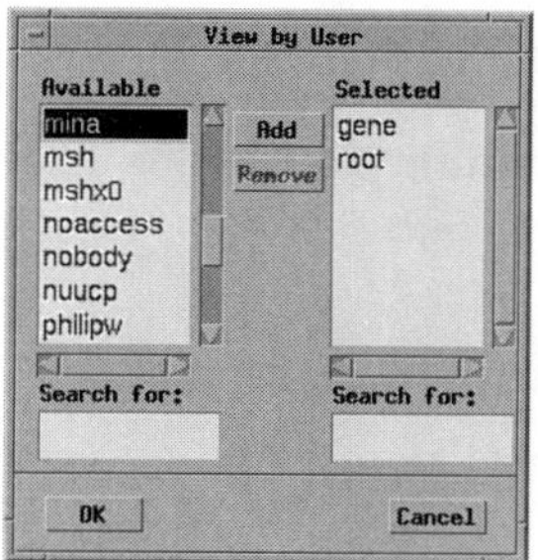

FIGURE 18.6 *View By User.*

The columns displayed in the Process Manager can be customized to the user's requirements. Several preselected settings are available: Default, Ownership, Times, Scheduling, Size, and Full Command. Each of these settings includes a different list of attribute columns. Any of these may be customized by adding other columns from the Available list or deleting from the Selected list. Figure 18.7 illustrates the Attributes selection window.

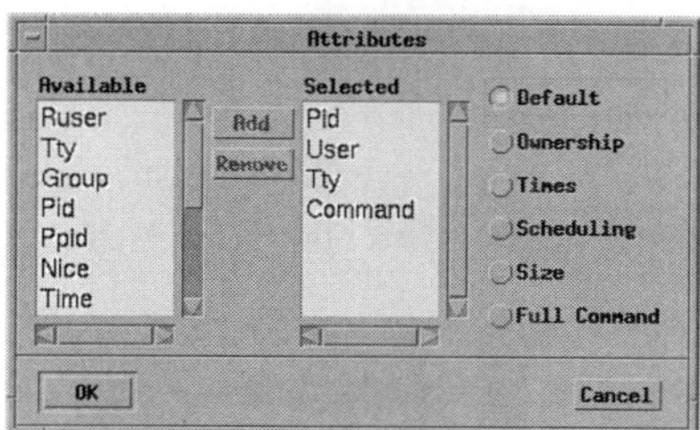

FIGURE 18.7 *Selecting the Display Attributes.*

Under the Options menu is the Customize Attributes option. This allows changing headings and column widths. Figure 18.8 illustrates this option.

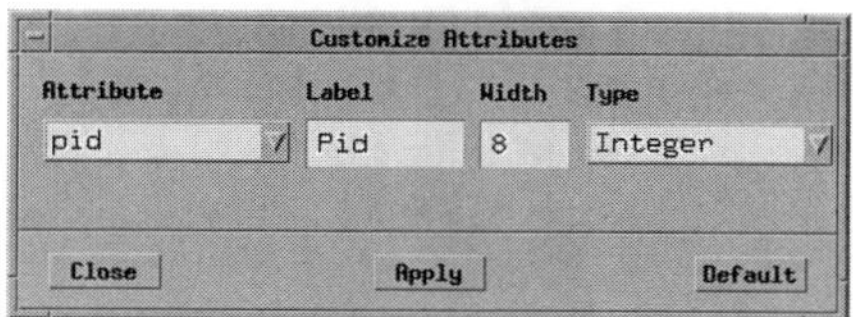

FIGURE 18.8 *Customize Attributes.*

Viewing Logins from the Command Line

From the command line there are two utilities for viewing logins. The who command lists the user name, terminal or pseudo-tty, and the date and time of login. The who command will provide the listing shown below:

```
$ who
root        pts006      Aug 14 09:58
gene        pts007      Aug 14 09:59
spopp       pts008      Aug 14 09:59
msh         pts009      Aug 14 10:00
root        dtremote    Aug 14 10:36
```

The w command provides the information from who plus additional data. The first line indicates the time, how long the system has been up, and the number of users logged in. The second part of the listing provides the user information—user name, terminal, login time, idle time (since last terminal use), the total Job CPU time for the process and all its child processes. The PCPU is the time that accumulates by all currently active processes. The final piece of information is the process that is running. Most of the processes show blank times, indicating that they have less than one second. The dtwm job on the bottom line is the Desktop Window Manager. The last line indicates that user root using a desktop on a remote system has been idle for 1 minute 19 seconds. The total Job CPU time for this user is 21 seconds and the process dtwm has accumulated 5 seconds. The man pages for the w command indicate that these totals may not always be accurate if background processes are also being run.

```
$ w
  11:13am  up  1:19,  5 users
User     tty        login@   idle  JCPU  PCPU              what
root     pts006     9:58am     44              more /etc/vfstab
gene     pts007     9:59am      8                          -ksh
spopp    pts008     9:59am   1:14                          -csh
msh      pts009    10:00am      6                             w
root     dtremote  10:36am   1:19  21    5                 dtwm
```

SCOadmin Login Sessions Viewer

An alternative to the command line view of who is logged in is the *SCOadmin Login Sessions Viewer*. The Login Sessions Viewer is executed from the SCOadmin menu. The only action that can be taken is to highlight a login session and select Logins, Examine. Figure 18.9 illustrates the Details window and the Login Sessions Viewer.

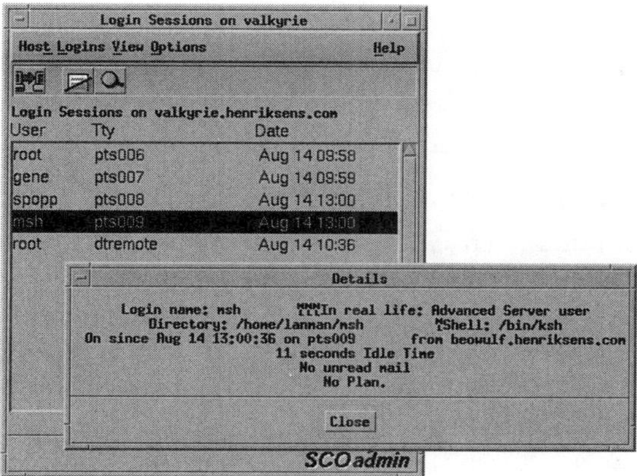

FIGURE 18.9 *The Details and the Login Sessions Viewer.*

Scheduling Processes

UnixWare 7 provides two scheduling methods. The `at` command schedules a one-time job for execution. The cron utility maintains tables of jobs to be run repeatedly.

The *at* Command

The `at` command is run from the command line. There is no graphical interface for `at`. The following simple `at` job shows how an `at` job is created.

```
# at 13:21
echo Hello > /dev/pts006
Control+D
UX:at: INFO: Job 903115260.a.0 at Fri Aug 14 13:21:00 1998
# Hello
```

The `at` job captures the user's environment variables and stores them in the `at` script to be run. These scripts are located in /var/spool/cron/atjobs.

Use of `at` is controlled by entries in the at.deny and at.allow files. If a user's name appears in at.allow, the user is permitted to use `at`. If an at.allow file exists and the user's name is not included, the user is denied `at` privileges. If no at.allow file exists, the at.deny file is examined. If the user's name is not in the at.deny, then the user has `at` privileges. If neither file exists, only root can use `at`. The at.deny and at.allow files are located in the /etc/cron.d directory.

Use the `-l` option to list jobs and the `-r` <*jobid*> to remove jobs.

The Cron Daemon

UNIX provides a method of scheduling repetitive tasks for the operating system. These tasks include system work file cleanups, tape backups, and other jobs. These are done through the cron facility.

Each user may have a file used by cron to schedule jobs. These files are called *crontabs* and have to be submitted to cron. The root user always has a crontab file by default. To make a copy of it, use the following command:

```
crontab -l > /.cronfile
```

This will run the crontab program with the list option (`-l`) and redirect the output from the screen to create a file (.cronfile) in the root directory. The file will be hidden from normal users because it begins with a dot.

After entries are made in an existing crontab file or a user starts a new crontab, the file should be submitted to cron:

```
crontab filename
```

An alternative method of modifying the crontab is to use `crontab -e` to edit the existing crontab with the ed line editor. By setting the `EDITOR` environment variable, another editor, such as vi, can be used.

Warning

Running crontab with no options and then exiting out will overwrite the existing crontab with a blank one. If you accidentally run crontab, press the Delete key; do not exit with a Ctrl+D.

The crontab table for root follows. The last line was added by the VisionFS installation.

```
#ident  "@(#)adm:common/cmd/.adm/root   1.1.11.1"
#ident  "$Header: root 1.2 91/07/24 $"
#
# The root crontab should be used to perform accounting data collection.
#
1,30 * * * * $TFADMIN /usr/bin/ps -p $$ >/dev/null
0 04 * * 0 /usr/vision/bin/visionfs checkpoint 1>/dev/null 2>/dev/console
```

The format of the crontab file is six fields per entry. Five fields determine the date and time of execution. The sixth field is the command to be executed. From left to right, the fields are:

Minutes after the hour: 0–59 are valid.

Hour of the day: 0–23 are valid.

Day of the month: 1–31 are valid.

Month of the year: 1–12 are valid.

Day of the week: 0–6 are valid, with 0 being Sunday.

An * represents all legitimate values for the given field. A range of values may be specified with a dash, such as `1-5`. A series of values may be separated by a comma, such as `0,4`.

Using the * value does not restrict that column in any way. If the column for day of the month uses an * and the day of the week is 1–5, the command will execute from Monday through Friday, without regard to the day of the month.

The last field is the command. The command should be specific with the pathname because the command is executed by cron, not by the user, and cron has no knowledge of the user's environment PATH variable. If the command file is a long one, put the command in a separate file and make the file executable. Place the name of the file in the command section of the crontab.

Manually creating cron entries requires some thought, but the scheduling is flexible enough for most cases.

The /etc/cron.d directory has the control files cron.allow and cron.deny. They are used in the same manner as the at.deny and at.allow.

SCOadmin Task Scheduler

The Task Scheduler provides a graphical front end to the crontab files. From the Task Scheduler, you may edit the tasks of other users. The Task Scheduler does not allow selecting multiple days per week, such as Tuesday and Thursday, but multiple entries can be made to work around that. For many administrators, the Task Scheduler will be a welcome addition to the graphical tools. Figure 18.10 illustrates the Task Scheduler.

If the selected Schedule Type is Date, the window shows Time in hours and minutes and the Month and Day. If the Schedule Type is Day of Week, the bottom box labeled Date is replaced with a Day of Week display.

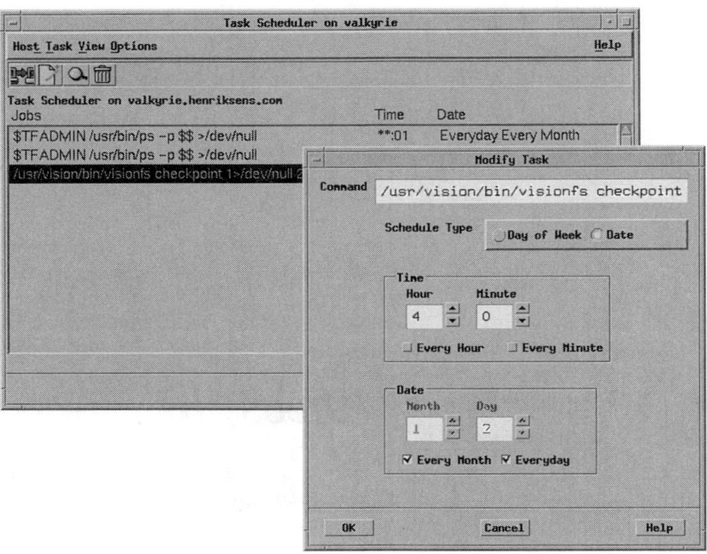

FIGURE 18.10 *The Task Scheduler.*

CHAPTER 19

Storage Devices, Filesystems, and Permissions

- **Storage devices**
  Learn how UnixWare 7 handles SCSI device naming and auto-recognizes them.
- **Filesystems**
  UnixWare 7 offers an array of filesystems. Understand what they are and how to manage them.
- **The Filesystem Manager**
  Look at the capabilities of the graphical administration tool for filesystem management.
- **Permissions**
  UnixWare 7 has standard UNIX permissions, plus an extension called Access Control Lists. Learn how to take advantage of Access Control Lists.

Storage Devices

The mass storage devices used on UnixWare 7 systems generally consist of hard disks, tapes, and CD-ROM drives. Use of tapes and tape drives is covered in Chapter 12, "Removable Media," as are floppy disks and CD-ROM drives. Hard disk drives, whether SCSI or EIDE, are accessed using the same device-naming scheme. EIDE drives that conform to ATAPI standards are seen by the system as SCSI drives.

Management of the hard drives requires an understanding of the hard disk configuration and nomenclature. Most of the disk management is performed from the command line, and the disk name is one of the arguments to the command.

Disk Partitions

Intel-based computers may have up to four primary partitions on a disk drive. Each partition may contain an operating system or data.

Within each partition, the operating system arranges the structure according to its needs. The primary disk has a Master Boot Record in track 0 that is used at boot time to locate the active partition. When located, the partition boot code in the active partition loads the operating system.

With UnixWare 7, the partitions are subdivided into *slices*. Slices have three main uses:

- The most common use for a slice from the user's perspective is to hold a filesystem.
- Slices may be used by the operating system as raw disk storage for swap, dump, and the partition boot slice.
- Slices may be reserved for an application, such as Oracle or Informix, that uses raw disk space to improve I/O throughput.

Tip

OpenServer 5 uses the `divvy` *command to create divisions within a partition. The OpenServer 5 divisions are the equivalent of a slice in UnixWare 7. The* `divvy` *command does not currently exist in UnixWare 7. The commands to add a disk in UnixWare are* `disksetup` *and* `diskadd`. *The commands to display or modify a partition are* `prtvtoc` *and* `edvtoc`.

The *Storage Device Interface (SDI)* is the framework used in UnixWare 7 for many of the storage device drivers. The purpose of the SDI is to provide a modular method of handling storage devices. The modularity ensures compatibility between current and future drivers and standardizes the way drivers are written.

The SDI is composed of two layers. The top layer is the device-specific portion and is called the *target driver*. The target driver controls the specific type (target) device and determines what actions must be taken to satisfy requests sent to the driver. Target drivers exist for hard disks (`sd01`), tape devices (`st01`),

CDROMs (`sc01`), WORM devices (`sw01`), and other mass storage devices. Man pages exist for each of these drivers with additional information.

The bottom layer of the SDI is the *Host Bus Adapter driver (HBA)*. The HBA receives the request from the target driver and sends the appropriate control signals to the device to satisfy the request from the target driver.

MultiPath IO (MPIO)

UnixWare 7 features MPIO to provide redundant access routes to SCSI storage devices. The MPIO drivers are layered above the target drivers. Figure 19.1 illustrates the UnixWare 7 I/O architecture. The Volume Table of Contents (VTOC) driver understands the subdivisions of the disk into partitions and slices. The MPIO driver tracks all possible paths to a storage device. The MPIO driver would not be present in a system with a single path to storage devices. The Redundant Array of Inexpensive Disks (RAID) driver would encompass the proprietary interface to the RAID devices. Each hardware manufacturer could provide a proprietary RAID driver to achieve the full capabilities of its device in UnixWare 7.

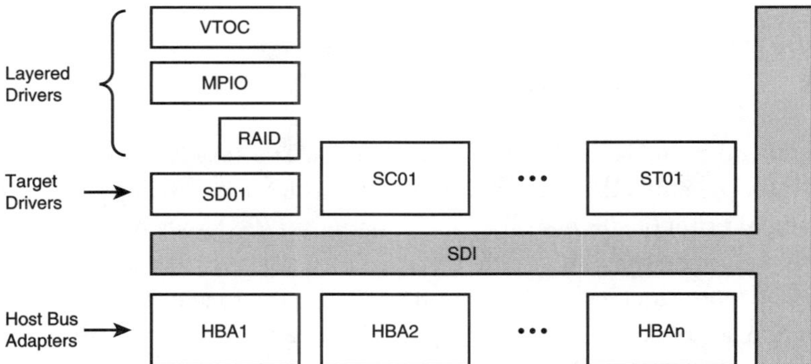

FIGURE 19.1 *The UnixWare 7 I/O architecture.*

With MPIO-supported hardware, multiple paths to storage devices are reported by the SDI to the MPIO driver. With multiple access paths to a storage device, failure of a single path will not terminate access to the storage device. The MPIO drivers can mark an access path as failed and continue to use the remaining paths. After the failed paths are repaired, the paths can become active again. The MPIO driver can perform load balancing by routing requests over multiple paths.

The *Data General Clariion RAID* is an example of the advanced storage devices that use MPIO. The Clariion supports all commercial RAID levels and has no single point of failure by virtue of its duplicate controllers, ports, and power supplies. Figure 19.2 illustrates the Clariion architecture. With the Clariion, one path to an array is active and the other is passive. If a port fails, the Clariion driver will mark the alternate path to the working port as an active path. The product-specific MPIO driver is responsible for maintaining the availability of paths to the storage devices based on the current condition of the hardware under its control.

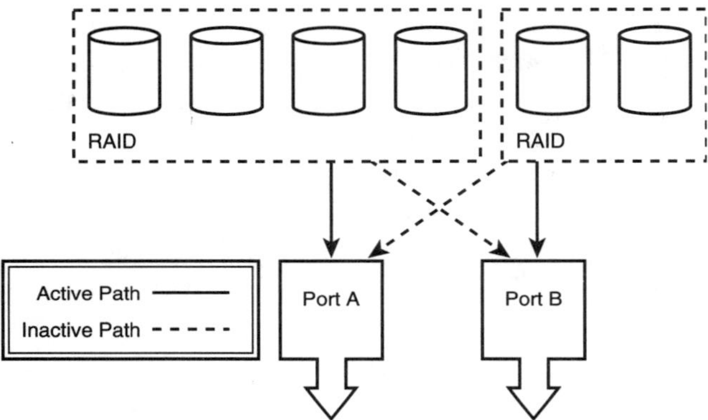

FIGURE 19.2 *The Data General Clariion RAID Architecture.*

The command to manage MPIO paths is `sdipath`. The `sdipath` command can list the multiple paths to a disk. Normally the MPIO driver will mark a path as failed when it cannot successfully use the path for I/O. However, a path can be placed in fail mode manually with `sdipath`. Once a failed path has been repaired, `sdipath` can be used to bring the failed route to active status. Information supplied by `sdipath` will provide the administrator with the status and the read and write requests per path.

MPIO increases the robustness of the I/O subsystem through redundant data paths and increases throughput by using multiple active paths to data stores simultaneously. High-end systems supporting RAID and failover, with redundant power supplies, controllers, and disk drives can use MPIO to improve performance and availability.

SCSI Device Names

The names for mass storage devices in UnixWare 7 follow the conventions of UnixWare 2. The name of a device describes its position in the SCSI hierarchy and a region on the disk. The devices can be found in the /dev/dsk and /dev/rdsk directories.

The format for the naming convention is

`c#b#t#d#s#`	hard disk slices
`c#b#t#d#p#`	hard disk partitions
`c#b#t#l#`	CD-ROM and tape devices

- `c#` is the controller number on which the device is located. `c0` is the first controller.
- `b#` is the bus number on the controller. Some controllers have multiple busses. `b0` is the first bus on the controller.
- `t#` is the target ID number of the device. This is usually set by a jumper or switch on the device. `t0` is target ID 0, the normal ID for a boot drive.
- `d#` is the drive number, normally `d0`. This is also known as the *logical unit number (LUN)*. For CD-ROM and tape devices, it is specified as `l#`.
- `p#` is the partition on the disk. `p0` refers to the whole disk; `p1`–`p4` refer to the four possible disk partitions.
- `s#` is the slice number within the UNIX partition. `s0` refers to the whole UNIX partition.

The whole disk of the primary SCSI disk (`t0`) on the first bus (`b0`) of the first SCSI controller (`c0`) would be `c0b0t0d0p0`. The partitions of that disk would range from `c0b0t0d0p1` through `c0b0t0d0p4`. A disk with an ID of 6 on the second bus would be `c0b1t6d0p0`.

To access the slices in the UNIX filesystem, use the `c#b#t#d#s#` format. The root filesystem of the UNIX partition is `c0b0t0d0s1` on the disk attached to controller 0, on bus 0, with an ID of 0 and a LUN of 0.

Tip

In OpenServer 5, there are devices in the /dev directory for each filesystem, such as /dev/u and /dev/ru. With the exception of /dev/root, /dev/boot, /dev/swap, and /dev/dump, these do not exist on UnixWare 7. All references to filesystems are in the /dev/dsk and /dev/rdsk directories.

Slices

Some slices on all UNIX partitions have preset, required definitions:

- *Slice 0*—The whole UNIX partition. The size is equal to the whole UNIX partition.

- *Slice 7*—The partition boot slice. Contains the UNIX boot code (not to be confused with the Master Boot Record or the /stand partition; the boot slice is the operating system boot loader), the VTOC information (partition slice layout), and the PDINFO (identification information). This slice occupies sectors 1 through 34 of each UNIX partition.

Tip

OpenServer 5 addressed this area as beginning at /dev/hd0a (on the primary disk), which encompassed the entire active partition. It was not an area with a unique entry in the /dev directory.

- *Slice 8*—The alternate sector slice. This slice is listed as `ALT SEC/TRK` in the `prtvtoc` listing. It is listed as `ALTS TABLE` in the install phase. This slice contains the information on remapped sectors, spare sectors, and other remapping information. This slice is optional. This is the equivalent of the badtrack table on OpenServer 5.
- *Slice 9*—In earlier versions of UNIX, including SVR4.0, slice 9 was used as an additional alternate track area. It can now be used for any purpose.

On the boot disk there are additional required slices:

- *Slice 1*—The root filesystem.
- *Slice 2*—The swap slice.
- *Slice 10*—The boot slice with a bfs filesystem. This is mounted as `/stand`. This slice contains the boot program that was loaded by the partition boot code in slice 7. It also includes unix, unix.old, resmgr, and other files necessary to get UnixWare loaded. The boot program is called stage3.blm. If you get a boot failure message referencing stage3.blm, it came during the load of the boot program from `/stand`.

Optionally, the following slices may occur on the boot disk:

- *Slice 3*—The /usr filesystem.
- *Slice 4*—The /home filesystem.
- *Slice 5*—Currently unused.
- *Slice 6*—The dump slice (for memory dumps instead of placing them in swap).
- *Slice 9*—Currently unused.

- *Slice 11*—The /var filesystem.
- *Slice 12*—The /home2 filesystem.
- *Slice 13*—The /tmp filesystem.
- *Slice 14*—The Volume Management public slice; used by the optional Veritas Volume Manager.
- *Slice 15*—The Volume Management private slice; used by the optional Veritas Volume Manager.

The maximum number of slices in a UNIX partition is 184 only when adding a non-boot drive. A primary partition can contain more than the default 16 slices, but you will have to use `prtvtoc` and `edvtoc` to do this after it is installed.

Tip

There is no /u filesystem created by default. It is possible to change the system to mount a `/u` *if your software requires one. A second alternative would be to create a symbolic link to* `/u` *linking it to* `/home`*:*

```
ln -s /home /u
```

Access to `/u` *should then place the user in* `/home`.

SCSI Device Scan

When UnixWare 7 starts the boot process, the `/etc/rc1` script runs. As a part of the `rc1` script, the /etc/scsi/pdimktab program makes a record of all SCSI devices found.

There is no need for the OpenServer 5 `mkdev hd` command. After a hard drive is added to the SCSI controller and the system is booted, the drive is available using the correct device name in `c#b#t#d#p#` format. This automatic recognition extends to SCSI tapes and CD-ROM drives. The device nodes are generated automatically.

The /etc/scsi directory contains the SCSI utilities and information on the SCSI devices. The sdi_scsi file has a listing of SCSI devices. These devices are picked up by `pdimktab` and inserted into the /etc/device.tab. The /etc/device.tab may disappear in a future release.

If a SCSI device is not in the /etc/device.tab, it cannot be mounted. Other devices are in the /etc/device.tab, including COM ports, pseudo-terminals, TCP devices, floppy disks, and so on. The `devattr` (device attributes) command lists information about a specific device from the /etc/device.tab file.

```
# devattr -v /dev/dsk/c0b0t0d0s0
addcmd='/etc/diskadd c0b0t0d0'
alias='disk1'
bdevice='/dev/dsk/c0b0t0d0s0'
bklib='SCSI'
cdevice='/dev/rdsk/c0b0t0d0s0'
desc='Disk Drive 1'
display='true'
displaycmd='/etc/prtvtoc /dev/rdsk/c0b0t0d0s0'
inquiry='SEAGATE ST52160N        0344'
pdimkdtab='true'
real_addr='c0b0t0d0sXX'
removecmd='/usr/lib/scsi/checkdevice c0b0t0d0s0 sd01'
scsi='true'
stamp='CEHKRJCDpOfE'
type='disk'
```

In addition to the `devattr` command, the `prtconf` (print configuration) command uses the device.tab file. The `prtconf` command has no arguments:

```
# prtconf
    SYSTEM CONFIGURATION:
    Memory Size: 80 Megabytes
    System Peripherals:
        Floppy Drive 1 - 1.44 MB 3.5
        Disk Drive 1 - SEAGATE  - ST52160N          - 2063 MB
        Disk Drive 2 - FUJITSU  - M1606S-512        - 1041 MB
        80387 Math Processor
```

For a listing containing only devices controlled by the SDI interface, run:

```
/sbin/sdiconfig -l
```

The listing on a SCSI-based system will appear similar to the following:

```
0:0,7,0: HBA     : (amd,1) AMD SCSI
  0,0,0: DISK    : SEAGATE ST52160N        0344
  0,1,0: DISK    : FUJITSU M1606S-512      6226
  0,2,0: TAPE    : ARCHIVE Python 25501 -XXX6500
  0,5,0: CDROM   : PHILIPS PCA80SC         V3-0
```

On an EIDE configuration, such as a Toshiba Tecra laptop, the listing will appear thusly:

```
0:0,7,0: HBA     : (ide,1) Generic ESDI/IDE/ATA
  0,0,0: DISK    : Generic IDE/ESDI        1.00
1:0,7,0: HBA     : (ide,2) Generic ESDI/IDE/ATA
  0,0,0: CDROM   : TOSHIBA CD-ROM XM-1402B 0186
```

For additional information on listing system information, see Chapter 15, "System Administration."

The Device Directory

The device directory (/dev) contains special device files for the system. Access to all devices is through the special device files rather than directly to devices. These files are pointers to access routines within the UnixWare 7 kernel.

Disk devices are located in /dev/dsk and /dev/rdsk. The /dev/dsk directory contains the block mode device pointers, and the /dev/rdsk directory contains the character mode pointers.

A listing of the /dev/dsk directory will appear like the following listing:

```
br--------    1 root    sys    7679,184 May 15 15:09    c0b0t0d0p0
brw-------    1 root    sys    7679,185 May 15 15:09    c0b0t0d0p1
brw-------    1 root    sys    7679,186 May 15 15:09    c0b0t0d0p2
brw-------    1 root    sys    7679,187 May 15 15:09    c0b0t0d0p3
brw-------    1 root    sys    7679,188 May 15 15:09    c0b0t0d0p4
brw-------    1 root    sys    7679,   0 May 15 15:09   c0b0t0d0s0
brw-------    1 root    sys    7679,   1 May 15 15:09   c0b0t0d0s1
brw-------    1 root    sys    7679,   2 May 15 15:09   c0b0t0d0s2
brw-------    1 root    sys    7679,   3 May 15 15:09   c0b0t0d0s3
brw-------    1 root    sys    7679,   4 May 15 15:09   c0b0t0d0s4
brw-------    1 root    sys    7679,   5 May 15 15:09   c0b0t0d0s5
brw-------    1 root    sys    7679,   6 May 15 15:09   c0b0t0d0s6
brw-------    1 root    sys    7679,   7 May 15 15:09   c0b0t0d0s7
brw-------    1 root    sys    7679,   8 May 15 15:09   c0b0t0d0s8
brw-------    1 root    sys    7679,   9 May 15 15:09   c0b0t0d0s9
brw-------    1 root    sys    7679,  10 May 15 15:09   c0b0t0d0sa
brw-------    1 root    sys    7679,  11 May 15 15:09   c0b0t0d0sb
brw-------    1 root    sys    7679,  12 May 15 15:09   c0b0t0d0sc
brw-------    1 root    sys    7679,  13 May 15 15:09   c0b0t0d0sd
brw-------    1 root    sys    7679,  14 May 15 15:09   c0b0t0d0se
brw-------    1 root    sys    7679,  15 May 15 15:09   c0b0t0d0sf
br--------    1 root    sys    7679,440 Jun 15 11:44    c0b0t1d0p0
brw-------    1 root    sys    7679,441 Jun 15 11:44    c0b0t1d0p1
brw-------    1 root    sys    7679,442 Jun 15 11:44    c0b0t1d0p2
brw-------    1 root    sys    7679,443 Jun 15 11:44    c0b0t1d0p3
brw-------    1 root    sys    7679,444 Jun 15 11:44    c0b0t1d0p4
brw-------    1 root    sys    7679,256 Jun 15 11:44    c0b0t1d0s0
...
brw-------    1 root    sys    7679,271 Jun 15 11:44    c0b0t1d0sf
```

Examining the abbreviated list of the /dev/dsk directory, the partitions and slices for both drives are shown. The major device number is 7679. The minor device numbers for the partitions on the first drive are 184 through 188, and the slices are numbered 0 through 15. Slice numbers can range from 0 to 183 allowing for 184 slices per disk partition. Unless the slices above 15 are created, the device nodes are not created. Each disk has 256 minor devices; disk 0's minor range is 0–255. Disk 1 minor devices start at 256. Unlike previous versions of UNIX, the major/minor device numbers are not fixed values. The vtoc driver with major device number 7679 is an exception to the rule. The major device number is created by a device driver's configuration routine return.

A channel number and resource manager key are used in lieu of the minor device number. User-level utilities see a major/minor device number pair, but these are fabricated from the device instance, channel number, and resource manager key.

The Volume Table of Contents (VTOC)

When installing a new disk using `diskadd` or `disksetup`, the Volume Table of Contents is created. This is the equivalent of the OpenServer 5 `divvy` function. The vtoc target driver uses the VTOC to manage the disk organization. After a disk is installed, the VTOC is managed through two tools: `prtvtoc` and `edvtoc`.

It is possible to use a non-active partition on disk for a single UNIX filesystem. There will be no VTOC table when this method is used. The method shown below is not officially supported but was provided by a SCO employee who uses it. His purpose in using this methodology is to isolate the data partition from the operating system because he frequently tests, crashes, and reloads the operating system.

Assume partition /dev/rdsk/c0b0t0d0p1 is the UnixWare 7 partition, and there is a second empty partition on that disk. The second partition can be referenced as /dev/rdsk/c0b0t0d0p2.

To use it as a filesystem, you can do the following:

```
mkfs -F vxfs (options you desire) /dev/rdsk/c0b0t0d0p2
```

You should be able to mount the newly created filesystem using

```
mount -F vxfs /dev/dsk/c0b0t0d0p2 /part2
```

There is no method for determining bad tracks or assigning alternate tracks because there is no ALT sector slice. The entire partition is available under the mount point, `/part2` in this example. If you reload the operating system, you would only need to mount the filesystem because it would already exist.

prtvtoc

The `prtvtoc` command prints information about the layout of the hard disk. The format for the command is

```
prtvtoc -ap [-f vtocfile] raw device
```

Use `prtvtoc` to print the contents of a VTOC:

```
#prtvtoc /dev/rdsk/c0b0t0d0s0
slice 0:   DISK         permissions:   VALID UNMOUNTABLE starting sector:   63 (cyl 0)         length:   4225032 (263.00 cyls)
slice 1:   ROOT         permissions:   VALID             starting sector:   337365 (cyl 21)    length:   1847475 (115.00 cyls)
slice 2:   SWAP         permissions:   VALID UNMOUNTABLE starting sector:   64260 (cyl 4)      length:   273105 (17.00 cyls)
slice 4:   HOME         permissions:   VALID             starting sector:   2184840 (cyl 136)length:   2008125 (125.00 cyls)
slice 7:   BOOT         permissions:   VALID UNMOUNTABLE starting sector:   63 (cyl 0)         length:   34 (0.00 cyls)
slice 8:   ALT SEC/TRK  permissions:   VALID UNMOUNTABLE starting sector:   97 (cyl 0)         length:   15968 (0.99 cyls)
slice 10:  STAND        permissions:   VALID             starting sector:   16065 (cyl 1)      length:   48195 (3.00 cyls)
slice 15:  VOLPRIVATE   permissions:   VALID UNMOUNTABLE starting sector:   4192965 (cyl 261)length:   16065 (1.00 cyls)
```

To obtain `prtvtoc` information suitable for use with edvtoc, use the optional `-f` *`filename`* option:

```
#prtvtoc -f vtocfile /dev/rdsk/c0b0t0d0s0

#SLICE   TAG    FLAGS    START     SIZE
 0       0x5    0x201    63        4225032
 1       0x2    0x200    337365    1847475
 2       0x3    0x201    64260     273105
 3       0x0    0x0      0         0
 4       0xb    0x200    2184840   2008125
 5       0x0    0x0      0         0
 6       0x0    0x0      0         0
 7       0x1    0x201    63        34
 8       0xd    0x201    97        15968
 9       0x0    0x0      0         0
10       0x9    0x200    16065     48195
11       0x0    0x0      0         0
12       0x0    0x0      0         0
13       0x0    0x0      0         0
14       0x0    0x0      0         0
15       0xf    0x201    4192965   16065
```

The TAG column defines the slice type:

```
· Boot                        0x01
· Root                        0x02
· Swap                        0x03
· Usr                         0x04
· whole partition             0x05
· Alternate sectors           0x06
· non-unix space              0x07
· Alternate tracks            0x08
· Stand                       0x09
· Var                         0x0a
· Home                        0x0b
· Dump                        0x0c
· Alt. Sector/track           0x0d
· Vol. Management public      0x0e
· Vol. Management private     0x0f
```

The FLAGS column is the permission flags associated with the slice. These are composed of a mathematical total of up to three values:

Unmountable partition	0x01
Read Only	0x10
Partition is valid to use	0x200

The root partition is 0x200, valid to use. The swap partition is 0x201, valid to use but unmountable.

The START and SIZE columns are the absolute sector numbers with the first sector number being zero. Slices should begin and end on cylinder boundaries whenever possible. To calculate these values manually, you will need the heads, cylinders, and sectors per track information.

In the preceding information, the disk has 63 sectors per track. With the exception of slice 8—the alternate sector's slice that immediately follows the boot code—all start numbers are evenly divisible by 63. With the exception of the boot and alternate sector's slices, all sizes are evenly divisible by 63.

The -p option to the prtvtoc command can be used to obtain information known as *Physical Disk Information (PDINFO)*. The PDINFO is stored in the partition boot slice and is used as a sanity check each time the disk drivers are initialized, usually boot time.

```
prtvtoc -p /dev/rdsk/c0b0t0d0s0

Device /dev/rdsk/c0b0t0d0s0
device type:           4 (DPT_SCSI_HD)
cylinders:             263                heads:               255
sectors/track:         63                 bytes/sector:        512
number of partitions:  16                 size of alts table: 2048
media stamp:           "CEHKRJCDpOfE"
```

The device type of 4 translates to DPT_SCSI_HD. The DPT stands for *Disk Parameter Type*. DPTs include

DPT_NOTDISK	0	Not a disk device
DPT_WINI	1	Winchester (IDE/EIDE)
DPT_FLOPPY	2	Floppy
DPT_OTHER	3	Other type of disk
DPT_SCSI_HD	4	SCSI disk
DPT_SCSI_OD	5	SCSI optical

The final option for the `prtvtoc` command displays the alternate sectors:

```
prtvtoc -a /dev/rdsk/c0b0t0d0s0

ALTERNATE SECTOR/TRACK MAPPING TABLE:

Bad Sector Start          Alternate Sector Start          Count
    1503229         ->        1503229                 1

      15962 alternate sector(s) left for allocation.
```

edvtoc

The `edvtoc` command is used to write a modified VTOC table to a disk. The format of the VTOC table is the same as that printed out by the `prtvtoc -f vtocfile` syntax:

```
edvtoc -f vtocfile /dev/rdsk/c0b0t1d0s0
```

To modify a VTOC on disk, use the following steps:

1. If the disk is other than the root disk, unmount the disk.
2. Use `prtvtoc -f` to get a copy of the current VTOC.
3. Edit the VTOC file and make any desired changes.
4. Run `edvtoc` using the edited file to write the new VTOC to disk.
5. If the disk was the root disk, reboot. If it was not a root disk, remount the filesystem.

Warning

Modifying the VTOC on a disk can result in the loss of some or all data on the partition. Back up the filesystems before using `edvtoc`.

A second use of `edvtoc` is to update the disk parameters (heads, sectors per track, and so on). This may be necessary when a disk is moved from one disk controller to another. Use the `-p` option to update the parameters:

```
edvtoc -p /dev/rdsk/c0b0t0d4s0
```

The final use of `edvtoc` is to change the disk stamp value with the `edvtoc -s stamp`. Use `prtvtoc -p` to print the PDINFO to see the current disk stamp, labeled as the *media stamp*. The only reason to use this option is to correct a stamp collision caused by two or more disks having the same disk stamp. The possibility of stamp collisions is small because the stamp is randomly generated.

If a duplicate stamp were generated, one of the devices would not be recognized by the I/O subsystem. If a stamp collision were suspected, executing `sdiconfig -l` would not show the device with the duplicate. If this occurs on an MPIO device, strange things could happen due to incoherent data if the MPIO device picked the wrong drive. To correct the problem under MPIO would require turning off the MPIO and reinitializing the disk or creating a stamp.

Filesystems

UnixWare 7 supports several types of filesystems. In addition to the normal disk-based filesystems, memory and special-purpose filesystems exist. The only filesystem backward-compatible to OpenServer 5 is the System 5 filesystem. The System 5 filesystem is the equivalent of the OpenServe 5 S51K filesystem.

Veritas Filesystem (vxfs)

The *Veritas filesystem (vxfs)* is the default for root and user filesystems and offers several advantages over older filesystems. The maximum file and filesystem sizes under vxfs is 1 terabyte (TB). To enable the large files, create the filesystem initially with the `largefile` option or use the `fsadm` command to modify the structure of the filesystem to allow large files.

The version 4 vxfs used in UnixWare 7 supports quotas. The quota service is turned on using the `quotaon` command. Filesystems must be mounted when `quotaon` is turned on for them. A file named *quotas* must be created in the root directory of each filesystem to have quotas. The file must be owned by root. The `edquota` command is used to edit the user's quotas.

To create quotas in /home:

1. Verify that /home is mounted.
2. Run touch `/home/quotas`.
3. Run `chown root /home/quotas`.
4. Run `quotaon -F vxfs /home`.
5. Run `edquota -F vxfs gene`.

The two lines show one quota that has been edited with limits replacing the default zeros and the new line for /home:

```
fs /home blocks (soft = 0, hard = 0) inodes (soft = 0, hard = 0)
fs / blocks (soft = 1000, hard = 1200) inodes (soft = 1000, hard = 1200)
```

A hard quota cannot be exceeded by the user. The soft quota can be exceeded with warnings given to the user. The user must reduce file usage below the soft quota within a given time period. When the user goes over the quota, error messages appear indicating no space is left on the device.

Extent based allocation is used by vxfs to assign multiple grouped blocks of space to a file rather than assign one block at a time. Extents reduce fragmentation and improve reads of multiple blocks in a single I/O.

Intent logging increases system recovery speed by forcing writes of impending changes to disk while buffering the actual writes. When a crash occurs, the intent log is examined to determine the necessity for checking filesystem integrity. Tools for working with vxfs filesystems include mkfs, fsck, quotaon, edquota, and fsadm. Several options for vxfs may be used in the `mount` command. For security, the `blkclear` option will write zeros to disk space allocated to files to avoid the possibility of old data from another file being left in a new file's data blocks.

Tip

Check the man pages on `mkfs_vxfs`, `mount_vxfs`, *and* `fsadm_vxfs` *for more information and pointers to other commands.*

The vxfs filesystem can be further enhanced with the Veritas Volume Manager. The enhancements to vxfs include the ability to group multiple disk slices that appear to the user and applications to be a single partition. Depending on the arrangement of the slices, the data can be arranged in several methods. UnixWare 7 Disk Mirroring and UnixWare 7 Online Data Manager (ODM) are layered products. ODM is included in the UnixWare 7 Enterprise Edition.

- *Disk spanning*—Disk space is concatenated into a single entity. Using concatenation, several smaller disks can be used to create a filesystem larger than any of the individual disks. The chance of failure increases as the number of disks increases. Failure of any disk destroys the entire filesystem. In concatenated filesystems each disk is filled and then data is stored on the next disk. This feature is a standard part of the UnixWare 7 vxfs filesystem capability.
- *Striping (RAID 0)*—Several disks are used with data written in stripes across each disk. Data is evenly distributed for better performance. No data redundancy is provided, and the failure of one disk destroys the entire filesystem.
- *Mirroring (RAID 1)*—Data written to one disk is mirrored to a second disk. If one drive fails, the other drive has a complete copy of the data.

- *Striping with parity (RAID 5)*—Data is written across all the disks in stripes with parity information stored for recovery if a single drive fails.
- *Striping with mirroring (RAID 0 + RAID 1)*—Stripes of data are written across drives and mirrored to another set of drives.

Boot Filesystem (bfs)

A *boot filesystem (bfs)* is created in slice 10 at system installation and mounted to /stand. The /stand is the boot area for UnixWare 7 and contains the files necessary to start the system. The /stand directory contains unix, unix.old, resmgr, bootmsgs, and so on. The size defaults to 20MB. This is not a user filesystem.

The bfs filesystem is supported through the Filesystem Manager GUI.

The structure of the bfs filesystem is simple. Data is written across the filesystem in contiguous blocks. The data block following the last block written is the next block to be used. For data blocks to be reused, one of two conditions must exist:

- The deleted file must have been the last file written.
- The system must detect the need for compaction and then compact the filesystem.

Compaction is performed when the system recognizes one of two conditions:

- The last data block in the filesystem has been reached and there are free blocks available.
- The system deletes a large file (500 or more blocks) and there is one file after it on the filesystem; and it is a small file (10 or fewer blocks).

The bfs filesystem is limited to having one file open for writing at any time. There are no subdirectories or special files allowed in a bfs filesystem. Attempting to create a subdirectory or special file returns an error message: `Operation not applicable.`

System 5 Filesystem (s5)

The s5 filesystem is the only OpenServer 5 filesystem (S51K) recognized by UnixWare 7. The s5 filesystem is supported through the Filesystem Manager GUI.

Extended System 5 Filesystem (ufs)

The *extended System 5 filesystem (ufs)* is a more complex version than the s5 filesystem. It is not supported through the Filesystem Manager, only on the command line.

Secure Filesystem (sfs)

The *secure filesystem (sfs)* is a variant of the ufs filesystem. It is supported by commands at the command line but not through the Filesystem Manager.

DOS Filesystem (dosfs)

The *DOS filesystem (dosfs)* provides compatibility with both DOS floppy disk and hard disk FAT16 partitions. Dosfs filesystems may be mounted and accessed using UNIX commands. The dosfs is supported through the Filesystem Manager GUI. Filenames are supported only in the DOS 8.3 format. To use FAT32, you will need Merge 4.

Memory Filesystem (memfs)

The *memory filesystem (memfs)* provides a high-performance, volatile filesystem. There are no tools to manage a memfs because, when dismounted, the filesystem and its contents disappear. When mounting a memfs, two options are available at mount time when using the `-o` option:

- `swapmax` sets the maximum amount of memory to be used.
- `rootmode` enables you to set permissions on the mount point. The default permissions are `0775`.

To create and mount a memfs on /mnt allowing a 1MB filesystem with read-write-execute privileges for Everyone with the sticky bit set for the directory:

```
mount -F memfs -o rootmode=1777,swapmax=1048576 /mnt /mnt
```

Warning

Do not place a space between the options in the -o clause. Using the syntax

```
-o rootmode=1777, swapmax=1048576
```

will create an error. There is no device file for the mount, so the directory on which the memfs is to be mounted is entered twice.

The option exists to allow read-only mounting of a memfs. No one seems to know why this option exists. It is not possible to create a memfs in read/write mode, load it with data, and then remount it in read-only mode. A read-only mount will result in memory being used for an empty filesystem.

CD-ROM Filesystem (cdfs)

The *CD-ROM filesystem (cdfs)* supports the Rock Ridge and High Sierra formats. Options exist to allow translation of names in case (upper and lower), executing setuid (SUID) programs, creating UIDs and GIDs for the files and directories on the CD, and other protection options.

CD-ROMs must be mounted read-only with either the `-r` or `-o ro` options.

If only a single CD-ROM drive exists on the system, the directory /dev/cdrom will contain the device name, such as `c0b0t5l0`, and possibly a second entry, such as `cdrom1`. To mount the CD-ROM on the /mnt directory in this case:

```
mount -F cdfs -r /dev/cdrom/cdrom1 /mnt
mount -F cdfs -o ro /dev/cdrom/c0b0t5l0 /mnt
```

Network File System (NFS)

The *Network File System (NFS)* is used to mount shared resources from a remote NFS server. The format for an NFS mount is

```
mount -F nfs <remotesystem>:/<sharedfile> /mount_point
mount -F nfs thor:/u /mnt
```

NetWare UNIX Filesystem (NUCFS)

The *NetWare UNIX filesystem (NUCFS)* provides UNIX access to NetWare shared files. Chapter 9, "Services for NetWare," covers the NUCFS in more detail.

Process Filesystem (procfs)

The *Process filesystem (procfs)* is mounted on /proc. The procfs is a pseudo-filesystem allowing access to the processes running on the system. A listing of the files in /proc will provide the process ID (PID) of each process or lightweight process currently running. The PID numbers are names of subdirectories that contain files with information concerning the processes. This is not a user filesystem.

If the /proc filesystem is not mounted, the `ps` command will return with no processes. If this problem appears, check the /etc/vfstab to be sure the entry for /proc appears.

Processor Statistics Filesystem (profs)

The *Processor Statistics filesystem (profs)* is mounted on the /processor/system directory. Information on the processor is stored in a file named 000 for the first processor. This is not a user filesystem. Profs is a pseudo-filesystem.

File Descriptor Filesystem (fd)

The *File Descriptor filesystem (fd)* is a pseudo-filesystem mounted on /dev/fd. The entries in /dev/fd are character-special devices for the current process's file descriptors. A benefit of the /dev/fd implementation is using standard-in (`stdin`) and standard-out (`stdout`) notations with commands that do not support these options.

Consider the following. A file called "names" contains first names in a single column:

```
Gene
Melissa
Mina
Susie
```

To compare the contents of names with the input from the keyboard:

```
diff names /dev/fd/0 > diff_file
```

If the input from the keyboard is

```
Gene
Melissa
Mina
```

then the diff_file will contain

```
4d3
< Susie
```

The /dev/fd descriptors could be put to innovative uses by shell programmers.

Manipulating and Managing Filesystems

Several commands are useful for checking on filesystems and converting or upgrading filesystems. Some of these commands will be familiar to both UnixWare 2 and OpenServer users.

> *Tip*
>
> *Unlike OpenServer 5, many commands in UnixWare 7 require the* `-F` ***`filesystemtype`*** *option.*

fstyp

The `fstyp` command will attempt to determine the filesystem type of a disk by running a module for each filesystem type being checked. The `fstyp` command is driven by heuristic methods and is not guaranteed to be accurate. If no match is found, the command returns an `unknown_fstype (no matches)` response. If the result indicates that the filesystem could be one of several types, an `unknown_fstype (multiple matches)` message is returned.

The `fstyp` command does not work on memfs, nfs, or pseudo-filesystems. Attempting to determine the filesystem type of /tmp, a memfs will return

```
/tmp not block or character special device
```

fsck

Filesystems that have not been unmounted properly or have suffered damage can be checked and repaired with `fsck`. If no special file is used as an argument, `fsck` will read through the /etc/vfstab and run an `fsck` on each filesystem with a listing in the `fsckdev` column that has a numeral in the `fsckpass` column.

Tip

It is recommended that the raw device (/dev/rdsk) entries be used rather than the block device (/dev/dsk) entries. If the filesystem is mounted, `fsck` *will not work on the block device. It is not recommended to run* `fsck` *on mounted filesystems.*

fsadm

The vxfs filesystem has a special command for management: `fsadm`. It allows reporting on disk and directory fragmentation, changing the size of a filesystem, reorganizing directories and file extents, and allowing support for large files. Large files are defined as being greater than 2GB in size. When setting the `largefile` option, be careful to check the backup command being used to ensure that it has been modified for use with large files. Use the man pages for the commands you use to verify large file support.

quota

The `quota` command allows listings of quotas by user or by filesystem. If quotas are in effect, the quota program can list disk quotas and usage for each user by specifying the username. Without a username, it will list warnings about filesystems with users over quota.

When users attempt to copy data into a filesystem in which they have exceeded their quota, they will receive messages like those below. The disk is not out of space; the user is out of space.

```
UX:cp: ERROR: Cannot create ./file1: No space left on device
UX:cp: ERROR: Cannot create ./file2: No space left on device
UX:cp: ERROR: Cannot create ./file3: No space left on device
```

To check on the user, run the `quota` command for the user:

```
quota -F vxfs gene
```

You will see the following response:

```
Block limit reached on /home4
File count limit reached on /home4
```

To check on the user's quotas on a particular filesystem, run `repquota`:

```
repquota -F vxfs /home4
```

You will see the following response:

```
                 Block limits                              File limits
User    used    soft    hard    timeleft   used          soft     hard     timeleft
gene    +-      192     100     200        7.0 days      64       100      200
```

User Gene is over the soft limit on blocks and has seven days left to correct the problem.

Converting Filesystems

Raw slices used for databases that maintain their own file I/O can be converted from OpenServer 5 to UnixWare 7 with the `sdimkosr5` command. This command reads the divvy table and creates a VTOC for the UNIX partition. Previously mapped bad blocks remain as bad blocks, but newly discovered bad blocks cannot be remapped. If an OpenServer 5 disk is connected to a UnixWare 7 system, UnixWare 7 will do a temporary divvy table conversion on-the-fly. Always back up data prior to converting a filesystem.

To upgrade earlier versions of Veritas filesystems to later versions, use `vxupgrade`. When upgraded, older versions of the drivers will not be able to mount the filesystem. Upgrades cannot be reversed. Filesystems may not be downgraded.

To convert supported filesystems to the Veritas filesystem, the `vxconvert` command may be used. The list of filesystem types that can be converted is very short. If you cannot convert the data, create a new vxfs filesystem and restore the data from the backup. A bug in early releases prevented vxconvert from working properly.

Mounting a Good Disk on Another System

With the automatic recognition of SCSI devices at boot time, mounting filesystems from another UnixWare 7 system is very simple. Install the disk and boot the computer. To locate the filesystems, use `prtvtoc` on the new disk. Create directories for the mounts and mount the filesystems:

```
mkdir /home/moredata
mount /dev/dsk/c0b0t3d0s1 /home/moredata
```

This is far easier than the OpenServer 5 routine of running `mkdev hd`.

To have the filesystem mounted automatically when rebooting, add entries to the /etc/vfstab.

Setting Up a New Hard Disk

Adding a new hard disk to UnixWare 7 requires only a couple of steps. Insert the new drive and boot the computer. If your system supports hot add of disks, the steps are slightly different and do not require rebooting.

UnixWare 7 allows hot swapping, hot adding, and hot removing of devices, although the underlying hardware must support the actions. It is possible to physically hot add a disk, CDROM, or tape drive to a SCSI bus.

Using the `sdiadd` command, devices can be added to the system. If adding a new device, `sdiadd` is not necessary if the device is added prior to booting.

One restriction on hot add and hot remove is the SCSI termination. A device that is the SCSI terminator may not be hot removed or added. If you anticipate using hot add or remove, use terminators at the cable ends that are independent of mass storage devices.

To hot add a disk device to an existing host bus adapter, type:

```
sdiadd c#b#t#d#s#
```

This will quiet the SCSI bus and allow plugging in the hard drive. Press the Enter key when the disk is attached to notify `sdiadd` that you are through so that the SCSI bus will start being used again. If no parameter is provided for the `sdiadd` command, it will find all new devices and add them to the system. While the bus is in the quiet mode, no data will travel over it.

If the disk that was added already had filesystems, mount them and add them to the /etc/vfstab file. If the disk added was new, use `diskadd` to complete the installation.

> **Tip**
>
> *The documentation on* `sdiadd` *and* `sdirm` *incorrectly includes the* `-h` *option. The functionality of* `-h` *has not been included in the commands.*

diskadd

The `diskadd` routine steps the administrator through the programs to add the new hard disk and its filesystems. To use `diskadd`, execute it with the disk number:

```
diskadd c#b#t#d#
```

where `c#b#t#d#` is the disk number to be added. When adding the second disk to the system, the disk number can be replaced with the numeral `1`. If the disk being added is on controller 0, bus 0, ID 2, and LUN 0, then the command would be

```
diskadd c0b0t2d0
```

The following would appear:

```
UX:diskadd: INFO: You have invoked the System V disk management (s5dm)
➥diskadd utility.
The purpose of this utility is to set up additional disk drives.
This utility can destroy the existing data on the disk.
Do you wish to continue?
(Type y for yes or n for no followed by ENTER):
```

First, `diskadd` will warn that this will overwrite the disk contents. After answering that you are aware of the consequences, fdisk is run.

fdisk

One addition to `fdisk` that is not in OpenServer 5 is the ability to overwrite the master boot code.

While this ability is not used often, it could be used to overwrite the master boot code if it has become infected by a virus. Any Intel-based operating system is subject to a master boot sector virus if booted from an infected DOS diskette.

You may select one of the following options:

0	Overwrite system master boot code
1	Create a partition
2	Change Active (Boot from) partition
3	Delete a partition
4	Exit (Update disk configuration and exit)
5	Cancel (Exit without updating disk configuration)

Select the appropriate options. After exiting fdisk, the `disksetup` command is run.

disksetup

The first prompt for `disksetup` is:

```
Surface analysis of your disk is recommended but not required.
Do you wish to skip surface analysis? (y/n)
```

Disk surface analysis is the equivalent of the OpenServer 5 badtrack routine. After the disk surface analysis, the process of dividing the disk into slices is begun. This will create the VTOC.

```
You will now be queried on the setup of your disk. After you have deter-
mined which slices will be created, you will be queried to designate the
sizes of the various slices.
How many slices/filesystems do you want created on the disk (1-13)?
```

Tip

Notice that `diskadd` *allows only 13 slices maximum.*

There are required slices already subtracted. To get 184 slices (actually 181 user defineable), run disksetup manually with the `-Ie` *option to get extended slice capability.*

For each slice/filesystem requested, the following dialog will appear:

```
Please enter the absolute pathname (e.g., /home3) for slice/filesystem 1
➥(1-32 chars)? /home3
Enter the filesystem type for this slice (vxfs,ufs,s5,sfs), type 'na' if
no filesystem is needed, or press <ENTER> to use the default (vxfs):
Specify the block size from the following list (1024, 2048, 4096, 8192),
or press <ENTER> to use the first one:
Should /home3 be automatically mounted during a reboot?
Type "no" to override auto-mount or press <ENTER> to enable the option:
```

After specifying the slices, the slices are sized.

```
You will now specify the size in cylinders of each slice.
(One megabyte of disk space is approximately 1 cylinder.)
There are now 932 cylinders available on your disk.
The filesystem type you have chosen is limited to 1048576 cylinders.
How many cylinders would you like for /home3 (0-932)?
Press <ENTER> for 0 cylinders: 450
```

After entering sizes for all slices, you are asked to confirm the allocations:

```
You have specified the following disk configuration:
A /home3 filesystem with 450 cylinders (450.0 MB)
A /home4 filesystem with 482 cylinders (482.0 MB)
Is this allocation acceptable to you (y/n)?
```

Answering **y** to the above question will bring the dialog shown below. `Disksetup` runs mkfs to create the filesystems. You are offered the option to change the inode allocation for each filesystem. The vxfs filesystem has a dynamic allocation of inodes. The inode allocation entered here is the initial allocation.

```
Filesystems will now be created on the needed slices.
Creating the /home3 filesystem on /dev/rdsk/c0b0t1d0s1.
Allocated approximately 115168 inodes for this file system. Specify a
new value or press <ENTER> to use the default:
Creating the /home4 filesystem on /dev/rdsk/c0b0t1d0s2
Allocated approximately 123360 inodes for this file system. Specify a
new value or press <ENTER> to use the default:
```

```
UX:diskadd: INFO: Diskadd for Disk Drive 2 DONE at Thu Jul 16 13:28:58
➥EDT 1998
```

The following lines were added to the /etc/vfstab after the execution of diskadd. Both filesystems were mounted automatically at the end of the process.

```
/dev/dsk/c0b0t1d0s1     /dev/rdsk/c0b0t1d0s1     /home3     vxfs     1     yes
➥    mincache=closesync     SYS_RANGE_MAX
/dev/dsk/c0b0t1d0s2     /dev/rdsk/c0b0t1d0s2     /home4     vxfs     1     yes
➥    mincache=closesync     SYS_RANGE_MAX
```

As an alternative, an automated disksetup can be run from the command line specifying the following:

- The raw disk device
- A defaults file that includes the slice layout
- That the device will be a system boot disk
- The partition boot code should be written without queries, prompts, or information

To install a primary disk that is currently mounted on `c0b0t1d0s0` with a default layout file named myslices, run

```
/usr/sbin/disksetup -B -b /etc/boot -d myslices /dev/rdsk/c0b0t1d0s0
```

where the myslices file would look like:

```
slice #   slicename          FStype   FSblksz   slicesize   minsz
 1        /                  vxfs     1024      35M         12
 2        /dev/swap          -        -         2m          8
 5        /home              vxfs     4096      40W         3
 10       /stand             bfs      512       5M          5
 13       /dev/volpublic     -        -         20M         0
 14       /dev/volprivate    -        -         256K        128
```

See the man pages on disksetup for more information on the slice layout file.

To write boot code to a disk:

```
/usr/sbin/disksetup -b /etc/boot /dev/rdsk/c0b0t1d0s0
```

If you cannot boot from the hard disk and need to rewrite the boot code, there are two methods you can use.

- Use the emergency boot media, get to a shell prompt, mount the root filesystem, chroot to the filesystem, and run `disksetup`.

- Use the install media to boot the system and, at the System Node name prompt, switch to `VT0>`, get to a shell prompt, mount the root filesystem, chroot, and run `disksetup`.

For a step-by-step guide, use the following steps, which specify the method from the install media:

1. Boot from the Install media.
2. At System Node Name prompt, switch to `VT0>`.
3. Put install CD-ROM into drive.
4. Mount `-F cdfs -r /dev/cdrom1 /cd-rom`.
5. Run `cd /cd-rom/.extra.d/etc/conf/mod.d`.
6. Run `modreg 4 vxfs`.
7. Run ``modadmin -l `pwd`/vxfs``.
8. Mount `-F vxfs /dev/dsk/c0b0t0d0s1 /mnt`.
9. If the mount fails with `No space left on device`, run

   `/cd-rom/.extra.d/etc/fs/vxfs/fsck /dev/rdsk/c0b0t0d0s1`

   and try step 8 again.
10. Chroot to the hard disk using `chroot /mnt /usr/bin/sh`.
11. Run `/usr/sbin/disksetup -b /etc/boot /dev/rdsk/c0b0t1d0s0`.

Removing a Disk Drive

When you need to remove a disk drive from UnixWare 7, use the `diskrm` command. This is a hard link to `diskadd`.

```
diskrm c#b#t#d#
```

Using `diskrm` will deconfigure the disk and its slices. It will also remove it from the vfstab.

Rebooting a system from which a disk has been physically, not logically, removed will remove it from the /etc/device.tab listing and make it unavailable for use. The disk will not be removed from the /etc/vfstab by autoconfiguration on boot.

You can hot remove a disk with `sdirm`. Like autoconfiguration, `sdirm` will not remove a disk from the /etc/vfstab. Use the Filesystem Manager to modify the vfstab.

Tip

Like `sdiadd`*, some documentation for* `sdirm` *refers to the* `-h` *option. The* `-h` *option does not exist.*

You may not remove disk 0 (`c0b0t0d0s0`).

To verify the disk number, use `prtvtoc`. For example, to check on disk 1, run:

```
prtvtoc /dev/rdsk/c0b0t1d0s0 ¦more
```

The Filesystem Manager

From the SCOadmin GUI, several filesystem management functions can be performed. This section will detail the use of the GUI tool. The GUI can be reached from the SCOadmin option on the front panel. Figure 19.3 illustrates the Filesystem Manager in the normal mount status display mode.

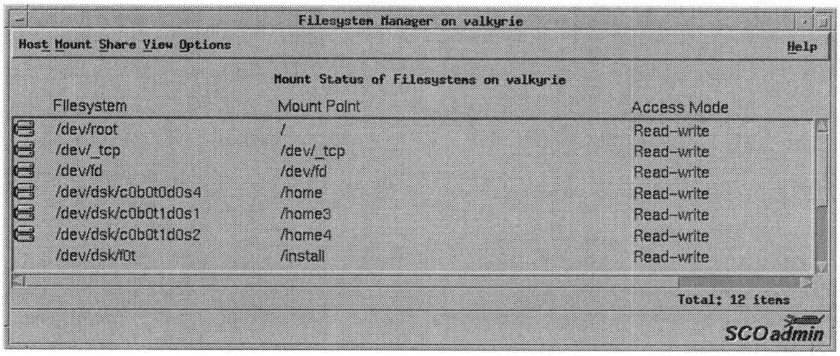

FIGURE 19.3 *The Filesystem Manager.*

Mount and Unmount

To mount a local filesystem, choose Mount, Local. Figure 19.4 illustrates the Mount Configuration Manager. Select a filesystem using the drop-down box. Enter a mount point, which can be any existing directory or the manager will create a new directory for you.

Optionally, enter a description for the mount. At the Filesystem Type prompt, click in the box and the system will identify the filesystem type. Set the access mode to read/write or read-only. Specify when to mount.

Two additional options can be set through the Advanced Options window. Not all mount options are available through the manager.

The first option is to set the mode of intent logging. Log mode is the preferred method. The other methods use delayed writes to the log, which could result in loss of file information in a crash. Clear Blocks is a security feature. The system will write zeros to disk space when it is allocated to a file.

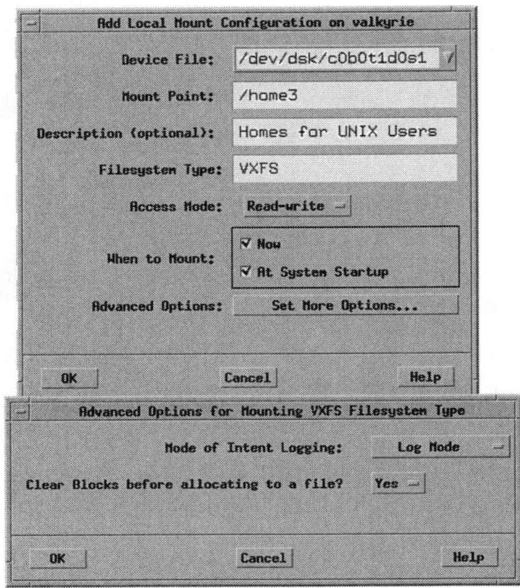

FIGURE 19.4 *The advanced options for a vxfs mount.*

When a filesystem has been mounted, highlight the filesystem by clicking it. Select the Mount option in the menu, and three additional options are offered:

- Modify Mount Configuration
- Remove Mount Configuration
- Unmount

The Modify Mount option allows changes to the mount configuration entered in the Add Local Mount Configuration. The window for modifying mount options is the same one used to add a new mount configuration.

The Remove Mount option will unmount the filesystem and remove the mount configuration from the /etc/vfstab file. The Remove Mount will display a window requesting confirmation as shown in Figure 19.5.

The Unmount option will unmount the filesystem without affecting the mount configuration information in the /etc/vfstab. This option can be used when performing other filesystem management functions. A window requesting confirmation of the unmount will be displayed, as shown in Figure 19.6.

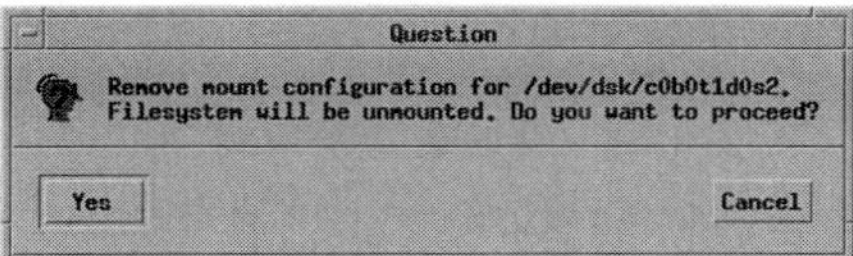

FIGURE 19.5 *The confirmation request for removing a mount configuration.*

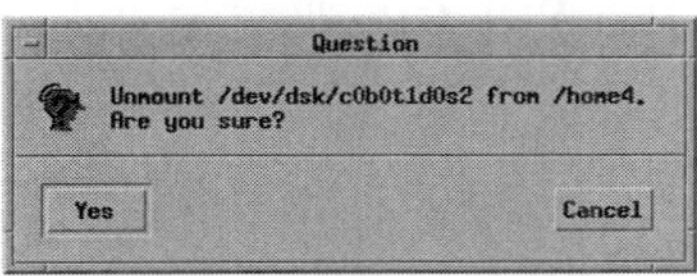

FIGURE 19.6 *The confirmation request for unmounting a filesystem.*

Remote Mounts and Shares

To share a filesystem or a file with a remote NFS client, select Share, NFS, Add Share Configuration. The windows shown in Figure 19.7 illustrate the process of adding an NFS share.

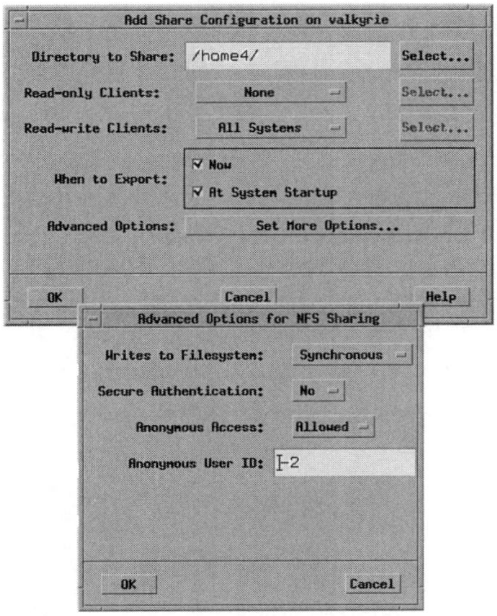

FIGURE 19.7 *Adding an NFS share.*

After a share has been established, select Share Status from the View menu on the Filesystem Manager. All shares will be shown. Highlight a share by clicking it and select Share. Three new menu options are available:

- Modify Share Configuration
- Remove Share configuration
- Unshare

These three options work in the same manner as those for the local mount configuration. Use the Modify Share option to change options on the share. This option uses the same windows as the Add Share Configuration.

Remove Share Configuration asks for confirmation. If you select yes, the share information in the /etc/dfs/dfstab and /etc/dfs/sharetab is removed. The sharetab and dfstab are the equivalent of the OpenServer 5 /etc/exports file.

The Unshare option does not have a confirmation window. Selecting Unshare will unshare the filesystem immediately. When the Unshare is completed, the Share option is available. The configuration file information in the /etc/dfs/sharetab is removed, indicating the directory is not currently shared; but the entry in the /etc/dfs/dfstab is not changed.

To mount remote NFS filesystems, select Mount, Add Mount Configuration, Remote. The windows shown in Figure 19.8 illustrate adding a remote NFS share to the local system. For more information on NFS mounting and sharing, see Chapter 6, "LAN Network Configuration."

Modifying Mount Configurations (vfstab)

The /etc/vfstab maintains information on filesystems and mount points for the local system. Remote mounts are maintained in the /etc/rmtab. The list of currently mounted filesystems is maintained in the /etc/mnttab.

The /etc/vfstab can be modified from the GUI Filesystem Manager or from the command line. The Filesystem Manager does not recheck the /etc/vfstab for changes while it is running, so you should not use the command line and the GUI simultaneously. The format for the file is

- The special device to be mounted

  example: /dev/root
- The device to use for fsck if the filesystem is not clean

  example: /dev/rroot
- The mount point

  example: /

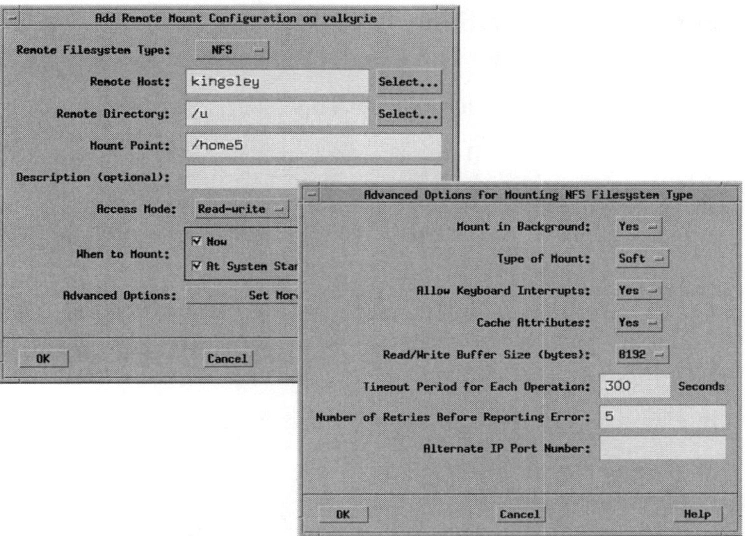

FIGURE 19.8 *Adding a remote NFS share.*

- The filesystem type

  example: vxfs

- The fsck pass numeral used to decide if fsck will be run automatically if needed

  example: 1

- Whether or not to automount the filesystem with `mountall`

  example: root is no, user filesystems is yes

- Mount options

  example: `mincache=closesync`

- The default filesystem level ceiling, used in enhanced security

  example: SYS_RANGE_MAX for root or - if not used

Administrators should not add additional data field entries to the file structure. The /etc/vfstab file may be edited to manually change the mount information. It is always wise to make a copy before changing a system file.

Viewing Other Mount Information

Options in the View menu, shown in Figure 19.9, include:

- *Mount Status*—Show mounted filesystems. This is the default.
- *Share Status*—Show shared filesystems.
- *Disk Usage*—Show the disk usage (total, used, and free) in megabytes and percentage used.
- *Inode Usage*—Show inode usage (free and used) and percent used.
- *Filesystem Type*—Show the filesystems and their types: vxfs, bfs, memfs, and so forth.
- *Set Auto Refresh*—Set the window to be refreshed at user-defined intervals.
- *Refresh Now*—Refresh the data.

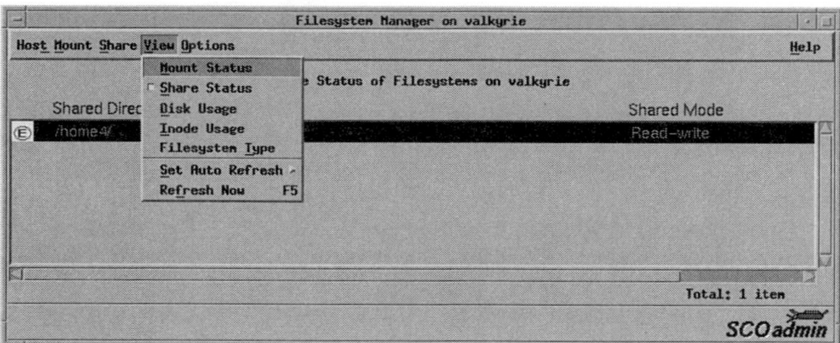

FIGURE 19.9 *Options for viewing filesystem data.*

File Permissions

UnixWare 7 uses standard UNIX file permissions, plus an extended capability called *Access Control Lists (ACLs)*. ACLs may only be used on sfs and vxfs filesystems.

Standard UNIX Permissions

The permissions used by UnixWare 7 are controlled by the UNIX `chmod` command. Both the octal and symbolic methods of setting permissions may be used.

The `chmod` command has a `-R` option to make it act recursively on subdirectories. To change permissions on the /home/gene directory and all files and subdirectories with /home/gene, the following command could be used:

```
chmod -R 750 /home/gene
```

The one restriction on the recursive action is with symbolic links that lie within the targeted directory structure. The symbolic link will be followed, and the permissions on the actual file at the end of the link will be changed. If the linked file is a directory, the directory will be changed, but not its files and subdirectories.

The chown command is used to change ownership of files. The UnixWare 7 version allows changing owners and groups simultaneously and performing the changes recursively. To change the user ownership and group ownership of a directory structure, run:

```
chown -R msh:other /home/melissa
```

Another option for the chown command is -h. This option will change the ownership of symbolic links rather than the standard action of following the link and changing ownership of the file.

Access Control Lists (ACLs)

ACLs provide an expansion of the user and group permissions on files and directories. ACLs pertain to additional users and groups other than those in the output of the ls -l command.

When a file is created, it has the standard UNIX permission bits set. An ACL is also created for the file. At creation time the ACL is not much more than the standard permissions.

Consider the file called myfile. Executing an l, the equivalent of ls -l, on myfile provides the following output:

```
# l myfile
-rwxr-x--x    1 gene     other           425 Jul 17 15:34 myfile
```

To see the default ACL set up for a new file, execute getacl on the file.

```
# getacl myfile
# file: myfile
# owner: gene
# group: other
user::rwx
group::r-x
class:r-x
other:--x
```

The # symbols in front of the three lines after the execution are provided by the getacl command. From the output of getacl, we can determine the same information as from the long listing. The filename and ownership are listed with the permissions for user, group, and other.

There is a fourth category named *class*. The class is the same as group at this point. The settings for class are the maximum that can be given to another user or group that will be added to the ACL.

With the minimal entry we have at this point, there is no increase in functionality over standard UNIX permissions.

The user and group entries both have double colons. The area between the colons is for user and group names, except in the case of the owner of the file.

Additional ACL Entries

If you need to grant rights to a user who is not a member of the group to which the file belongs and the user needs more rights than the rights of other, you can add *ACL entries*.

Additional ACL entries can be used to grant or deny rights to specific users or groups. The entry below grants read, write, and execute access to a user named Susie.

```
user:susie:rwx
```

The following entry would deny access to the group named editors:

```
group:editors:---
```

As new ACL entries are made, the class permissions may no longer equal the original group permissions. This allows the permissions for additional ACLs to change as required.

Default Entries

Default entries can be applied to directories. The effect of a default ACL is for new files created in the directory to inherit the default settings. If the new file is a directory, it will inherit the non-default settings and the default settings so that permissions on the new directory are the same as the parent directory.

If a group of users needs access to files in a directory, it is simple enough to set the ACLs on the files to give them access to the files. When new files are created in the directory, the ACLs will need to be added to the new files. The setting of default ACLs solves the problem. If three users not related to the owner or group that owns the directory need read access to all files created in the directory, default ACLs can be added to the directory and the files will inherit the defaults.

```
default:user:mina:r--
default:user:harold:r--
default:user:katie:r--
```

If the ownership and permissions on the directory were set to

```
drwxr-x--- gene authors
```

the default ACLs would allow Mina, Harold, and Katie to read new files even though they may not be members of the group authors.

setacl

The `setacl` command is used to add and delete ACLs. To create a new entry or to modify an existing ACL, use the `-m` option. The syntax is

```
setacl -m u[ser]:username:perms file
setacl -m g[roup]:groupname:perms file
```

Referring back to the myfile file, check the output of the `l` and `getacl` command:

```
# l myfile
-rwxr-x---    1 gene     other              424 Jul 17 16:46 myfile
# getacl myfile
# file: myfile
# owner: gene
# group: other
user::rwx
group::r-x
class:r-x
other:---
```

Now when we execute a `setacl` command, we can see the difference:

```
setacl -m g:authors:r-- myfile
# l myfile
-rwxr-x---+   1 gene     other              424 Jul 17 16:46 myfile
# getacl myfile
# file: myfile
# owner: gene
# group: other
user::rwx
group::r-x
group:authors:r--
class:r-x
other:---
```

You can now see that the ACL contains the entry for the group authors with read-only permission. Suppose the person changing the permissions does not know the maximum available permissions that can be granted by the class permissions (`r-x`) and tries to provide more access than is allowed.

```
# setacl -m g:editors:rwx myfile
# getacl myfile
# file: myfile
# owner: gene
```

```
# group: other
user::rwx
group::r-x
group:authors:r--
group:editors:rwx        #effective:r-x
class:r-x
other:---
```

Note that the permissions for the editors group are established at rwx with an effective permission of r-x. This limitation is in keeping with the class permission, which sets the maximum permission allowed.

It is possible to change the class permission to match the new permission being granted. The -r option to setacl causes the class permission to be recalculated.

```
# setacl -r -m g:auditors:rwx myfile
# l myfile
-rwxrwx---+   1 gene     other          424 Jul 17 16:46 myfile
# getacl myfile
# file: myfile
# owner: gene
# group: other
user::rwx
group::r-x
group:auditors:rwx
group:authors:r--
group:editors:rwx
class:rwx
other:---
```

Notice that after the addition of the new ACL with the -r option, the permissions on the file have changed. Group now shows rwx. The rwx is representative of the class, not the group. The editors that formerly had been given rwx and were restricted to r-x now have their full permissions. The original group maintains its original r-x permissions.

How would you know if ACLs had been set on a file? Notice the + symbol at the end of the permissions on the long listing.

Deleting ACLs

The ACLs that have been set can be removed with the -d option to setacl. If the -r option is included, the class ACL will be recomputed. In the example we have used, deleting the ACL for the two groups with permissions greater than the class was originally set for will return the class permission and the long listing permissions back to their original settings.

Duplicating Complex ACLs

After you have determined a set of ACLs that fit your requirements, you may need to duplicate those settings or something very close to those settings. Do not manually re-create the ACLs for every directory or file.

Use `getacl` to create a file on disk:

```
getacl myfile > myfile.acl
```

Edit the file myfile.acl and change the settings as you require. Apply the settings as shown below:

```
setacl -r -f myfile.acl myotherfile
```

While ACLs may appear to be similar to the Windows method of setting permissions, these permissions are not portable to a Windows view of the UNIX filesystem using Advanced File and Print Server.

CHAPTER 20

Mailers

- sendmail
  Learn what mail transport is used by UnixWare 7.
- `mfck`
  Find out how to check, repair, and convert mail folders between sendmail and MMDF formats using `mfck`.
- Mail Manager
  Learn to use the Mail Manager to configure mail services on your system.
- Virtual Domain User Manager
  Learn how to add users to virtual domains configured on your system.
- Mail-related administration
  Learn how to handle mail forwarding, Internet mail, preprocessing, and more.
- MUAs
  Find out what Mail User Agents (MUAs) come with UnixWare 7.
- UnixWare 7 and Windows Mail
  Learn how to retrieve email from your UnixWare 7 host using mail clients for Windows.

sendmail

The mail transport used by UnixWare 7 is sendmail. It is a quite complicated, extensive subject when fully examined. Books on sendmail are available if you want to learn all of its ins and outs.

Tip

If you are unable to deliver mail outside your local host, are using sendmail, and are not using DNS, make sure the /etc/service.switch file exists and contains the line `hosts files`*. If this file does not exist or does not have the* `hosts files` *reference, create the file or add the line as needed.*

You will also need to comment out the lines in /etc/rc2.d/S81sendmail that check for networking services and remove and re-create the /etc/service.switch file. Alternately, in UnixWare 7.0.1, look for the # AUTO = YES line in /etc/service.switch, and change the YES to NO to disable this behavior.

Configuration of sendmail

While the Mail Manager provides a graphical, user-friendly way to configure sendmail, it can also be configured from the command line. The man pages on sendmail offer an overview of command line options to sendmail.

The configuration of sendmail is controlled by the /etc/sendmail.cf file. This file can be modified with a text editor if desired. It can also be copied between UnixWare 7 systems with identical configurations, but only if you did not modify the host name in the Mail Manager because the default host name is not stored in the /etc/sendmail.cf file, but an overridden name is. This causes the /etc/sendmail.cf file to become machine specific rather than machine name independent. The /etc/default/mail file can be used for system-wide mail configuration settings; at this time, only folder management options are contained in /etc/default/mail.

By default, UnixWare 7 sendmail is configured to support local and SMTP mail delivery.

Tip

UnixWare 7's sendmail.cf format is different from that of OpenServer 5. If you use a sendmail.cf file with a non-UnixWare 7 layout, the Mail Manager will not function correctly with the file. This does not prevent sendmail from working, but it does mean that you cannot use the Mail Manager if you are bringing the sendmail.cf file from a non-UnixWare 7 system.

mfck

`mfck` is a utility designed to check and repair damaged mail folders, as well as convert folders between different formats.

Check and Repair Mail Folders

`mfck` with no options checks the validity of mail folders and prompts you to accept or reject any necessary repairs. Multiple folders can be checked and repaired with a single command. The selected folders are given as arguments to `mfck`.

You can run `mfck` with the `-y` or `-n` options to avoid answering prompts to perform repairs. The `-y` option answers yes to all prompts, and the `-n` option answers no to all prompts.

For instance, to check and repair a folder in /var/mail/msh without responding to prompts, use

```
# mfck -y /var/mail/msh
```

Conversion for sendmail/MMDF

The `-c` option to `mfck` converts mail folders between the specified formats. Currently, only sendmail and MMDF formats are supported. The format arguments are case sensitive and must be specified after the `-c` option, followed by the list of one or more folders to be converted. To convert /var/mail/msh from MMDF to sendmail, use

```
# mfck -c sendmail /var/mail/msh
```

This utility is particularly useful in preserving mail folders when moving to UnixWare 7 from OpenServer 5, which used MMDF as the default mail transport.

Mail Manager

The Mail Manager is accessed through SCOadmin. It provides a graphical tool for administering sendmail (see Figure 20.1).

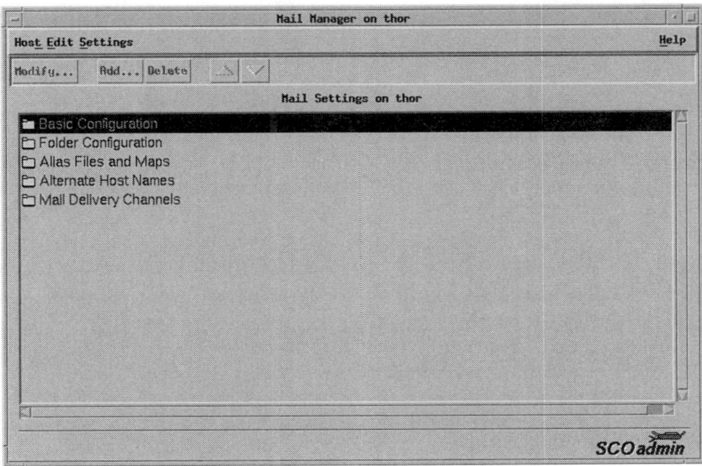

FIGURE 20.1 *Starting the Mail Manager.*

You can open and close the folders by single-clicking them. The elements within the folders can be modified by double-clicking the desired element, or single-clicking to highlight it and then clicking the Modify button or selecting Edit, Modify from the menu.

Basic Configuration

The Basic Configuration folder (shown in Figure 20.2) allows you to change these four settings:

- Host Name
- Mail Comes From
- Domain Table Enabled
- Domain Table File

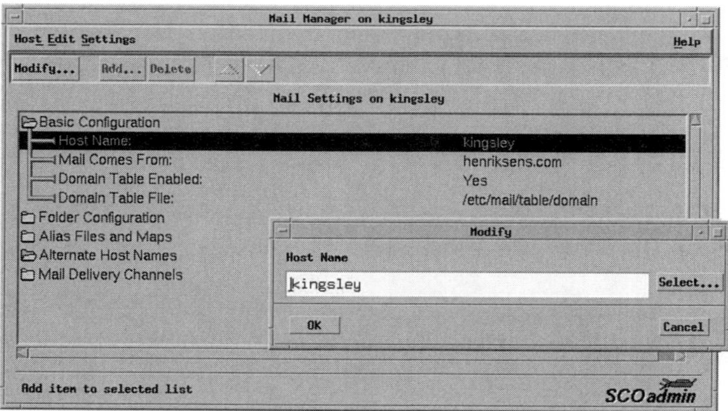

FIGURE 20.2 *The Basic Configuration folder.*

Host Name

For most systems, the host name will not need to be modified. It defaults to the local host. Changing the host name will result in sendmail treating messages that originate on your system as though they came from the host you specified. This can cause confusion when replying to messages or trying to determine where they really originated.

Mail Comes From

The Mail Comes From field is used for masquerading. *Masquerading*, or *domain hiding*, allows mail originating from a host to appear as though it is coming from the domain in which the host resides. For example, mail sent by the user msh on the host kingsley appears to come from `msh@henriksens.com` rather than `msh@kingsley.henriksens.com`.

The Mail Comes From field defaults to the local host name. To use masquerading, set it to the domain from which you wish mail to appear to originate. By default, masquerading is disabled for the root account. To enable masquerading for root, modify the /etc/sendmail.cf file and change the line `CEroot` to `CE`. You can also add usernames here for whom you wish to disable masquerading. Usernames should be separated by a space.

Domain Table

The domain table is disabled by default. If it is enabled, the domain table file is used for sendmail. This file maps domain names to their locations and is particularly useful when names have been changed. The old domain name can be mapped to the new one.

It can also be used to map short host names to fully qualified ones, as well as to specify a route for sending mail to a specific domain.

Folder Configuration

The Folder Configuration portion of the Mail Manager is used to specify the locations of mail folders, their formats, and how maintenance of the folders will be handled (see Figure 20.3).

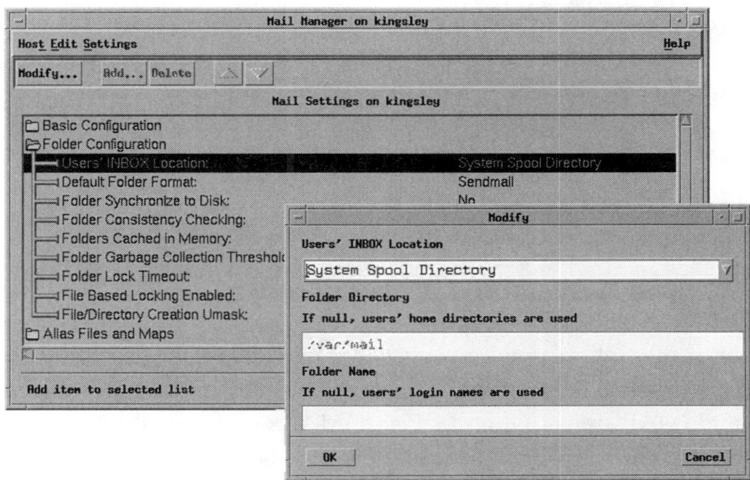

FIGURE 20.3 *Folder configuration.*

Users' INBOX Location

The directory and filenames to be used for storing the users' mail are defined here. If the filename is null, the username is used. The default is the System Spool Directory with a null filename. You may also select the user's home directory or a custom location.

Default Folder Format

There are two available formats: MMDF and sendmail. The default is sendmail; MMDF support is included for compatibility with OpenServer 5 mailboxes. UnixWare 7 Mail User Agents (MUAs) automatically recognize either file format (MMDF or Sendmail) and preserve it, with the exception of dtmail, which does not recognize MMDF format. You can use `mfck` to convert existing folders to sendmail format from MMDF (see the section on `mfck` earlier in this chapter).

Folder Synchronize to Disk

Selecting this option increases reliability in case of a system crash, but decreases throughput.

Folder Consistency Checking

You should select this option only if you are using an MUA that modifies folders without changing the size or time stamp of the file.

Folders Cached in Memory

Mail performance may be improved by caching folders in memory, but this results in less memory being available for other system functions. This feature is currently not fully functional in UnixWare 7. Turning on this option increases the amount of information cached in memory, but does not read in the entire folder, as was originally intended.

> *Warning*
>
> *Do not use this option when RAM is limited.*

Folder Garbage Collection Threshold

This option comes into play with the use of the *message store*, a technology designed to reduce the disk accesses for mail server operations, especially in the POP and IMAP arenas. Older POP and IMAP servers would parse the entire inbox every time a client connected to the host. Given even a few users with large mail folders who checked mail every 10 minutes, server performance could be seriously impacted. The UnixWare 7 message store eliminated the need for parsing the inbox at connect time.

However, there remains the issue of rebuilding mail folders to remove deleted messages. You can set a percentage that determines how often to remove deleted messages from a mail folder by rebuilding the folder, which is known as *garbage collection*. The threshold represents the percentage of bytes that must be valid when a mailbox is closed. When a message is deleted through the mail client, it is marked as Deleted, but remains in the mail folder as unused or invalid bytes. When the percentage of valid bytes in the mail folder drops below the Garbage Collection Threshold, the mail folder is rebuilt.

Setting this value to 0% means that garbage collection never occurs, and 100% means that the folder is rebuilt on every close if any messages were deleted. Lower threshold values result in better performance because less time is spent rebuilding folders, but more disk space is wasted. A value of 50% is recommended.

Neither Pine nor dtmail support the use of a message store, so the Garbage Collection Threshold should be set to 100% if you use these clients. This value can be overridden for individual users by creating a file called .maildef in the user's home directory and setting the `MS1_EXPUNGE_THRESHOLD` parameter to the value desired for that user. For instance, to set the threshold to 100% for a particular user, insert the line `MS1_EXPUNGE_THRESHOLD=100` in the user's .maildef file. The parameter is case sensitive.

Folder Lock Timeout

This is a message store parameter whose value determines the length of time sendmail waits for access to a folder. It may need to be increased on overloaded systems.

File Based Locking Enabled

You should enable file-based locking if you are using MUAs that do not use kernel-based locking. While none of the MUAs supplied with UnixWare 7 requires file-based locking, some freeware mailers do.

File/Directory Creation Umask

This option determines the default umask used when files and directories are created for use with the mail system.

Alias Files and Maps

Aliasing allows you to direct mail to individual users. You can use this to map a single user to an alias (for example, mail sent to `info@henriksens.com` is directed to `msh@kingsley.henriksens.com`), or to create an alias for a group of users (for example, mail sent to `all@henriksens.com` is directed to `msh@kingsley.henriksens.com`, `gene@thor.henriksens.com`, `mina@valkyrie.henriksens.com`, and `susie@valkyrie.henriksens.com`). This feature can also be used to filter mail through programs or shell scripts.

Selecting this option from the Mail Manager opens the window shown in Figure 20.4. You can specify the location of the alias folder, which defaults to /etc/mail/aliases. This file can be edited directly using your favorite editor (vi), or you can click on the Edit Alias File button for a graphical edit window. The file consists of an alias name, a colon, and the destination for that alias. Multiple usernames are separated by commas. The alias files and maps are searched in the order specified in the window.

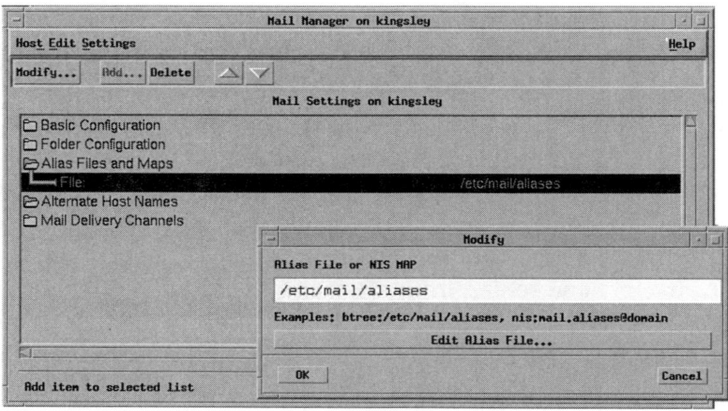

FIGURE 20.4 *Specifying an alias file.*

When you need to add new users to an alias, you can either edit the aliases file or select User, Subscribe from the Mail Manager menu. You can then enter the username and specify to which alias to add the new user.

When retiring a user, you can select User, Retire from the Mail Manager menu and enter the username to be retired. This will remove this username from all aliases to which it belonged. You are also given the opportunity to redirect mail that may still arrive addressed to this user. Click the Redirect Mail button and specify the redirection address.

Alternate Host Names

This is a primitive virtual domain feature and is not the recommended way to enable virtual domains in UnixWare 7. For information on creating a virtual domain, see the Virtual Domains section in Chapter 8, "Browsers and Intranets."

To add a new alternate host name, click this folder and then click the Add button. You can type a host name into the box, or click Select to choose from the hosts listed in /etc/hosts (see Figure 20.5).

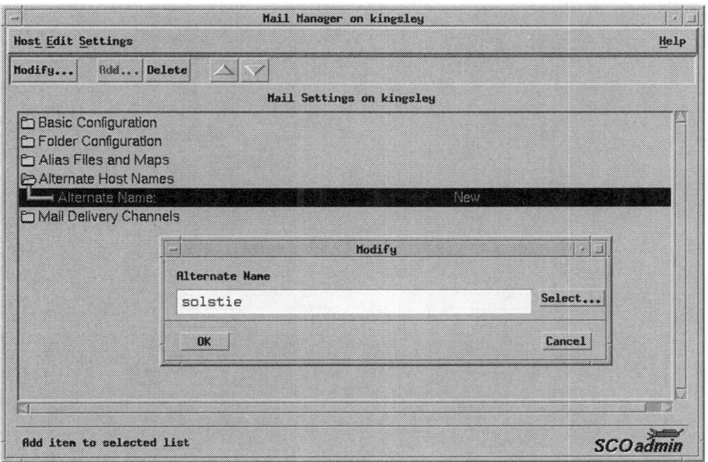

FIGURE 20.5 *Alternate host names.*

Mail Delivery Channels

The idea of channels is borrowed from OpenServer 5's MMDF. Sendmail has a built-in concept of *mailers*, which are programs to which mail for a certain set of mail addresses is passed for delivery. The most well-known mailers are the SMTP and local mailers, which are responsible for network and local delivery, respectively. A *channel* is a combination of a mailer and the associated /etc/sendmail.cf code that detects the addresses for each mailer. The goal of providing these channels within the GUI admin tool is to reduce the necessity of hand editing /etc/sendmail.cf. Essentially, it is a programming language and requires a sendmail guru to modify it.

The following three channels are configured by default (see Figure 20.6):

- *Local*—Delivers mail to local users.
- *SMTP*—Delivers mail over TCP/IP networks using DNS and SMTP.
- *Badhost*—A delay channel that queues messages that temporarily fail because the name server is not available or the host is not responding. Alternatively, it can be configured to forward mail for unknown hosts to a *smarter* mail host (one with more routing information) for delivery.

If you are not using DNS, see the tip in the "sendmail" section of this chapter regarding non-DNS mail delivery.

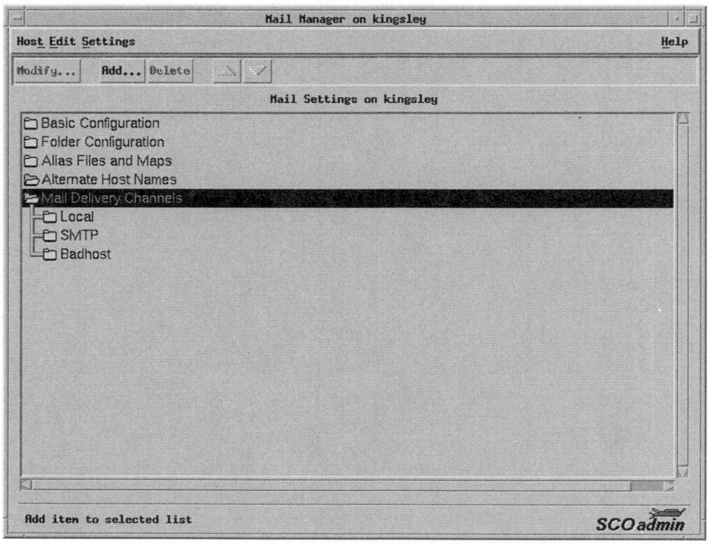

FIGURE 20.6 *Mail delivery channels.*

Three other channels are available for activation through the Settings portion of the main menu. They are

- *UUCP*—Delivers mail to hosts configured in /etc/uucp/Systems.
- *Baduser*—Delivers mail addressed to unknown users to a smarter machine (useful for centralizing alias definitions on a single server).
- *Multihome*—For use with virtual domains.

To add other channels, select the Mail Delivery Channels folder, then choose Edit, Add from the menu. You can modify channels by clicking the desired channel, then double-clicking the attribute you wish to modify (see Figure 20.7). Alternatively, single-click to select the attribute, then either click the Modify button or select Edit, Modify from the menu.

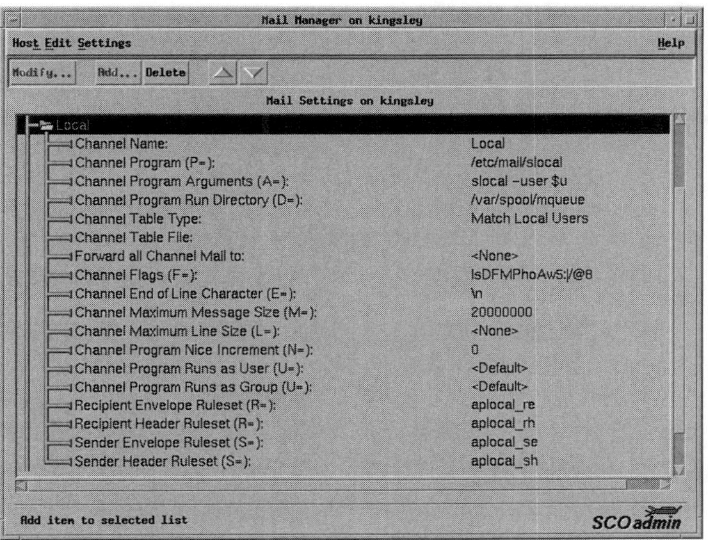

FIGURE 20.7 *Mail delivery channel attributes.*

Virtual Domain User Manager

If you have created virtual domains, you can manage users within those domains with the Virtual Domain User Manager. It is accessed through SCOadmin. The main window lists all configured virtual domains. To add users to a domain, click to highlight the desired domain and click the Users button, or select Edit, Users from the menu. Click Add User and select a username from the list of valid user accounts currently configured on the system; then enter the virtual username to be associated with that account (see Figure 20.8). The system user defines the account to which mail will be directed when mail is addressed to the virtual user for the virtual domain selected. For example, given a virtual domain of `solstie.henriksens.com` on the `kingsley.henriksens.com` system, and an entry in the Virtual User Manager mapping the system user msh to the virtual user melissa, mail addressed to `melissa@solstie.henriksens.com` will be delivered to `msh@kingsley.henriksens.com`.

Alias lists are maintained for each virtual domain. Click Mail Aliases or select Edit, Mail Aliases to maintain virtual domain aliases. The aliases for virtual domains work in the same way as standard aliases.

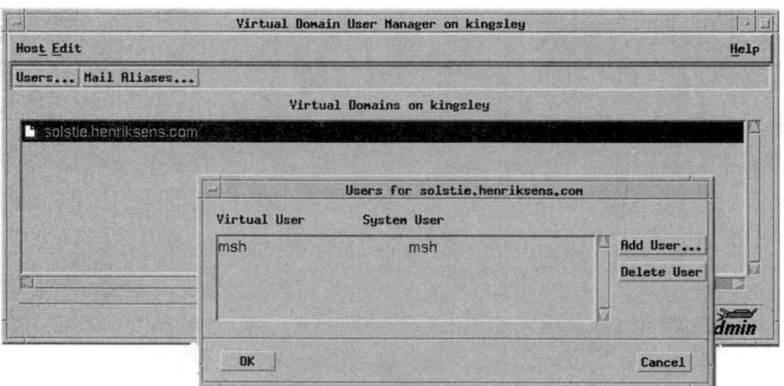

FIGURE 20.8 *Using the Virtual Domain User Manager.*

Mail-Related Administration

You may need to perform some additional configuration in order to allow servers on the Internet to find your mail server. You can also configure preprocessing of mail, set up vacation notification, and forward mail, as well as control whether the POP and IMAP services are enabled.

Internet Mail

If you have attached your network to the Internet, you may need to add *MX records* to your DNS server. MX records are used for identifying mail exchangers on the Internet. While most servers will try delivering mail to a host with the same name as the destination, some will not find your mail server unless an MX record exists.

You can create MX records that list your gateway, as well as one or two other machines outside your domain that are willing to queue your mail if your Internet connection is lost. The records have the following format:

```
Name        IN    MX    Priority        Host
```

`Name` is the destination name for the mail (that is, your domain). In DNS, the `@` symbol is used to represent the current domain.

`Priority` is a number from 0 to 32,767 assigned to this mail exchanger within your list of servers. Highest priority is given to the lowest number (your mail server is priority 0, backup servers have lower priorities/higher numbers).

`Host` is the name of the host that should receive the mail. If you are using mail servers outside your domain, they will queue the mail until your mail server is reachable.

The primary mail server might have an entry similar to

```
@     IN     MX     0     kingsley.henriksens.com
```

Preprocessing Mail

Incoming mail can be processed according to a set of criteria entered in the .maildelivery file of a user's home directory. Each line contains the following five fields:

header pattern action result string

The *header* is the message header line that is searched. The *pattern* is the text searched for in the header line, and is not case sensitive. The *action* is either `file`, in which case the message will be appended to the specified file, or `pipe`, which directs the message to the specified command. The *result* is either `A` (which means that, if the action was successful, the message is not delivered to the user's mailbox) or `R` (which means that the message is delivered regardless). The *string* is the file or command that is to be used.

For instance, the following line will send all mail with `urgent` contained in the subject line to the default printer, as well as placing a copy in the user's mailbox:

```
Subject     urgent     pipe     R     lp
```

This can be a useful tool for blocking *spam* (unsolicited mass email). See the man pages on mail delivery for more information.

Vacation Notification

UnixWare 7 uses the Vacation Notification Manager to set up return messaging when users will be unable to retrieve email. Any user can run this manager to set up his own vacation notices. The command `/etc/mail/admin/vacation` will start the manager, which is shown in Figure 20.9.

This manager is also accessible from the front panel of the CDE desktop by clicking the up arrow above the mailbox icon to open the Mail menu, then selecting Vacation.

The default subject and message can be modified. A list of addresses to which notices were sent is maintained. Enable this feature by selecting On and clicking OK. This configures a .maildelivery file in the user's home directory. Disable vacation notification by starting the manager, selecting Off, and clicking OK.

A notification is sent to each address only once, regardless of the number of messages received from that address. This prevents two users' vacation notices from entering a loop.

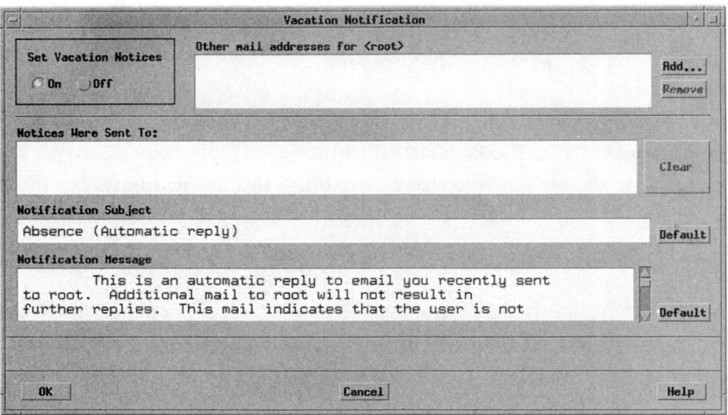

FIGURE 20.9 *Setting up vacation notification.*

Author's Note

The vacation notice will be sent in response to any email sent to the user, as well as to any aliases to which the user belongs.

Mail Forwarding

To forward user mail to another destination, place a .forward file in the user's home directory. The only information needed in the file is the new address.

For instance, to forward all mail sent to `mina@valkyrie.henriksens.com` to mina on `server.another.com`, create a .forward file in the home directory for mina on valkyrie with the entry

```
mina@server.another.com
```

The .forward file resides in the user's home directory, regardless of the location of his mailbox.

Enabling and Disabling POP and IMAP Mail

By default the POP3 (/etc/popper) and IMAP4 (/etc/imapd) servers are configured to be run by inetd. To disable these servers, edit /etc/inetd.conf and comment out the lines that contain the servers:

```
#pop-3    stream  tcp     nowait  root    /usr/sbin/in.tcpd       /etc/popper
#imap-4   stream  tcp     nowait  root    /usr/sbin/in.tcpd       /etc/imapd
```

You can create accounts for POP and IMAP clients to retrieve email without being able to login to your system. Set the login shell to `/bin/false` to create a non-login account. By default, /bin/false is not presented as an option when selecting a login shell; however, it can be manually typed into the login shell field.

Mail User Agents (MUAs)

An *MUA* is the client side of mail delivery, as opposed to the *MTA (Mail Transport Agent)*, which is the server side. MUAs use two main protocols, POP and IMAP, and may be enabled for MIME format. Several MUAs come with UnixWare 7; mailx, pine, dtmail, and Netscape mail are discussed in the following sections.

POP and IMAP

The *Post Office Protocol (POP)* and *Internet Message Access Protocol (IMAP)* daemons handle communication between the MTA and the MUA. There are a few basic differences between POP and IMAP.

POP allows one-way transfer from a mail server to the client. Mail is stored on the client machine after it has been read. It is then removed from the server unless the POP client has been configured to leave mail on the server after it has been read. Therefore, if you retrieve mail from different locations, it is stored on whichever machine you were using when you read it.

IMAP allows bidirectional transfer between a mail server and the client. The read messages are stored on a server as well as on the client. If you move stored messages (such as between folders), the changes are uploaded to the server the next time you connect to it. There are several advantages to leaving the primary copy of your inbox on the server:

- The ability to use more than one machine to read mail
- Preservation of mail in the event of the loss or corruption of a client machine
- The inclusion of your mail in the backup of the server, which is usually more complete and frequent than backups of client machines.

MIME

Some MUAs support the *Multipurpose Internet Mail Extension (MIME)* format. It is used for attaching files to your mail. Most MUAs can be configured to automatically open selected attachments with the appropriate program (spreadsheet, word processor, and the like).

mailx

The traditional UNIX command line mail is mailx. On UnixWare 7, mailx supports MIME and IMAP4. The `-R` option to mailx instructs mailx to read mail from a remote host. See the man page on mailx for more information.

pine

pine is a character-based, menu-driven mail reader. It supports MIME and IMAP4.

dtmail

dtmail is a graphical mail system that runs in X Windows. It is MIME compatible and has an icon on the CDE desktop. dtmail does not support IMAP and POP.

Netscape

The Netscape Web browser that is included with UnixWare 7 includes a graphical mail program with MIME, POP, and HTML capabilities. Netscape version 4 or later also supports IMAP.

UnixWare 7 and Windows Mail

Any mail client that supports POP or IMAP protocols can retrieve mail from a UnixWare 7 server. This includes mail clients for Windows. The protocols handle the communication. See the section in this chapter on POP and IMAP for a brief overview of the differences between these protocols. You need only to create a user account, if one doesn't already exist, for the mail recipient. The system running the client must be able to communicate with the UnixWare 7 system. A good way to verify connectivity is with the `ping` command.

Each mail client is different, but the configuration consists of providing a few essential pieces of information:

- Mail server (your UnixWare 7 system)
- Username
- Password

The incoming (POP) mail server and outgoing (SMTP) mail server will be the same in most cases; your UnixWare 7 handles both incoming and outgoing mail delivery.

Author's Note

Using Eudora Pro on Windows 95, I provided the Setup Wizard with the three pieces of information listed above (server name, username, and password) and was able to retrieve mail without any further configuration.

CHAPTER 21

Performance Tuning

- Monitoring performance
  Find out about the tools available to monitor your system.
- Analyzing the results
  Learn what to do with the data about your system.
- Tuning the system
  Learn how to modify your system to fix the problems.

Monitoring Performance

To determine how to get the maximum benefit from your hardware, system performance must be monitored. You may find bottlenecks that can be alleviated by tuning parameters or changing the way that you place demands on the system. You may find that your system would benefit from hardware upgrades instead of, or in addition to, other changes. By monitoring your system's performance, you can identify where the problems are occurring; this, in turn, tells you which parameters to tune, workloads to spread, or hardware to upgrade.

There are three primary ways to monitor your system's performance. The System Monitor offers a graphical representation through the desktop. `sar` provides a wide range of data about your system from the command line. The real time performance monitor (`rtpm`) provides a character-based readout similar to the data available from `sar`, but it updates the screen in real time.

System Monitor

For a graphical report on system activity, select SCOadmin, System, System Monitor. The System Monitor allows you to select which aspects of system performance you want to view.

You can set the reporting interval in seconds or choose to add a vertical and/or horizontal grid to the graph by selecting Actions, Options. Other choices available through the Action menu are to log the data to a file, play back logged data, and save your settings.

To select which aspects of the system to monitor, click the desired types of data in the List of System Monitor options, which is just below the graph. You can also select the color that data will be displayed in by clicking the List of Colors, or you can change the scale for non-percentage figures by clicking a different Scale number.

Monitoring CPU Usage

Four indicators of CPU usage are available:

- User time
- System time
- Wait I/O time
- Idle time

User time is the percentage of the time the CPU spends executing user mode programs, whereas system time tracks time spent executing kernel mode programs. The idle time should be the inverse of the combination of user, system, and wait I/O times. While the time spent waiting on I/O is a report of CPU usage, it is not an indicator of a need for increased CPU power. For a full explanation, see the sections on analyzing the results. Figure 21.1 illustrates a reporting of user, system, and idle time.

Monitoring I/O

The only real I/O indicator available from the System Monitor is CPU wait I/O time. This may or may not indicate an I/O problem; for a more complete explanation, see the later section on analyzing the results. Also see the section on monitoring I/O with the `sar` command for more options in identifying I/O problems. Figure 21.2 shows a reporting of the time the CPU spent waiting on I/O.

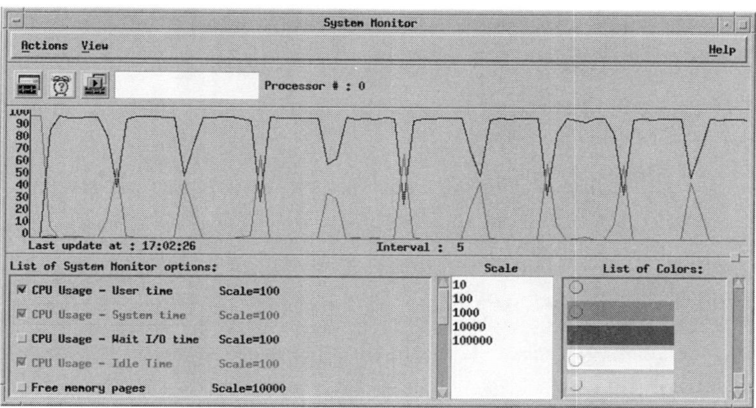

FIGURE 21.1 *Monitoring CPU usage.*

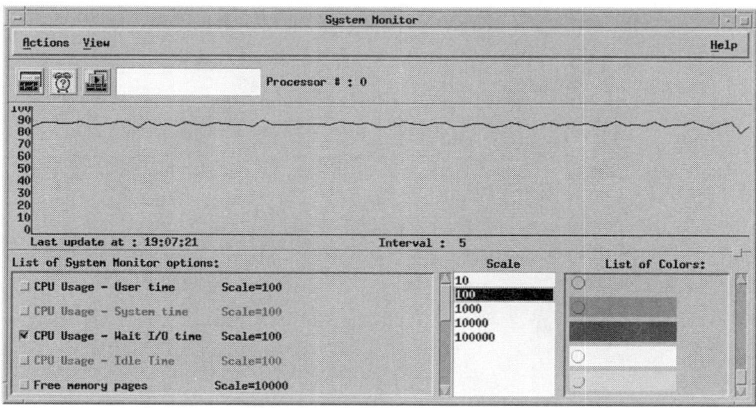

FIGURE 21.2 *Monitoring I/O wait time.*

Monitoring Memory Usage

There are several parameters that may be monitored for memory usage through the System Monitor. Following is a list of memory-related resources:

- *Free Memory Pages*—Average number of 4,096 byte pages available to user processes (256 pages is equal to 1MB)
- *Free Blocks for Swapping*—Number of 512-byte blocks available on disk for page swapping (2,048 blocks is equal to 1MB)
- *Page-in requests/per sec*—Number of page-in requests received per second
- *Page-out requests/per sec*—Number of page-out requests received per second

- *System swap in/per sec*—The number of transfers per second from the swap area on disk into memory
- *System swap out/per sec*—The number of transfers per second to the swap area on disk from memory
- *Block swap in/per sec*—The number of blocks transferred per second into memory from the disk swap area
- *Block swap out/per sec*—The number of blocks transferred per second from memory into the disk swap area
- *Process switching/per sec*—The number of process switches per second in and out of the CPU

Figure 21.3 shows the free memory pages and free blocks for swapping.

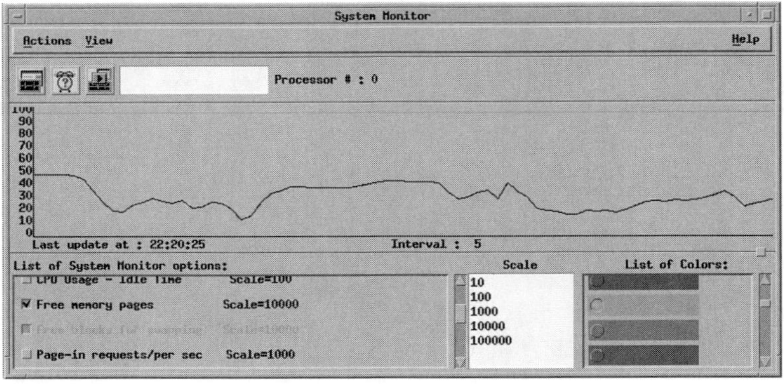

FIGURE 21.3 *Monitoring memory usage.*

Setting Alarms

You can set alarms in the System Monitor to alert you when the system goes above or below limits that you have defined.

To set alarms, select View, Alarms. Select the resource to monitor. You can specify the type of alarm, which is either *Beep*, to create an audible alarm, or *Flash Header*, for a visible alarm. If you select Flash Header, an alarm icon will appear next to the resource if it goes above or below the limit. Enter values in either or both of the Alarm Above or Alarm Below boxes, and click OK.

Logging and Playing Back Data

To log data using the System Monitor, select Actions, Log Data to File. Enter the filename you wish to use, and click OK. To stop logging, select Actions, Stop Logging Data.

To play back the logged data, select Actions, Playback Log Data. Select the filename to which you saved data, and click OK. You can end the playback by clicking Cancel.

The *sar* Command

The `sar` command, which stands for *system activity report*, can be used to report on a wide range of system activities. Different options will allow you to view different aspects of your system's performance.

`sar` can be used in several ways:

- By default, reports the current day's activity at 20-minute intervals
- Reports current activity in user-defined intervals for a specified number of iterations
- Reports historical activity as saved by the `sa1` shell script

For a complete description of capabilities, see the man page for `sar`.

sa1

The `sa1` command collects and stores data in the /var/adm/sa directory in files named sa##, where ## is the day of the month. For example, data from the 10th of this month will be stored in /var/adm/sa/sa10. The previous month's files are overwritten for the current month, which results in one month of history information being available.

To direct the `sar` command to report on data stored in one of these files, rather than on current activity, use the `-f` option followed by the filename (for example, `sar -f /var/adm/sa/sa01`). An entry exists by default in the sys crontab (/usr/spool/cron/crontabs/sys) to run `sa1` daily to collect and store history information.

sa2

If a readable report is desired in addition to, or instead of, data for use with `sar`, use the `sa2` command. An entry exists by default in the sys crontab (/usr/spool/cron/crontabs/sys) to run `sa2` daily. The reports are stored in the same directory as the data files, /var/adm/sa. The files are named sar##, where ## is the day of the month.

Monitoring CPU Usage

The -u option to sar is used to monitor processor utilization and is the default if no options are specified. On multiprocessor machines, aggregate information for all processors is displayed by default. Use the -P option followed by the processor ID to monitor a single processor.

The columns report percentages of CPU time devoted to user processes, system processes, waiting for I/O, and idle time. Following is the output from the sar command on a single-processor machine, which is reporting every 20 seconds for 10 iterations.

```
# sar -u 20 10
UnixWare valkyrie 5 7 i386     10/05/98

16:57:00   %usr     %sys     %wio   %idle
16:57:20    100        0        0       0
16:57:40     82       18        0       0
16:58:00    100        0        0       0
16:58:20     82       18        0       0
16:58:40    100        0        0       0
16:59:00     82       18        0       0
16:59:20    100        0        0       0
16:59:40     82       18        0       0
17:00:00     95        5        0       0
17:00:20     86       14        0       0
Average      91        9        0       0
```

The -q option to sar reports on the buildup of processes waiting on the CPU; this includes the number of runable processes in memory (runq) and the percentage of time the run queue is occupied (%runocc).

```
# sar -q 20 10

UnixWare valkyrie 5 7 i386     10/05/98

17:14:31      prunq   %prunocc      runq     %runocc       swpq %swpocc
17:14:51        1.2         30       2.3         100
17:15:11        2.0        100
17:15:31        1.0         25       2.2         100
17:15:51        2.0        100
17:16:11        1.0         20       2.3         100
17:16:31        2.0        100
17:16:51        1.0         30       2.3         100
17:17:11        1.0          5       2.0         100
17:17:31        1.0         15       2.2         100
17:17:51        1.0         10       2.1         100
Average         1.0         13       2.1         100
```

Monitoring I/O

The `%wio` column in the `sar -u` output can be useful in monitoring I/O. The `-d` and `-b` options also provide I/O information.

The `-d` option to `sar` reports hard disk activity, including:

- Percentage of time the disk is busy (`%busy`)
- Average number of queued requests (`avque`)
- Average time that transfer requests wait on queue in milliseconds (`avwait`)
- Average service time for transfer requests in milliseconds (`avserv`)

```
# sar -d 20 10

UnixWare valkyrie 5 7 i386    10/05/98

19:38:57 device   %busy    avque    r+w/s    blks/s  avwait   avserv
19:39:17 sd011       93      1.5       89      1610     4.9     10.4
19:39:37 sd011       93      1.2       90      1658     1.9     10.3
19:39:57 sd011       93      1.2       90      1613     1.6     10.3
19:40:17 sd011       93      1.3       90      1622     2.7     10.3
19:40:37 sd011       93      1.2       89      1602     2.1     10.4
19:40:57 sd011       93      1.2       90      1643     1.9     10.4
19:41:17 sd011       92      1.4       89      1629     4.1     10.4
19:41:37 sd011       93      1.2       89      1621     2.0     10.4
19:41:57 sd011       93      1.3       89      1601     2.7     10.4
19:42:17 sd011       93      1.5       89      1644     4.8     10.4
Average  sd011       93      1.3       89      1624     2.9     10.4
```

The `-b` option reports buffer activity, including read and write cache hit ratios (`%rcache/%wcache`).

```
# sar -b 20 10

UnixWare valkyrie 5 7 i386    10/05/98

19:33:32  bread/s  lread/s  %rcache  bwrit/s  lwrit/s  %wcache  pread/s  pwrite/s
19:33:52        0        1      100        1        1        0        0         0
19:34:12        0        7      100        2        4       41        0         0
19:34:32        0        1      100        1        1        4        0         0
19:34:52        0        1      100        0        0        0        0         0
19:35:12        0        2      100        1        1       34        0         0
19:35:32        0        6      100        3        4       21        0         0
19:35:52        0        1      100        1        1        0        0         0
19:36:12        0        3      100        2        2       21        0         0
19:36:32        0        1      100        1        1        0        0         0
19:36:52        0        1      100        1        1        0        0         0
Average         0        2      100        1        2       20        0         0
```

Monitoring Memory Usage

When physical memory on a system is exhausted, swap space on disk is used to meet the additional memory requirements. *Virtual memory* is the total of physical memory plus swap space. *Paging* is the process of moving the contents of physical memory to and from the swap areas and file systems on disk.

Running `sar` with the `-r` option reports free memory in a count of 4KB pages and free swap space in 512-byte blocks.

OpenServer 5 Tip

In OpenServer 5, `sar -r` *reported the amount of swap space on disk. In UnixWare 7, it reports the swap space in virtual memory (RAM plus swap).*

```
# sar -r 5 10

UnixWare valkyrie 5 7 i386     10/05/98

20:32:47    freemem      freeswap
20:32:52       3984         29971
20:32:57       3404         29320
20:33:02       3153         28830
20:33:07       3372         28892
20:33:12       3433         28795
20:33:17       3281         28133
20:33:22       3622         28078
20:33:27       3686         27880
20:33:32       3759         27881
20:33:37       3787         27862
Average        3548         28564
```

The output of `sar` with the `-w` option includes the number of transfers to and from memory (`swpin/s` and `swpot/s`) and the number of pages transferred for swapins and swapouts (`pswin/s` and `pswot/s`).

```
# sar -w 20 10

UnixWare thor 5 7.0.1 i386     10/06/98

11:20:03   swpin/s  pswin/s  swpot/s  pswot/s  vpswout/s   pswch/s
11:20:23      0.00      0.0     0.25      9.4       41.4       302
11:20:43      0.05      0.0     0.50     35.9      185.5       352
11:21:03      0.00      0.0     0.50     34.9      276.6       297
11:21:23      0.10      0.1     0.45     22.0      155.5       298
11:21:43      0.05      0.0     0.00      0.0        0.0       254
11:22:03      0.00      0.0     0.00      0.0        0.0       248
11:22:23      0.00      0.0     0.35     22.7      159.5       191
11:22:43      0.15      0.1     0.54     47.9      215.7       124
11:23:03      0.25      0.2     0.05      4.9       30.7       117
11:23:23      0.20      0.2     0.40     29.5      158.0       233
Average       0.08      0.1     0.30     20.8      122.4       241
```

Using sar with the -p option reports on paging activity, including page-in requests per second (pgin/s) and pages paged in per second (ppgin/s).

```
# sar -p 5 10

UnixWare valkyrie 5 7 i386    10/05/98

20:30:47   atch/s  atfree/s  atmiss/s  pgin/s  ppgin/s   pflt/s   vflt/s   slock/s
20:30:52     0.00      0.00      0.00    0.00     0.00     0.00     0.60      0.00
20:30:57     0.20      0.20      0.20    0.20     0.20     0.00     1.79      0.00
20:31:02     1.59      1.59      0.00    0.00     0.00     0.00     0.80      0.00
20:31:07   701.19    156.75     29.76   21.23    46.83   464.09   202.98      0.00
20:31:12  1126.10    186.65     16.73    6.37    14.14   835.06   147.01      0.00
20:31:17     0.00      0.00      0.00    0.00     0.00     0.00     0.00      0.00
20:31:22     0.00      0.00      0.00    0.00     0.00     0.00     0.00      0.00
20:31:27   602.59     89.44      5.38    0.00     0.00   461.16    68.53      0.00
20:31:32     9.96      9.36      0.60    0.20     0.20     0.40     9.76      0.00
20:31:37   122.31     50.40      6.37    8.57    17.73    59.56    64.54      0.00
Average    256.57     49.48      5.91    3.66     7.93   182.14    49.66      0.00
```

Tip

The swap command is a quick way to determine whether physical memory is being exhausted. It reports the swap device, the number of blocks available, and the number currently free. If the number of blocks free is less than the number available, swap space is being used.

```
# swap -l
path                 dev      swaplo    blocks     free
/dev/swap          7679,2          0    257040   209952
```

The Real Time Performance Monitor (*rtpm*)

The rtpm is an interactive, real time performance monitoring tool. You can customize this screen to get the information you want and set up preferences in a startup file (see Figure 21.4). There are over 400 individual counters that may be tracked using rtpm. You can use subscreens to view specific aspects of your system, including CPU, memory, paging, file system, I/O, NetWare, and TCP/IP. See the man pages on rtpm for a complete description.

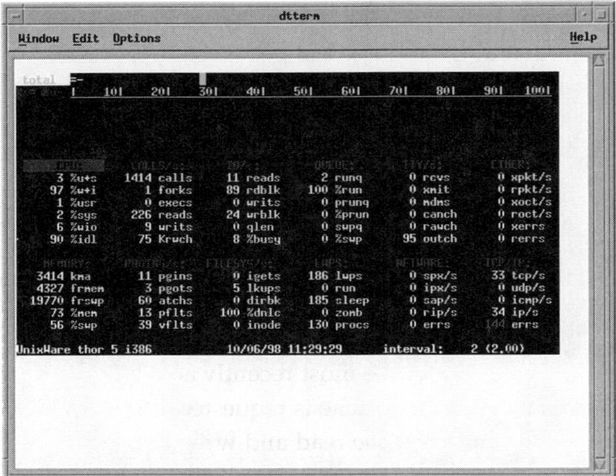

FIGURE 21.4 *Real time display of system performance with* `rtpm`.

Analyzing the Results

After you have collected data on your system's performance, you need to decide what it all means. Following are some general guidelines for what values might indicate bottlenecks in different areas. There are also programs available to analyze your `sar` data, such as SarCheck.

Suggested Guidelines

While there are no hard and fast rules, there are some guidelines as to what performance levels are acceptable and what might indicate a problem. This is especially true of the indicators that are reported in terms of percentages.

CPU Usage

CPU system time should not be more than two times user time; if it is, system resources are not being used efficiently.

CPU idle time, as reported by `sar -u`, should be greater than 10% at a minimum and preferably 30% or higher. In the output of `sar -q`, the `%runq-sz` should not be higher than 2%, and the `%runocc` should be less than 90%.

The CPU should spend less than 10% of its time waiting on I/O. Higher I/O wait times usually indicate that the processor is waiting on the disk. A high I/O wait time should be investigated to determine whether the disk access time is indeed the problem, or whether other factors, such as swapping, are contributing to this problem. Either way, the effect is that processor time is being wasted while waiting on other resources.

I/O Usage

If a high percentage (greater than 10%) of CPU time is being spent waiting for I/O, the problem may be a disk bottleneck. To further investigate, examine the output from `sar -d`. A `%busy` figure averaging greater than 50% can indicate a disk bottleneck. The `avserv` column shows service time after a request has reached the disk. The `avwait` column shows the average wait time for an I/O request to be serviced. The `avque` column reports the average length of the wait queue for an I/O request.

Another factor to consider when examining I/O problems is the buffer cache. This is maintained by the system to make the transfer of data between memory and the disk more efficient by keeping the most recently accessed data in memory. When data that is held in the buffer cache is requested, the need for access to the disk is eliminated. `sar -b` reports the read and write hit rates (`rcache/wcache`). Effective use of the buffer cache results in high figures in these columns. If you are not getting cache hits, consider increasing the size of the buffer cache.

If the disk performance seems acceptable, but you have unacceptable levels of CPU time devoted to waiting for I/O, you may have a memory bottleneck.

Memory Usage

Paging and swapping are indications of insufficient RAM because they occur when physical memory has been exhausted.

The following are the resources available for examination through the System Monitor and recommended threshold values.

Greater than 200:

- Free Memory Pages
- Free Blocks for Swapping

Less than 5:

- Page-in requests/per sec
- Page-out requests/per sec

Less than 1:

- System swap in/per sec
- System swap out/per sec

- Block swap in/per sec
- Block swap out/per sec

Process switching per second should be less than 100 on a 4- to 6-user system.

You may have a RAM bottleneck if any of the following occurs:

- Frequent swapping or page-outs as indicated by `sar -p` and/or `sar -w`
- Low available RAM as reported by `sar -r`
- Use of swap space as indicated by `swap -l`

A RAM bottleneck can result in high CPU time spent waiting for I/O because swap space on the disk is being forced to handle what would be better handled in RAM. A hardware solution to a RAM bottleneck is to add more RAM to the system.

The *sysdef* Command

The `sysdef` command reports current configuration information. With no options, it examines the default bootable kernel (/stand/unix). To examine a file other than the default, use the `-n` option followed by the filename of a valid bootable kernel. The `-i` option will report the configuration of the kernel currently running in memory (/dev/kmem).

> *Tip*
>
> *This command provides information that is good to print out for your system log.*

Third-Party Tools

There are also third-party tools available to analyze system performance data. One is *SarCheck* from Aurora Software, Inc. It reports on possible bottlenecks and makes recommendations. It will not make any changes to your system; it is purely an analysis tool. SarCheck for UnixWare 7 is in beta test at the time of this writing. For information on this program, go to `www.sarcheck.com`.

Tuning the System

After the problems have been identified, they need to be corrected in order to improve system performance. Some solutions are hardware related, and some involve tuning kernel parameters. A third option is to manage the load on the system by scheduling jobs to be run at less busy times using `at` or `cron`.

Author's Note

It is a good idea to change only a few parameters at a time rather than making massive changes in a single-kernel rebuild. After sweeping changes, you don't know which changes resulted in the increased or decreased system performance.

CPU Tuning

There are several hardware solutions to CPU bottlenecks. Using intelligent serial cards takes some of the load off the CPU. Disk controllers that use DMA (Direct Memory Access) to transfer data to and from memory also reduce the demands on the processor. Upgrading the CPU itself or adding CPUs to multiprocessor systems is another solution.

On the kernel side, you can reduce the value of the `MAXUP` parameter. This parameter governs how many processes each user can run. The default is 80. This may need to be tuned if individual users generate more than the default number of processes.

I/O Tuning

If the `avserv` is a problem, it can be reduced by getting faster disks and/or caching controllers.

If your system has multiple disks, look for unbalanced loads across the `avwait` and `avque` columns. You may be able to remedy this problem by rearranging the location of data. Try placing databases, swap, and temp files, or other high-usage files to a lower-demand disk.

If the `avque` is consistently greater than 1, and the `avwait` greater than 0, consider adding additional disks and/or controllers.

Some kernel parameters that can be tuned to increase I/O performance are discussed below.

NBUF

The `NBUF` parameter controls the size of the buffer cache. Increasing `NBUF` reduces writes to the disk. When you modify `NBUF`, you also need to modify `NHBUF`, which is used to search for a buffer in the *hash queue*. Hash queues contain addresses of the disk blocks that are in memory. For single-processor systems, `NHBUF` should be set to the power of 2 that is less than or equal to half of `NBUF`. The objective is to keep the list in each queue very short.

FDFLUSHR

`FDFLUSHR` is the interval in seconds to check the need to write the buffer cache and file pages to disk. The default is 1.

NAUTOUP

`NAUTOUP` is the number of seconds between filesystem updates. The default is 60 seconds. Increasing `NAUTOUP` can improve performance, but also increases the risk of data loss in a system crash.

RAM Tuning

If you find that the RAM is a bottleneck, you can implement a hardware solution by adding more memory.

To try to alleviate a RAM bottleneck without adding more physical memory, decrease the size of `NBUF`, which reduces the buffer cache. As noted in the I/O tuning section above, `NHBUF` should also be modified when `NBUF` is changed.

System Tuner

The *System Tuner* is the preferred method for changing tunable kernel parameters. However, not all kernel parameters are available via the system tuner; the `idtune` command is used for such parameters. A backup copy of the current kernel should be made before using the System Tuner. Do this by logging in as root and copying /stand/unix to /stand/unix.before.

Author's Note

I find it comforting to make a copy of the /etc/conf directory structure, which contains all of the tunables information, in case I want to return to square one after an unfortunate tuning episode. The files in /etc/conf should not be edited directly.

The System Tuner is accessed through SCOadmin, System, and is shown in Figure 21.5.

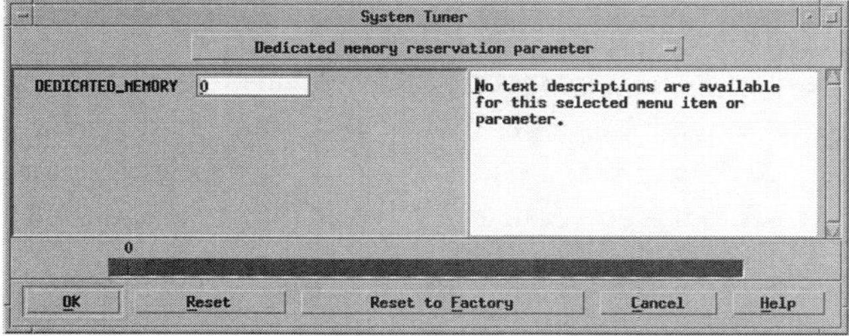

FIGURE 21.5 *Tuning kernel parameters with the System Tuner.*

To select a different category of tunables, click the box at the top of the window and choose the desired category (see Figure 21.6).

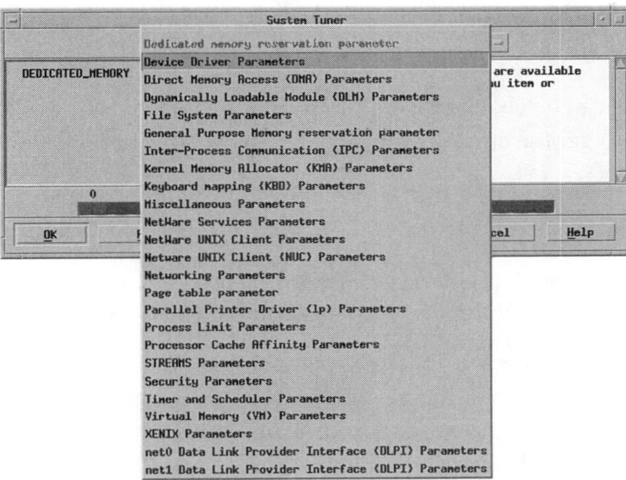

FIGURE 21.6 *Selecting from available tunables.*

To change a parameter, enter the new value. You can choose Reset to return parameters to their previous settings, or Reset to Factory to return to the original settings.

After changing the value, click OK. You will be prompted to rebuild the kernel. If you select Yes, it will be rebuilt immediately. Selecting No will cause a rebuild on the next boot.

If you chose to rebuild the kernel, you will then be prompted to reboot the system. Select OK to reboot so that the new parameters will take effect. Selecting Cancel will result in the new parameters taking effect at the next reboot.

Autotuning

One of the features of UnixWare 7 is *autotuning*; some kernel parameters are autotuned based on the amount of memory in your system. For autotuned parameters, a table stores the current, default, maximum, and minimum values appropriate for your system. These parameters are stored in the /etc/conf/autotune.d directory, and the table is passed to the kernel to allow autotuning at boot time. There are multiple files in this directory that contain the parameters for such areas as kernel, mem, and net0.

Normally, you should not need to change autotuned parameters. If you do, however, use the `idtune` command as described in the following section. Before changing any of these parameters, use `idtune` to view the current, default, maximum, and minimum values. The `-g` option to `idtune` displays these parameters in the order listed above. The maximum and minimum values do not apply to string tunables.

The *idtune* Command

Tunable parameters can be changed using the `idtune` command. You can also use this command to get the current value of existing tunable parameters.

To see the current value of the `VXFSNINODE` parameter, use:

```
# /etc/conf/bin/idtune -g VXFSNINODE
```

The values listed are those that will be used at the next build time unless overridden by the `-c` option, which reports the values in the current kernel.

Several options can be used when changing parameters. The `-m` option will change the value, but only if the change will result in an increase in the parameter. The `-f` option will force the change and suppression of all confirmation messages and does not apply to string tunables. The `-d` option sets the parameter to the default value. To change the `VXFSNINODE` parameter to 8000, use

```
# /etc/conf/bin/idtune VXFSNINODE 8000
```

When changing parameters, you are prompted for confirmation unless the `-f` option is used.

The `-c` option is used with options that update the values. It specifies that the change is made to both the stune and stune.current files in the /etc/conf/cf.d directory. This could result in the new loadable kernel modules being inconsistent with the currently running kernel and should be used with caution.

Changes made to kernel parameters will not take effect until the kernel has been rebuilt and the system rebooted. To rebuild the kernel, use

```
# /etc/conf/bin/idbuild -B
```

This causes the kernel to be rebuilt immediately. If you omit the `-B` option, the kernel is rebuilt during the next system boot.

CHAPTER 22

Security

- System security
  Learn about security profiles and how to use them.
- User security
  Find out how to govern user access to your system.
- Network security
  Learn to use tools to make your network more secure.

System Security

Administrators should keep in mind that a system is vulnerable when the host is placed in an easily accessible location. In the same way, sensitive information is at risk when backups are not stored securely.

Beyond physical security, there are several ways in which UnixWare 7 helps administrators to govern access to the systems under their control.

Security Profiles

UnixWare 7 offers four predefined security profiles:

- Low
- Traditional
- Improved
- High

Each has a directory named with the security level that resides in /etc/security/seclevel (for example, /etc/security/seclevel/low) and contains the default configuration for the given level, which can be modified to suit your needs, if desired.

You can create your own security profile by creating a directory with the desired name, copying the etc_def and script files from an existing directory, and modifying these files to suit your needs.

The following sections discuss the defaults for the predefined security profiles. The root account is able to override some password restrictions, but they are enforced by the system when the user logs in or tries to change his or her password.

Low Security

Low security is the least restrictive. It is recommended for systems that are not publicly accessible and that have a small number of cooperating users. With low security:

- A maximum of 99 unsuccessful login attempts may be made before the login terminates; for a non-network login, the user will be able to attempt to log in after the minimum delay for login attempts is reached, whereas the connection is dropped for a network login.
- There is no minimum delay between login attempts on a terminal.
- Logins must be completed within a maximum of 300 seconds.
- umask defaults to `022` (results in Read and Execute permissions for group members as well as other users).
- User accounts can be deleted, and UIDs can be reused.
- Passwords are not required on accounts (although they are recommended) and never expire.
- The minimum password length is one.
- The maximum generated password length is eight.
- Remote printing is allowed.
- All networking services are enabled.

Traditional Security

Traditional security is recommended for systems on which standard UNIX security is desired. With traditional security:

- A maximum of 99 unsuccessful login attempts may be made before the login terminates.
- There is a minimum delay of 10 seconds between login attempts on a terminal.
- Logins must be completed within a maximum of 60 seconds.
- umask defaults to `022` (results in Read and Execute permissions for group members as well as other users).
- User accounts can be deleted, and UIDs can be reused.
- Passwords are not required on accounts (although they are recommended) and never expire.
- The minimum password length is three.
- The maximum generated password length is eight.
- Remote printing is allowed.
- All networking services are enabled.

Improved Security

Improved security is recommended for systems on which groups of users can share information. With improved security:

- A maximum of five unsuccessful login attempts may be made before the login terminates.
- There is a minimum delay of 20 seconds between login attempts on a terminal.
- Logins must be completed within a maximum of 60 seconds.
- umask defaults to `027` (results in read and execute permissions for group members, and no permissions for other users).
- User accounts can be deleted, and UIDs can be reused after sufficient aging.
- Passwords are required on accounts and have a maximum life of 24 days.
- The minimum password length is six.
- The maximum generated password length is 10.
- Remote printing is not allowed.
- Most networking services are enabled.

High Security

High security is recommended for systems on which many users access confidential information individually. With high security:

- A maximum of three unsuccessful login attempts may be made before the login terminates.
- There is a minimum delay of 20 seconds between login attempts on a terminal.
- Logins must be completed within a maximum of 60 seconds.
- umask defaults to `077` (results in no permissions for group members or other users).
- User accounts can be deleted, but UIDs cannot be reused.
- Passwords are required on accounts and have a maximum life of 12 days.
- The minimum password length is eight.
- The maximum generated password length is 10.
- Remote printing is not allowed.
- Networking services are limited.

Changing Security Profiles

While you are allowed to change security profiles to one that is more restrictive than your current setting, it is not recommended. While the system was at a lower profile, security may have been compromised in some way that would allow users or other systems access that is not allowed by the new profile. For example, login or other scripts could have been altered in such a way as to provide a hole in the security to allow a user more access than is authorized by the system administrator.

Tip

It is desirable to set the security profile at the time of installation to the highest you might decide to use. It can be relaxed to a lower security level later without risk of compromise. It is recommended that a system be reinstalled to move to a more restrictive security profile.

The security profile on a system can be changed through SCOadmin, System, Security Profile Manager. Clicking on the current security profile opens a selection box with the current profile highlighted. Only the four predefined security profiles are available through the Security Profile Manager. You can select a profile to which to change the system, then click Host, Save, or press Ctrl+S to apply the change (see Figure 22.1).

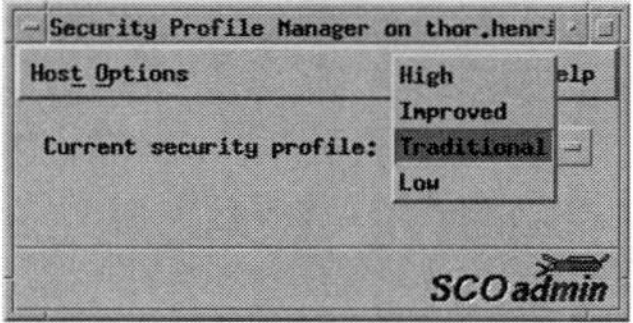

FIGURE 22.1 *Changing the security profile.*

If you select a higher security profile, you are warned that security may have been compromised while at the lower settings (see Figure 22.2), but are still allowed to make the change.

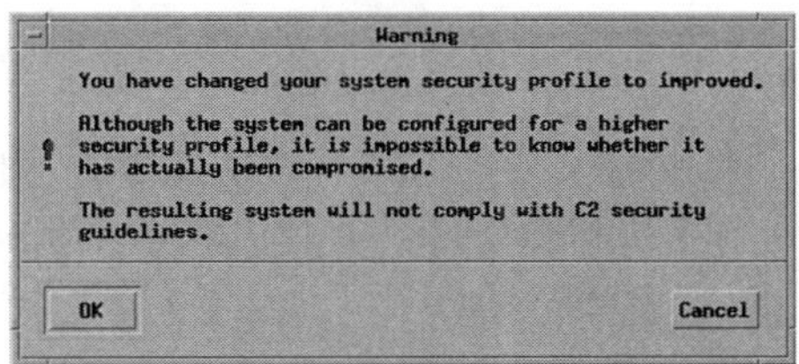

FIGURE 22.2 *Warning when increasing security.*

You can also change security levels with the `relax` command. This command enables you to use security profiles other than low, traditional, improved, or high. For instance, to relax the security level to one you have created in a directory called my_profile, use

```
#relax my_profile
```

The system will have to be rebooted before the changes take effect. You will be prompted to press Enter during the boot process to rebuild the kernel to effect the changes, or Esc to abandon the rebuild.

Verifying Security Integrity

The `secdefs` command can be used to report the current security profile. It can also verify whether any parameters have been changed such that they no longer comply with the current profile.

Executing `secdefs` with no arguments will return the name of the security profile that most closely matches current settings. It will also report how many differences exist between the current settings and the closest matching profile.

```
# secdefs
traditional (0 differences)
```

To see a listing of the differences between the current and closest matching settings, use the -v option to secdefs.

secdefs with the -a option will list all security profiles and the number of differences between the current settings and those defined for each profile.

```
# secdefs -a
traditional (0 differences)
my_profile (7 differences)
low (8 differences)
improved (12 differences)
high (18 differences)
```

To see a listing of the differences between a given profile and the current settings, use the -v option to secdefs followed by the name of the security profile to which to compare.

Restricting Login Shells

The only login shells that are permitted are those listed in /etc/shells. To disallow a particular shell, remove it from the file or comment the line out by placing a pound sign (#) at the beginning of the line.

Adding Secondary Passwords

You can define a password that is required for some connections. This password must be entered in addition to a regular login and password. One use for secondary passwords is to keep one frequently changed password that users must know in order to access their usual accounts from an offsite location. Another is to allow only some users dialup access, while all others must be onsite to access their accounts.

Create entries in /etc/dialups to define which login devices will be prompted for the secondary password. There should be one entry per line.

The /etc/d_passwd file maps passwords to executables (login shells). Create an entry for each executable that you want to have its own password. There should be one entry per line containing the full pathname of the executable program followed by a colon, the encrypted password, and another colon. If an entry exists but has no password, there will be no secondary prompt. If a device is listed in /etc/dialups but no entry exists in /etc/d_passwd for the login shell used, it will default to the password for /usr/bin/sh, if it exists.

To generate an encrypted password, use the makekey command. You will need to provide an eight-character password string, followed by two more digits or letters to use as a salt for the encryption. For instance, to generate an encrypted password of `dialpass` with a salt of `99`, enter

```
#echo dialpass99 ¦ /usr/lib/makekey; echo
```

Author's Note

Because of U.S. export restrictions, `makekey` *is only available in the United States and Canada. An alternate way to get an encrypted password is to create a dummy user account, assign it the desired password, and copy the encrypted version of the password from the /etc/shadow file.*

The system responds with an encrypted password string, in this case `99MhefDWzrlHY`. Enter this string in the password field for the desired shell.

For more on secondary passwords, see the man pages for `d_passwd`.

OpenServer 5 Tip

Dial-up passwords in OpenServer 5 were created with the `-m` *option to the* `passwd` *command. This is no longer a valid option.*

Verifying File Privileges

The file privilege database is maintained by the system in /etc/security/tcb/privs. It is possible that file privileges can be modified in such a way that the file privilege database is inaccurate.

To check the file privilege database, use the `initprivs` command. It will report any errors in the database. You can fix the errors reported by `initprivs` by running the `setpriv` command with the `-x` option:

```
#/etc/security/tools/setpriv -x
```

User Security

User privileges on a system can be governed in a number of ways. Several that can be used alone or in concert are described in the following sections.

System Owner Privileges

User accounts can be granted system owner privileges. The system owner can perform system administration tasks and has the following privileges:

- *Shut Down System*—Use the Shutdown Manager to shut down the system.
- *Administer Printers*—Use the Printer Manager to add, configure, and remove printers.
- *Administer File Systems*—Use the Filesystem Manager to add, configure, and manage filesystems.

- *Change System Tunables*—Use the System Tuner Manager to change tunable kernel parameters.
- *Monitor System Resources*—Use the System Monitor to view usage of system resources.
- *Administer Intranet*—Use the Network Configuration Manager to configure and manage network connections to remote systems.

These privileges are available to the system owner from the desktop only; this account cannot perform system administration tasks from the command line.

These authorizations can be added to and removed from user accounts through SCOadmin, Account Manager. Highlight the user account to be modified, and select Users, Authorizations. Selecting the Account Has Owner Privileges box will assign the privileges, as shown in Figure 22.3.

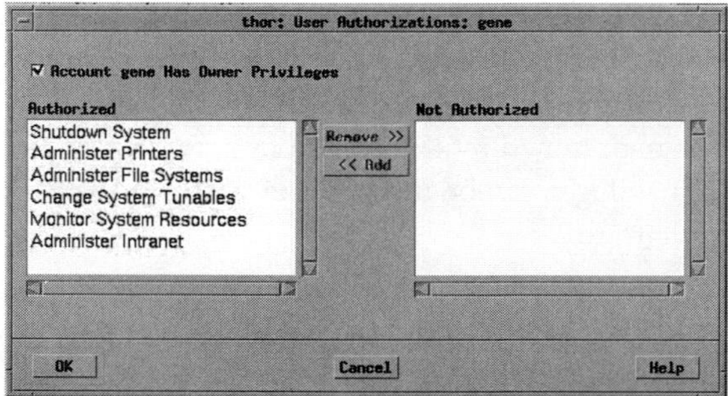

FIGURE 22.3 *Assigning system owner privileges.*

To apply the changes, click OK. You may also apply only some of these privileges.

To add privileges, either double-click the privilege to be added from the Not Authorized list, or click once to highlight the privilege and click the Add button.

To remove privileges, either double-click the privilege to be removed from the Authorized list, or click once to highlight the privilege and click the Remove button.

You can also assign system owner privileges at the command line with `make-owner`. When executed with an argument of a single-user account, system owner privileges are assigned to the specified user. When used with a minus sign (–) before the user account, system owner privileges are removed from the specified user. To transfer owner permissions from one user to another, execute `make-owner` with the new user account name followed by the old user account name. For example, to transfer system owner privileges from gene to larry, use

```
#/usr/lib/scoadmin/account/make-owner larry gene
```

This adds larry as a system owner and assigns the associated privileges to his account. gene is no longer a system owner, but the privileges remain in his account. When viewing his privileges through the Account Manager, the owner privileges are still in the authorized list, but the box identifying the account as a system owner is no longer selected.

> *Tip*
>
> *See the man pages on* `make-owner` *for a complete description of this command, including how to add other privileges to those associated with system owners.*

Authorizations that can be assigned are stored in /usr/lib/scoadmin/account/PrivTable. The authorizations associated with each account are stored in the /usr/lib/scoadmin/account/Users directory, with a file named for each account with privileges assigned to it.

Roles and Command Access

Roles can be defined to encompass groups of permissions. You can then assign one or more roles to a user account. By using roles you can eliminate the need for any users to know the root password.

Adding and Removing Roles

The `adminrole` command is used with the `-n` option to create a new role. For example, to create a role called pkgadm, use

```
#adminrole -n pkgadm
```

To list the commands associated with an existing role, use `adminrole` with no options followed by the name of the role. To remove a role, use the `-d` option to `adminrole`.

Associating Commands with a Role

After a role has been created, you can define which commands are associated with it. The allprivs privilege must be given along with the desired commands to allow non-root users to execute root-only commands.

To add commands to a role, use the `adminrole` command with the `-a` option, followed by the command, its path, and the privilege associated with the command. For example, to add the `pkgadd` command to the role of `pkgadm`, use

```
#adminrole -a pkgadd:/usr/sbin/pkgadd:allprivs pkgadm
```

Use the `-r` option to `adminrole` to remove commands from a role. To remove the `pkgadd` command from the role of `pkgadm`, use

```
#adminrole -r pkgadd pkgadm
```

Assigning Roles to Users

The `adminuser` command assigns the defined roles to user accounts. A database of users and their assigned roles is kept in /etc/security/tfm. The first time you assign a role to a user account, add the `-n` option to `adminuser` to create an entry in the database. Otherwise, use `adminuser` with the `-o` option followed by the role and user. For instance, to assign the `pkgadm` role to the user harold, who has not been previously assigned any roles, use

```
#adminuser -n -o pkgadm harold
```

To remove a role from a user, execute `adminuser` with the `-d` option:

```
#adminuser -d pkgadm harold
```

Executing Root-Only Commands

The `tfadmin` command is used for non-root users to execute root-only commands. For example, for harold to use the `pkgadd` command to install the Apache Web server from the primary CD-ROM, he would enter

```
#/sbin/tfadmin pkgadd -d cdrom1 apache
```

When you assigned a user an administrative role, you also assigned the allprivs privilege that was associated with the command(s) in that role. This results in an entry in the file privilege database. If users are not able to run the `tfadmin` command, there may be an inconsistency in this database. See the previous section on verifying file privileges for instructions on checking and correcting such inconsistencies.

SUID and SGID

When the SUID (set user ID) and/or SGID (set group ID) bits are set on a binary file, the program is executed with the UID and/or GID of the file, rather than those of the user executing the program. During the execution of the program, the user has the access to files, processes, and resources associated with the owner and/or group of the program file. SUID and SGID do not work on shell scripts.

When SUID and/or SGID is set, an `s` appears in the user and/or group permissions of the file. To set SUID bits, use the `chmod` command with a leading 4 before the standard three-digit mode. To set SGID bits, use the `chmod` command with a leading 2. To remove SUID and SGID bits, execute `chmod` with a standard three-digit mode.

For example, given a file in /etc/usrapp named runlist, setting the SUID bit gives the following result:

```
# l
total 0
---x--x--x    1 root     sys              0 Oct  4 11:46 runlist
# chmod 4111 runlist
# l
total 0
---s--x--x    1 root     sys              0 Oct  4 11:46 runlist
```

Alternately, setting the SGID bit results in permissions as follows:

```
# chmod 2111 runlist
# l
total 0
---x--s--x    1 root     sys              0 Oct  4 11:46 runlist
```

Using `chmod` with a leading 6 sets both the SUID and SGID bits.

The Sticky Bit

The *sticky bit* allows users in a common group to add files to a directory, but remove only the files that they own, even if the mode is such that they could otherwise remove any files in the directory. It appears as a `t` in the last character of the file mode if it would otherwise be an `x`, or a `T` if the last character would otherwise be a `-` (other users have no permissions on the directory). As always, root can delete files regardless of permissions settings.

To add a sticky bit to a directory, use the `chmod` command with a 1 preceding the usual three-digit mode. To remove the sticky bit, execute `chmod` without the leading 1. For example, to set the sticky bit on a directory such that members of the group sys can add files and remove their own files, but other users have no access, use

```
# chmod 1770 userapp
# l -d userapp
drwxrwx--T    2 root     sys             96 Oct  4 12:13 userapp
```

Users can set and remove sticky bits on directories that they own. Root can set and remove sticky bits on any directory.

Restricting Root Logins

Root logins can be restricted to the console only. The root account will not be allowed access from any other location. To set this feature, edit the /etc/default/login file and add the following entry:

```
CONSOLE=/dev/console
```

This feature is set by default with improved and high security profiles.

Monitoring Use of the *su* Command

To enable logging of attempts to use the su command, both successful and unsuccessful, verify that the following entry exists in /etc/default/su:

```
SULOG=/var/adm/sulog
```

You can then check the sulog in /var/adm to monitor su attempts. If the attempt was successful, a plus sign (+) appears after the date and time. If unsuccessful, a minus sign (-) is recorded.

If you wish to have attempts reported to the console as well, be sure the CONSOLE=/dev/console entry is uncommented.

As with the restricted root login capability, this feature is set by default with improved and high security profiles.

Network Security

In addition to handling security through system and user controls, you can use several tools to increase network security. Restricting FTP access, TCP wrappers, packet filtering, and proxy servers are all tools in creating a more secure network environment.

ftpusers

Individual user accounts can be restricted from FTP access by entering the usernames in /etc/ftpusers, one per line. By default, root is restricted from FTP access.

User accounts can also be restricted through the FTP Server Manager by selecting View, Denied Users to display currently denied accounts. Then use the Edit menu to add or delete users from this list.

TCP Wrappers

UnixWare 7 provides a service called *TCP wrappers.* This enables you to control access to a host on a per-system and per-service basis. The in.tcpd daemon handles TCP wrappers.

Configuring /etc/inet/inetd.conf

The in.tcpd daemon starts some services by default. The /etc/inet/inetd.conf file can be modified to use in.tcpd to start services that would otherwise be started by inetd.

The service to be started is given as an argument to in.tcpd program. In the excerpt from /etc/inet/inetd.conf that follows, there are two lines each for telnet and ftp services. The first, which is active, uses in.tcpd to start the service, thereby enabling the use of TCP wrappers. The second, which starts with # and is therefore merely a comment, illustrates the services being started directly. Were the services started directly, access could not be controlled by TCP wrappers.

```
ftp      stream   tcp   nowait   root      /usr/sbin/in.tcpd    in.ftpd -a
#ftp     stream   tcp   nowait   root      /usr/sbin/in.ftpd    in.ftpd -a
telnet   stream   tcp   nowait   root      /usr/sbin/in.tcpd    in.telnetd
#telnet  stream   tcp   nowait   root   /usr/sbin/in.telnetd    in.telnetd
```

Configuring hosts.allow and hosts.deny

TCP wrappers control access with two files:

/etc/inet/hosts.allow

/etc/inet/hosts.deny

These files contain rules that in.tcpd applies to service requests to determine whether to grant access.

When a service request is received, in.tcpd first checks the hosts.allow file. If the host requesting service is allowed to use that service, either by explicit statement or by a rule containing wildcards, the service daemon is invoked immediately. Otherwise, the hosts.deny file is checked.

If the host is denied from using the requested service by a rule in hosts.deny, the service daemon is not invoked. If the host is not denied service in the hosts.deny file, the service is invoked by default. In other words, TCP wrappers allow access to services unless instructed otherwise.

Although the files are named hosts.allow and hosts.deny, rules to allow or deny service can be placed in either file. The rules in the hosts.allow file will be applied before hosts.deny is read, however. Therefore, if a service is denied by a rule in hosts.deny but allowed by a conflicting rule in hosts.allow, the service daemon will be invoked because the allow file is read and acted upon first.

The rules in hosts.allow and hosts.deny should be formatted as follows:

```
daemon_list : client_list [: options] [:allow ¦ deny]
```

Entries in hosts.allow are assumed to be rules to allow access unless `deny` is explicitly stated. The opposite is true of entries in hosts.deny.

Elements of the daemon_list (services) and client_list (hosts) fields can be separated by spaces or commas. Exceptions to list items can be specified using the `EXCEPT` token.

Wildcards can be used to specify hosts. `ALL` matches everything. `LOCAL` matches all hosts whose names do not contain a dot character. On systems using DNS, however, all host names contain a dot character, and `LOCAL` will not match any hosts.

`KNOWN` and `UNKNOWN` can be used to specify hosts whose names and addresses are known and unknown, respectively. These are not necessarily consistent, however, because of the possibility of temporary problems with a name server.

Other wildcard patterns for matching hosts are

- Leading dot character (.). A host will match if the last elements of its name match the specified pattern. For example, `kingsley.henriksens.com` matches the `".henriksens.com"` pattern.
- Trailing dot character (.). A host will match if the first elements match the specified pattern. For example, 10.1.1.103 matches the "10.1." pattern.
- Leading at sign (@). A host will match if it is in the NIS netgroup specified.
- Network address/netmask pair. A host will match if its network, subject to the specified netmask, matches the specified network address. For example, the pattern 10.1.1.0/255.255.255.0 matches all addresses in the range 10.1.1.0 through 10.1.1.255.

Because of the ability to place either allow or deny rules in either of the hosts.allow or hosts.deny files, specific configurations can often be achieved in several different ways. They may use either the hosts.allow or hosts.deny file exclusively or use both files in concert.

For example, one way to configure a system in which only hosts on the 10.1.1 the network can access services, and only the host 10.1.1.103 is authorized for telnet, is to add the following entries to the /etc/inet/hosts.allow file:

```
in.telnetd: ALL EXCEPT 10.1.1.103: DENY
ALL: 10.1.1.0/255.255.255.0
ALL: ALL: DENY
```

By ending the hosts.allow file with an `ALL: ALL: DENY` rule or by placing an `ALL: ALL` rule in the hosts.deny file, you can ensure that only specifically allowed services will be accessible to the specified hosts. Without such a rule, any services not explicitly denied will be allowed.

In addition to governing access to services, TCP wrappers can be used to perform actions as a part of the rule. For instance, perhaps the root user wishes to be notified of failed telnet attempts. The previous line to deny telnet requests can be modified as follows:

```
in.telnetd: ALL EXCEPT 10.1.1.103: spawn ( echo "telnet attempted from %a" ¦
 /bin/mail -s "telnet attempt" root ) &: DENY
```

This will result in a mail message being sent to root with the IP address (%a) of the host that attempted to use telnet. Other variable substitutions can be found in the man pages for hosts_access. These include the name of the daemon process (%d), the client host name (%n), and the server host name (%N).

Because TCP wrappers control service requests, a new restriction put into place will not affect current instances of services because the service requested has already been invoked.

Packet Filters

Another method of restricting network access is the use of *packet filters*. While TCP wrappers restrict access to particular services (or all services) on a given host, packet filters restrict which packets are allowed to pass through the host.

Thus, a router can use packet filters to stop unauthorized hosts on one network from reaching another network to which the router is connected, or from accessing specific services on that network. For this reason, packet filtering can be used as a tool in creating a firewall.

Packet Filter Configuration

Packet filters can be configured on a UnixWare 7 system provided it has one of the following:

- LAN network interface using an MDI network adapter driver
- WAN network interface using the PPP serial line protocol provided by UnixWare 7

Because packets can travel both into and out of a host, packet filters can be configured for either incoming or outgoing packets, or both.

In addition, two different types of filters can be used. *Allow filters* allow packets matching the specified rules to pass through and drop all other packets. *Block filters* drop packets matching the specified rules and allow all other packets to pass through. Allow filters are more secure because they are more restrictive; only explicitly allowed packets will be passed on.

Packet filters can be administered through SCOadmin, Networking, Packet Filter Manager.

To specify an interface to administer, select Filter, Interface from the initial Packet Filter Manager window. A window listing the available interfaces will open from which you may select one to configure (see Figure 22.4).

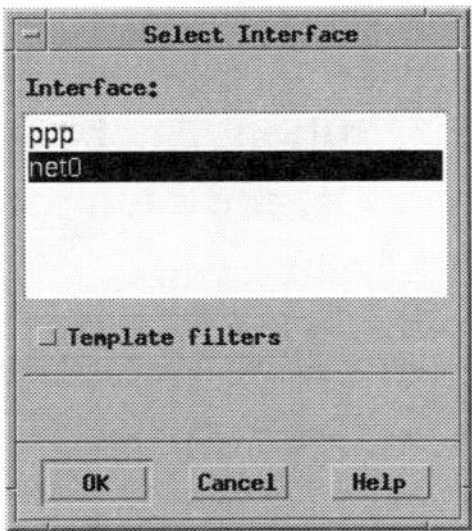

FIGURE 22.4 *Selecting an interface.*

Template Packet Filters

Several template packet filters are preconfigured. You can use these as is or as a starting point for modification to suit your needs. To see them, click the Template Filters box when selecting an interface. The filter names indicate their function. The template filters for IP are shown in Figure 22.5.

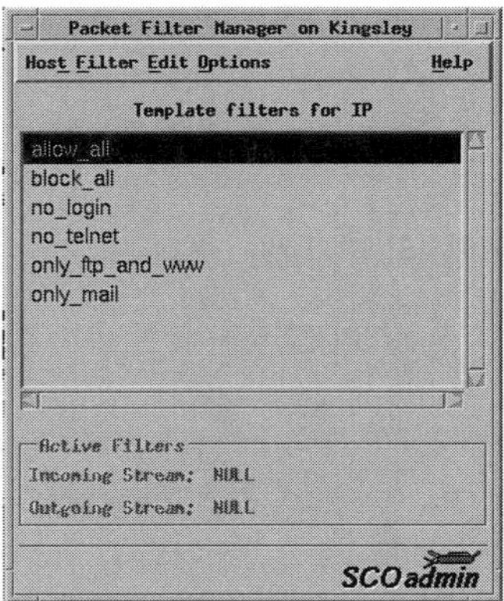

FIGURE 22.5 *Template packet filters.*

To copy a template filter, select Edit, Copy. This will open the window shown in Figure 22.6. You can then specify to which interface to copy the filter and what it should be named.

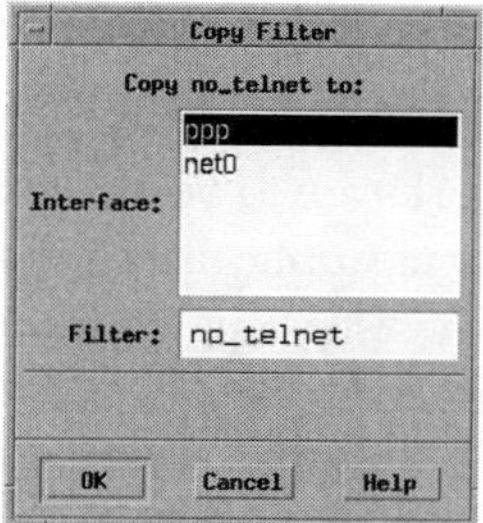

FIGURE 22.6 *Copying a packet filter.*

Adding Packet Filters

To add a new packet filter, select the appropriate interface to add, then choose Edit, Add. The window shown in Figure 22.7 will prompt for a name for the new filter.

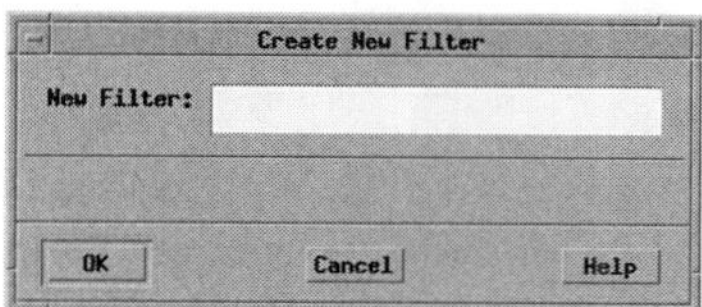

FIGURE 22.7 *Adding a new packet filter.*

After a name has been entered, you can configure the filter. The first choice to make is whether to Block or Allow matching packets.

After determining the filter method, you need to specify the services and ports to be affected by this filter. You can either highlight the Specific ports and services, select All, or highlight those to be excluded from the new filter. If you click either Specific or All Except, the Add button is made active.

The Add option is to be used for adding new ports and services to the list of possible selections; the Modify and Delete buttons also refer to the list from which you can choose services. To select an item in the list for the new filter, click the item to highlight it. If you wish to specify more than one item, hold the Ctrl key while clicking subsequent items. Simply clicking additional items without pressing Ctrl will change the selected item to the one just clicked, rather than adding the clicked item to those already selected.

The directions to which the filter is applied are specified by clicking From and/or To. This is not the same as specifying a filter as Incoming and/or Outgoing; rather, it refers to the direction of the service request. In restricting telnet, for example, From would affect telnet requests coming to the host being configured *from* other hosts and/or networks; To would affect telnet requests going out from the host being configured *to* other hosts and/or networks.

Finally, you need to specify which hosts and/or networks are to be affected by the filter. As with the services, you can define the filter as applicable to specific hosts/networks, all hosts/networks, or all hosts/networks except those specified. The Add, Modify, and Delete buttons are again referring to additions, modifications, and deletions of the list from which you may choose. To actually select hosts or networks, click to highlight them. To make multiple selections, hold the Ctrl key while clicking subsequent items.

Figure 22.8 illustrates the window in which all of these properties may be configured.

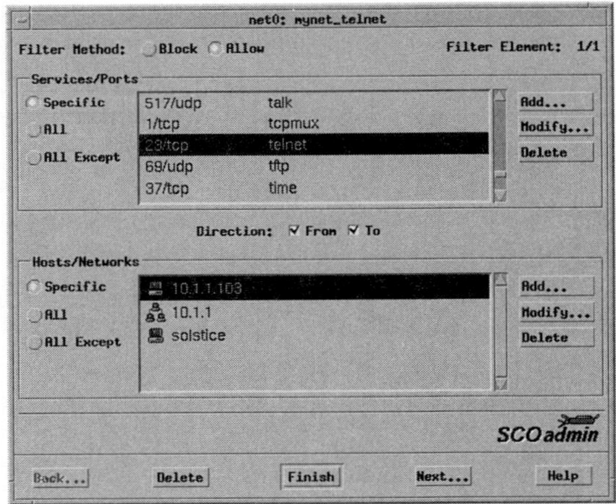

FIGURE 22.8 *Setting packet filter configuration.*

To add a host to the list from which you may select, click the Add button. The window shown in Figure 22.9 will open to allow you to either specify a new host or network, or to select a host from the list of those defined in /etc/hosts or by the DNS server. To add a network, click Network and enter the network number (for example, 10.1.2). To add a single host, select Host and enter either the host name or IP address.

Alternatively, to select the host from those defined in /etc/hosts, click the Select button. A window like that shown in Figure 22.10 will open containing all of the hosts defined in /etc/hosts. You can choose to have the list sorted by name or IP address. Click to highlight the host to be added to the list, then click OK.

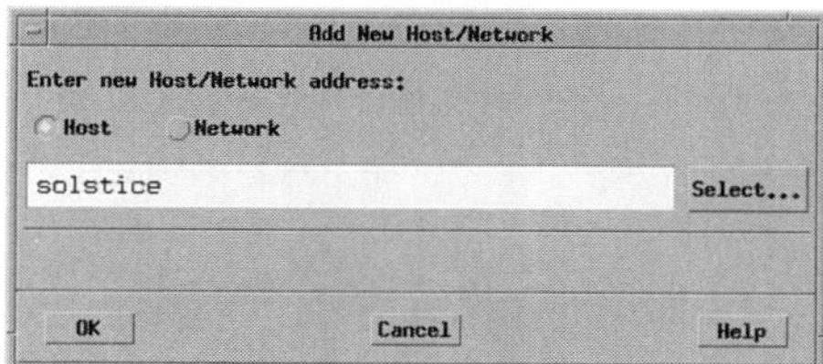

FIGURE 22.9 *Adding a host to the packet filtering selection list.*

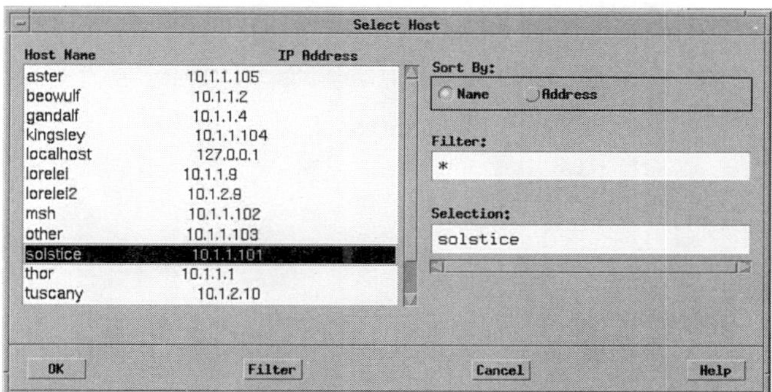

FIGURE 22.10 *Selecting a host from those defined in /etc/hosts.*

After you have configured the packet filter to behave as desired, click the Finish button. You will be given three choices (see Figure 22.11):

- Saving the configuration and returning to the Packet Filter Manager
- Simply returning to the Manager and abandoning the configuration
- Canceling the choice to finish and continuing with the configuration

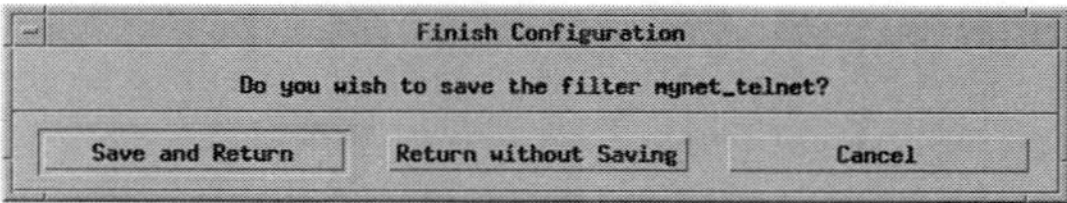

FIGURE 22.11 *Saving the specified configuration.*

Modifying Packet Filters

After you have either copied a template filter or added a new filter, you can choose to modify it. The windows and options are essentially the same as those for setting up a new filter, but give the existing filter as a starting point.

Loading Packet Filters

While packet filters for PPP interfaces may be configured through the Packet Filter Manager, they must be loaded using the PPP Manager. The options for loading and unloading selected packet filters are grayed out when a PPP interface is selected.

For non-PPP interfaces, a defined packet filter may be loaded by clicking the desired packet filter and selecting Filter, Load. The window shown in Figure 22.12 will open to allow you to specify whether the filter should be applied to incoming or outgoing packets, or both.

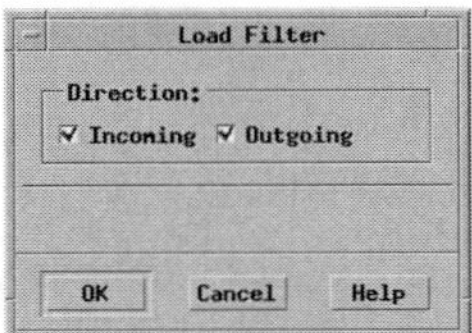

FIGURE 22.12 *Loading a filter.*

When you load a filter, it is immediately applied. Therefore, if a current action is no longer allowed, it stops in mid-stream. For instance, an X session that is blocked during a session will stop being able to send or echo input, and the screen will no longer be refreshed.

Unloading Packet Filters

To unload an active packet filter, click to highlight it, then select Filter, Unload (see Figure 22.13). As with loading, the change is immediately applied.

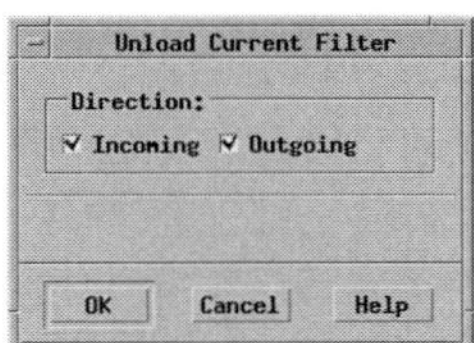

FIGURE 22.13 *Unloading a filter.*

Proxy Servers

A host that is connected to multiple networks can be configured to act as a *proxy server*. It will handle requests sent to it (for example, Web services) as if it were requesting the information itself. Other hosts that are connected to the proxy server will send requests to it rather than to the final destination.

This enables an isolated network to have Web access from every host, while only one host (the proxy server) actually needs to have an Internet address. It can also be used in concert with packet filtering to increase security. The machines using the proxy server can safely reject packets from machines outside their own isolated network, while still having Web access.

Netscape Proxy Server

The Netscape Proxy Server is available as an Optional Service to UnixWare 7. It can be used on an evaluation basis for 60 days.

To install the Netscape Proxy Server, insert the Optional Services CD-ROM and use the `pkgadd` command (that is, `pkgadd...`). Select both the server and the documentation packages, and select the Automatic configuration. This uses the 60-day evaluation license by default. If you have purchased a license for this service, you can enter it through the License Manager after the installation.

When the installation is complete, enable the Netscape Proxy Server with the following command:

```
#nsproxy enable
```

The Netscape Proxy Server listens on port 8080 by default.

Squid

A second option is to use the *Squid proxy server*, which is free and comes on the Skunkware CD-ROM. To install Squid, insert the Skunkware 7 CD-ROM, and use a `pkgadd` command similar to

```
#pkgadd -d cdrom1 squid
```

When the package has been installed, you will need to make two modifications to the configuration file /usr/local/squid/etc/squid.conf:

1. Change the http_port to `8080`.
2. Comment out the `httpd_accel` directive.

These changes will make Squid act as the primary proxy server, rather than as an httpd accelerator on port 80, which looks for the real proxy server on port 8080.

To start Squid, use the following command:

```
#/usr/local/squid/bin/RunCache &
```

Squid will then run until the next shutdown. To start Squid at boot time, put the `RunCache` command in a script in the /etc/rc2.d directory.

Configuring Browsers

When you have a proxy server running on the desired host, you need to let the browsers that will use that proxy server know where to find it.

For example, in Netscape Communicator 4, select Edit, Preferences to open the Preferences window. Double-click Advanced; then click on Proxies. Select Manual Proxy Configuration, then click the View button. To proxy HTTP services, enter the IP address (or host name, if defined in the hosts file on the system being configured) of the host running the proxy server into the HTTP box with `8080` as the port.

PART IV

Disaster Recovery

CHAPTER 23

Emergency Recovery

- Emergency Recovery Diskettes
  Learn how to use the Emergency Recovery Diskettes and determine what they tell you.
- Restoring the master boot record
  Find out in this chapter how to restore the master boot record without restoring the entire system.
- Restoring the root filesystem
  Determine how to restore a root filesystem or an entire primary hard disk from the emergency recovery tapes.
- The inside details of the Emergency Diskettes
  If you want the inside details, here is what happens during recovery and what is contained in the Emergency Recovery Diskettes.
- Restoring non-root filesystems
  Learn how to check and re-create non-root filesystems.
- SCO ARCserve/Open from Cheyenne
  Find out what the ARCserve package brings to the emergency recovery procedure.

Recovering a UnixWare 7 System

Nothing raises the FUD (fear, uncertainty, and doubt) factor like a system failure. When the system does not boot and messages such as `No OS` or `Non-system disk or disk error` appear on the console, you can only hope that you have a set of diskettes and tapes that will allow total recovery. To further increase the tension, Hewlett-Packard reports that businesses suffering an irretrievable loss of all business data have a 94% probability of going out of business within two years.

In Chapter 14, "Wrapping Up the Install," the creation of Emergency Recovery Diskettes (ERDs) and tapes is covered. Chapter 12, "Removable Media," covers the backup of data. The first step in any system recovery is to have diskettes that allow booting the system. The recovery diskettes should have been tested before this point.

The UnixWare 7 Emergency Recovery Diskettes

Before starting on the recovery process, you should assemble all of the diskettes and tapes necessary to recover the system.

The recovery diskettes consist of a two-diskette set. You should have these for each system. These diskettes and the tapes are system specific. SCO specifically states that you should create separate diskettes for each system. There is no generic version of these as there is in OpenServer 5.

> *Author's Note*
>
> *The diskettes I created on my Compaq DeskPro XL5100 will fail when I attempt to boot my Compaq Prosignia 300, even though both have all SCSI peripherals and use the Compaq SCSI controller. They do seem to work on either of the pair of DeskPro XL5100s.*

Booting from the Emergency Recovery Diskettes

To boot the system, insert the first diskette and power on the system. As the system boots, the `Starting UnixWare` message is displayed. You can break out to the `[Boot]` prompt by pressing any key while the `Starting UnixWare` message is displayed. To continue booting, type **`boot`** and press the Enter key.

> *OpenServer 5 Tip*
>
> *UnixWare 7's recovery process is very different from OpenServer 5. The two diskettes are not called the "root and boot" floppies for good reason. Once you boot, you are running entirely in memory; the second diskette is not a root filesystem, as in the OpenServer 5 root and boot floppies. You cannot boot the hard disk copy of UNIX or use the hard disk root filesystem as the booted root filesystem from the floppy boot because no static driver for the hard disk is loaded into the recovery kernel. The dynamic driver that accesses the hard disk for tape recovery is loaded after the second diskette is read.*

After the system reads the first diskette, the message

```
Insert the second emergency recovery diskette and press ENTER
```

is displayed.

After pressing the Enter key, the message

```
Reading the second emergency recovery floppy
```

is displayed. After the second diskette is read, the system no longer needs the floppy disk drive.

Hard Disk Sanity

If the hard drive is in good condition, the message

```
The hard disk is sane. Press ENTER to continue.
```

will appear on the screen. If the hard disk has problems, the message will read

```
The hard disk is NOT sane. Press ENTER to continue.
```

The `hard disk is sane` message reveals the following:

- A valid master boot record exists.
- A valid UNIX partition exists.
- Valid slice information exists within the UNIX partition.
- The filesystems are clean and pass fsck.

This check does not verify the partition boot code in the UnixWare 7 partition.

The Emergency Recovery Menu

Pressing the Enter key after the `hard disk sanity` message provides the following menu:

Emergency Recovery Menu

Mount File Systems

Unmount File Systems

Access UnixWare Shell

Restore Disk(s)

Reboot

If the disk is not considered sane, the Mount File Systems option will not appear. If the option is available, it will mount the filesystems under the /mnt directory.

The Unmount File Systems option will unmount the filesystems mounted in the first option. This option does not appear if the disk is not sane.

The Access UnixWare Shell option provides access to the command line. Because the floppy disk is not in use at this time, a diskette with additional tools may be mounted.

If the hard disk was sane and the filesystems mounted, all the programs on the hard disk are now available for use (just remember to preface the path name with `/mnt`). If you need to use the hard disk commands extensively, use the `chroot /mnt ksh -o vi` command to change the root to `/mnt` so the normal paths are available. To return to the menu from the shell:

1. Type **`exit`** and press Enter.
2. Press Alt+SysReq.
3. Press F1.

The Restore Disks option is used to restore the disks from the emergency recovery tape.

Booting Without the Emergency Diskettes

What do you do if you arrive at a site with a crashed system and no one has the ERDs? What do you do if the ERDs fail when you attempt to boot?

It is possible to boot from the original boot diskettes and break out to a shell. If the site does not have the original diskettes, see Chapter 4, "Installation of UnixWare 7," on re-creating boot diskettes.

To boot from the original diskettes:

1. Boot the system from the first diskette. (Starting with version 7.0.1, a message appears here for selecting the install language.)
2. Insert diskette 2 when prompted.
3. Press F8 to defer licensing and choose an evaluation license.
4. If necessary, load the Host Bus Adapter (HBA) diskette.
5. Enter the Device Configuration Utility (DCU) if necessary, or press F10 to continue.

> *Tip*
>
> *It is necessary to go this far in the install procedure to get the host bus adapter drivers loaded.*

6. When the `System node name` prompt is displayed, insert the UnixWare 7 operating system CD into the CD-ROM drive.
7. Switch to virtual terminal zero (VT0) by pressing Ctrl+Alt+Esc. You can switch back to the install menu with Ctrl+Alt+F1.
8. Mount the CD-ROM using the following command:
   ```
   mount -F cdfs -r /dev/cdrom1 /cd-rom
   ```
9. Assuming the root filesystem is vxfs, register the vxfs filesystem module:
   ```
   modreg 4 vxfs
   ```
10. Load the vxfs filesystem module:
    ```
    modadmin -l /cd-rom/.extra.d/etc/conf/mod.d/vxfs
    ```
    This will return a `US:modadmin: INFO` message.
11. Mount the hard disk. The following command uses controller 0, bus 0, target ID 0, and LUN 0. If your system disk is not the same, use the correct device. Note that the UnixWare 7 root slice is always slice #1.
    ```
    mount -F vxfs /dev/dsk/c0b0t0d0s1 /mnt
    ```
12. If the mount fails, you may need to run fsck and repeat the `mount` command.
    ```
    /cd-rom/.extra.d/etc/fs/vxfs/fsck /dev/dsk/c0b0t0d0s1
    ```

When the hard disk is mounted, you will have access to additional commands.

Author's Note

On the 7.0.0 version, I had no trouble with mounting the hard drive. On the Early Access Product (EAP) version of 7.0.1, I was forced to run the `fsck` command in step 12 before mounting the disk drive. I would receive a `No space on device` message if I attempted the mount without the `fsck`. Once mounted, I could not unmount it with the `umount /mnt` command. It would claim that `/mnt` was busy.

Restoring the Master Boot Record

If the message displayed by the system at boot was `No OS` or `Non-system disk or disk error`, the boot block or Master Boot Record (MBR) may have been corrupted. Restoring the MBR and partition table can be done without restoring the entire emergency tape.

1. Boot from the emergency diskettes. Select the option to Access the UnixWare shell. You could get to the shell prompt with the original install media by the method explained previously if the ERDs are not available.

2. The `fdisk` command is now available. If the drive is mounted, you may be able to run fdisk with no options and access the information. If not mounted, specify the hard disk, usually /dev/rdsk/c0b0t0d0p0. Partition 0 refers to the whole disk.

3. When you run the `fdisk` command, if the partition table is also corrupt, `fdisk` will prompt with the partition table parameters that specify a 100% UNIX disk. If you know there are other partitions, you must know the parameters to restore the partition table. If you do not know the parameters, you have two choices:

   - Restore the emergency recovery tape.

   - Extract the first archive from the tape and find the partition table parameters. The format of the files in the archive is given later in this chapter. To extract the first archive:

     ```
     cpio -icvdumB -I /dev/rmt/ctape1
     ```

   The ctape1 may be different on your system.

The fdisk program will re-create the partition table. Re-execute fdisk. Select option 0 to overwrite the master boot record. Select option 4 to update and exit.

To reboot, press Esc.

Restoring the Root Filesystem

To restore the root filesystem, insert the first emergency_rec tape and select Restore Disk(s) from the Emergency Recovery menu.

The restore procedure will access the tapes and restore the disk to the logical condition that existed when the tape was made. This step will replace the MBR and the partition boot code. The filesystems are then restored to disk.

The following messages are displayed during the restore process:

```
Reading the original disk configuration information.

Setting up the hard disk(s) to match the original configuration.

Restoring the disk(s). This will take several minutes.

Disk(s) is(are) successfully restored. Press ENTER to continue.
```

To reboot, press Esc or select Reboot from the menu. Remove diskettes, CDs, and tapes before rebooting.

After rebooting, switch to the character-based console screen (Ctrl+Alt, then

Esc). You will probably see many error messages starting with

```
UX:initprivs: WARNING
```

This is caused by the changing of last update times on the restored files. The dates and times do not match the stored values in the file privilege database. To fix the problem, run the `setpriv` command:

```
/etc/security/tools/setpriv -x
```

On reboot the problems should not reappear.

Author's Note

In experimenting with restores, I found that the restore correctly worked with a newly formatted hard drive as well as one with an fdisk partition table that did not match the original partition table. Where I had a problem was with an fdisk that showed no partition. For some reason, I received a disk error. Creating a partition, even a DOS partition that encompassed the entire disk, solved the problem. The restore program is looking for a valid partition table. SCO has reported this to be a bug; it should be fixed in a future release.

The Inside Details on the Emergency Diskettes and Tapes

Author's Note

This section was written for those support people who want to know more than how to restore. It is for those techies who want to know what is happening when they restore so they can work around problems and have as much opportunity as possible to save a failed system.

The `emergency_disk` command used to create the emergency diskettes works with the contents of the /usr/lib/drf directory. The `prep_flop` script prepares the files to be copied. The `cut_flop` script copies the files and small bootable filesystem to the floppies.

Warning

Do not make changes to these scripts unless you make backup copies and have an alternate set of emergency floppies. If you need additional programs available when booting from these diskettes, create your own mountable diskette with your chosen files.

The Emergency Diskettes

The emergency diskettes contain a floppy boot loader and a series of compressed cpio archives. You cannot mount them as filesystems to look at them. Diskette 1, the bootable diskette, has a small boot filesystem on it. Attempting to mount this diskette yields an error message referring to an unknown filesystem. Diskette 2 contains compressed cpio archives.

The commands available on the emergency diskettes are

```
cat     chroot   cpio      date    dd        echo    edvtoc    fdisk
find    fsck     grep      ksh     labelit   ln      ls        mkdir
mkfs    mount    prtvtoc   rm      stty      vi
```

Warning

Some of these are limited-function shell aliases for the regular UnixWare 7 commands. If the hard disk is functional, you have access to the fully functional commands on the hard disk. If not, you can use the magic diskette or a diskette that you have created for the purpose.

The Emergency Tapes

The `emergency_rec` command can create tapes in two formats: cpio and dd. The dd option (`emergency_rec -e`) copies the entire primary hard drive to tape. The cpio tape copy (`execute emergency_rec` without the `-e` option) is the default method of execution.

Both tapes contain a cpio archive at the start of the tape that contains disk layout information. Using the `cpio` command, you can extract files from the tape.

Tip

Remember that the ARCserve system starts up automatically and does not share the tape drive with other commands. Executing cpio while the ARCserve programs are running will yield a cpio that sits and does nothing: No action, no errors, no tape access. To stop ARCserve, run the `astop` command. When finished with cpio, restart ARCserve with the `astart` command. When creating the tapes and diskettes, you must be in single-user mode, so ARCserve is not running.

The files located in the first archive are for restoring the disk drive to the state it was in at the time the tape was created. These files are boot, disksetup, fd_cmds_11, fd_cmds_12, layout_1, and part_dd_1.

To extract these files, use cpio:

```
cpio -icvdumB -I /dev/rmt/ctape1
```

The files will be placed in a directory named .extra.d. Under this directory is a directory named Drf_Rec.

The boot file is the partition boot program. This is a copy of /etc/boot. The disk setup program copies the boot program to the partition boot sector and creates the slices in the UnixWare 7 partition.

Warning

The following files came from a 2GB disk drive with a UnixWare 7 partition, an NT partition (listed by UnixWare 7 fdisk as "Other"), and a Compaq system partition. The partition information below should not be used on any other system. It is shown for illustration purposes only.

The fd_cmds_11 is a script file used to reconstruct the fdisk partition table. If you had no information on the current fdisk partitioning before the crash, this file will restore that partitioning for you. The Compaq system partition is the line `c 4 0 1`; it starts at cylinder 0 and has a length of 1. The `c 1 65 190 1` line is the UnixWare 7 partition starting at cylinder 65 and has a length of 190. The NT partition is the missing area between cylinder 1 and 65.

```
fdisk -L $1 >/tmp/fdisk_out <<-END
c 4 0 1
c 1 65 190 1
s
END
```

The layout_1 file contains the slice layout within the UnixWare 7 partition.

```
1     /            vxfs    1024    618502K    1R
2     /dev/swap    -       -       128520K    1R
4     /home        vxfs    1024    313267K    1R
10    /stand       bfs     512     24097K     1R
11    /var         vxfs    1024    232942K    1R
12    /home2       vxfs    1024    200812K    1R
```

The `part_dd_1` contains data only if multiple partitions exist on the hard disk. The p number can range from 1 to 4. The UnixWare 7 partition on this disk is listed as partition 1 by fdisk.

```
/dev/rdsk/c0b0t0d0p1   p1
```

The cpio Format

The cpio format consists of two cpio archives. The first has the disk and partition layout information discussed in the previous section, "The Emergency Tapes." The second archive has the UnixWare 7 filesystems from the first hard disk and, if they exist on the second hard drive, the /home, /home2, /var, and /usr filesystems. See Chapter 14 for more information on the contents of the tape.

The dd Tape

When the `-e` option is used to create the emergency_rec tape, the first archive is the cpio disk format information. The second archive is a dd copy of the entire hard drive.

Author's Note

I created a dd format tape for a disk with a 100MB DOS partition and a 900MB UnixWare 7 partition. I then deleted both partitions, created a new 1000MB DOS partition, and reformatted the entire disk. Next I performed a restore. I was able to boot into both UnixWare 7 and DOS.

To use the dd restore, the new disk has to be larger than the original disk. I used two 2GB SCSI disks from the same manufacturer with different model numbers and got errors trying to restore to one of the disks. If you make a dd tape, I would also make a cpio version in case you have to replace the disk. Restoring a 1GB tape to a 2GB disk works. Running fdisk yielded the expected results: 50% of the disk was used by the restored partition parameters.

Restoring Non-Root Filesystems

If a non-root filesystem fails, the recovery is generally not as difficult as for a root filesystem. The first tool in the recovery arsenal is fsck.

Run fsck on the problem filesystem:

```
fsck /dev/rdsk/c0b0t0d0s4
```

You can determine the device name of your filesystem by running the `mount` command. If the problem filesystem is not mounted, run `prtvtoc` on the problem disk:

```
prtvtoc /dev/dsk/c0b0t0d0s0
```

The slice number is the s number in the device name.

Make sure the filesystem being checked is not mounted. If the filesystem is mounted, a copy of the superblock is kept in memory. You may repair the filesystem on disk; but as soon as the operating system synchronizes the in-memory superblock with the copy on disk, the repaired disk copy is overwritten.

If fsck repairs errors, re-execute until no more errors are found. If fsck fails or continues to report errors, you will need to re-create the filesystem.

Use the `mkfs` command to re-create the filesystem. The parameters for `mkfs` to re-create a particular filesystem can be determined by running `mkfs -m` on the slice:

```
mkfs -m /dev/rdsk/c0b0t0d0s4
```

This will return output similar to:

```
mkfs -F vxfs -o ninode=65536,bsize=1024,version=4,inosize=256,
logsize=1024,nolargefiles /dev/rdsk/c0b0t0d0s4 2425814
```

Tip

As a system administrator, it would be wise to run `mkfs -m` *on each filesystem and store the output in your system log book. You do keep a system log book, don't you?*

If you have saved the output of `mkfs` from each filesystem, then you can run the command to re-create the filesystem.

Run fsck on the newly created filesystem to ensure that it is valid. If fsck fails, you may have physical damage.

After the new filesystem is proven by fsck to be clean, mount it and prepare to restore the data. The method of restoration depends on the method used to back up the filesystem. Use tar, cpio, ARCserve, or other products to restore the files to the filesystem.

As a precaution, you may want to unmount the filesystem and re-check with fsck. There is no reason to turn users loose to enter data if there is any doubt about the stability of the data storage.

ARCserve

At the present time, Cheyenne ARCserve/Open for UnixWare 7 does not provide an emergency recovery capability. A future release is planned that will have disaster recovery capabilities. The anticipated date of release is mid-1999 at the earliest.

CHAPTER 24

Migrating to UnixWare 7

- Migrating your system
  Learn where to go for information on migrating to UnixWare 7.
- Migrating from OpenServer 5
  Learn the differences in files and directories between OpenServer 5 and UnixWare 7. See how to use the `ap` command to migrate users. Learn about program compatibility.
- Migrating from UnixWare 2
  Learn about the few directory and file changes. See how to migrate users.

Migrating Your System

You may have purchased an upgrade license for UnixWare 7, but there is no in-place upgrade for the operating system on your computer. In this case, you must do a fresh install. When you perform a fresh install, all user settings, printer configurations, and other customized settings will disappear. Migration tools are currently limited, but more will be provided in future releases of UnixWare 7. A graphical Migration Wizard is under development. The Wizard will allow you to save many configuration settings from OpenServer 5 and move them to UnixWare 7. SCO plans to include other operating systems on the "move from" list eventually.

As SCO builds new migration tools, they will be listed on the Web at `www.sco.com/security/sectools.html`. As new security tools are created, they will be made available at this site.

If you are migrating to UnixWare 7 on a new system, your problems may be reduced by having the original system available for reference and copying files. If you are planning to install UnixWare 7 on your existing system, you will want to save as many files as you can to ease the configuration of your new system.

As a software developer migrating applications to UnixWare 7, you will want to take advantage of the SCO Developer Program. SCO provides a quarterly newsletter called *CoreDump* plus other benefits, such as discounted products for developers. Contact SCO at `devprog@sco.com` for more information. SCO's Web site has developer information at `www.sco.com/developer`. The articles in the *CoreDump* newsletter include such topics as "UnixWare 7 Compatibility Modules" on how binaries designed for UnixWare 7 can run on UnixWare 2 and OpenServer 5.

Author's Note

In this chapter, we have listed file and directory differences. These lists vary from those in the UnixWare 7 documentation. We have verified that the list of commands and directories with full path names are correct as of version 7.0.1.

Tip

An excellent document, titled "Upgrading Your System to UnixWare 7," is located in the /info/upgrade directory on the first CD in the installation set.

The upgrade document is accessible from UNIX or Windows. The information exists in three forms:

- *upgrade.txt, a simple text format version*
- *upgrade.ps, a PostScript copy for printing*
- *upgrade.html, a hypertext version*

This document lists all the files that should be migrated from OpenServer or UnixWare 2 to UnixWare 7 for many functional areas, such as uucp, DNS, TCP, and the like.

Migrating from OpenServer 5

OpenServer 5 users will appreciate the familiar SCOadmin GUI but will see many differences in the file structure and commands. Throughout this book, OpenServer 5 notes have been included to highlight differences. Many commands have changed and some have disappeared. Before attempting to run shell scripts on UnixWare 7, you may want to scan the list of command changes. You may also need to revise customized .profile, .login, or other user startup scripts.

Preserving Previous Settings

As a method of preserving customized settings from OpenServer 5, the script below was created by J.P. Radley, a longtime SCO supporter involved with the CompuServe SCO Forum. This script can be used as a model on which to build your own. Many of the directories will be in different locations on UnixWare 7; and some of the settings, such as the X Desktop on OpenServer 5, will not carry over to the CDE desktop on UnixWare 7. The X Desktop settings may be used with the UnixWare 7 X Desktop. The following script was originally designed for carrying settings from one version of OpenServer 5 to the next. Copy the files to /home on the UnixWare 7 system and determine which files you need for upgrading. You may also want to get a copy of this script from `ftp.jpr.com`.

```
#!/bin/sh: << NEVERMIND# savefiles -- JPRadley  29 October 1997  v. 1.3.0

        LUBRICATING AN OPERATING SYSTEM UPGRADE

While SCO's OSR 5.0.4 and 5.0.5 now permits an In-Place Upgrade (IPU)
from OSR 5.0.0 or 5.0.2, it probably should be avoided. You are relying
on the system engineers who wrote the scripts for the IUP to have thought
of every possible file, nook, and cranny where changes were made for
whatever local purposes and reasons. The odds are that you will still
find some local changes in some rarely touched files will be obliterated
by an IUP, and if you don't remember what the files were or what the
changes were, you'll spend a great long time searching through your back-
up tapes to find what you need.
I devised a script to save copies of everything I think was localized to
my /u/filesystem; in many upgrades, or new OS installations, only the
root filesystem changes, so whatever is in secondary filesystems will
still be around, and surely easier to retrieve than playing back a backup
tape.
Note that while I prefer avoiding IPUs, this script is useful whether you
go the IPU route or do a fresh install of the operating system.
Be sure that you edit this: this reflects *my* needs, and every system is
different. In particular, you'll note that I've saved no MMDF-related
files, because I don't use them. And because I don't place my atdialer
text files in /usr/lib/uucp/defaults, I don't save that directory (my
atdialer text files have remained in /etc/default, which I do save.)
It is very important that you do not save a morass of symbolic links: you
want the contents of the files, not a pointer. I use BackupEDGE, whose h
flag takes care of this; the alternate tar command should do, though. Run
savefiles before you make your complete Master backups, which of course
you would be foolish to not have prior to upgrading. And if you are going
to re-run divvy and change your filesystem sizes, then you'll get the
/u/r files back from the tape on your first restore.
NEVERMIND
```

```
# cut out from line 1 up to and including this line if desired
#!/bin/sh
# @(#)savefiles -- JPRadley  29 October 1997  v. 1.3.0
#
# @(#)copy likely useful files to the /u filesystem, so as to retrieve
# @(#)them readily after a fresh install, without having to constantly
# @(#)run through a giant Master backup tape looking for one little
thing.
#
# some of the saved files will just be copied back in (e.g., spool files)
# others will be points of reference for editing the new OS's files
(e.g.,
# rc2.d files)
#
# note to others: this is *my* personal list of stuff to save and
reminders
# of what to do after installing a new OS on the root filesystem.
#
# edit to suit *your* site's local peculiarities!!!
#
# reminder -- after installing the new OS:
#  check for existence of /mnt, /cdrom, /tmp, /usr/tmp
#  run ap -r -f /u/r/ap.userlist to recoup old set of users
#  install BackupEDGE, gds, Specialix, xdev, scoadmsh, other
supplements...
#  remake symlinks, including at least:
#     /usr/local         /u
#     /appl              /u/appl
#     /usr/lib/sendmail     /u/bin/smail
#     various atdialer links
#     interchange var/spool and /usr/spool?

rm -fr /u/r         # 'r'?  Whatever... that's my mnemonic for 'recover'
mkdir -p /u/r
/tcb/bin/ap -gd > /u/r/ap.userlist     # to remake passwd,group,tcb files

# I *think* this is everything I'll need after the new OS is installed :-)

sort << EndOfList > /u/r/savedfilelist
./-i
./.Xdefaults-jpradley
./.crontab
./.cshrc
./.deliver
./.elm
./.forward
./.hushlogin
./.ksh
./.less
./.lesskey
./.login
```

```
./.lynxrc
./.mailrc
./.muttcolors
./.muttrc
./.ncftp
./.netrc
./.odtpref
./.pgp
./.profile
./.rhosts
./.sh_history
./.signature
./.signaturel
./.tcshrc
./.xdt_dir
./.xdtsupCheck
./Mail
./Main.dt
./etc/X0.hosts
./etc/cleanup
./etc/conf/init.d
./etc/conf/node.d/snd
./etc/conf/node.d/si
./etc/conf/node.d/xi
./etc/conf/pack.d/snd
./etc/conf/sdevice.d/snd
./etc/csh.cshrc
./etc/cshrc
./etc/default
./etc/edge.failed
./etc/edge.exclude
./etc/edge.passed
./etc/gettydefs
./etc/group
./etc/hosts
./etc/hosts.allow
./etc/init.d
./etc/inetd.conf
./etc/inittab
./etc/magic
./etc/named.boot
./etc/passwd
./etc/perms/fp
./etc/perms/text
./etc/ppphosts
./etc/profile
./etc/rc
./etc/rc.d
./etc/rc0
./etc/rc0.d
./etc/rc1
./etc/rc2
```

```
./etc/rc2.d
./etc/rc3
./etc/resolv.conf
./etc/services
./etc/shells
./etc/syslog.conf
./etc/tcp
./etc/termcap
./etc/ttys
./etc/ttytype
./usr/adm/awksyslog
./usr/adm/ftpd
./usr/bin/buildit
./usr/bin/diction
./usr/bin/diffmk
./usr/bin/eqn
./usr/bin/explain
./usr/bin/grabit
./usr/bin/hyphen
./usr/bin/it
./usr/bin/look
./usr/bin/mm
./usr/bin/mmcheck
./usr/bin/mmt
./usr/bin/neqn
./usr/bin/nroff
./usr/bin/prep
./usr/bin/ptx
./usr/bin/soelim
./usr/bin/style
./usr/bin/tbl
./usr/bin/troff
./usr/dict
./usr/games
./usr/internet/ip/0.0.0.0/sco_ftp
./usr/internet/lib/mailcap
./usr/internet/lib/mime.types
./usr/internet/ns_httpd/docs
./usr/ktx2
./usr/lib/X11/app-defaults/Ghostview
./usr/lib/X11/app-defaults/ScoTerm
./usr/lib/X11/config
./usr/lib/X11/vtwm
./usr/lib/audio
./usr/lib/dict.d
./usr/lib/dprog
./usr/lib/edge
./usr/lib/font
./usr/lib/macros
./usr/lib/mkdev/audio
./usr/lib/mkuser
./usr/lib/mstppp/Accounts
```

```
./usr/lib/mstppp/Autostart
./usr/lib/mstppp/Devices
./usr/lib/mstppp/Filter
./usr/lib/mstppp/IPPool
./usr/lib/mstppp/Systems
./usr/lib/spell
./usr/lib/style1
./usr/lib/style2
./usr/lib/style3
./usr/lib/suftab
./usr/lib/term
./usr/lib/terminfo/an43.src
./usr/lib/terminfo/ansi.src
./usr/lib/tmac
./usr/lib/uucp/Devices
./usr/lib/uucp/Permissions
./usr/lib/uucp/Systems
./usr/lib/uucp/dialWB
./usr/lib/xc
./usr/spool/cron
./usr/spool/fax
./usr/spool/lp
./usr/spool/mail
./usr/spool/smail
./usr/spool/uucplogins
./usr/spool/uucppublic
EndOfList

# use of BackupEDGE's h flag is *obligatory*, so as to save file contents,
# and not just a bunch of symlinks. :-)

cd ; edge cahfF - /u/r/savedfilelist ¦ (cd /u/r ; edge xvf -)

# or use this:
#cd ; tar cLPfF - /u/r/savedfilelist ¦ (cd /u/r ; tar xvf -)

#EOF savefiles
```

Many of the items in the savefiles script may not apply to your installation. You may have directories or files that are applicable to your installation that should be added. Remember that if you use full path names to directories, such as /u, that do not exist in UnixWare 7, they may wind up in root; and root may be too small to hold the files. You may want to link /u to /home if copying files that belong in /u.

Warning

Do not replace the UnixWare 7 `inittab` *and* `rc` *components with their OpenServer 5 counterparts. Use the OpenServer 5 scripts to determine if you want to customize the startup or shutdown. Many system files in OpenServer 5 are not compatible with UnixWare 7.*

Differences in Commands

Some of the commands in OpenServer 5 have different options or syntax in UnixWare 7. Commands that applied to OpenServer 5 specific functions have been dropped. We will now look at some of these commands in more detail.

Equivalent Commands

Table 24.1 shows the OpenServer 5 command on the left and the equivalent UnixWare 7 command on the right. In some cases there is no one-to-one direct correlation.

TABLE 24.1 COMMAND EQUIVALENTS

SCO OpenServer 5 Command	UnixWare 7 Equivalent
`doscmd`	`dos(1)` (Subcommands are the same.) In UnixWare 7.0.1, and for future releases, the dos command has been deleted. For DOS compatibility, see the Skunkware CD for the mtools package.
`bootos(HW)`	`boot(1M)` Use the `KERNEL` argument to specify the kernel to boot.
`mkdev(ADM)`	`dcu(1M)` The main functionality is in `dcu(1M)` and `resmgr(1M)`.
`mkdev hd`	`diskadd(1M)`
`divvy(ADM)`	`disksetup(1M)` Use `prtvtoc(1M)` and `edvtoc(1M)` to edit the disk's VTOC.
`badtrk(ADM)`	`disksetup(1M)`
`custom(ADM)`	`pkgadd(1M)` Use for SCO UnixWare 2 and UnixWare 7 packages.
`enable(ADM)` and `disable(ADM)`	`pmadm(1M)` and `sacadm(1M)` for terminals (`enable` and `disable` work on printers only.)
`coltbl(ADM)`	`colltbl(1M)`
`configure(ADM)`	The `idtools` commands. See `idconfupdate(1M)`, `idinstall(1M)`, `idmkinit(1M)` and `idtune(1M)`.

`cpuonoff(ADM)`	`psradm(1M)`
	To activate and deactivate processors.
	`psrinfo(1M)`
	To show the current state of processors.

`cpusar(ADM)`	`sar(1M)` (base command)

SCO OpenServer 5 Command	UnixWare 7 Equivalent
haltsys(ADM)	halt(1Mbsd) (Must have BSD package installed.)
integrity(ADM)	pkgchk(1M)
link_unix(ADM)	idbuild(1M)
multiscreen(M)	Configure using vtlmgr(1).
nwpasswd(NWG)	Use NetWare UNIX Client (NUC) to change passwords.
p_fsck (fsck(ADM))	fsck(1M) (-P option)
rc2(ADM):	rc2(1M):
I01MOUNTSYS	S01MOUNTSYS
P00ANNOUNCE	K00ANNOUNCE
P75cron	S75cron
P70uucp	S70uucp
reboot(ADM)	halt(1Mbsd)
rlogind(ADMN)	in.rlogind (See rlogind(1Mtcp).)
routed(ADMN)	in.routed (See routed(1Mtcp).)
rusersd(NADM)	rpc.rusersd (See rusersd(1Mtcp).)
rwalld(NADM)	rpc.rwalld (See rwalld(1Mtcp).)
rwhod(NADM)	rpc.rwhod (See rwhod(1Mtcp).)
slist(NWG)	nlist(1nuc)
telnetd(ADMN)	in.telnetd (See telnetd(1Mtcp).)
tftpd(ADMN)	in.tftpd (See tftpd(1Mtcp).)
timed(ADMN)	in.timed (See timed(1Mtcp).)
ulist(NWG)	Use NetWare UNIX Client (NUC) utilities to view all the users on a NetWare server.
uuclean(ADM)	uucleanup(1Mbnu)
xntpd(NADM)	in.xntpd (See rwalld(1Mtcp).)

Commands with Different Functionality

The list in Table 24.2 has OpenServer 5 commands on the left and the equivalent UnixWare 7 commands on the right. In this list the command names are the same, but the functionality is changed.

TABLE 24.2 COMMANDS WITH SAME NAMES AND CHANGED FUNCTIONALITY

SCO OpenServer 5 Command	UnixWare Functionality Name
`ct(HW)`	`ct(1bnu)`
`crash(ADM)`	`crash(1M)` (Functionality is substantially different.)
`custom(ADM)`	`custom(1Mxnx)` (Included for compatibility to install SCO OpenServer packages only. Use `pkgadd(1M)` to install SCO UnixWare 2 and UnixWare 7 packages.) Custom+ formatted files will not install.
`boot(HW)`	`boot(1M)` (boot program)
`debug(HW)`	(boot debugger) No equivalent.
`dbx(CP)`	command-line `debug(1)`; also see "A guide to debug for dbx oriented user-level users." If started in a graphical environment, (program debugger) debug will launch its graphical interface rather than the command-line interface; this can be overridden using `debug -ic` to start the debugger.
`dbxtra(CP) dbXtra(CP)`	`debug(1)` If started in a graphical environment, (graphical front-ends) debug will launch its graphical interface for (dbx) rather than the command-line interface.
`rc0(ADM), rc2(ADM)`	`rc0(1M), rc1(1M), rc2(1M), rc3(1M)` (See manual pages for details.)
`rsh`	`rsh(1tcp)` (remote shell)
/etc/TZ	/etc/TZ (time zone directory)

Commands for OpenServer 5 Compatibility

The following SCO OpenServer commands are available for backward compatibility only. Set the `OSRCMDS` variable to

```
(OSRCMDS=on ; export OSRCMDS)
```

to run applications that use the SCO OpenServer versions of these commands. Most of these exist in the UnixWare 7 system with slightly different functionality. In the case of rsh, it is a restricted shell in OpenServer 5 and the remote shell in UnixWare 7. These are located in /OpenServer/bin.

```
compress        pg
cpio            rksh
csh             rsh
dd              sh
egrep           sort
fgrep           tar
grep            uncompress
ksh             zcat
more
```

Commands No Longer Available

The following SCO OpenServer commands are not available. Many of these commands were used in OpenServer 5–specific functions.

```
aio(HW), aioinfo(ADM), aiokinit(ADM), aiomemlock(F)
ale(ADM)
apm(ADM)
asktime(ADM)
asroot(ADM)
atcronsh(ADM)
audit(S), auditd(ADM), auditcmd(ADM), auditsh(ADM)
authck(ADM), authsh(ADM), auths
backupsh(ADM)
badblk(ADM), badtrk(ADM)
bshrink(ADM)
btmnt(ADM)
chtype(ADM) (unretire(ADM))
clri(ADM)
clorex
cps(ADM) (fixmog(ADM))
customextract(ADM), customquery(ADM)
displayintr(ADM)
divvy(ADM)
dkinit(ADM), dparam(ADM)
dnvt(PADM)
dumpsave(ADM)
ecc(ADM)
eisa(ADM)
idaddld(ADM), idas(M), iddeftune(ADM), idld(M), idmkreg(ADM),
idscsi(ADM), idmkvidi(ADM)
idleout(ADM)
```

```
initcond(ADM)
initscript(ADM)
intbb(ADM)
ismpx
isverify(M)
jterm, jwin
kbmode(ADM)
kernel(ADM)
layers
marry
mcart
menumerge(ADM)
mpsar(ADM)
mpstat(ADM)
mscreen(M)
mthread(ADM)
nd(ADM)
netutil(ADM)
nlogin(PADM)
nping(PADM)
nwpasswd(NWG)
nwvolumes(NWG)
nwwho(NWG)
passwdupd(ADM)
pcpio
pipe(ADM), pipestat(ADM)
reduce(ADM)
relax(ADM)
remote
report.expire(ADM), report.login(ADM), report.term(ADM)
rmgroup(ADM), rmpasswd(ADM), rmuser(ADM)
sconf(ADM)
sd(ADM), sdd(ADM)
sddate
setconf(ADM)
sfmt(ADM)
shl
showsvcs(PADM)
slist(NWG)
smmck(ADM)
ssoPathMap(CDMT)
swconfig(ADM)
sysadmsh(ADM)
```

```
tcbck(ADM)
termupd(ADM), ttyupd(ADM)
ttylock(ADM), ttyunlock(ADM)
u370(ADM), u3b(ADM) u3b15(ADM), u3b2(ADM) u3b5(ADM)
ulist(NWG)
undelete
unretire (ADM)
vax(ADM) (in machid (ADM))
vmstat
xbackup (ADM), xdump(ADM), xdumpdir(ADM)
```

Differences in Directories

Locations of many OpenServer 5 files and directories have been moved to locations in keeping with the System 4 standards (see Table 24.3).

TABLE 24.3 FILES THAT HAVE MOVED TO NEW DIRECTORIES

OpenServer 5	UnixWare 7
/bin/[*]	/bin/[*]
-	/sbin/[*]
-	/share/[*]
/etc/bcheckrc	/sbin/bcheckrc
/etc/chroot	/usr/sbin/chroot
/etc/crash	/usr/sbin/crash
/etc/cron	/usr/sbin/cron
/etc/dcopy	/usr/sbin/dcopy
/etc/default/filesys	/etc/vfstab
/etc/default/lang	/etc/default/locale (/etc/default/lang exists for backward compatibility)
/etc/devnm	/sbin/devnm /usr/sbin/dfsck
/etc/ff	/usr/sbin/ff
/etc/fsck	/sbin/fsck
/etc/fsdb	/sbin/fsdb
/etc/fstyp	/sbin/fstyp
/etc/fuser	/usr/sbin/fuser
/etc/exports	/etc/dfs/dfstab
/etc/getty	/lib/saf/ttymon
/etc/gettydefs	/etc/ttydefs
/etc/grpck	/usr/sbin/grpck
/etc/init	/sbin/init

continues

TABLE 24.3 CONTINUED

OpenServer 5	UnixWare 7
/etc/install	/usr/sbin/install
/etc/killall	/usr/sbin/killall
/etc/labelit	/sbin/labelit
/etc/ldsysdump	/usr/sbin/ldsysdump
/etc/link	/usr/sbin/link
/etc/log/[*]	/var/adm/log/[*]
/usr/lib/mail/aliases	/etc/mail/aliases
/etc/mkfs	/sbin/mkfs
/etc/mknod	/sbin/mknod
/etc/mount	/sbin/mount
/etc/mountall	/sbin/mountall
/etc/mvdir	/usr/sbin/mvdir
/etc/ncheck	/usr/sbin/ncheck
/etc/prfdc	/usr/sbin/prfdc
/etc/prfld	/usr/sbin/prfld
/etc/prfpr	/usr/sbin/prfpr
/etc/prfsnap	/usr/sbin/prfsnap
/etc/prfstat	/usr/sbin/prfstat
/etc/pwck	/usr/sbin/pwck
/etc/rc0	/sbin/rc0
/etc/rc1	/sbin/rc1
/etc/rc2	/sbin/rc2
/etc/rc3	/sbin/rc3
/etc/rc6	/sbin/rc6
/etc/setclk	/sbin/setclk
/etc/setmnt	/sbin/setmnt
/etc/shutdown	/sbin/shutdown
/etc/swap	/sbin/swap
/etc/sysdef	/usr/sbin/sysdef
/etc/termcap	/share/lib/termcap
/etc/uadmin	/sbin/uadmin
/etc/umount	/sbin/umount
/etc/umountall	/sbin/umountall
/etc/unlink	/usr/sbin/unlink
/etc/utmp	/var/adm/utmp

OpenServer 5	UnixWare 7
/etc/volcopy	/usr/sbin/volcopy
/etc/wall	/usr/sbin/wall
/etc/whodo	/usr/sbin/whodo
/etc/wtmp	/var/adm/wtmp
/bin/telinit	/sbin/init
/shlib/[*]	/lib/[*]
/usr/adm/[*]	/var/adm/[*]
/usr/bin/nlsadmin	/usr/sbin/nlsadmin
/usr/bin/strace	/usr/sbin/strace
/usr/bin/strclean	/usr/sbin/strclean
/usr/bin/strerr	/usr/sbin/strerr
/usr/lib/cron/.proto	/etc/cron.d/.proto
/usr/lib/cron/at.allow	/etc/cron.d/at.allow
/usr/lib/cron/cron.allow	/etc/cron.d/cron.allow
/usr/lib/cron/queuedefs	/etc/cron.d/queuedefs
/usr/lib/lex/[*]	/usr/ccs/lib/lex/[*]
/usr/lib/spell/spellhist	/var/adm/spellhist
/usr/lib/spell/hlista	/share/lib/spell/hlista
/usr/lib/spell/hstop	/share/lib/spell/hstop
/usr/lib/terminfo/[*]	/share/lib/terminfo/[*]
/usr/lib/uucp/Devconfig	/etc/uucp/Devconfig (Note that links to /usr/lib still exist for these /etc/uucp files.)
/usr/lib/uucp/Devices	/etc/uucp/Devices
/usr/lib/uucp/Dialcodes	/etc/uucp/Dialcodes
/usr/lib/uucp/Dialers	/etc/uucp/Dialers
/usr/lib/uucp/Permissions	/etc/uucp/Permissions
/usr/lib/uucp/Poll	/etc/uucp/Poll
/usr/lib/uucp/Sysfiles.eg	/etc/uucp/Sysfiles
/usr/lib/uucp/Systems	/etc/uucp/Systems
/usr/mail/[*]	/var/mail/[*]
/usr/man/[*]	/lib/scohelp/en_US.ISO8859-1/man
/usr/net/nls/dbfconv	/lib/saf/dbfconv
/usr/net/nls/listen	/lib/saf/listen
/usr/pub/[*]	/share/lib/[*]
/usr/spool/[*]	/var/spool/[*]
/usr/tmp/[*]	/var/tmp/[*]

Executing OpenServer 5 Binaries on UnixWare 7

UnixWare 7 provides binary compatibility with many OpenServer 5 applications. In UnixWare 7.0.1, the XENIX compatibility code was removed from the operating system.

This code had formerly been contractually required by Microsoft dating back to the early SCO XENIX days. A European court overturned the contract, allowing SCO to reduce the royalty payments to Microsoft.

As part of the XENIX compatibility, the DOS commands (`doscp`, `dosls`, and so forth) were removed along with many system calls used by XENIX software. You should test any old software that may have been written using XENIX system calls. These programs should work on 7.0.0 and not on 7.0.1.

Some software checks to see if the operating system level is version 3.2. Software that makes this check can be installed and run by setting the `SCOMPAT` environment variable before installing or running the software:

```
SCOMPAT=3.2;export SCOMPAT
```

If your old applications will not run on UnixWare 7 and you have the source code to the applications, recompile them using the UnixWare 7 UnixWare/OpenServer Development Kit (UDK).

Author's Note

I used `rcp` to copy Informix SE and an application we had developed on OpenServer 5 to UnixWare 7. We had no problems with running the application.

Some software that was developed under SCO UNIX version 3.2v4.2 will run properly but displays error messages at startup. As many as two screens of messages may appear. The error messages are

```
libc: setlocale: LC_CTYPE: LANG= syntax error in /etc/default/lang

libc: setlocale: LC_CTYPE: no LANG= line in /etc/default/lang
```

The executable that gave these errors is a COBOL application. With the default character-based `TERM` setting of AT386-ie, the function keys work properly at the console. Programmatic attempts to change the background color were erratic. Any spot on the screen not changed by a new screen would not get the new background color. According to the developer, the source code called for complete redisplay; but the Microfocus compiler may be intelligently deciding what to redraw. Attempts to use `ansi` and `ansic` for the `TERM` setting resulted in no scan code support for the function keys.

To use an OpenServer 5 version of ScoTerm in the graphical login, download TLS701 from SCO's Web site. This Technical Library Supplement (TLS) is not fully supported. It will provide an executable script and the X11 files to run the compatible ScoTerm window.

Some applications developed under OpenServer 5 APIs may not operate properly. Examples of those applications follow:

- Certain X Desktop APIs
- MooLIT APIs
- Security APIs, such as old NCSA C2 interfaces
- SCO ISAM
- Certain XENIX 286 APIs

It is best to test each application under UnixWare 7 before committing to an upgrade.

Contact your vendors for UnixWare 7 versions of software for third-party hardware such as intelligent serial port adapters, multi-console adapters, and other hardware that came with operating-specific drivers. Vendors of software that runs on earlier SCO releases should have new versions for UnixWare 7.

Migrating System Configuration Files from OpenServer 5

Files can be moved from OpenServer to UnixWare 7 by tape or over the network. If you choose to use tape, remember that ARCserve/Open will take control of the tape drive. Unless you stop ARCserve/Open with the `astop` command, your `cpio` or `tar` command will sit there doing nothing. If using `cpio`, it is important to use the `c` option for standard ASCII headers to ensure compatibility.

Migrating Users

UnixWare 7.0.1 has the `ap` (account profile) command ported from OpenServer 5. Use the `ap` command on OpenServer 5 to create a file of information on accounts you want to move to UnixWare 7. The UnixWare 7 `ap` command is limited at the present time to reading in a file and creating accounts; it cannot unload the accounts information. The option to unload, `-d`, is present in the documentation, but not active.

To create a list of accounts to migrate on the OpenServer 5 system, use

```
ap -gd > userlist
```

The result will be a list of user and group information suitable for use with the `ap -r` command to restore user accounts. Use your favorite editor to remove undesired accounts such as system accounts like root, adm, and uucp, from the file. The file should look like the following listing:

```
larry:x:202:50:Larry Bell:/u/larry:/bin/ksh
larry:u_name=larry:u_id#202:\
     :u_pwd=E8BSZzIcxnKVMnWccP7Z1yIg:\
     :u_type=general:u_succhg#901405424:u_pswduser=larry:u_lock@:\
     :chkent:
group::50:
ENDOFGROUPS::0:
andrew:x:203:50::/u/andrew:/bin/ksh
andrew:u_name=andrew:u_id#203:\
     :u_pwd=6yFMewtfDoFpc:\
     :u_type=general:u_succhg#900095342:u_pswduser=andrew:u_lock@:\
     :chkent:
group::50:
ENDOFGROUPS::0:
lonzie:x:204:50::/u/lonzie:/bin/ksh
lonzie:u_name=lonzie:u_id#204:\
     :u_pwd=2hsS1w434E.Ak:\
     :u_type=general:u_succhg#900112955:u_pswduser=lonzie:u_lock@:\
     :chkent:
group::50:
ENDOFGROUPS::0:
```

You may need to edit the file to change the location of home directories. Move the file to the UnixWare 7 system and execute `ap -r -f` *`userlist`*, where *`userlist`* is the name of the file. Appropriate warnings and errors will be shown. In the following messages the group `group` already exists with gid 102. If the group name exists, the group ID (gid) is not changed to the new group ID. Check group names before adding the new accounts.

```
UX:ap: WARNING: Group group already exists with a different group ID, 102
not 50
UX:ap: INFO: Group ID 50 ignored
```

Using the `ap` command does not create home directories. It is not necessary to re-create user passwords; they are migrated to the UnixWare 7 system with no problem. If a name being migrated already exists in the UnixWare 7 password file, it will not be overwritten; you will see an error message:

```
UX:ap: ERROR: Existing entry for <username> not overwritten
```

Migrating from UnixWare 2

UnixWare 2 provides a good match for UnixWare 7 with relation to commands and directories. While some have changed, the list of differences is much shorter than for OpenServer 5.

Differences in Directories

The list of renamed directories is short by comparison to the OpenServer 5 list (see Table 24.4).

TABLE 24.4 RENAMED DIRECTORIES AND FILES

SCO UnixWare 2	UnixWare 7
/usr/lib/saf/ttymon	/lib/saf/ttymon
/etc/gettydefs	/etc/ttydefs
/usr/sbin/swap	/sbin/swap
/usr/share/lib/termcap	/share/lib/termcap
/usr/lbin/[*]	/lbin/[*]
/usr/lib/[*]	/lib/[*]
/usr/share/[*]	/share/[*]
/usr/share/lib/spell/hlista	/share/lib/spell/hlista
/usr/share/lib/spell/hstop	/share/lib/spell/hstop
/usr/share/lib/terminfo/[*]	/share/lib/terminfo/[*]
/usr/share/man/[*]	/lib/scohelp/en_US.ISO8859-1/man
/usr/lib/saf/dbfconv	/lib/saf/dbfconv
/usr/lib/saf/listen	/lib/saf/listen
/usr/share/lib/[*]	/share/lib/[*]

Executing UnixWare 2 Binaries on UnixWare 7

UnixWare 2 should provide easy migration of executables. Applications that use the Destiny desktop will not migrate to UnixWare 7.

Migrating Users

The `ap` command was not part of the UnixWare 2 commands. It is being ported to UnixWare 2. Look for `ap` to appear on SCO's Web site at `www.sco.com/security/sectools.html`.

If you have to migrate users prior to getting `ap`, you can use the Accounts Manager to create the new accounts. If you have a large number of accounts to migrate, you can use your favorite UNIX editor to manually paste them into the /etc/passwd, /etc/shadow, and /etc/group files. After you have pasted them, run the `creatiadb` command to correct the identification authentication database.

Author's Note

I have manually edited the /etc/passwd and /etc/shadow file and run `creatiadb`*, and I have been able to use the login accounts. Some SCO techs have recommended this not be done. It does work, though. Make sure that the group ID for the user is in the /etc/group file and that the home directory is set correctly. Back up before you do this. Check for the* `ap` *program and use it in preference to manual edits.*

PART V

Appendixes

Appendix A

SCO Resources on the Web

The SCO Corporate Web Site

`www.sco.com`

The main Web page features the latest news from SCO, as shown in Figure A.1. A search engine is provided for searching the Web site; however, this is not the search to use for technical problems. The search engine provides the ability to locate information on SCO products, press announcements, and the like. A selection box provides access to 13 international SCO Web sites in native languages.

Author's Note

SCO currently has 13 international Web sites in native languages. The Web sites are similar in structure, although the graphics may be different. Where a Web site is described as `www.sco.com/products`, *it may appear as* `www.sco.it/italia/produ` *or* `www.sco.de/deutsch/produ`, *depending on the country.*

Products

`www.sco.com/products`

Descriptions of all SCO products are provided for your information.

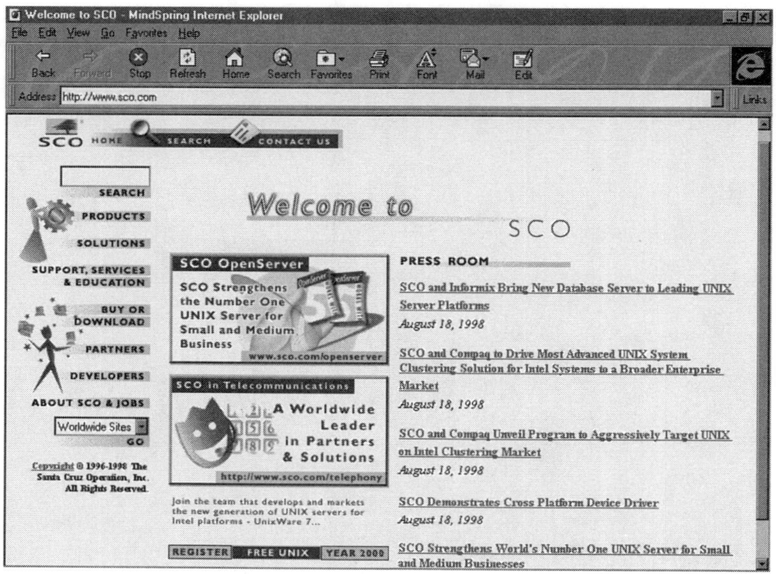

FIGURE A.1 *The SCO corporate Web site.*

Solutions

`www.sco.com/solutions`

Success stories for government and business are highlighted along with the third-party applications. The third-party applications link to the SCO directory, which is a list of third-party applications available on SCO UNIX. Developers may add their own applications here.

Hardware Compatibility

`www.sco.com/chwp`

Check out the compatibility of hardware for any of the SCO products before you purchase the hardware. Hardware compatibility is available from SCO OpenServer to UnixWare 7. Also included are Tarantella and ARCserve Open. Searches can be performed by product category, manufacturer, and SCO product, as shown in Figure A.2.

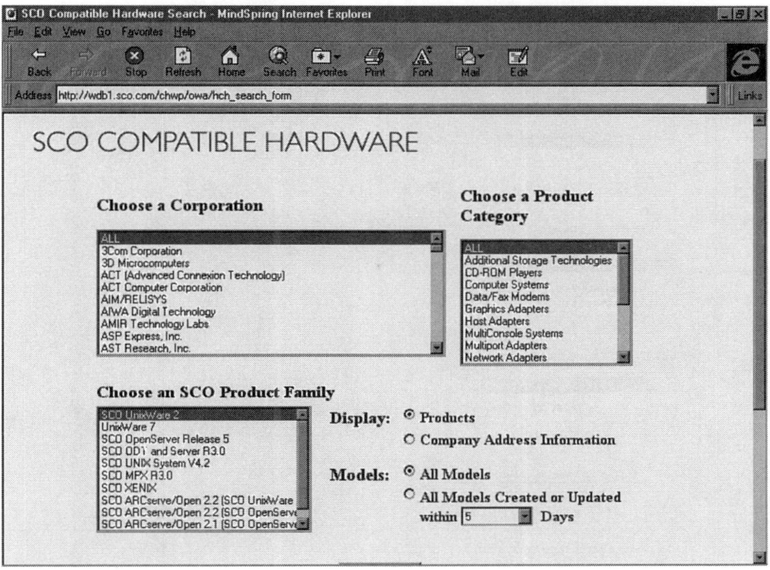

FIGURE A.2 *The SCO compatible hardware Web pages.*

Support, Services, and Education

`www.sco.com/support`

Support is available from SCO or the Authorized Support Centers. SCO services are detailed here (see Figure A.3). The Authorized Support Centers are sites that specialize in SCO support. Each has trained personnel and a support agreement with SCO to guarantee customers that the support provided is high quality.

SCO Advanced Education Centers provide SCO-authorized training. The instructors have all passed the SCO certification examinations with a higher score than the requirement for an Advanced Certified Engineer. Both authors have taught at SCO education centers and highly recommend the courses. See `www.sco.com/Training/train.html` for information on a training center near you.

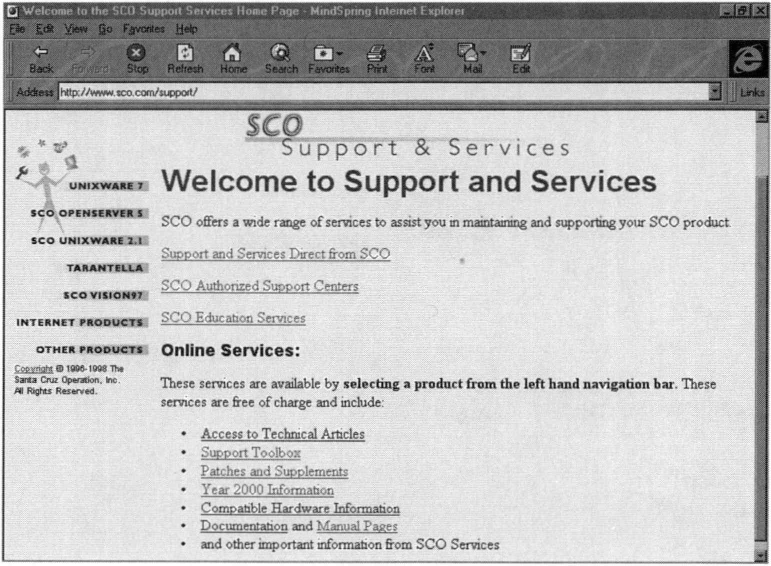

FIGURE A.3 *The support Web page.*

On the Support page are several very important links for technically oriented users. These links provide access to up-to-date troubleshooting and downloads. There are also links down the left side by product to allow you to narrow your search quickly. Clicking UnixWare 7 provides links to all UnixWare 7 patches, documentation, and more.

Access to Technical Articles

You can search SCO's Technical Articles database, formerly known as the *IT scripts*. These are the same scripts SCO support uses to answer calls. The improved search capabilities include searching by product for articles created in the previous 7, 14, or 30 days.

Support Toolbox

The Support Toolbox is shown in Figure A.4. The Toolbox includes a minimum patch listing to provide you with a list of the patches that should be installed on each product. The New Supplements section reports all the latest supplements available, saving you the time of searching for news of supplement releases.

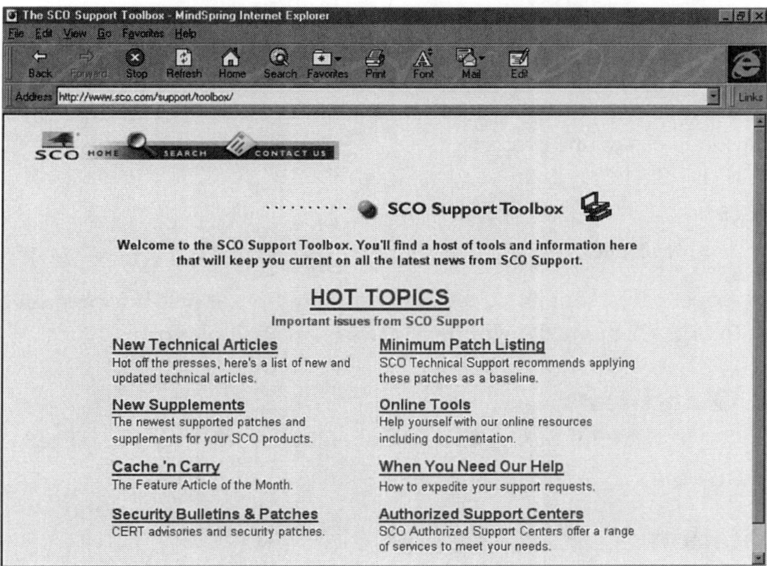

FIGURE A.4 *The Support Toolbox.*

Online Tools

`www.sco.com/support/toolbox`

The Online Tools page provides links to documentation and manual pages, VisionFS documentation, NetNews, FTP download sites, and other technical necessities. The Minimum Patch Listing provides a list of SCO products and the current patch levels.

Year 2000 Information

`www.sco.com/year2000`

From the Y2K page, you can download the SCO White Paper on Year 2000 plus find links to other Y2K sites.

Buy or Evaluate

`www.sco.com/buyeval`

Many SCO products are available for evaluation. You can get licenses for free UnixWare, OpenServer, and many other products for non-commercial use.

Partners

www.sco.com/partners

Information of interest to SCO resellers is available at this site. Some of the information is password protected.

Developers

www.sco.com/developer

The developers area contains the CoreDump newsletter and information of interest to organizations developing software on SCO platforms.

About SCO and Jobs

If you want to work for SCO, all the job openings worldwide are posted on the Web site.

Documentation

For complete documentation on UnixWare 7, visit SCO's documentation site

doc.sco.com

For a complete list of online documentation, see

www.sco.com/documentation

Downloads

To download the Vision products for evaluation or licensing, go to

www.sco.com/vision/eval

Many SCO optional products are available for download. ARCserve Open, Netscape, Java products, SCO Doctor, and more are located on SCO's Web site at:

www.sco.com/download

The SCO Skunkware is free software made available by SCO. It is not supported. Skunkware offers tools and games for SCO operating systems:

www.sco.com/skunkware

Appendix B

References

File and Print Sharing

Henriksen, Gene. 1998. *Windows NT and UNIX Integration*. Indianapolis, IN: Macmillan Technical Publishing.

SCO. 1996. *Introducing VisionFS*. Santa Cruz, CA: SCO.

Networking

Albitz, P. and C. Liu. 1996. *DNS and BIND*, Second Edition. Sebastopol, CA: O'Reilly & Associates.

Comer, D. 1995. *Internetworking with TCP/IP*, Volume 1. Englewood Cliffs, NJ: Prentice Hall.

Costales, B. and E. Allman. 1997. *Sendmail*, Second Edition. Sebastopol, CA: O'Reilly & Associates.

Derfler Jr., F. 1995. *Guide to Connectivity*, Third Edition. Emeryville, CA: Ziff-Davis.

Derfler Jr., F. and L. Freed. 1993. *Get a Grip on Network Cabling*. Emeryville, CA: Ziff-Davis.

Goodheart, B. and J. Cox. 1994. *The Magic Garden Explained: The Internals of UNIX System V Release 4, An Open Systems Design*. Englewood Cliffs, NJ: Prentice Hall.

Hunt, C. 1995. *Networking Personal Computers with TCP/IP*. Sebastopol, CA: O'Reilly & Associates.

Hunt, C. 1997. *TCP/IP Network Administration*, Second Edition. Sebastopol, CA: O'Reilly & Associates.

O'Reilly, Tim and Grace Todino. 1992. *Managing UUCP and UseNet*, Tenth Edition. Sebastopol, CA: O'Reilly & Associates.

Stern, H. 1991. *Managing NFS and NIS*. Sebastopol, CA: O'Reilly & Associates.

SCO Reference Materials

SCO course materials:

Advanced File and Print Server

Configuration and Maintenance

Configuring SCO Internet FastStart

UnixWare 7 Administration: New Features

UnixWare 7 Administration I: User Services

UnixWare 7 Administration II: System Installation

UnixWare 7 Network Administration

SCO course materials are provided with courses taught by SCO Advanced Education Centers (AECs). Appendix A, "SCO Resources on the Web," lists the Web address for the AEC page.

SCO documents provided with UnixWare 7:

UnixWare 7 Runtime Release Notes

UnixWare 7 Installation Guide

SCOhelp (online documentation)

Man pages

System Tuning

Course materials for UnixWare 7 Internals are available from

The Computer Classroom
1700 East Woodfield Road, Suite 905
Schaumburg, IL 60173
800-603-8988

Index

Symbols

A

D

E

F

G

H

J

K-L

M

N

O

P

Q-R

S

U

V

W

X-Z